Hinc venti dociles resono se carcere solvunt,
Et cantum accepta pro libertate refundunt.

(Inscription on an Organ. From 'Opera Poetica'
by Jean Baptiste de Santeul 1630-1697)

Gordon,
with every good wish for a
happy retirement; albeit over
a year late!

Peter

20/XÄ/90

Hence from this recounting from
the docile winds are loosed and
the docile winds are loosed and
their liberty
stay a melody for their liberty
received.

For the 1878 Paris International Exhibition, London reed organ-builder James Hillier of Camden Town built this instrument which he called an "Orchestrophone". It was a C-C compass two-manual American organ having 25 stops controlling 13 sets of reeds each of two and a half octaves. There were two knee swells and two heel-movement combination pedals

Harmonium

THE HISTORY OF
THE REED ORGAN
AND ITS MAKERS

ARTHUR   W.   J.   G.   ORD-HUME

Illustrated by the author

DAVID & CHARLES
Newton Abbot   London

British Library Cataloguing in Publication Data

Ord-Hume, Arthur W. J. G.
   Harmonium: the history of the reed organ and
   its makers.
   1. Reed-organ—History
   I. Title
   786.9′4′I9   ML 597

   ISBN 0–7153–8885–1

Printed in Great Britain
by Redwood Burn, Trowbridge, Wilts
for David & Charles Publishers plc
Brunel House   Newton Abbot   Devon

Contents

List of Plates

List of Line Illustrations

ADDITIONAL ILLUSTRATIONS

Preface

The reed organ appears somehow to have eluded the attention of musical historians. While there are plenty of dictionary references and a few popular handbooks, nobody seems ever to have gone into the history and development of these fascinating little instruments. This present work attempts to rectify this anomaly.

In the way of things, much of the minutae of history and development is forever lost and what little remains of the early days of reed-organ-building is similarly disappearing into the mists of time. What is even sadder is that the era of the harmonium and American organ really has receded into the past and, other than as collectors' items, they have virtually disappeared from our musical horizons. Apart from a flurry of 1950s portable reed organs and notwithstanding a production of small, plastic-cased and electrically-blown modern harmoniums from Japan, there is no serious move to bring the instrument into the twenty-first century. Thoroughly eradicated by the electronic organ and then by the diminutive, multi-voiced portable keyboard, the cost of manufacturing and maintaining a harmonium today, plus its limitations in the light of solid-state circuitry, dictates that it has departed the contemporary scene. When, in years to come, the special music which was written for it comes to be played, it will have to be prefaced with an introductory comment as to what a harmonium was, for the younger generations may not know.

This is another reason for the present work, in that it has taken rather more than twenty years to piece together the information. When the job was begun, there were still many reed organ builders alive. Now, two decades later, most have gone to join the Great Majority and their stories remain solely in notebooks or on recording tapes. Years ago, standing in an ancient north London building and watching an elderly man lovingly rebuilding a century-old harmonium, the author became aware that he was watching the last stages of a once-great industry moving inexorably into the realms of history. It was at that moment that a decision was taken to try to research the early beginnings, the development and the heyday of this interesting and often misunderstood instrument.

Harmoniums can be found all over the world. In a tiny church far above the Arctic Circle in the very north of Russia, the author found an old St Petersburg-made instrument still in use. In the Church of St George at Arreton on the Isle of Wight, despite the presence of a Victorian pipe organ of 1886, there are two small harmoniums, one a London-made Kelly and the other unidentified but serving today's congregation as a showcase stand. In far-off Tasmania, there stands within Longford's Christ Church a seraphine made more than one and a half centuries ago in north London. And it was here, in May 1838, that St George's Anglican Church, Battery Point, Hobart, was consecrated, the singing of several ladies accompanied by one Miss Logan on a seraphine. Such instruments were undoubtedly costly luxuries then, for when it was sold thirteen years later it fetched £21, and £46.5s. was raised by public subscription in order to buy a new patent harmonium with twelve stops. Harmoniums, their makers and their markets knew no boundaries!

And here at home, as the nineteenth century drew to a close, the daily musical service held in the crypt chapel of St Paul's Cathedral in London was still sung to the accompaniment of a harmonium; by 1899, though, it had gone in the face of a pipe organ by the Positive Organ Company.

Harmoniums represent an inescapable, unforgettable part of our musical and devotional heritage. The larger suction organ, called so many things from 'parlor organ' upwards and downwards yet best known by the generic term 'American organ', became almost a cult artefact. Yet it all began with the simple free reed and the little keyboard pressure organ. The manufacture of these instruments became a major industry with makers in every part of the world. Men spent their lives designing, building, improving, striving to make a better reed organ. An account of these endeavours ought to be preserved before it is too late. They form a small but important chapter in our musical and industrial history.

This book is, then, a little tribute to those events of the past. And maybe at the end of it all, we will be able to look afresh at this, the simple little reed organ, maligned by many in the higher echelons of music, this scrap of an instrument which impertinently set out to emulate its grander pipe-organ relative — and in some ways actually succeeded. Harmoniums certainly brought music to many who could not afford a piano, and to many a church and chapel which lacked the means to provide any other form of accompaniment for worship.

WHEATSTONE'S HARMONIUMS (English), in solid oak cases manufactured by them, have the full compass of keys, are of the best quality of tone, best workmanship and material, and do not require tuning.

Guineas.

New Patent, 5 octaves, from CC, double pedals (the best and cheapest Harmonium made) . . . 6
With 1 stop, oak case (reduced price) 9
Piccolo Piano Model, 1 stop, polished, with unique wind indicator 10
(*With soft and distinct tones, and projecting finger-board.*)
With 2 stops, 1 set and a half of vibrators (polished case) 12
(*The extra upper half set of vibrators adds greatly to the effect of the treble, and produces a beautiful diapason-like quality of sound.*)
With 3 stops, large size, organ tones (polished case) 15
With 5 stops, 2 sets of vibrators (ditto) 22
With 8 stops, 2 sets of vibrators (ditto) 24
With 10 stops, 3 sets of vibrators (ditto) 30
(*The best and most effective instrument made.*)

For particular description of the above and other Harmoniums, in rosewood and mahogany cases, see Messrs. Wheatstone & Co.'s Illustrated Catalogue, which may be had of them gratis and post-free.

The only Exhibition Prize Medallist for Harmoniums, 1851.

An extensive assortment of French Harmoniums, by Alexandre (including all the latest improvements), at prices from 5 to 150 guineas.

WHEATSTONE & CO.,
Inventors & Patentees of the Concertina,
20 CONDUIT ST., REGENT ST., LONDON.
The Original Manufacturers and Importers of the Harmoniums.

Catalogue of the Great Exhibition, London, 1851

Introduction

It is difficult today to cast one's mind back some one and a half centuries to the early days of the harmonium and to realise what an impact the instrument had on a significant number of people and their appreciation of music. Indeed, the simple little reed organ came to play an important part — literally — in the lives of our forefathers. Even in our own youth, as many of us will recall perhaps with a smile, there was the school harmonium with leaky bellows and one pedal immutably lying flat on the floor. In the local chapel, perhaps, we sang hymns to an aged specimen which suffered from an occasional cyphering note plus a clutch of other important ones which never quite sounded.

When first it made its hesitant appearance under a variety of names invented before anybody could really think of a good name for it, the harmonium was greeted with curiosity and casual interest by people from all walks of life. Generally smaller, as well as lighter, than a piano, it was cheaper and did not require to be tuned regularly. For the Victorian home, its mellow sounds and choice of voices provided a form of musical expression which had hitherto been unknown. It was these new advantages which elevated the harmonium to almost instant acceptance, in particular among those who could not afford a piano, and generated the conditions for the birth of the industry which thrived for a century not just in Britain but also in America and on the Continent.

But not everybody liked the instrument and it was initially shunned by serious musicians. It was not until makers such as Alexandre, Debain and Mustel of France imbued the harmonium with additional characteristics which elevated it to what the purists of the time considered to be a 'real' musical instrument, that the musical dictionaries — particularly that of Sir George Grove in 1879 — began to accord the harmonium serious attention.

The developments in the United States were equally significant and several outstanding brands of the so-called American organ were produced, in particular by quality manufacturers such as Mason & Hamlin, Estey and Vocalion. Along with the name 'American organ' 'parlor organ' or 'pump organ', we find a confusing multiplicity of terminology such as 'suction harmonium', 'pressure harmonium', 'cottage organ', 'normal harmonium', 'melodeon', 'seraphine' and so on. These names can be a source of confusion to novice and expert alike; we will endeavour to sort them out as we go.

What, one might well question, is there to say about this relic of the past—this rather low-brow if not downright working class clavier? Indeed, is there anything worth telling about it, or is it not better that it be allowed to fade into obscurity like half-pint milk-bottles and spinning tops? There is much more to the reed organ than that and a growing number of collectors and historians alike have come to appreciate that the early examples of these instruments have indeed played a significant part in musical history, contributing to a tale which is well worth recounting before it is too late.

The harmonium and its precursers such as the seraphine and melodeon quickly became associated with the smaller church and chapel and over the years to come this was fostered with the construction of small, compact-folding portable organs. Unlike the piano, these were not highly susceptible to changes in temperature and humidity, so that it was easier to transport them considerable distances without great risk of harm. To this day, many very elderly instruments still exist to bear witness to this, for instance the fine church at Longford in Tasmania has a well-used and now-unplayable seraphine built in Camden Town, London, in 1823 and now correctly preserved as a part of the church's musical heritage.

It is this use which perhaps gives us a clue as to why the reed organ was invented in the first place. The sustained tone of the organ pipe had already been known and appreciated for over 2,000 years, and the organ itself offered an advantage over percussion and plucked keyboard string instruments. Coveted as organ-tone was, however, the large and expensive pipe organ remained out of the reach of the musical majority. As early as 1772 Adam Walker sought to solve the need with his 'Celestina' described as 'a new method of producing continued tones upon an instrument.' Shaped like a harpsichord and played from a keyboard or pinned barrel, the Celestina (British Patent No 1020 of 29 July) used bowed strings.

The word 'wheezing' seems almost inevitably bound up with the harmonium in our recollections today. While this may have been true with a poorly maintained example, the harmonium was a robust and important instrument of music. In fact the oft-maligned early harmonium was just the start of an extraordinary industry which, in the space of less than a century, developed and improved it out of all proportion. The result of all this effort was the American organ, which was really not even an American invention. The noble creation of a Frenchman, it was an American maker who capitalised on his work and set off a massive demand which encouraged builders of American organs all over the world. The American organ emerged as an instrument of extreme musical beauty and sensitivity which could be called upon to interpret even orchestral music. With the perfection of reed-voicing and tonal balance and design, the harmonium became not so much an acceptable orchestral instrument as a veritable orchestra in itself.

Outwardly it reflected the bourgeois taste in decoration, but it was soon to develop a lush style of its own which was quite unmistakable in overall effect although every maker had his own interpretations of the rules of case design. The ornate cabinet, however, did nothing to enhance the musical performance, though the general public seldom seemed to understand that an impressive-looking organ case did not necessarily contain an impressive-sounding instrument. Shelves for knick-knacks and racks for magazines, holders for candles and in some cases a row of dummy organ pipes in gilded wood or painted tin, all helped to elevate the reed organ to the dizzy heights of the picture rail in the Victorian home, when the actual organ part of the case was seldom higher than the row of artificial-ivory covered keys.

It is said that in mining communities in Wales, the man of the family would always judge the merits of an organ by the number of stop-knobs and also by lifting up one end. If it was heavy, then it had to be good. Manufacturers got wise to this quite quickly - and built their cases heavier. And many stop-knobs did no more than operate mutes or shades which produced but marginal effect on the sound produced. The number of knobs, like the curlicues on the mirror'd and finial'd cabinet, were meaningless non-musical assets in so many instances. Instruments with one and a half or two and a half sets of reeds could have up to a dozen or more 'stops' for, unlike the pipe organ, the number of knobs bore almost no relationship to the number of sets of reeds nor to the tones produced. The Cornish organ company of America provided one stop-knob for every octave on the organ; thus their two-to four-row organs might have sixteen or eighteen stop-knobs.'

But long before such multiple-reed sets, the burgeoning harmonium had just one row of reeds and little in the way of pretention. It was born in the backstreet workshops of craftsmen using no more than hand tools. The Victorian age had yet to come, but the very first steam railways were already extending their cast-iron tracks across the land. This was an important spur to commerce and industry, for the network of stage coaches and mail coaches were already on the way out. The significance of London as a rail terminal was already established by 1837, yet it was thought unwise for locomotives to enter the stations. The London and North Western Railway engines, for example, terminated at Camden Town, from whence the carriages were hauled up and down the mile long slope into Euston by an endless rope 4,080yd long and driven by a huge stationary steam engine with a 20ft diameter wheel. Camden Town, soon to become the centre of London's piano and harmonium industry, was thus a sort of staging post for the railway.

The 1831 census shows that the metropolis had a population of one and a half million people. London barely extended north of the Oxford road - now called Oxford Street - and the Portland Place of today was a little row of cottages with small gardens attached. On Sundays, the men who occupied them could be seen at work in these gardens or taking their tea there, passing the time of day with their still-country neighbours. And northwards from there, apart from the farm buildings on what was one day to become the Regent's Park, there was hardly a building let alone another person until you came to that fine stretch of water on the fringes of north west London, the Welsh Harp. If you did not want to venture so far, you could scramble through the hedge and cross a ditch to climb Primrose Hill with its heavily wooded crest. The suburban sprawl was only just beginning as the market gardens of Hackney and the fields around the eleven-miles-across city began to succumb to the speculative builders.

Into this environment, where on Saturdays you could go to the Great Room attached to Messrs. Flight & Robson's organ works in St Martin's Lane and hear the blind organist Purkiss playing on the giant Apollonicon barrel and finger organ, came the harmonium builders and the harmonium players. It was a fruitful age redolent with inventors, improvers and visionaries, and this melting-pot of talent combined to cement the transition from the harsh-toned and, consequently, ill-named seraphine, to the subtlety of the developed harmonium. The work carried out in London, Paris and North America all contributed to the production of a very fine instrument. The Vocalion, precursor of the Aeolian Orchestrelle player organ, the Mustel and its German counterpart, the Scheola, and the work of makers such as Holt and Humphreys left no doubt in the minds of the purists that the reed organ was a genuine musical interpretor.

In the past, attempts to chart the history of the reed organ have been sharply divided between the efforts of the musical historian who has concentrated on a brief overview of the instrument, its significant developments and the music written for it, and those of the enthusiast who has access to a great deal of information about a few of the instrument's many builders. Between these two approaches, the library of works on the reed organ is still small. A clutch of useful catalogue reprints and a few general books on some of the major American makers is, in the main, the whole corpus. Robert F. Gellerman's 1973 illustrated study of American reed organs remains the only significant work.

The approach of this book is first to examine the history of the instrument and then to describe its development in the major countries which acted as host to its creation. A detailed chapter on makers and designers is also included with the suggestion that this should be considered as part of the general reading rather than purely reserved as a reference section. It incorporates a deal of additional information not included in the historical chapters which precede it.

Arthur W. J. G. Ord-Hume, London

CHAPTER 1

The History of the Free Reed
in Musical Instruments

As far as music and musical instruments are concerned, a reed is a thin, flexible piece of some material secured firmly at one end and free to move at the other. Normally, the movement is such that the reed can move freely within the confines of a closely cut slot. When a current of air is allowed to impinge upon it in a certain way, the wind bypasses the reed by flexing it to open and close the slot in which it is fitted. The result is a rapid to-and-fro vibration. This vibration may be at such a frequency that, when suitably amplified as, for example, by a specially-shaped acoustic chamber, it is audible. The size, weight and proportion of the reed and, to a certain extent, the amount of wind impinging upon it, have the ability to modify the quality of the sound produced.

The reed in music comes in two distinct types - the free reed and the beating reed. The former vibrates inside an opening which is virtually the same size as the reed and only marginally bigger so that the sides of the hole do not interfere with the movement of the reed. The latter type vibrates against an opening which is smaller than the reed so that it effectively beats against the surrounds of the opening at every cycle of movement. There is another form of reed found in musical instruments - this is the double reed as used in, for example, the oboe and the bagpipe chanter. Here, the two reeds are made to beat against each other, so forming a variant of the beating-reed classification.

The simplest reed-produced sounds are made without the need for openings to channel the wind or a frame within which the reed can move. They are in fact produced by strings. The once-popular aeolian harp - a resonant soundbox across which strings were stretched so that the wind could set them in motion - was no more than a primitive reed instrument. Another form of aeolian harp free-reed sound with which we are all familiar is the musical tones produced by the wind in telephone wires, amplified by placing the ear to the side of the pole.

A long blade of grass stretched between the sides of the thumbs is another example; here the reed formed by the blade of grass can be tensioned slightly by bending the thumbs, so raising and lowering the pitch of the sound. And, by cupping the hands so as to provide a resonant chamber, the sound of the reed can be modified. Unlike the other type of reed described, which is secured at one end, this form of reed is secured at each end and the centre length is allowed to vibrate about its fixed ends. Again, using a piece of thick grass, thin grass, or even paper, alters the characteristic of the sound in another way. In fact this is a subtle use of the reed principle since, depending on the shape of the cavity created between the thumbs, the grass reed can be proved to be both beating and free - or neither. On the other hand, the kazoo-like comb and tissuepaper has the attributes of a beating reed, yet is no more than a buzz whose pitch is governed by the pressure of blowing and the shape of the mouth.

The most popular of the free-reed instruments, and one which appears in various guises in many parts of the world, is the Jew's harp. A Chinese work of the twelfth century, says the *Oxford Companion to Music* without quoting the particular work, 'shows it in much its present shape'. The name and its origins are confused: the *Oxford Companion* referred to above calls it 'Jew's Harp' and quotes alternatives as 'Jews' Harp' or 'Jews Harp', playing the finer points with the apostrophies. However, other sources, both past and present, prefer to call it the 'jaw's harp' because, presumably, this won't offend anybody and after all it is held in the cavity between the jaws, ie the mouth. Be that as it may, the one-time accepted German word *Judenharfe* happens to translate directly as 'Jew's Harp.' Today it is known as *Maultrommel* in Germany, *guimbarde* in France and *scacciapensieri* in Italy. The old Latin name was *crembalum*, retained in the *Syntagma musicum de organographia* of Michael Praetorius as late as 1619. The vexed question of what to call it may be settled by reverting to its first-recorded name - Jew's trump or trumpe - which goes back to 1545 and was in regular use until the late eighteenth century.

Makers of Jew's harps have always been few in number. At the beginning of this century, there were half a dozen in southern Germany, one in Birmingham, England, and John Smith's unusual enterprise - the only such factory in the United States - situated at Bath-on-the-Hudson. By 1935, the only surviving factory was in Birmingham - that of M. Troman & Co, Bridge Works, Curson Street.

The instrument, simple though it may be, actually demonstrates all the principles of the developed reed organ in that the tone of the sound can be modified by the shape of the mouth while playing. While the Jew's harp has but one pitch, the wide variety of implied pitches possible is again governed by the shape and size of the mouth cavity, cheeks, tongue and lips. The series of harmonics which it produces is virtually the same as that of the trumpet which explains why in many languages its name is associated with that instrument. The first, second and third harmonics are suppressed, but those from fourth to tenth sound clearly.

The earliest forms of Jew's harps are to be found in various forms all over south-east Asia; the European instrument came from Asia and a representation of one in a sculpture on Exeter Cathedral is dated around 1350. Marcuse relates that an actual instrument was located during the excavations of the remains of Tannenberg Castle, Hessen, which was destroyed in 1399.

In 1827 and 1828, the youthful Charles Eulenstein, born in Heilbronn, Württemberg, demonstrated his prowess with the Jew's harp in London when he astonished the masses by playing sixteen of them and producing 'extremely beautiful effects'. However, the metal of the instruments, plus his continual practising, finally eroded his teeth to the point where he could not play because of the pain. His performances attracted the attention of another Charles who was the same age and who, destined to be knighted as Sir Charles Wheatstone, became a renowned scientist and inventor. To him goes credit for two somewhat diverse concepts - the electric automatic telegraph and the concertina. More to the point, though, is his claim to having invented a mouth-blown free-reed instrument which offered a choice of musical pitches. This he called the 'Symphonium.'

While there were other small free-reed instruments which predated it, Wheatstone's Symphonium of 1825 is considered to be the progenitor of the mouth organ or harmonica. By 1830, the first recognisable mouth organs were being produced in Trossingen, Germany.

Before discussing these later free-reed instruments, though, there is one extraordinary free-reed musical instrument which is without doubt the earliest known device of this type and, because it is still with us today, forms a most valuable document for study in the history of the free reed.

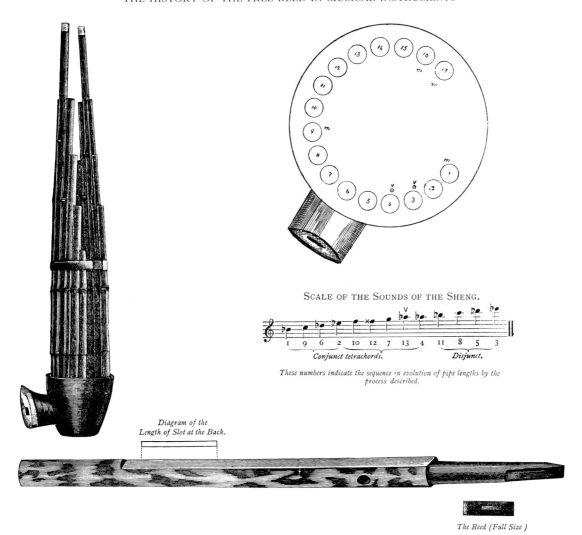

SCALE OF THE SOUNDS OF THE SHENG.

Conjunct tetrachords.   *Disjunct.*

These numbers indicate the sequence in evolution of pipe lengths by the process described.

Diagram of the Length of Slot at the Back.

The Reed (Full Size)

Fig. 1. The Chinese *sheng*, an instrument of great antiquity still being made and played today. Note that the arrangement of the pipes around the gourd which forms its body is not chromatic: the musical scale can be compared with the order of the pipes in the instrument. Pipes 1, 9, 16 and 17 are non-playing dummies placed purely for aesthetic reasons of symmetry

This is a Chinese instrument which was mentioned around 1100BC although it was not depicted until the sixth century AD. Indeed, it is said to be much older than the earlier of these dates, having been invented by the Chinese Emperor Huang Tei around 2500BC. It is called, variously, the *cheng* or *sheng* (pronounced 'sung') and was originally known as the 'bird's nest'.

Without delving into the mystique of its mythology, the sheng is indeed one of the most remarkable free-reed organs in the world since, by a novel quirk of its design, it works in a most peculiar manner. There are thirteen speaking pipes made of hollow bamboo, each of a different length and all being contained together at one end in a hollowed-out gourd. To ensure symmetry, the total number of pipes is usually seventeen, the additional four being only dummies. The curious

17

part of the sheng concerns its reeds and the method of sounding them. They are made of copper, are quite flat with their frames, and each is mounted some two-thirds along the length of its respective pipe. At a set distance between each reed position and the base of the pipe where it enters the gourd, there is a hole in the side of the pipe.

The sheng operates on the principle of the American organ in that air is sucked out through a mouthpiece. The air is drawn out continually, but none of the pipes will speak until the finger-hole in the side of the pipe is closed. The instrument is played in a series of slow chords, the player's fingers covering several pipe-holes at one time as the instrument is cupped in the hand.

A version of the sheng, seen recently in London, retains many of the attributes of the primitive instrument described here, but is played with a series of mechanical keys like those of a flute and the performer blows into the mouthpiece to produce a striking and quite unusual sound.

Just how the technique of vibrating free reed tongues reached Europe is a mystery. It has been

BY HIS MAJESTY'S   ROYAL LETTERS PATENT.

MESSRS. DAY & MYERS,

SOLE PATENTEES OF THE

ÆOLOPHON AND SERAPHINE,

Beg to call the attention of the Public to the merits of *their* instruments. The principle on which the tone is produced in the Seraphine, as well as its shape, is too well known to require explanation. The Æolophon differs from the Seraphine in the form of the springs, producing the sound in the bass, these springs being made curved ; the result of which is a superior quality and body of tone, and much greater rapidity of articulation than can be obtained from the Seraphine spring. The appéarance of the Æolophon is similar to that of a cottage pianoforte, the upper part being made use of to give expression to the instrument, by means of powerful swells. The springs in *all the instruments* manufactured by Messrs. Day and Myers, are made of steel, of the same temper as the main spring of a watch, and rendered impervious to rust by peculiar preparation. To the use of tempered steel is to be attributed the fact, that Messrs. Day and Myers's instruments stand in tune for several years together, *an excellence that cannot be possessed by instruments in which the springs are of any other metal.* Another important advantage resulting from the use of tempered steel, combined with superior workmanship, is, that the articulation is sufficiently perfect to place very rapid music within the range of these instruments, whilst at the same time their powers are such as to render them capable of expressing all that is grand and solemn.

Messrs. Day and Myers wish especially to direct the attention of the public to an instrument of enlarged powers, which they have lately perfected, called the

GRAND DOUBLE ÆOLOPHON,

This instrument, as its name indicates, consists of two sets of springs, one an octave higher than the other ; by this means producing a volume of sound equal to that of an organ of considerable size, yet so perfectly under the control of the performer, that when required, its delicacy is not exceeded by even the smaller instrument. In the GRAND DOUBLE ÆO-LOPHON will be found beauty of tone, combined with variety, power, and compactness. The comparatively small cost of this instrument, with the saving of expense in tuning, will give to the GRAND DOUBLE ÆOLOPHON the preference in point of economy, to all other assistants in congregational harmony, whilst its quickness of articulation renders it suitable for the performance of rapid orchestral music.

This instrument may be had in a variety of shapes, so as to suit any situation in which it may have to be placed.

Organists and organ builders are invited to hear Messrs. Day and Myers's Æolophon pedals, or substitutes for the pedal-pipe of large organs. They consist of eighteen double notes, the lowest of which is GG, the pedal to which being depressed, brings into action two tones, the GG, and the GGG, and so on for the other seventeen pedals, each producing hereby the effect of two pipes, the length of which in the lowest pedal would be 20 feet and 10 feet respectively. The smallness of the instrument producing this effect, together with its economy, places pedal notes within the reach of parties possessing organs, who have hitherto been prevented from using them, by either the largeness of the space required by pedal pipes, or their necessarily great expense.

An exhibition of the capabilities of all these instruments, by an eminent performer, takes place at 12 o'clock, daily, at the Manufactory, 37, POULTRY, LONDON, where the Patentees will be glad to receive the visits of the musical public.

Fig. 2. From the first issue of "The Musical World" published on 18th March 1836, comes this fulsome advertisement from Day & Myers which tells us a good deal as to how the instruments were made. Note that the reference to "springs" is the contemporary way of referring to reeds. The steel reeds must indeed have sounded brash

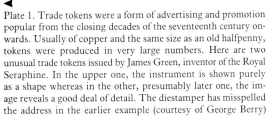

Plate 1. Trade tokens were a form of advertising and promotion popular from the closing decades of the seventeenth century onwards. Usually of copper and the same size as an old halfpenny, tokens were produced in very large numbers. Here are two unusual trade tokens issued by James Green, inventor of the Royal Seraphine. In the upper one, the instrument is shown purely as a shape whereas in the other, presumably later one, the image reveals a good deal of detail. The diestamper has misspelled the address in the earlier example (courtesy of George Berry)

Plate 2. A major difference between the appearance of the seraphine and that of the later harmonium concerns the pedals. The seraphine almost always had one small blowing pedal as distinct from the twin foot treadles of Debain-style reed organs. Here is a seraphine bearing the nameplate of Gunther & Horwood, Camden Town, London. The instrument has an F-F compass and appears to date from the period 1823 to 1829 (see details in Chapter 10). The instrument stands derelict but otherwise preserved in Christ Church (Anglican) at Longford near Launceston, Tasmania. B A Clark and J M S Johnson in their book "Pipe Organs of Tasmania" date the instrument as c.1844 and, in mis-spelling the name of the maker, state that it "cost 60 pounds" (Author)

Plate 3. Detail of the nameplate on the instrument seen in Plate 2. This address seems to have been used by a variety of piano and harmonium makers over a period of years (Author)

suggested that the knowledge was brought back by the Venetian merchant and traveller Marco Polo (1254-1324) from one of his journeys to the Far East. This seems more likely than the alternative suggestion, put forward by some, that the principle was discovered independently in Europe where the first written record was made in 1619 by Michael Praetorius in the second volume of his *Syntagma Musicum*. There he described an organ register in the following words: 'This tongue is no longer cut directly out of a pipe tube but is an independent part mounted on a slot through which it is vibrating.' The unique tone colour of the vibrating reed must have been greeted with excitement; it was an entirely new sound in Europe and was to play a unique and significant part in satisfying the musical taste of the people for the next two centuries. This in turn led to a variety of experiments by many craftsmen, some directed immediately towards musical instruments, others, like those of Christian Gottlieb Kratzenstein, towards the chimera of the artificial larynx which might be made to utter words.

The regal, in general use by the fifteenth century was, on the other hand, a beating-reed organ. In certain ways it was the forerunner of the portable harmonium and 'Bible' harmoniums of the 1880s, in that it could be carried under the arm.

Despite Mersenne's early seventeenth century description, the free reed remained unexploited except in pipe-organ building where it was occasionally employed experimentally as a soft reed stop to offset trumpet and cornet stops with their beating reeds. Early in the nineteenth century, though, there was a resurgence of interest and it can be safely assumed that by the end of the first decade of the nineteenth century, the principle of the vibrating reed and its practical potential were both widely known. By 1829, both the mouth organ and the accordion had appeared in somewhat primitive but nevertheless readily identifiable guises. The former is thought to have been the work of Christian Friedrich Ludwig Buschmann in 1821 - he was actually trying to perfect a Jew's-harp tuning device when he stumbled upon the 'mouth aeolian'. The latter stemmed from the work of artisans such as Buschmann (1822) and Cyrillus Demian or Damian of Vienna (1825). Indeed, it was Damian's addition of chords to be played from the left-hand side which gave the instrument the name 'accordion'. The original diatonic instrument was enlarged around the middle of the last century by the provision of a chromatic keyboard by the Viennese musician Gustav Walter (1835-1910). After the accordion came the concertina, an instrument for the invention of which Sir Charles Wheatstone is accredited in 1829.

Some of the early inventions which translated these small and intrinsically simple instruments into the harmonium and upwards are discussed in the following chapter.

IMPROVED SERAPHINE. MESSRS. KIRKMAN and WHITE, respectfully acqnaint the Musical Public, particularly the Clergy and Profession, that they have now on Sale an assortment of their Improved Seraphines, adapted either for the Drawing Room or Chapel with or without German Pedals. These extraordinary Instruments are used at the Italian Opera House and other Theatres ; may be heard at the Manufactory, 3, Soho Square, next door to the Bazaar.

THE ROYAL SERAPHINE. J. GREEN, Inventor and Sole Manufacturer, 33, Soho Square, respectfully recommends those who wish to form a judgement of the effects in the Opera of Quasimodo, and Don Juan of Austria, at the Theatre Royal, Covent Garden: Its introduction there affords an exemplification of its applicability to all purposes of a Church Organ, and for the accompaniment of a mass of voices. Its various capabilities in diversity of tone and delicacy of expression, admirably adapting it for domestic purposes, may be heard at any time at Mr. GREEN'S Music Warehouse, 33, Soho Square.

SERAPHINES.—METZLER and Co.. 105, Wardour Street, respectfully invite the attention of the musical public to their improved Seraphines, adapted either for the Concert Room, Drawing Room, or Place of Worship:—the various qualities of their tone —delicate and soft, or powerful, at the pleasure of the performer—renders them capable of giving effect to any Organ music, at a price less than one fourth the cost of an organ of the same power and depth of tone.

Fig. 3. Three revealing advertisements from "The Musical World" published in London in 1836. The first two, from April that year, are from the same page and show Kirkman & White advertising their "Improved Seraphine" while John Green states that he is the "inventor and sole manufacturer" of the Royal Seraphine. The third notice, a few months later, comes from Metzler

CHAPTER 2

The Early Beginnings of
the Harmonium

In general, the improvements which took place in the evolution of the reed organ can be divided into two types: first there were those which concerned the embellishment, appearance, enlargement and ease of manufacture; secondly there were those which concerned ease of playing, musical enhancement and tonal development. Generally speaking, the greater part of the first category emanated from the United States while the significant part of the second category came from France and Great Britain, for it was within these countries, and perhaps no more so than in Britain during the later years, that the reed organ was seen as a serious musical instrument. These evolutionary developments will be discussed in the chapters which follow. What concerns us here is how the practical reed organ came to be invented.

The free reed as applied to keyboard instruments experienced a hesitant start but can be said to date from at least the middle of the eighteenth century. But although there were several experimenters who contributed to this early evolution, the first person to employ the free reed with any measure of lasting success appears to have been Gabriel-Joseph Grenié (1756-1837) who built his *orgue expressif* in Paris in 1810. Fétis relates that Grénie had already devoted considerable time to experiments with both beating and free reeds as early as 1798. In the letters-patent of 1810, Grenié mentions the earlier work of Sébastien Érard (born at Strasburg, Alsace, in 1752) and the Abbé Vogler (George Joseph Vogler, born at Würzburg in 1749) to create an organ using free-reed pipes which was capable of expression. In these instruments, the free reed was mounted in the side of a trumpet-shaped wooden resonator developed from the type of resonator used with beating-reed organ stops.

Vogler constructed his Orchestrion in 1789. This was a small organ of four manuals each with 63 keys and a 39-note pedal, but whether it used free or beating reeds is uncertain. It was built for him in Holland by the Swedish organ builder, Rackwitz. Rackwitz had been an assistant to the Copenhagen organ builder, Kirschnigk, who worked between 1763 and 1770 and who had carried out experiments with free reeds in conjunction with a piano as an additional register. Johann Nepomuk Maelzel, better known as the man who pirated the Dutch organ builder Winkel's invention of the metronome and made ear-trumpets for the ailing Beethoven, also took an interest in free reeds and their potential as a result of coming into contact with Vogler and his work. As might be expected, Maelzel tried them out for himself and used free-reed pipes in the construction of one of his early Panharmonicons which he showed in Paris in 1807.

How much influence was exerted on Grenié by the earlier work and ideas of Vogler and Maelzel is uncertain though, as already mentioned, Grenié gave credit to Vogler and to Érard about whose

Plate 4. The elegant, almost classical lines of the "Improved Seraphine" manufactured by Joseph Kirkman and Thomas White of 30, Soho Square, London, c.1840-2. Dimensions are 38ins by 34ins by 21ins. The name appears on a white label and the casework is of rich hued mahogany, there being carved columns either side of the front and carved supports. Ivory-covered keys with moulded boxwood fronts. Compass F-F, 5 octaves. One set of reeds at 8ft pitch. There are 3 pedals: 1 = bellows; 2 = increase wind flow; 3 = swell (from the collection of R L Mitchell of J G Morley)

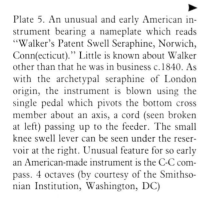

Plate 5. An unusual and early American instrument bearing a nameplate which reads "Walker's Patent Swell Seraphine, Norwich, Conn(ecticut)." Little is known about Walker other than that he was in business c.1840. As with the archetypal seraphine of London origin, the instrument is blown using the single pedal which pivots the bottom cross member about an axis, a cord (seen broken at left) passing up to the feeder. The small knee swell lever can be seen under the reservoir at the right. Unusual feature for so early an American-made instrument is the C-C compass. 4 octaves (by courtesy of the Smithsonian Institution, Washington, DC)

own experiments nothing is known. Grenié certainly received inspiration from the great work on organ building published between 1766 and 1778 by Dom Bedos de Celles - *L'art du facteur d'orgues* - which contains a useful section on free-reed pipes.

There is considerable significance in the fact that the Dutch organ-building genius, Diederich Nicolaus Winkel (born 24 August 1777, died 28 September 1826) employed precisely this sort of free-reed pipe in the extraordinary and innovative mechanical organs he built in the years which preceded the construction of his Componium in 1824. Of the surviving Winkel instruments, one (in the Nationaal Museum van Speelklok tot Pierement, Utrecht) uses both the Grenié-type of reed pipe and also the locking-bellows reservoir and expression feeders which were a feature of Grenié's *orgue expressif*. After Maelzel's pirating of Winkel's metronome, Winkel in retaliation set out to create a mechanical organ which would exceed the performance of the Panharmonicon.

Bernard Eschenbach (1769-1852) used free reeds in his Eolodicon of 1800, a description of which appeared in *Le Breton*, no 164, of 13 December 1827:

> Recemment, M. Eschembach [sic], dans son Eolodicon, a imaginé, en trouvant le principe de sa decouverte dans la harpe d'Eole et la guimbarde, de produire a volonté les vibrations sonores par un soufflet employé a faire vibrer, non des cordes tendues, mais des ressorts metalliques fixés par une extrémité et libres de l'autre.

Eschenbach's work inspired his cousin, the piano and organ builder Johann Caspar Schlimbach, to make his own keyboard instrument containing metal reeds. This was in 1810. Schlimbach's organ was unusual in that the bellows were operated by the knee. He called the instrument the 'Aeoline'. While contemporay references note that the instrument was inspired by aeolian harps and Jew's harps, this should not be interpreted as suggesting that the instrument was unworthy of a place in reed organ history. Writers of the time had no yardsticks by which to describe such an instrument in terms other than those with which they were familiar. Even so, Schlimbach's invention was but an experimental venture into free reeds, and it was left to others to make more definable steps forward. Schlimbach's work was taken on by the organ builder Voit of Schweinfurt.

Johann Christian Dietz, a distinguished mechanician, was born at Darmstadt in 1778 and in a fruitful life produced a number of musical instruments including one in 1805 which he called the 'Melodion.' This was an unusual instrument in that, although it used free reeds, they were set in motion not by air but by contact with a friction cylinder. The race was now on to perfect the keyboard reed instrument and inventors and their inventions came thick and fast. Lichtenthal in his dictionary published in 1839 stated that he believed the first of these to have been the work of Eschenbach, adding: 'Le son de cet instrument est produit par l'air gui agit sur des languettes en acier... Dans quelques églises d'Allemagne, on s'en sert pour accompagner le chant.'

In 1818, Antoine Haeckl of Vienna built his Physharmonica which was intended to be placed under a piano and played with the right hand to imitate 'les solos de hautbois que la main gauche devait accompagner sur le piano.' The instrument had four octaves and c to c4 compass. It was taken on concert tours by a well-known Viennese professor of music, Hieronimus Payer. Meanwhile, numerous imitations and variations were produced, among them models by Davrainville, the organ builder from Nantes who was renowned for his high-quality mechanical pipe organs. His reed organs were built in 1825 and 1826. But it fell to Johann Christian Dietz of Paris to make the next significant improvement with his 'Aerophone' of 1828. This featured deep resonant chambers for the reeds, which imparted a louder sound to the instrument.

One year later, the Thuringian Friedrich Sturm (1797-1883) took the components of the reed organ and mounted them in a piano-like case. This he called his 'Aeolodicon', and among the many who sang its praises in Berlin was Spontini who, in 1831, wrote that the instrument had a most commendable facility for reproducing crescendo and diminuendo depending on the force exerted on the pedals. The basic pitch of the reed organ was the same as that of the piano, namely 8ft. Sturm noted the improved brilliance to the music when a 4ft register was added and it seems likely that he was the first to make use of such a facility.

In 1834, the famous French organ builder Aristide Cavaillé-Coll (1811-99) also experimented with the possibility of producing expression from the free-reed organ with his 'Poikilorgue' of 1834 which resembled a square piano.

Napoleon Fourneaux was born at Leard in the Ardennes on 21 May 1808 and trained as a clockmaker. At the age of twenty-two, he came to Paris and built a small free-reed instrument which he called an 'Accordeon'. By 1836 he was making mechanical organs and experimenting with free-reed organs, manufacturing in 1838 a two-manual instrument with a 16ft register. He died very young on 19 July 1846, leaving to his son, also named Napoleon and born in 1830, the task of quantifying his experiments. This the younger Fourneaux did with two important published works on the *orgue-expressif* published in 1854 - *Traité théorètique et pratique de l'accord des instruments a sons fixes* and *Petit traité de l'orgue expressif*. Napoleon junior also built free-reed instruments.

Christian Friedrich Ludwig Buschmann, like Sturm, was a Thuringian, born on 17 June 1805. He nade musical instruments in Hamburg. His father Friedrich Buschmann is remembered for his invention of a glass harmonica, but he also made a number of free-reed instruments which are preserved today in the University of Leipzig. One was the 'Terpodion' and another the 'Aeoline'. Another Buschmann, Jean-David (1775-1852), made similar instruments including one which resembled the Melodeon created by Dietz. However, it differed in one important detail, namely that it had the abilitity to produce crescendo and diminuendo. J.-D. Buschmann called his instrument the 'Uranion' and a description of it was published in *Allgemeine musikalische Zeitung*, 12th year, No 30, p469, 1809.

After this extensive period of trial and error, the world was poised for the invention which would act as the catalyst and produce the definitive instrument. Haeckl was enjoying a measure of success with his Physharmonica, and somewhat jealously guarded its design and manufacture. One might say that this instrument was almost the equivalent in stature of the seraphine in Britain. Several authorities say that the earliest traceable British patent is in the name of Joseph Storer who, together with John Myers, was granted a patent on 20 July 1839 for 'improvements [to] seraphines.' This is not correct, for John Green received British Patent No 7154 as early as July 1836 (see chapter 10). Green had been a traveller with the musical-instrument maker, music publisher and keyboard composer Muzio Clementi in London and this would probably have brought him into contact with the then-current line of thought in France regarding the free reed in keyboard instruments. This does not mean that he was the true inventor and it is likely that the instrument existed prior to that date but sadly its first creator remains unknown. That it was inspired by developments in France and Germany seems most likely. Where Myers and Storer fit into this early picture is also uncertain. Their business began the year following Green's patent and their patent for improvements did not come until 1839. Did they know of the work of Green? It seems more than likely, for the musical-instrument fraternity in London was a close-knit community.

John Green may not have patented his improvements immediately; in those times it was seldom essential to hasten to gain such protection. This is significant, for Green is said to have introduced to the market what he called his 'Royal Seraphine' in 1833 or 1834. This instrument incorporated a swell effect created not so much by varying the wind pressure but using the pipe-organ technique

Plate 6. Early harmonium by an unknown maker. In the collection of the Smithsonian Institution, this is considered to be German and is dated as c.1855. It is more likely to have been made in America by a German immigrant. The most unusual feature has to be the means of operating the bellows, the complex treadles being moved backwards and forwards to pump feeders hinged along a line parallel to the keyboard and at the front of the instrument. Was this inspired by the velocipede? C-C compass. 4 octaves (by courtesy of the Smithsonian Institution, Washington, DC)

Plate 7. An early stage in the perfection of the reed organ and its tone was reached in this, the Vocalion organ, which was made c.1886 by William Hill of London and built to the specification of James Baillie Hamilton. The first instrument of this type was shown at the 1885 Inventions Exhibition in London. The instrument, which works on pressure, has a compass of 58 notes C-A comprising 320 reeds running straight through without a break. There are 12 stops which are as follows: swell organ: cremona 8ft, dulciana 8ft, octave, sub octave, vox humana, swell to great |coupler|; great organ: wood wind |sic| 8ft, claribel 8ft, diapason 8ft; pedal organ: bourdon 16ft, violone 16ft, great to pedal |coupler|. The bass reeds are in the overhang of the case front (from the collection of Phil and Pam Fluke)

25

of enclosing the reeds in a box with a movable swell-shutter to mute the sound on demand. Green continued to make various improvements over the following years.

When, in 1841, Wardle Evans produced his 'Organo Harmonica', the previous instruments were largely rendered obsolete. Evans went on to manufacture his invention as an increasingly refined and competent musical instrument (see page 23). Indeed, there are many today who would prefer to consider that Evans was the true inventor of the developed reed organ. However, while Evans's instrument was much further along the road to success than its predecessors, the design which came to be considered the standard by which all subsequent reed organs would be judged came from France.

Alexandre François Debain was born in Paris in 1809 and trained as a cabinet maker. However, he abandoned this at the age of sixteen and became apprenticed to the musical-instrument maker, Charles Joseph Sax. Shortly after completing his apprenticeship, he worked for several Parisian piano factories, his prodigious talent earning for him successively important positions. In 1820 he began repairing organs, and by 1830 had his own business making pianos and organs. Among his inventions was a machine called the "Stenographer' which would write down improvisations as they were played on the keyboard.

He then began making small single-row reed organs and, after considerable experimentation, developed his instrument into a single-manual organ having four rows of reeds each divided into bass and treble. The year was 1842 and Debain patented it under the name 'Harmonium'. This instrument, with its then-novel method of dividing its reed ranks into two portions, was the true progenitor of all that followed, and 'harmonium' finally became the generic term for the instrument. However, just as Haeckl tried to reserve for his own use the name he gave to his reed organ, so did Debain try to protect the name of his invention. Sadly, for the progress of the instrument, his patenting of the name 'Harmonium' obliged his contemporaries to seek other descriptions for their inventions, thereby delaying the acceptance of the name. And while 'harmonium' came to be accepted in Britain, it took some while to gain acceptance in France where the non- aligned name 'orgue expressif' was commercially preferred.

Debain's invention consisted of an instrument operated by air at a pressure above that of the surrounding atmosphere, and having four rows or ranks of free reeds. Each of these rows comprised reeds of different quality and included two 8ft, one 4ft and one 16ft pitch. Although these rows went through the whole compass of the keyboard, each row was mechanically divided, not exactly in half, so that it was possible to select, for example, different stops for the melody than for the bass.

From then onwards, this became the classical format of the 'four-rank harmonium' as it was called by contemporary musicians and in contemporary tutors. The task of producing the practical small reed organ working on air at pressure had been completed. Now came the period of its refinement and perfection. On the path to this stage in development there had been a variety of names used for the instrument, and even in the decades to come there were still some fanciful names to emerge. The more significant of these are listed with brief details in Appendix 3.

The first British manufacturer to adopt the use of the name 'harmonium' appears to have been Wheatstone & Co who advertised as such in the catalogue of the Great Exhibition of 1851.

"Musique Adresses Universel", 1930

CHAPTER 3

The Development of the Instrument in Europe

From the previous chapter, it is obvious that Alexandre Debain was not the inventor of the reed organ, nor did he claim to be the inventor of the best keyboard reed organ. What he did was to place the tonal and mechanical components of the instrument in a logical position so that they conformed to a layout which was at once both musically acceptable and replicable. On top of this, he patented various other improvements including a way of producing differing sounds by modifying the reed channels and cells, the whole being under the command of one keyboard. He also devised the expression stop whereby the reservoir of the bellows is locked so that the action of the feeders can directly affect the sound of the reeds.

Among the features which Debain devised was the arrangement of the rows of reeds in a reed organ. Hitherto, these had all been set in one row in the reed pan, sometimes erroneously called the sound-board. Debain showed how the rows could be built up as a series of stepped terraces, the key action acting in the centre with some reed rows in the front and others at the back. This was adopted by most reed-organ makers, both for harmoniums and American organs, across the world.

Another important manufacturer in France was Jacob Alexandre, a French Jew, who was born on 11 June 1804 and worked in Paris as a musical-instrument maker. He built the portable style of reed organ. One of his senior workers was Louis-Pierre-Alexandre Martin from Sourdun, also called Martin de Provins. In 1841, Martin invented the percussion device (see page 76) wherein the reed is struck by a small felt-covered wooden hammer in a mechanical action similar to that of a piano so as to produce a bell-like sound and promptness of speech. Besides this, Martin also invented one significant extra improvement to the reed organ - the *prolongment* whereby the notes of the lowest octave of the keyboard could be used as a pedal-point. Each key, once depressed, could be locked down until a second key was depressed, whereupon the first key would be released and the second retained in the playing position. Martin's initial invention covered the control of this by a knee-board rather like the later swell pedal. Jacob Alexandre's son Édouard later transferred the control of this feature to a draw-stop so that, when prolongment was selected, the pedal-point effect could be brought into play (see also page 63).

Another of Alexandre's workers experimented with suction-powered reed organs, but although some were built, the French did not believe the instrument to be commercially viable. The employee took the idea to America where Mason & Hamlin capitalised on it, making their first suction-powered model in 1861. The sound which the new organ produced was considered more suitable for the American love of devotional tone in the organ. Mason & Hamlin exhibited it in Paris at the 1867 exhibition, and so started the harmonium's gradual fall from favour. It took many years to come, but it began as early as the late 1860s and, despite a rapidly expanding market, the American organ took a proportionally larger and larger share. Most makers of instruments in Europe were forced into competition, and so had to produce American organs themselves.

In April of 1888, *Musical Opinion* reported the passing of Alexandre:

We have... to announce the demise of another French manufacturer whose instruments are well known in England. M. Édouard Alexandre, the head of the firm of Alexandre organ and harmonium makers, died at Paris on the 9th ult. Soon after the establishment of the firm by the late Jacob Alexandre, about the 'twenties', its name became known as makers of cheap instruments, the hundred franc organ being a speciality. In due time, Jacob's son entered the firm, which was henceforth known as Alexandre Père et Fils. The English Patent Office, from 1854 downwards, contains the records of many patents taken out by M. Édouard Alexandre, who also, at the commencement of his business career, purchased the

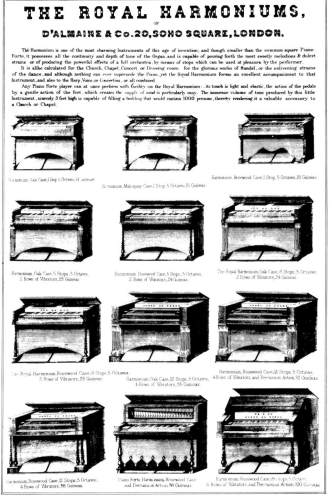

Fig. 4. D'Almaine in London advertised these instruments on the back page of a folio of sheet music c.1850-60. The early style of very large foot treadles which dominated the front elevation of these early harmoniums is clearly shown here

patent rights of M. Martin. The firm have at various times gained many awards, among the most noticeable of which was the medal of honour at the French Exhibition of 1855. A few years after this the great factory at Ivry was established. M. Ed. Alexandre's wife, Charlotte Dreyfus, was a well- known performer on the harmonium. Before the death of the elder Alexandre, which occurred some twelve years ago, the firm had been much injured by the appearance in the market of the American organ, which, as it well known, was invented by one of Jacob Alexandre's own workmen in 1835. The head of the firm, however, did not take kindly to the invention, although he made a few specimens. Nevertheless, the inventor met with better acknowledgement in America, where he took his ideas. We believe that Messrs. Mason & Hamlin first developed the American organ, and with what success may be seen by the beautiful specimens by numerous manufacturers of this instrument now in the market.

A third French manufacturer who played a vital part in the refinement of the instrument was Victor Mustel (1815-90). Mustel was a maker who was imbued with a true artistic devotion. As early as 1854 he had made several major improvements to the sound of the reed organ. These were the Forte fixe, the Forte expressif, the Harpe éolienne and the so-called Double expression (see page 33). Mustel's two sons, Charles and Auguste, devoted their lives to the perfection of the harmonium and to Charles goes credit for the invention of the Metaphone in 1878. This was a mechanical device which, by the use of shutters, allowed certain sets of reeds - usually those placed at the back of the organ pan - to be closed off. This produced a sort of sound-box so that the speaking reed could produce two forms of sound, the ordinary, natural sound or with the metaphone selected so that the reed could speak into the sound chamber thereby producing a quite different tone. The metaphone system came in two forms; early specimens used a form of roller blind to uncover the chamber, but models were also made at various times using louvres rather like the pipe organ swell-box.

The forte fixe and the forte expressif served as separate swell-shutters which could be used in conjunction with the metaphone to increase the volume of sound produced. The forte fixes shutters were controlled directly by the operation of stop knobs. However, the forte fixe were governed by the amount of pressure being produced in the instrument by the performer using the pedals. This meant that when pedalling gently and playing *pianissimo*, the shutters were closed. However, when pedalling hard, the forte expressif shutters would open in sympathy. Naturally they could be overridden by the stop selection knob.

The harpe éolienne and voix céleste, which were soon to be found on so many organs all over the world, comprised two reeds for each note, the second in each pair being tuned very slightly sharp so that the sound of the two reeds produced a pleasing beat or waver; no mechanical 'vox humana' fan ever created quite the sound of a true voix celeste stop and that of Mustel was extremely good. It is probable that to Mustel should also go credit for establishing the ideal position for the tonal break in the keyboard, bass to treble, as being between E and F on a CC instrument (see Appendix 1).

A significant change occurred with French builders between 1880 and 1900, namely the adoption of standard pitch. Whereas many of the earlier instruments had been tuned to somewhat arbitrary local pitch standards - and therefore made both bad accompaniment and difficult export instruments, Europe was coming round to adopting Kammerton or 'chamber pitch.' Although this was ratified at a conference in Vienna in 1885, it was in effect what had been called 'French pitch' for some while, a pitch appreciably lower than that used in Germany and based on A = 435. Prior to the adoption of French pitch in America (where it was known as 'international pitch') American reed organs were tuned to a variety of pitches between the high German and the low French. Mustel spearheaded a move to conformity in the manner in which he resolutely produced at French pitch. However, pitch was rising: the New Philharmonic pitch of A is 439 and the military bands'

Old Philharmonic Pitch of A is 452.5. What we today loosely call concert pitch, where A is 440 only, came into universal use in 1939, yet Mustel, recognising the trend, was tuning to this pitch by the turn of the century. Several earlier instruments, one dating from about 1888, are known at this pitch, although it seems likely these were altered at a later date for accompaniment duty. Mustel's far-sightedness was greeted first with diffidence but then with enthusiasm by makers across Europe, and A = 440 was virtually every maker's yardstick by 1914.

Two of Mustel's early employees were the German brothers, Julius and Paul Schiedmayer. Prior to working for Victor Mustel they had worked with Alexandre. They returned to Stuttgart in 1853 to set up manufacturing harmoniums there. However it seems they retained considerable contact with Mustel, for when they introduced their most sophisticated harmoniums at the end of the nineteenth century, it was to the Mustel design that they turned. When the Scheola player reed organ appeared, this was little more than a Mustel to which Schiedmayers added their own case and upperwork. Virtually every other detail was Mustel, and the belief is that they took delivery of Mustel organs for conversion in their Stuttgart factory. Schiedmayers also became involved in interesting experimental reed-organ work (see page 47).

Other European makers joined the increasing number of harmonium producers, among them Nyström in Karlstad, Sweden, in 1865. One of J. P. Nyström's apprentices was Theodore Mannborg who returned to Germany and opened up a harmonium factory at Borna in Saxony in 1889, five years later moving his workshop to Leipzig.

The demand for harmoniums in Britain was large: Alexandre alone was sending 7,000 annually in the decade 1860-70. Soon, though, the increase in British-manufactured organs plus the effect of the mounting penetration of the American organ eroded this demand. Even so, by 1879 Alexandre had made 110,000 instruments. By comparison, the annual production of American organs had, by that year, reached 40,000.

In Britain, the harmonium underwent a similar process of evolution at the hands of a number of craftsmen such as the brothers Snell, Wardle Evans, Charles Kelly and Thomas Croger. To Evans goes credit for doing most for the harmonium in England. An inventor and skilful craftsman, his work is still appreciated to this day. His double-manual harmoniums enjoyed quite a vogue among amateur organists and a small reed instrument named the Orchestrina-di-camera, with its quite charming imitations of the tone of the flute, oboe, clarinet, bassoon and French horn, was a typical example of his skill in reed voicing.

Charles Kelly was described by his contemporaries as the 'cheery father of a cheery son.' The father ran what he called a 'pianoforte bazaar' at 11 Charles Street, Middlesex Hospital. But it was as a first-class maker of harmoniums that he is chiefly remembered. His instruments were supplied to Queen Victoria and to other members of the Royal Family, and he exhibited them with success at the Paris Exposition of 1867.

It was in the 1860s that the harmonium achieved its zenith of popularity in Britain, and every music shop stocked them in large numbers. Joseph Wallis of 135 Euston Road strongly promoted the instruments imported from Christophe & Étienne, both of whom were one-time Alexandre employees. But, although this was the high point of the harmonium's career, the American organ, first exhibited at that same Paris show, was, as we have seen, attracting attention. The situation was worrying on the one hand, yet presented a golden opportunity on the other. It fired makers' inspiration to make similar models and, by the 1880s, both pressure and suction-reed organs were established in production in Britain. One maker, John Jones of Bristol, actually incorporated both pressure and suction into one of his two-manual Bristol Organs which entered production in 1885. He was granted a patent (No 9860) for this in 1884, his specification stating that:

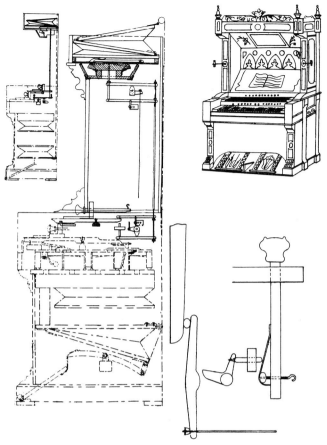

Fig. 5. John Jones of Bristol was granted British Patent No 9860 of 7 July 1884 for a combined harmonium and American organ. The suction organ was mounted in the upper part of the case above the pressure section

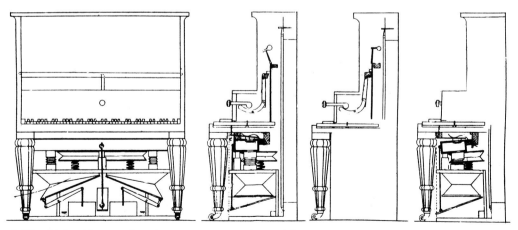

Fig. 6. Combining pianos and reed organs was a popular goal for many Victorian inventors. Southampton music teacher Isaac Pritchard was granted British Patent No 7865 of 17 May 1884 for this design. The central knob above the keyboard disengaged the piano action

the two instruments together constituting an instrument of two manuals having the exhaust or American organ quality in the upper or swell manual and the pressure or harmonium system in the lower or great organ, the object in view being to obtain effects of contrast of quality in the tones (such as are produced in large church organs) for the better study of classical or concerted music and to enable those who possess a harmonium of superior quality to combine with it the means of producing the delicate shadings of tone and combinations only possible with the exhaust system.

The same idea occurred to a number of other makers, although Jones was probably the first to produce such a dual-system organ. Even so, it was fifteen years before Mannborg produced his dual-system three-manual organ which he showed at the 1900 World Exhibition in Paris. Schiedmayer built a strange instrument called the 'Organ-pedal Harmonium' which operated like a normal suction harmonium with the player pedalling in the normal way, or, with the aid of an assistant turning a hand crankshaft, could be used as a pedal organ (an organ with a pedal clavier) using both suction and pressure.

Another British maker of high-quality harmoniums was Gilbert Bauer who was active in the 1860s in Ogle Street and later in King's Road, St Pancras. He was probably one of the earliest to make harmoniums with pedal boards and to this day is remembered for his well-made, technically complex and musically excellent instruments. Bauer learned his trade in Paris and, when he opened up his London workshop, he employed mainly French craftsmen.

Mustel's perfection of the prolongment or pedal-point feature first created by Martin was not the only such device. Edward Snell who, with his brother William, manufactured harmoniums extensively at various addresses in north London for around half a century, invented a pedal-point

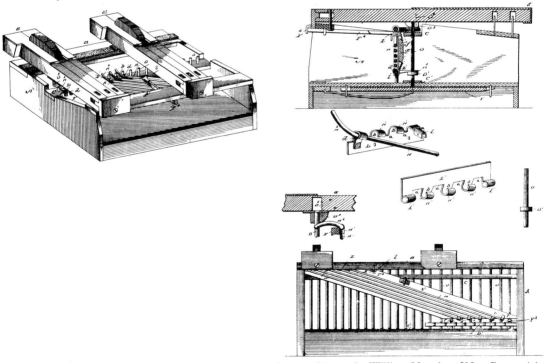

Fig. 7. One of the many devices to serve as an octave coupler was this one by William Murphy of New Brunswick, Canada, for which a British Patent No 2261 of 16 February 1886 was granted. Samuel Howard (of Melody attachment fame) had produced a practical coupler some eight years earlier

32

feature for his harmoniums in 1861. This he called the 'tirasse-tenuto' or pedal substitute. History has a habit of tripping over itself at times; in 1886 great claims were made by an American manufacturer who said he had invented a pedal-point stop of this self-same sort. Martin had done just that for Alexandre probably back in the 1850s, and Snell had produced his own variant in 1861.

A means of making a melody stand out from the accompaniment was in many ways an admission that the harmonium was not an easy instrument to play musically. When played as a one-rank instrument, it was simple enough; but once there were choices of pitch to contend with via the stops, if the instrument was played with, for example, more than an 8ft pitch selected, the fundamental melody notes could find themselves lost amidst accompaniment notes played effectively in octaves. This is readily understood if one imagines an 8ft, 4ft and 2ft stop selected. If one now plays middle C, then the notes which sound are middle C, the C an octave above and the C an octave above that - the three notes representing in effect three octaves. Add to this a 16ft bourdon or bass stop and there is then a fourth C playing, this one an octave below middle C.

Faced with this sort of musical quagmire, trying to make the melody so that it could be clearly heard was often quite a problem, particularly if the player used a number of stops of differing pitches without appreciating the difficulties such registration might cause. In 1853, Victor Mustel had turned his attention to the question of allowing the melody to stand out. This is what he had achieved with his double-expression which was in reality the division of the keyboard into two portions each with its own effective swell. The division of the keyboard became commonplace throughout the world of reed-organ making after it was patented in 1854.

The next invention to aid in emphasising the melody came from William Dawes, an inventor and engineer from Leeds who created a melody attachment by the use of which the top note of a melody could be made to stand out above the accompaniment. This was patented in 1864 and Dawes also patented a pedal bass developed from the same principle which could be used as a pedal substitute. This operated in virtually the same way as the prolongment of Alexandre's worker Louis Martin and the tirasse-tenuto of Edward Snell.

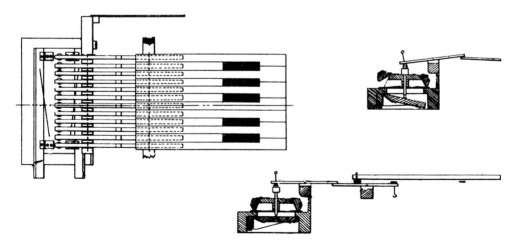

Fig. 8. The most significant improvement to the American organ was the invention of the so-called superoctave coupler for which Samuel Jenkinson, a North London organ-builder, was granted British Patent No 3115 of 13 February 1894. Like so many good ideas, it was a very simple device, yet one which considerably enhanced the performance of the instrument to which it was fitted. It comprised a small box containing a single octave of reeds which could produce an octave above the highest octave available on the keyboard

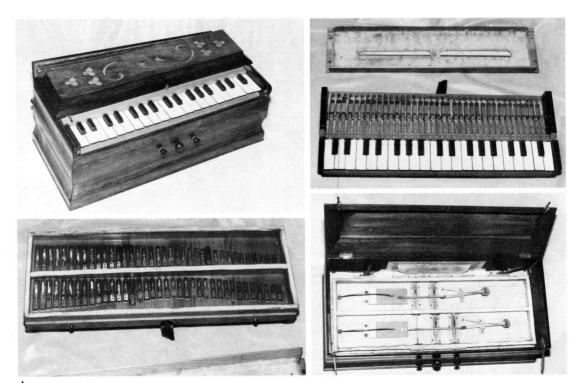

Plate 8. Miniature harmonium or harmoniflute made in France c.1850-60. There is no name on this instrument but stamped inside the windchest is the name "Savart" - probably the name of the craftsman who made the chest. Bellows lined with early French ledger paper. Compass G-G, 2 rows of reeds, each controlled by a drawstop. Central drawstop is a *grand jeu* producing an almost musette tone. Centrally above keys is a tiny lever which, when drawn out, opens a swell shutter. Distance between keyboard octave is 130mm. Bellows worked by one hand or by an assistant from behind. By lifting up the fretted top behind the keyboard, the keyboard and its little swell box can be removed |top right|. The keyboard is formed directly on top of the reed pan |lower left|. Note that several of the reeds have been replaced, one with an American organ reed. With the keyboard out, the nicely-made stop mechanism on top of the bellows board is exposed |lower right| (Author's collection)

◀

Plate 9. Early production 4-rank Debain harmonium showing the full-width foot treadles which characterised these formative instruments. Compare with the illustrations of the earlier seraphines. Produced around 1865, this has a 5- octave C-C compass and is tuned to the French pitch A = 435 (Staatliches Institut für Musikforschung, Preussischer Kulturbesitz Musikinstrumenten-Museum, Berlin)

SUPER OCTAVE COUPLER

Jenkinson's

PATENTS.

WE hold all the Patents on this grand Improvement in American Organs. Do not conclude the purchase of an American Organ before you have seen and heard the SUPER OCTAVE COUPLER, which makes a five octave organ into a six octave, a ten oct. organ into a twelve oct., and a fifteen oct. organ into an eighteen oct. Gives twelve more notes to each row of five octave reeds; it doubles the power to the top note on the organ; prevents the nasty breaks in the top octave.

When a Dealer tells you that this improvement is no use, take his statement with a grain or two of salt: he has old stock to sell. When George Stevenson's railway started, he was told that it was of no use.

Giving Twelve more Notes, F♯ to F (including semitones).

WE can produce testimonials from the largest Dealers in the United Kingdom; and several of the American makers are in treaty with us to use the improvement in their organs; one of them has concluded, and is using it.

This is one of the best improvements ever made in the American Organ. Buyers should see and try it before purchasing, as it is better to purchase an organ with the SUPER OCTAVE COUPLER complete than to have it fixed afterwards. We are constantly being asked to fix it to old organs.

FACTORY: 45, HAMPSTEAD ROAD, LONDON, N.W.

Fig. 9. This advertisement appeared in "Musical Opinion" in January, 1898, and shows the coupler fitted to a keyboard. Note that the front keyboard strip is removed to reveal the extra reed box in place under the keys

Dawes's melody attachment, of which J. Humphreys & Son were the sole makers, operated in a quite ingenious way using what is best described as a cascade valve system, so that, even when a chord was played, only the top note would sound, the others following sequentially as each note opened the controlling valve of its next successor down the scale. The attachment operated only under certain selected conditions such as when the melody system was operated in conjunction with certain stops. In, for example, a three-row organ, when the melody stop was selected, the three rows only operated on the reeds in the upper portion of the compass where, under normal conditions, the melody lies, while the accompaniment was suitably subdued. This meant that the melody notes were made to stand out and were thus accentuated. It also meant that the player had to allow for this fact, otherwise portions of the accompaniment or counter-melody would be subject to the same melodic treatment. The stop could be cancelled by the use of the knee-swell which allowed the three (or other number of) sets of reeds to act throughout the whole compass. Humphreys were still making instruments with this attachment as late as 1909, some of them two-manual organs.

Another way of achieving emphasis was double touch, where the melody might be highlighted by depressing the key slightly further than normal to bring in an extra rank of reeds. This was claimed as an English invention, the work of Augustus Tamplin, a professor of music. However,

Plate 10. Elegant small harmonium by Kaufmann of Dresden, 4-octaves C-C compass, two individual feeders supplying air through hollow central column. This style was originated by Debain in Paris, c.1852 who used a three-legged cast-iron stand to support one of his portable "harmoniflute" lap-organs. This specimen dates from late 19th-early 20th century (Staatliches Institut für Musikforschung, Preussischer Kulturbesitz Musikinstrumenten-Museum, Berlin)

► Plate 11. Minister's portable bible organ made in the shape of a book |above right| which could be carried under the arm.When opened |above left|, the bellows feeder has to be pushed down against its internal spring to charge the adjacent direct-acting reservoir. One row of reeds only (Author's collection)

Plate 12. Table organ produced by M Kasriel, Paris in the early 1890s. The instrument was patented in England (British Patent No 8827 of 3rd May 1895) by Joseph Wallis & Son of London in conjunction with Kasriel and marketed as the Wallis Patent Table Organ. This elegantly-finished and nicely-designed instrument was made in very large numbers yet few seem to survive today. It was blown using a detachable foot strap which pumped the feeder. F-G compass. 3 octaves and a fifth (courtesy of the Smithsonian Institution, Washington, DC)

Brooman secured a British Patent for just this much earlier in 1860 (see chapter 10).

The work of Samuel Howard of Manchester played an important part in the isolation of melody in the American organ. Between 1897 and 1901, he applied for a number of patents for such a scheme. His operating principle was ingenious and fairly simple. In his first scheme, rather like that of Dawes, the highest notes would sound on the melody or solo stop. However, in its developed form, the player could select whether it was the upper note or the lowest note of a melody or chord which should stand out. One or more stops in an organ would be equipped with this improvement so that, when the stop to which the melody device was applied was selected, that register would sound only the upper or melody notes. Unlike Dawes' cascade-type valves, Howard's Melody Attachment was a wholly mechanical device yet was an outstanding success. This development is described in chapter 10.

Among the earliest of devices to enhance the performance of the reed organ was the octave coupler. This came in several types and styles, the most common being a hinged-roller board under the keyboard which, when lifted up to contact the keys, allowed a series of small angled rods, each with a lever at both ends, to come into contact with the key being played, so allowing the other end of the rod to depress another key an octave above, or occasionally an octave below. The actual inventor is unknown but *Pinet's Harmonium Tuner*, published in 1913, describes a very early piano-sized reed organ incorporating an octave coupler:

> Even before Debain... instruments of the harmonium class had been made. For instance at the Paris 1900 Exhibition, in the historical section, a small instrument was shown, containing 5 octaves of free reeds of eight feet pitch, which was exhibited by Mr. Bilde and was the property of the Convent of the Augustines de la Miséricorde, 39 Rue Tournefer. This instrument was given to the Community in 1825 by Charles X himself, and is deserving of a brief description.
>
> The article resembles a modern upright piano, the feeders are directly under the sound-board, the wind reservoir is placed in the upper part of the case, and pressure is given by means of two springs fixed to a cross beam under the top cover, the blowing pedals are of cast iron and are adapted to the shape of the foot (it is amusing to note that the Americans claim the credit of having designed this pedal for their sewing machine).
>
> The construction of the sound-board is absolutely similar to that of Debain, except that the reeds are arranged in two rows instead of one. It is not a cavity board cut out of the solid. The wind inlet where the reed is placed is the same shape as at present, but the resonating cavities are wider, they are 15 mm. in the treble and 20 mm. in the bass and generally a centimetre less than the length of the frame of the reed. The outlet apertures for the wind are round, and the sound-board is made of

Fig. 10. A highly refined improvement to the American organ was Samuel Howard's so-called melody device by which a solo effect could be brought out on a single manual instrument. Howard, granted British Patent No 14,744 of 18 July 1899 for his invention, devised a simpler and cheaper method of achieving what William Dawes had done in 1864 with his seminal invention of the system whereby a melody line could be made to stand out above the accompaniment on a single manual reed organ. It was Samuel Howard who devised the practical octave coupler for which he was granted a patent in 1878. This notice appeared in May 1898

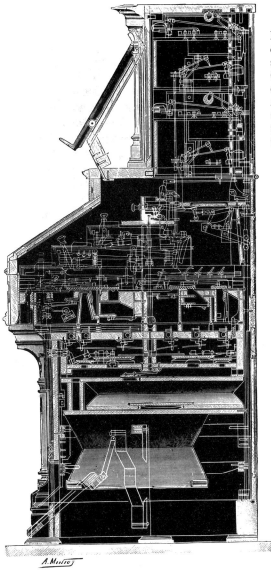

Fig. 11. Mustel in Paris continued to manufacture outstanding and complex harmoniums right up into the 1930s. This section of a three-manual instrument of 1910 shows the Celeste action - a percussion system of hammer-struck tuned steel bars like a xylophone - in the upper part of the case. Also visible at the keyboards are the side levers (rather like small daggers) which operated the prolongement action. The two heel-operated combination pedals, one for full organ and the other for key registers, can also be seen

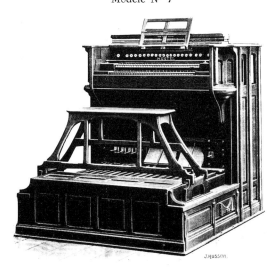

Modèle N° 7

Fig. 12. Mustel also produced this as a practice organ with pedals. The Model 7 of 1910 had 11 rows comprising 616 reeds. The lower keyboard offered eight 8ft stops and two 4ft stops. The upper one offered three 8ft, two 4ft and two 16ft. There was independent expression for each manual and, as well as coupling both manuals, the pedal organ could be coupled to the first manual. The Mustel organs were among the very finest built in Europe. However, while unquestionably a capable organ, despite the glowing tribute by organist Auguste Reinhard, it still featured the old-style and impractical straight pedal-board and a goodly measure of tonal Franco-Victoriana

Auguste REINHARD

L'Orgue Mustel marque le point culminant de la construction dont il représente le perfectionnement le plus accompli dans ce domaine.

The Mustel-Organ indicates the highest point of organ manufacture and represents the most perfect improvement done in this domain.

August REINHARD

Das Mustel-Harmonium bezeichnet für die Gegenwart den Hohepunkt des Harmoniumbaues und ist in überwiegendem Masse das Vollkommenste, was bis heute auf diesem Gebiete geleistet worden ist.

August REINHARD

chestnut and oak. The keys operate the pallets by means of thin plungers or rods. The reeds, made entirely by hand, are of solid brass not cast but cut out of thick metal a little shorter than our 8ft No. 2 set, having wider tongues than No. 5, particularly in the bass. The rivetting is very neatly done and the frames are cut away below. The reeds have retained their quality, and give a very round tone.

An interesting feature in this instrument is that it *possesses an octave coupler*, the invention of which is claimed by the Americans. This coupler works very well and acts by means of a slide which engages with the tail of the pallet, the latter being shaped like a round accordion valve - and the depression of the key causes the valve of the upper octave to lift accordingly without noise or the chance of missing, the pull being effected by small strips of silk which fold back when the slide returns to its place and the coupler is put out of action.

Unfortunately the name is not known of the skilful maker of this ingenious instrument, which contradicts many points in the none too precise history of the harmonium.

This description makes quite fascinating reading and it appears, from the manner it which it is written, that the author had himself seen the piece very recently. It would be interesting to know if it is still in existence somewhere. As far as octave couplers are concerned, however, by the 1870s they was in wide use in American organs and harmoniums both in Europe and the United States. Generally, it was used in the treble; but it was quite often also applied in the bass.

The purpose of the octave coupler was to brighten the upper register and to help isolate the melody line from the accompaniment in a sort of up-dated Dawes system. But there was a problem with it in that it worked perfectly for all but the last octave of the keyboard beyond which there was no octave of reeds to couple to. Samuel Jenkinson who built organs in north London applied himself to this shortcoming and, realising that all that was missing was an octave of reeds at the very top end, provided just that in his 'super-octave coupler' which he patented in 1894. It was the most significant of all British inventions and was soon in use by makers all over the world, including the United States. The device comprised a box containing the 'missing' twelve notes which was fitted onto the reed-organ table so that the coupler could now double up an octave even on the highest keyboard note.

Later on, there is a description of the fan tremulant or vox humana stop to replace the simple diaphragm or pulsed pneumatic tremulant of the harmonium. This was made in a variety of forms by British and American makers in lieu of the proper 'voix celeste' using an extra row (or more often half a row since the celeste did not run through the whole organ) tuned a regular beat flat - the stop invented by Mustel (see page 29). The earliest models were American designed and involved a series of valves to set the vibrato-inducing revolving vane in motion. However, it was James Harrison of Thomas Harrison & Son in north London who devised the vox humana which was soon to be adopted almost universally. This dispensed with valves of the former type and provided suction (or pressure) to a multi-bladed fan contained in a narrow, tight-fitting housing. This wind motor was quick to start, steady in speed and drew little power from the organ. There was a mechanical brake which instantly stopped the fan and rotor when the vox humana stop was cancelled. Harrison's device, British Patent No 8476 of 1885, was soon to form a part of of almost every suction reed organ built. Prior to this, the pipe-organ technique of a box with a rubber-cloth diaphragm and a rocking weighted pallet was employed. Among the very many who adopted Harrison's design was the Aeolian Co of New York for its player reed organs.

The attempts to improve the sounds produced by the free reed in the keyboard organ were continuous on both sides of the Atlantic. In the States, various claims were made for the manner in which the reeds were mounted, ranging from having different reeds in the same cell so that they interacted, through to the so-called 'qualifying tubes' extensively promoted by Clough & Warren. These were the invention of an employee, one Scribner, in 1882, and comprised a tapered box

„Schiedmayer, Pianofortefabrik",

vormals J. & P. Schiedmayer, Stuttgart.

Schiedmayer=Harmonium

mit 5½ Zungenreihen, Perkussion, 23 Registerzügen und 2 Kniedrückern.

Hector Berlioz sagt in seiner Instrumentationslehre:

„Das Harmonium ist zugleich ein Instrument für die Kirche und für das Theater, für den Salon und für den Konzertsaal. Wie viele Provinzialtheater Frankreichs und selbst Deutschlands, welche keine Orgel besitzen, fanden sich, seitdem Meyerbeer, Halévy, Verdi, Gounod etc. in ihren dramatischen Werken die Orgel angewendet haben, in Verlegenheit, auf welche Weise sie dieselbe ersetzen sollten! Zu wie vielen Verstümmelungen der Partituren hat dieser Mangel einer Orgel nicht Veranlassung gegeben! Heutzutage könnte nichts die Theaterdirektoren wegen Duldung ähnlicher Missethaten entschuldigen, weil sie für sehr mässige Kosten statt einer Orgel ein Harmonium haben können, welches jene beinahe vollständig ersetzt. Ebenso verhält es sich mit den kleinen Kirchen, wohin die Musik bis jetzt noch nicht gedrungen ist; ein von einem einsichtigen Musiker gespieltes Harmonium kann und muss dort die harmonische Bildung einführen und mit der Zeit jenes widerliche Geheul verdrängen, das sich daselbst noch mit dem Gottesdienste vermengt."

Fig. 13. The Stuttgart business of Schiedmayer produced the Hlavac-Konzert Harmonium in 1880. This particular model had two manuals, C-C compass, 5½ rows of reeds covering six octaves and providing eight octaves (by the use of full-range couplers). The lower manual offered three 8ft registers and one 16ft divided between bass and treble. The upper manual offered three 8ft registers, two 4ft, one 2ft and one 16ft. The whole was controlled by 23 stop knobs. Two knee swells each offered a double function: the first degree of movement selected bass (left) or treble (right) prolongment, the second stage or full movement of the left knee swell gave *grand jeu* while that of the right selected full-compass prolongement. The illustration is from Riehm, 1897

or chamber through which the air passed to each reed. This principle was later used successfully in the Vocalion patents for the Orchestrelle tone ranks. The manner in which the sound left the organ played a considerable part in the quality of the sound produced. Vertically mounted reeds were tried in the States (one maker, Smith of Boston, built instruments in which the whole action was vertical) and mutes of different materials were experimented with as were the methods of controlling them. All these attempts sought to do something to the sound after it had been produced and left the reed.

There were also various experiments to try to improve the sound quality and volume of the reeds themselves. A Scottish inventor, John Baillie-Hamilton, along with several others, tried to enhance the sound of the reed by attaching springs or wires to it. The upshot was a new type of reed organ which they called the the 'Vocalion.' The first actual demonstrations were given in 1875 and produced what was described as a beautiful and very peculiar quality of sound. Despite this encouraging result, the manufacture of the Vocalion proved both expensive and labour intensive: it did not lend itself to the mass production methods already operating in the reed organ industry. The original concept of the Vocalion was therefore abandoned. However, Baillie-Hamilton found that much of the quality of sound produced by his unusual device could be achieved by using broad reeds and adjusting the sizes and cubic capacities of the reed cells. After some years in Britain, he went to Canada and the United States where he ultimately founded the Vocalion Organ Manufacturing Co. In 1883 he patented what he termed 'unison-bar' reeds which comprised two elements attached to the same stem. There followed a series of successful, if still expensive, Vocalion organs which were more or less conventional harmoniums built using Baillie- Hamilton's new reed and pan form. So successful were the tonal characteristics of his organs that when Aeolian began making the Orchestrelle, Vocalion was the supplier of the complete tone-ranks. Ultimately,

Fig. 14. Organs by Bell and Karn feature in this department store catalogue page. The reference to Earl Dufferin - Lord Blackwood - dates this as between 1888 and 1902 and is probably c.1890

Vocalion became part of the Aeolian empire and Baillie-Hamilton and his company disappeared.

After the discovery of the principles of reed voicing (see chapter 2), the odd design byways such as Baillie-Hamilton's multiple reeds along with Merritt Gally's eccentric but accoustically clever 'superior power' reeds - some Y-shaped in plan - faded into oblivion. Trayser of Germany, though, formed his reeds in octaves of fourteen out of one plate; but otherwise conventionally. The French invention of actually striking the reed was jealously guarded by Alexandre and, although percussion was used by many other builders including, in later years, Aeolian (who misguidedly called it a 'pizzicato' stop), he was able to claim a worthwhile licence fee for many years.

The small harmonium, something between the accordeon and the full-sized reed organ, seems always to have been in demand. From the very small table keyboard organs of the 1830s came Debain's handsome single-pedestal instruments of 1850-60. These featured a single foot-board pedal attached to a cast-iron base which worked a concussion or accordeon-type multi-fold bellows at the back of the windchest. Kaufmann of Dresden (with his own Physharmonika) and Hüller & Stiegler of Leipzig were among those who later adapted this style into a thoroughly practical little 4-octave harmonium with two direct-acting foot bellows (the actual top board of each feeder being the foot board) which fed wind up through a hollow central ornamental column direct to the wind-chest bellows (see Plate 10).

As with other makers such as Estey in America, and Gebrüder Hug in Leipzig, the demand for small and portable organs encouraged manufacturers to make folding harmoniums. These were

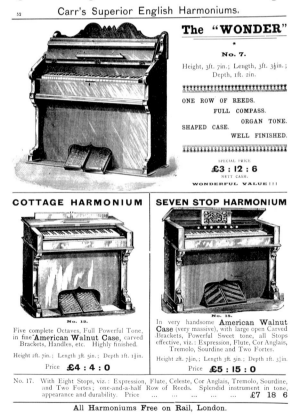

Fig. 15. From a department store catalogue comes this notice of stock harmoniums. These are typical of the instruments available in the closing decade of the last century

◄ Plate 13. Single-manual Mustel organ dating from November, 1881. Style is similar to the Model 2 but is without metaphones or prolongment. It is tuned to the French pitch, A = 435. There are seven sets of reeds totalling 430 controlled by 18 stops (courtesy of Keith C Jarrett)

Plate 14. Two-manual Mustel organ bearing the date 6th August 1926. The pitch is A = 440 and there are 11 sets of reeds totalling 586 controlled by 23 stops including metaphones, percussion and two prolongments. There is a heel pedal for full organ. These heel pedals are formed by the extended divider between the foot treadles and originally Mustel made these much shorter. In this form they were less easy to operate while pedalling and so, after about 1911, they were extended almost to the full length of the blowing pedals. The two small square knee swells are seen here in the closed position (courtesy of Keith C Jarrett)

▶

◄ Plate 15. Mustel Celeste two-manual reed organ. The upper manual plays on a series of tuned steel glockenspiel bars arranged with their hammer action in the upper portion of the cabinet. This percussion effect can be played separately or, using a coupler, in conjunction with the reed organ itself. The action, arranged in two staggered rows, is visible in the picture below which also shows the prolongment and metaphone stop levers in the keyboard cheeks. The two heel swell/full organ pedals can be seen to the left side of each bellows treadle. The angled music desk folds up flat to form the front panel of the upper case. Mustel's cabinetwork was always outstanding (formerly in the collection of the Author, now owned by Professor James Bratton of Denver, Colorado)

made in large quantities by R. F. Stevens of London in particular. Sad to say, when only a few years ago one of London's musical instrument wholesalers had a call for portable harmoniums, they had to be ordered not from London but from India!

By the start of the 1890s, there was a general feeling that British reed organ manufacturers were losing out rapidly to American organ competition. Although even then British instruments were musically superior in performance, the mass market lay in other directions. The editor of *Musical Opinion* took up his pen in the issue of July, 1891 and fired a broadside at the industry:

> Undoubtedly... the reed organ business is undergoing a radical change, and it is an interesting question whether the western organ manufacturers will be enabled to still further extend their trade. That the reed organ industry in this country is not developing at the rate of the piano industry is without question. Possibly our enterprising organ makers may manage to hold their own by finding new markets, and we must not lose sight of the fact that there is a strong and growing demand for American organs in England, Germany, and the English colonies.

This inspired Malcolm & Co to design, patent and manufacture their own special American organ action by mid-1893. *Musical Opinion* reported in December that year:

> The advantages of the invention are such that both sides are free from any appendages,- an advantage in case the action has to be taken out of an instrument. However, the inventor (Mr. Green, the manager) claims that, as the levers are worked by the aid of rollers, it is not within the range of probability that the action need be removed. All the parts are made in duplicate; therefore should a dealer desire to renew one, he has only to touch a button, release the affected part and write for a new part. The patent also provides that the vox humana stop is made as 'springy' as its fellow stops.

The criticism of our reed organ industry in 1891 may have been justified so far as the common or garden reed organ was concerned. At the other end of the scale, though, our industry was certainly not lagging behind, but truly led the world. It was realised that the reed organ, built to Royal College of Organists' specification with concave, radiating pedal board, could be used as a practice instrument by the church organist and even as a creditable replacement for the church organ. American organs and harmoniums had always found a place in chapels and churches, and all makers produced styles which they fondly believed would meet the needs of the church.

The specifications for pipe organs drawn up by the Royal College of Organists appeared in 1881, and the opportunity to create reed organs for the professional player was rapidly grasped. It was, though, only a limited number of makers who really made good instruments of this style and then not all of them to RCO recommendations. Among the makers who made instruments aimed at the professional were Estey and Mason & Hamlin in America; Mustel, Mannborg, Trayser (who later abandoned reed organ making when at the height of perfection), and Schiedmayer in Europe; and Arthur J. Spencer, John Holt, R. F. Stevens, Sames, Jones and Wedlake in England. Spencer produced the University two- and three-manual reed organs over a long period of time, he and John Holt catering both fully and virtually exclusively for this small and specialised market sector.

Holt's instruments came in a variety of styles ranging in price from 36 guineas up to £295 for a three-manual and pedal model with hand-blowing lever or electric pump. Holt's son joined the business of Rushworth & Dreaper and designed for them the Apollo, a much-improved version of his father's organ. This came in a variety of styles and cost from £190 upwards. The Canadian company of Thomas also made instruments to RCO standard and the 'Student's Practice Model' with two manuals and a pedal clavier had a compass of CC to c4, 61 notes, 6 sets of reeds and 12 stops, the price, added the 1908 advertisements of UK agent Charles E. Cartman of Manchester,

PORTABLE HARMONIUM,
Model 21.

No. 1.—4 octaves, 2 Rows of Reeds, 5 Stops	...	£15	10	0
„ 2.—3½ „ 2 „ „ 3 „	...	13	10	0
„ 3.—4 „ 1 „ „ No Stops	...	10	10	0

The above are all in very strong solid oak cases, dove-tailed and brass-bound, fitted with strong bellows, large strong iron drop handles. Very powerful tone. Well constructed throughout of best materials. Exceedingly strong and durable.

Measurements, Nos. 1 and 3 when shut down :

Length, 2 ft. 8 in., Height, 1 ft. 5 in., Depth, 1 ft. 3 in.
No. 2, „ 2 ft. 4 in., „ 1 ft. 5 in., „ 1 ft. 3 in.

Fig. 16. London maker R F Stevens was a prolific producer of harmoniums. This portable chapel organ dating from c.1925 is typical of many he and other similar makers produced over the years

on application. As an interesting anomaly, although the American makers of these organs tried to meet the demands of the British market, their models did not conform to the essential RCO designs as regards the pedal-board. In 1907, Farrand were advertising their two-manual instrument, described as 'Positively the Most Perfect Reed Organ yet Produced... it is the Nearest Possible Approach to a Real Pipe Organ,' with a straight pedal-board: Mason & Hamlin and Estey also perpetuated the impractical, ill-designed and obsolete pedal-clavier layout.

If the British industry did in any way lag behind that of America as regards the popular market,

◄ ►

Plate 16. Chapel organ by John Malcolm & Co, Kentish Town, London. Dated 20-9-01. 5 octaves, F-F compass, 28 bass, 33 treble. $2\frac{1}{2}$ sets of reeds plus 13 notes sub-bass, total 168 reeds. 12 stops, 2 knee swells, bass coupler, treble coupler. Walnut case with pew-shaped sides, mounted designs front and back |see above| and trundle carrying handles |picture left|. Sold by Monte Francis, Colchester, Essex. A late example of a British reed organ with an F compass (from the collection of Phil and Pam Fluke)

◄

◄ ►

Plate 17. Two-manual flat-top harmonium by Ph J Trayser & Cie of Stuttgart c.1875. 20 stops, $5\frac{1}{2}$ sets of reeds. Compass C to C. 29 bass, 32 treble notes. Total number of reeds = 337. Ebonised case has carved work plus brass inlay beneath the stop knobs. The two knee swells close in flush in the same manner as Mustel. All controls within organ are of brass in the French style. Ivory keys with bone fronts. Pencil note reads: "tuned and repaired by A Thornton, May, 1916". Organ is seen open |above| and closed |left|. Case number 19077 (from the collection of Phil and Pam Fluke)

46

that of France was virtually moribund by the beginning of this century. There were precious few new inventions or improvements from other than the house of Mustel. It is thus not surprising that, even by 1903, French harmonium makers were feeling the pinch from transatlantic competition (see quotation on page 93). The size of their industry was spelled out by *Musical Opinion* for April, 1905:

> The average annual value of the musical instruments made in Paris during the last six years has been twenty-three million francs, divided among three hundred and sixty makers, employing no fewer than five thousand workmen. Paris turns out every year one million three hundred and twenty thousand francs-worth of accordions. Pianos figure for eleven million four hundred thousand francs; organs and harmoniums for nearly five millions and a half...

No account of the history of the reed organ in Europe would be complete without reference to some of the unusual instruments devised experimentally to exploit its potential. Perzina's mutant instrument which used hammer-struck reeds instead of wind of any sort must be excluded from this brief survey. At a time when acoustical inventors Emanuel Moór and Paul von Jankó were experimenting with quarter and micro-tones in the field of keyboard music, a professor of physics called Arthur von Oettingen (born at Dorpat in northern Germany in 1836; lived and worked in Leipzig where he died in 1920) contrived a quarter-tone enharmonic harmonium which he called the 'Orthotonophonium.' This had a compass of 57 notes or not quite 5 octaves, each octave being divided into 53 notes. The keys were in 5 interspersed and interacting vertical rows, there being 4 tones to each of the 13 notes of the octave, plus the octave of the first note to make 53 - 13 times 4 plus 1. The correct octave of any note in any pitch was instantly accessible by use of a small plunger. Patented in 1914, it was made by Schiedmayer of Stuttgart: one can be seen in the musical instrument museum collection of the Staatliches Institut für Musikforschung Preussischer Kulturbesitz in West Berlin. Other similar devices were conceived by Bosanquet, Brown (designed by Poole), Helmholtz and Kewitsch (see chapter 10). Hans von Bülow gave to these the apt name 'enharmonium.'

Another oddity was the variable-touch harmonium patented by Brooman in which the deeper a key was pressed, the more sound the note produced (see chapter 10).

In the mid-1970s, an attempt to revive the reed organ in Britain was made by the Jacot Reed Organ Co of Birmingham; but in spite of good design and built-in electric suction unit, the whole organ business was on the brink of the electronic revolution, a move started (or popularised) by Hammond in the 1930s. The instrument had reached its peak in the first quarter of the present century at the hands of makers such as Holt and Apollo. It endured a period of recession during the World War I when what little production there was went for military and war-time use. After the war, the needs of the world were very different. Portable harmoniums were in greater demand than American organs in an age dominated by the attraction of the player piano and the gramophone and phonograph. The coming of radio was a final nail in the coffin of the mass-market popular reed organ. Although there was some post-World War I revival and Britain's reed-organ industry was for a while sustained by makers such as Holt, Rushworth & Dreaper (Apollo) and Stevens - in the case of the latter until as late as the 1950s - the reed organ industry had come to a closedown. Initially, the problem was one of economics. In the early part of this century, London sundries house J. & J. Goddard of 68 Tottenham Court Road sold 5-octave sets of untuned American organ reeds 2ft, 4ft, 8ft and 16ft at 5s 6d a set; by the 1960s the price was 80s a set. Five-octave organ keyboards with celluloid-covered keys cost 10s 6d; post-World War II price was £10. The cost of leather, rubber cloth, screws, keyboards - all had skyrocketted. Nobody will ever again be able to build a reed organ as a commercial proposition.

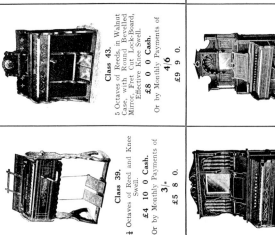

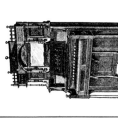

Fig. 17. The London business of Boyd was formed before 1903 for the manufacture of reed organs, pianos and player pianos. This notice, from the inside front cover of the "Boyd Tutor for American Organ and Harmonium", dates from around 1904 and shows both pressure and suction instruments

Fig. 18. Rushworth & Dreaper's Apollo pedal reed organ was a development of the John Holt pedal organ and represented probably the zenith of the British development of the reed organ. It was a perfect substitute for a church organ and could be used in church organ practice and teaching. This full-page notice appeared in "Musical Opinion" for June, 1913

CHAPTER 4

The American Industry
and its Achievements

Mention has already been made of the belief that most of the improvements to the reed organ which were carried out in the United States tended to be concerned with the mechanics and production of the instrument. In fairness, it should be emphasised that this happened at a much earlier stage than British or French production. The demand for instruments in America became so great, not just for the home market but for export, that better means of production and newer, more saleable styles were uppermost in the minds of American factories. The salient features in the way of improvement such as the coupler, sub-bass, vox humana and improved mechanics were all pioneered in America. The responsibility for the refinement of the reed organ as an instrument of music was, though, left to Britain, France and, to a lesser extent Germany.

The start of the reed organ business in the States was, like the burgeoning days of any new invention destined to become a great industry, something of a haphazard affair. There were many makers up and down the United States who were turning out small instruments which ranged from lap-organs up to the larger-sized keyboard or button reed organ which became known as a 'melodeon'. In Britain, however, 'melodeon' was another name for the accordeon. Also the vagaries of spelling produced 'melodion' and 'accordion'; where important, original spellings are followed in this book.

What is puzzling is how the reed organ reached America. Was it a seminal concept, or was it the development of an external stimulus? Nobody seems ever to have analysed just how the free reed came to become so popular with these instrument makers as early as the time of Peaseley in 1818 as related further on. American authorities on the subject have conveniently ignored this highly important consideration. In the absence of any information whatsoever, one might be justified in forming the opinion that it originated from an immigrant with knowledge of the very early work in Europe. A report published in 1892 suggests that the first US patent for a reed organ was granted in 1812 and the first reed organs built in America appeared in 1818. The early lap-organs, such as those made by Prescott and others, bore more than a passing resemblance to the rather primitive contemporary European product; all the main features were there although, once established in America, European and American products naturally tended to progress down different paths. In 1778 a Huguenot emigrant left Jersey in the Channel Islands as a child with his parents. His name was James A. Bazin and he settled in Canton, Massachusetts, where he made lap-organs and elbow melodeons in the French style. Much later, in 1842 and 1853, he was granted patents for improvements to reed organs.

The discovery that the tone of a reed could be modified according to the shape of the cell in

Case 85, with Pipe Top.

Resonant case, with pipe Organ Top, and heavy gilt pipes; richly carved, paneled and ornamented. Accompanied by BLACK WALNUT BENCH.
Length, with handle, 6 ft. 7 in.; without, 5 ft. 9 in. Height, 10 ft. 7 in. Depth, 3 ft. Weight, lbs.lbs. (Boxed, in two boxes, 000 lbs.)
Style 801—*ACTION 41, IN CASE 85, WITH PIPE ORGAN TOP. TWO MANUAL AND PEDAL BASE ORGAN; TWENTY*
THREE STOPS. C Scale. *For specifications of contents, see under Style 800, on last previous page.*

Fig. 19. From the Mason & Hamlin catalogue of October 1884 comes this handsome instrument with dummy pipe top and flat pedal board. The organ proper extends no further upwards than the top of the music desk

which it was placed is said to have been an American invention, and an exhaustive search has failed to produce information to the contrary. It is thus impossible to disprove this claim which was the subject of letters patent granted to Aaron Merrill Peaseley in 1818. The original papers, signed by James Monroe, President of the United States, and John Quincy Adams, Secretary of State, were preserved in the archives of the Mason & Hamlin Organ Company of Boston and New York. Peaseley styled his invention 'an improvement in organs'. Like so many new inventions, it attracted little attention and probably its primitive tone did little to warrant popularity.

Interestingly enough, early though this was, Peaseley was certainly not the first to use free reeds in America. A Boston pipe-organ builder, Ebenezer Goodrich, incorporated free-reed stops into some of his organs in the early 1800s and in 1809 built an entire reed-playing organ. Meanwhile, although the name seraphine was seldom used in the United States, a New York musical instrument maker Lewis Zwahlen was granted a patent on 5 May 1832, for a 'seraphina or harmonicon organ'. At this time, imports from Britain were quite common and it may be that Zwahlen, on seeing an imported seraphine, saw how he might improve upon it. As mentioned earlier, the inventor of the seraphine remains uncertain, but it seems to have made its first appearance towards the end of the 1820s. John Green's improvement, it will be remembered, came in 1833.

Some twenty-five years after Peaseley's invention - namely around 1843 - Jeremiah Carhart, then working for a melodeon maker named George A. Prince in Buffalo, New York, made use of suction or exhaust bellows in place of the pressure bellows hitherto commonly used. He also made numerous other detail changes to the instrument. Carhart, although he was not the originator of the exhaust bellows - even in Peaseley's original patent we find the suggestion that either a 'force or exhaust bellows' might be used - was granted United States Patent No 4912 on 28 December 1846 for this invention. He was working for Prince at the time and shrewdly did not assign rights

CARPENTER,

"LIBRARY ORGAN."

Containing the Celebrated Carpenter Organ Action.

Something Entirely New! The Æsthetic Taste Gratified!

THIS IS ONLY ONE OF ONE HUNDRED DIFFERENT STYLES.

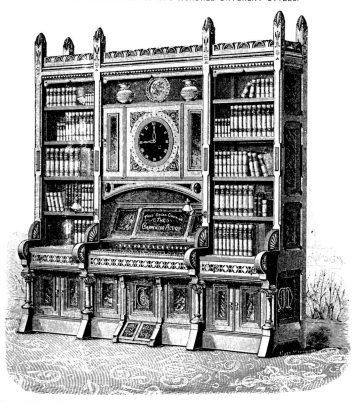

THIS effective and beautiful design in the modern Queen Anne Style is intended to meet the demands of those desiring an instrument of special elegance, and in harmony with the fittings and furnishings of the Study or Library Room, combining as it does, in a substantial and tasteful manner, the Organ, the Library cases, and the cabinet for bric-a-brac and articles of virtu.

It is well adapted to find favor in homes of culture and refinement, and will be championed by the music lover and connoisseur.

The composition is one of well balanced proportions, chaste subordination of ornamentation, and of artistic arrangement in constructive details, imparting to the design a rich simplicity and substantial worth.

This beautiful organ contains the Celebrated Carpenter Organ Action. The action is to an Organ what the works are to a watch. The merits of the Carpenter Organ were fully proved on page 158 of the YOUTH'S COMPANION of April 20th, to which special attention is directed.

A beautiful 80-page Catalogue, the finest of its kind ever published, is now ready and will be sent free to all applying for it.

Nearly all reliable dealers sell the Carpenter Organs, but if any do not have them to show you, write to us for a Catalogue and information where you can see them. DO NOT BUY ANY ORGAN UNTIL YOU HAVE EXAMINED "THE CARPENTER." In writing for a Catalogue always state that you saw this advertisement, in the *Youth's Companion.*

Address or call on E. P. CARPENTER, Worcester, Mass., U. S. A.

Fig. 20. The combination of musical instruments with another artefact, decorative or otherwise, was a fairly common characteristic of the United States in the last century. Sewing machines combined with an organette were at one end of the scale: Carpenter's Library Organ of 1882. This extraordinary instrument was advertised in the "Youth's Companion" for April that year (courtesy of the Ottenheim Collection)

to his employer, but instead charged a royalty to him and other reed-organ makers for the use of his patent. In addition to the exhaust bellows, Carhart also sought patent protection for the reed pan for the reed organ.

Both these features were certainly not original and to attempt to patent them appears naive in the extreme. Was Jeremiah Carhart a charlatan who capitalised on the fact that, thanks to the fire which destroyed all American patent records before 1836, there was no way of checking the originality of his claims, or did he just happen to think he was genuinely the first? There is no way of telling, but certainly by 1860, by which time people had begun to recall the long-prior claim by Peaseley, Carhart's claim had been disputed and his patents declared void.

Nevertheless, Carhart, as far as America was concerned, was the first inventor in that country to capitalise on the suction bellows in such a manner that the tone of the instrument might be bettered. From that moment onwards, suction bellows rapidly gained acceptance. The principle was also to lie at the very foundation of the piano-player and player-piano industry, then still half a century away.

Despite this unfortunate affair, Carhart's influence on the development of the reed organ in America cannot be over-emphasised. No doubt much of this was due to the fact that he was working with what was then America's leading reed-organ maker, George Prince. Certainly Carhart was experimenting with various methods of applying the free reed from around 1836. He did invent and successfully patent a machine for boring reed pans. He supplied organs and reeds to the trade and in addition built reed organs in large quantities. And, in the burgeoning days, Carhart gave his first reed organ the name 'Melodeon', apparently being the first to use this term. Just as 'harmonium' became generic from Debain in France, 'melodeon' became the generic term in America from thence forward.

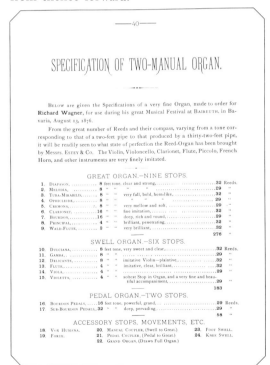

Fig. 21. From the Jacob Estey Company's catalogue of c.1878 comes this specification of an instrument which they built for Wagner for the Bayreuth Music Festival of 1876. Perhaps only Wagner would have wanted a 32ft Sub-Bourdon'.

Mannborgs Großes Ausstellungs-Harmonium
für die Weltausstellung Paris 1900.

Plate 18. The Leipzig maker Mannborg built this three-manual instrument for the Paris Exhibition of 1900. 5 octaves, C-C compass, 30-note pedal organ C-F compass. Probably the most complex reed organ ever built, it featured a unique blending of reed and pipe-organ technologies. Manual 1 operated a 5-row pressure reed organ comprising flute 8ft, melodia 8ft, oboe 8ft, bourdon 16ft and piccolo 4ft. Manual 2 operated an 8-row suction reed organ comprising diapason 8ft, flute d'amour 8ft, english horn 8ft, clarinette 16ft, viola dolce 4ft, waldflote 2ft, cornette-echo 8ft, aeolian harp 8ft. Manual 3 operated a three-rank pipe organ comprising gedackt 8ft (wood), posaune 16ft (metal), principal 4ft (metal). The pedals played a 5-row suction reed organ offering subbass 16ft, posaune 16ft, trompete 8ft, octave 4ft, bombardon 32ft. Accessories included prolongment, octave coupler, three manual couplers, three pedal couplers, no fewer than 10 full organ selectors, three kneeboards for swells and 6 pneumatic combinations. Electric blowing/suction was provided. The problem of keeping both reeds and pipes in tune dissuaded builders from making these hybrid instruments commercially. This illustration comes from the Mannborg catalogue and is the only one known (courtesy of Phil and Pam Fluke)

Case 139.

Paneled front and ends, ornamental antes; lamp stands, etc.; finished back.

Length, 5ft. 11 in. Depth, 2 ft. 2 in. Height, 3 ft. 6 in. (to top of full-board, 2 ft. 6 in.). Weight, 160 lbs. (Boxed, 310 lbs.)

Style 2209.—ACTION 69, IN CASE 139. FIVE OCTAVE, SEVEN STOPS. F SCALE.

Bass.	Treble.
DIAPASON, 8 ft.	MELODIA, 8 ft.
VIOLA, 4 ft.	SERAPHONE, 8 ft.
	VOX CELESTE, 8 ft.

TREMULANT. *Throughout.* FULL ORGAN (*Knee Stop*).

KNEE SWELL.

Having four sets of reeds, of two and a half octaves each.

Style 2208.—ACTION 73, IN CASE 139. FIVE OCTAVE, NINE STOPS. F SCALE.

Bass.	Treble.
DIAPASON, 8 ft.	MELODIA, 8 ft.
VIOLA, 4 ft.	FLUTE, 4 ft.
VIOLA DOLCE, 4 ft.	CLARABELLA, 8 ft.
DULCIANA, 8 ft.	

FULL ORGAN (*Knee Stop*). VOX HUMANA.

Throughout.

KNEE SWELL.

Having four sets of reeds of two and a half octaves each.

Case 139, with Extended Top A.

With GOLD BRONZE decorations.

Height, 5ft. Weight, 175 lbs. Top can be packed in box with organ.

Style 2207.—ACTION 59, IN CASE 139. FIVE OCTAVE, ELEVEN STOPS. F SCALE.

Bass.	Treble.
VIOLA, 4 ft.	OBOE, 8 ft.
VIOLA DOLCE, 4 ft.	CLARIONET, 8 ft.
DIAPASON, 8 ft.	MELODIA, 8 ft.
DULCIANA, 8 ft.	CLARABELLA, 8 ft.
	VOX CELESTE, 8 ft.

TREMULANT. *Throughout.* FULL ORGAN (*Knee Stop*).

KNEE SWELL.

Having four sets of reeds of two and a half octaves each.

Style 2206.—ACTION 8, IN CASE 139. FIVE OCTAVE, TEN STOPS. F SCALE.

Bass.	Treble.
VIOLA, 4 ft.	SERAPHONE, 8 ft.
VIOLA DOLCE, 4 ft.	VOX CELESTE, 8 ft.
DIAPASON, 8 ft.	MELODIA, 8 ft.

Throughout.

TREMULANT. FULL ORGAN (*Knee Stop*).

FORTE, DIA. MEL. FORTE, VIO. SER.

KNEE SWELL.

Having four sets of reeds of two and a half octaves each.

Case 139, with Extended Top B.

Large extended top, with music portfolio, bric-a-brac shelves, etc.

Height, 5 ft. 9 in. Weight, 180 lbs. (Boxed, 350 lbs.) The top is packed in box with organ.

Style 3301.—ACTION 44, IN CASE 139. FIVE OCTAVE, ELEVEN STOPS. F SCALE.

Bass.	Treble.
VIOLA, 4 ft.	FLUTE, 4 ft.
VIOLA DOLCE, 4 ft.	SERAPHONE, 8 ft.
DIAPASON, 8 ft.	VOIX CELESTE, 8 ft.
	MELODIA, 8 ft.

Throughout.

VOX HUMANA. FULL ORGAN (*Knee Stop*).

FORTE, DIA. MEL. FORTE, VIO. FL. SER.

KNEE SWELL.

Having five sets of reeds of two and a half octaves each.

Style 3300.—ACTION 199, IN CASE 139. PLAIN. FIVE OCTAVE, TWELVE STOPS. F SCALE.

Bass.	Treble.
VIOLA, 4 ft.	SERAPHONE, 8 ft.
VIOLA DOLCE, 4 ft.	VOIX CELESTE, 8 ft.
DIAPASON, 8 ft.	MELODIA, 8 ft.
SUB-BASS, 16 ft.	

Throughout.

FULL ORGAN OCTAVE COUPLER (*Knee Stop*).

TREMULANT, FORTE, MEL. DIA.

FORTE, VIO. SER.

KNEE SWELL.

Having four sets of reeds of two and a half octaves each; one set of one octave.

Case 139, with Extended Top C.

Imitation pipe top; pipes and decorations in GOLD BRONZE.

Height, 6ft. Weight, 195 lbs. (Boxed, 370 lbs.) This set requires an extra packing box.

Style 3310.—ACTION 75, IN CASE 139. FIVE OCTAVE, TWELVE STOPS. F SCALE.

Bass.	Treble.
VIOLA, 4 ft.	OBOE, 8 ft.
VIOLA DOLCE, 4 ft.	CLARIONET, 8 ft.
DIAPASON, 8 ft.	MELODIA, 8 ft.
DULCIANA, 8 ft.	CLARABELLA, 8 ft.
EOLIAN HARP, 2 ft.	VOX CELESTE, 8 ft.

TREMULANT. *Throughout.* FULL ORGAN (*Knee Stop*).

KNEE SWELL.

Having six sets of reeds of two and a half octaves each.

Style 447.—ACTION 50, IN CASE 139. FIVE OCTAVE, THIRTEEN STOPS. F SCALE.

Bass.	Treble.
VIOLA, 4 ft.	FLUTE, 4 ft.
DIAPASON, 8 ft.	MELODIA, 8 ft.
SUB-BASS, 16 ft.	VOIX CELESTE, 8 ft.
VIOLA DOLCE, 8 ft.	SERAPHONE, 8 ft.

Throughout.

OCTAVE COUPLER. FULL ORGAN

(*Coupling 16ft*).

VOX HUMANA. KNEE SWELL.

TREMULANT, FORTE, VIO FL. SER.

FORTE, DIA. MEL.

Having five sets of reeds, of two and a half octaves each; one set of one octave.

Fig. 22. The outward appearance of an organ should never be considered indicative of the style or content of the instrument itself. Here are two pages from the October 1884 Mason & Hamlin catalogue showing how the changes could be rung on case style and action (courtesy of C M Lindars)

The next significant development in America came from a young man named Emmons Hamlin who was also working for George A. Prince of Buffalo. Prince started his business around 1846, and by 1866 claimed to be the oldest establishment in the United States to be making melodeons. While working for him, Hamlin discovered that, by giving the tongue of the reed a slight bend and a twist at the free end, the reed sounded more promptly and the quality of tone produced was improved. Hamlin thus perfected for the reed the art of voicing, which hitherto had been considered impossible. Prior to that, any change in the tone of a reed had been considered dependent only on its proportions and the material of the reed itself. His new technique was applied to Prince's organs and earned them a reputation which exceeded that of other, contemporary makers. Largely due to this development, Prince became the most significant maker around the middle of the nineteenth century. Henceforth, every maker tried hard to improve on the technique of reed voicing with varying degrees of success.

Shortly after this, Hamlin formed a partnership with Henry Mason and so began the business of Mason & Hamlin in 1854. The new business developed what at first it called the 'organ-harmonium' but which soon became styled the American cabinet organ. By the early 1870s, Mason & Hamlin was exporting to every part of the world, the value of exports to Europe alone exceeding $100,000.

While this business thrived, so did that of Jacob Estey. Estey bought out a Brattleboro, Vermont, melodeon-manufacturing business founded in 1846 by Samuel H. Jones, Riley Burditt (later known as Burdett) and another. This was in 1846. The two manufacturers were consistently the most prolific in America, and both were responsible for many valuable improvements to the tone and construction of the instrument.

In 1870, about 32,000 organs were made in America. This compared with 23,000 pianofortes. The increased popularity of the instrument in that country between 1860 and 1870 was most noticeable as, in 1860, production had been around one-third of that total. The reason for the expansion was, according to *Great Industries of the United States* published in 1872, the 'great improvements made in the instrument itself'. In the words of this compendium of industrial progress:

> Formerly it was a mere 'convenience' for lack of something better, and mainly because nothing more satisfactory was available. Now the instrument is worthy from its intrinsic merit, and has favor with cultivated musicians, as well as the people. There can be little doubt that it has not yet reached its greatest popularity, because not sufficient time has yet elapsed to make it generally known... It is comparatively very cheap. A good instrument, though quite small, is now furnished at fifty dollars; and from this it increases in size, capacity, elegance, and price, to styles which are worth thousands of dollars each.

The days of the cheap American-made organ were numbered; in 1877 workers in the manufacturing centres of Worcester and Chicago began to press for higher wages. Inflexibility on the part of employers led to a series of lengthy and bitter strikes in that and the following year. The dispute was settled by an agreement to higher wages which, coinciding with a rise in the cost of materials, resulted in a rise of between 5% and 10% in the cost of pianos and organs. The recession of the late 1870s had already depressed sales and the industry suffered from price-cutting, low profit margins and minimal investment. Only in 1879-80 did the trade begin to pick up once more.

Even in the nineteenth century, the American reed organ industry was bedevilled with the ramifications of high finance, with mergers and takeovers. As in the eighteenth century church and chamber barrel-organ industry in London, workers moved from maker to maker, taking with them skills, bee-like to pollinate and expand a craft which was rapidly becoming an industry.

Partnerships were formed, dissolved, re-convened with fresh partners; and gradually the interests of bankers and financiers took a greater part in shaping individual manufacturer's fortunes.

There were also claims, counter-claims, litigation, law suits. For more than a decade, Estey was embroiled with Riley Burdett over who had been the first to create a reed pan with two-and-a-half sets of reeds, the half set starting at the tenor f and running through the treble in special reed cells so placed that they could tonally react with the other reeds, and tuned slightly sharp to form a celeste effect. The case ran from the early 1870s and involved charges of tampering with the evidence and mutilation of exhibits - an early reed organ made by one Arvid Dayton of Wolcottville, Connecticut, in around 1865 - the bribing of witnesses; graft in high places and subterfuge. It was claimed that an Estey employee, Henry K. White, discovered the celeste effect in tuning in 1865 and that Burdett, who had tried to patent the process in 1867, had been ill-advised. The Supreme Court of the United States had to sort out this peculiar and bitter case, reversing the earlier decisions of a circuit judge and district judge and finding Burdett's claims against Estey unfounded. Meanwhile, Arvid Dayton had been making celeste-tuned organs without bothering to patent the idea since 1855. The whole story of this strange case is told in *Estey Reed Organs on Parade* by Robert B. Whiting.

New inventions and patents went hand-in-hand throughout the American reed-organ industry. To Estey goes the credit for making the first cardboard fan tremulant or imitation vox humana attachment, subsequently improved upon and fitted to just about every organ made after the 1870s. Estey's first was patented in 1865 and was crank-driven from a special third foot treadle; the player had to master switching pedals in mid-music in order to use this. Every maker worth his pedals sought to invent and patent; Estey netted patent protection for a number of improvements, one being the 'Patent Vox Jubilante', described as a 'new and beautiful stop, peculiar to Estey Organs. The character of the tone is marked and wonderfully effective... This is accomplished by an extra set of reeds, ingeniously arranged and peculiarly tuned... With this attachment... the most thrilling effects can be produced..' There was also the 'Patent Harmonic Attachment' which was an octave coupler 'used on a single manual, and doubles the power of the instrument without increasing its size or number of reeds...' Additionally, the 'Patent Manual Sub-Bass' used 'an independent set of large and powerful Sub Bass Reeds... The manner in which this set of reeds is placed upon the air chamber increases the volume of tone at least one-third... The invention is covered by three patents.' After that there was a 'Patent Organ Bellows', 'Patent Reed Board' and 'Patent Knee-Swell' along with various others. Another reed-organ maker, Carpenter, also held a number of patents, but the most significant of these was one for a divided octave coupler.

There was always news of fresh developments in the company field, together with continuous effort to design and produce more and larger instruments. If the reed organ was originally the poor man's piano, then many a reed-organ maker decided to capitalise on it and make pianos as well; after all, the skills were similar. From *Musical Opinion* for April 1889 comes a story of such a move:

> The Burdett Organ Co. (Limited), of Erie, Pa., have recently written to one of their leading agents in Pennsylvania, that since they announced their intention of merging their organ making into piano making, they have received so many new orders for their organs, that they may yet determine to arrange to manufacture both organs and pianos. The new Burdett piano will be on the market in time for the fall trade.

The founder of that company, though, was not to enjoy the new-found success for long. These men lead active lives, sailing the Atlantic to set up new markets, travelling across the country

Plate 19. Mannborg also made more conventional chapel organs such as this model, also taken from the turn-of-the-century company prospectus. All this maker's instruments were tuned to A = 435. This two-manual suction instrument in its Gothic-style case is but one example of the extraordinarily broad range of case styles Mannborg could offer which included baroque, rococo, jugenstil and art nouveau (courtesy of Phil and Pam Fluke)

MASON & HAMLIN
AMERICAN ORGANS.

Specification of

THE "QUEEN'S MODEL,"

AS SUPPLIED TO

HER MOST GRACIOUS MAJESTY
THE QUEEN.

This Organ has been especially manufactured by the Mason and Hamlin Organ Company, and has been pronounced by competent Musicians "the best American Organ that has yet been produced." The tone, which is very round, full and sweet, is full of religious feeling, and a more perfect imitation of a Pipe Organ is not known.

The Queen's Model is of the full Compass of 5 Octaves, C to C, and contains Three-and-a-half complete sets of Reeds, 16 ft. throughout, 8 ft. throughout, 4 ft. throughout, and a Solo set of Reeds of 16 ft. in the Treble.

Bass Stops.	Treble Stops.
Bourdon, 16 ft.	Clarinet, 16 ft.
Sub Bass, 16 ft.	Musette, 16 ft.
Diapason, 8 ft.	Voix Céleste, 16 ft.
Viola, 4 ft.	Melodia, 8 ft.
Viola Dolce, 4 ft.	Piccolo, 4 ft.

Throughout.

VOX HUMANA. OCTAVE COUPLER (Up). FULL ORGAN (Knee Stop).

Also THE PATENT COMBINATION KNEE SWELL.
(The only effective Swell that has been invented.)

New Illustrated Catalogue Now Ready.

METZLER & CO., 42, GREAT MARLBOROUGH STREET, LONDON, W.
MAY BE HAD OF ALL MUSIC SELLERS.

Fig. 24. Metzler supplied this Mason & Hamlin model to Queen Victoria

---

MASON & HAMLIN'S
NEW PEDAL ORGAN,

FOR ORGAN PRACTICE.

TESTIMONIAL FROM EDOUARD BATISTE.

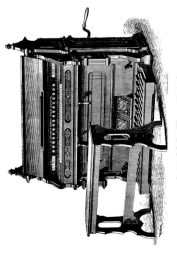

STYLE 510.

Chapel design; panelled front, back and ends; resonant top with exterior swells, controlled by the knee or foot. Accompanied by BLACK WALNUT BENCH.

Length, 4 ft. 11 in.; (with Blow handle, 5 ft. 10 in.) Depth, 2 ft. 8 in. Height, 4 ft. 10 in.
Weight, 467 lbs. (With Stool, in Packing Case, 650 lbs.)

CONTAINING FIVE OCTAVES, EIGHTEEN STOPS, AND COMPLETE PEDAL ORGAN OF THIRTY NOTES IN COMPASS.

Bass.		Treble.	
DIAPASON, 8 ft.	VIOLA, 4 ft.	MELODIA, 8 ft.	FLUTE, 4 ft.	SERAPHONE, 8 ft.
VIOLA DOLCE, 4 ft.	CONTRA BASSO, 16 ft.	CORNO, 16 ft.	VOIX CÉLESTE, 8 ft.	

Throughout.
PEDAL COUPLER.
OCTAVE COUPLER.
FULL ORGAN (Knee Stop).
VOX HUMANA.
FORTE DIA. MEL. KNEE SWELL.
FORTE, VIO. FL. SER.

Pedals.
BOURDON, 16 ft.
BOURDON DOLCE, 16 ft.
FULL ORGAN (Pedal Stop).
FOOT SWELL.

Having four sets of reeds of three octaves each, and three sets of two octave each, in Manual ; and one set of thirty notes in Pedals. With Blow Handle at back. The FULL ORGANS and SWELLS in this instrument can be independently operated by either knee or foot, and the Organ can be fully supplied with wind by the performer, having BLOW PEDALS conveniently placed above Pedal Key-board, or wind can be supplied by a second person using Blow Handle.

TO BE HAD OF ALL MUSICSELLERS.

No. 11.

Fig. 23. Tonally capable instruments for use in chapels did not demand the dummy pipe approach. Usually the back of the case was presented to the congregation and so invariably was neatly and decoratively finished, and the organist had to be able to see over the top of the case. The result was the almost pew-like case style favoured by many as typified by this Mason & Hamlin instrument for chapel or organ practice (courtesy of R H S Carpenter)

by horse and waggon, and generally imparting a great strain to their bodies and health. From *Musical Opinion* for March 1890:

BURDETT ORGAN CO

The American papers inform us that Mr. Riley Burdett of the Burdett Organ Company, died in Chicago, on January 26th, of pneumonia. He was born in Brattleboro, Vt., about the year 1819. In 1865, in Chicago, he became head of the R. Burdett Organ Company, which manufactured an instrument - the Burdett celeste organ - that became famous nearly the world over. The great fire of 1871 swept the works of the company out of existence, and the firm moved to Erie, where a new organisation was effected, under the style of the Burdett Organ Company (Limited), by Mr. Burdett, Mr. C. C. Converse, and others; Mr. Burdett devoting his time to organ invention, while Mr. Converse was, and now is, the company's business manager. It is this institution that gave Erie probably a more widely extended name than any other establishment, as its products were sent to every country on the globe. Mr. Burdett, it is believed, did more to perfect this popular instrument than any other man, as he was granted twenty-six patents affecting the movement, tone, construction, material, &c., all connected with the Burdett organ. For several years past Mr. Burdett has not given any time or attention to factory matters, the condition of his health being such as to prevent his doing so. His death does not affect the company's interests nor plans, nor the future of the instrument with which he was for so many years identified.

And just a few months later, in May, the same periodical had to record another sad event:

ESTEY ORGAN COMPANY

The death is announced, on April 15th, of Mr. Jacob Estey, founder of the Estey industries as Brattleboro, United States, and the manufacturer of the well known reed organ that bears his name. The deceased gentleman, although seventy-six years of age, was at his factory as usual, but the rupture of a blood vessel sent him to his house, where he died in an hour or so. Jacob Estey came of poor parentage, and was originally apprenticed to a plumber. He ultimately started a plumbing business in Brattleboro, and continued it till about 1855, when he appears, in conjunction with a Mr. Carpenter, to have turned his attention to the manufacture of 'melodions,' the American name for the ordinary harmonium. Mr. Carpenter retired in favour of one Hines, which latter made way for Mr. H. P. Green. So the deceased gentleman had a good choice of partners'. Thus matters went on till 1866, when the reed organ business - at that time employing over a hundred hands - migrated to Flat Street, his son (Julius) and his son-in-law (Levi K. Fuller) being taken into the firm. Since then the progress of the business has been upward and onward, over one fifth of a million instruments having already been sold. America is losing her pioneers in the American organ trade, for Mr. Riley Burdette [sic] died - also over three score and ten - about a couple of months ago. Strange to say, one of the most remarkable episodes of the latter gentleman's career was his protracted litigation with the Estey house, the suit being carried on for years. Mr. Burdette was granted an injunction against the Esteys, who therefore adopted new plans for placing the reeds.

The death of Estey's Levi K. Fuller was recorded in *Musical Opinion* for November 1886.

The year 1890 was indeed a sad one for many reed-organ builders on the other side of the Atlantic. From *Musical Opinion* for July 1890 we learn of the passing of another of the key figures of the industry in a fulsome tribute which also provides a deal of information about the formation of the company of which he was a founder:

MASON & HAMLIN PIANO & ORGAN CO
Death of Mr. Henry Mason

Henry Mason, the founder and president of the Mason & Hamlin Organ and Piano Co., breathed his last in Boston, the city of his birth, on Thursday, May 15th.

Though the result had been sadly anticipated, yet, when the final announcement was made, the sorrow and grief of relatives and friends was not the less severe, though consoled by the thought that the intense sufferings, so patiently and uncomplainingly borne, had at last ceased. This is the spirit in which the family of Mr. Mason met the inevitable, and in this spirit we offer them our condolences in their great grief. Henry Mason was born on October 10th, 1831, in the city of Boston, and was the youngest of the four sons of the late Dr. Lowell Mason, whose church compositions are so well and favourably known. It may be said that he was to the manner born, and after an ordinary school education, evincing a strong musical bent, he contemplated adopting the musical profession as a calling, but was strongly dissuaded by his father. This, perhaps, was fortunate, and though the profession may have lost one of its brilliant lights, the cause of music was more greatly benefited by the subsequent career of the deceased. Though he had never taken a full quarter's music lessons, still he was an excellent pianist and organist, and gave freely of his services to several churches in the vicinity of his native city, and notably Dr. Alexander's church in Boston.

STYLE 804.

Quartered Oak Resonant Case, with decorated Pipes; richly carved, panelled and ornamented. Accompanied by Oak Organ Stool. Decidedly superior to small Pipe Organs, and unquestionably the most perfect instrument of its class. Stops running throughout on the plan of the Pipe Organ.

Length, with handle, 7 ft.; without, 6 ft. 4 in.   Height, 10 ft. 10 in.   Depth, 3 ft. 2 in.

For specification, see New Catalogue, gratis and post free.

Price £280.

Fig. 25. Occasionally, dummy pipe tops could be designed to look less line an afterthought and more like the real thing. Mason & Hamlin's Style 804 of 1892 actually looks just right (courtesy of F H Miller)

60

Abandoning, therefore, all thoughts of a musical career, he started in business life at seventeen years of age as an office boy in a Boston hardware store, and in that humble capacity swept the store and made the fires when half of Boston was asleep. Here he remained for a few years, when he went abroad and studied the German and French languages, living most of the time in a musical atmosphere, while his brother William was studying music with Liszt and other masters.

Returning to America in 1854 he associated himself with one Emmons Hamlin, and formed the firm of Mason & Hamlin, which has since grown to world wide reputation. The combined capital (mostly borrowed) of the new firm was eight thousand dollars, but the combination was an excellent one; Mr. Hamlin being an expert mechanic, and Mr. Mason, as was subsequently proven, a rare business man and excellent musician. Mr. Hamlin had previously been a tuner in the employ of Messrs. Geo. A. Prince & Co., manufacturers of melodeons, in Buffalo.

Scarcely six months had elapsed since the organization of the new firm before Mr. Mason, whose motto was 'upward and onward', informed his partner that they would have to make a better instrument, as he was not content to follow, but to lead, and he believed that something superior to the melodeon could be made. Shortly thereafter they discovered the art of *voicing reeds*, which did more than anything else to bring the 'cabinet organ' (a word coined by Mason & Hamlin in 1860) to its present state of perfection. From this discovery the reputation and prosperity of the firm grew apace. While paying strict attention to business, Mr. Mason could still find time to favour the readers of the Boston *Traveler* and other Boston papers with well written musical criticism.

Their first establishment was located at Cambridge Street, from whence they moved to 277, Washington Street, over the piano warerooms of Messrs. Hallett & Davis, and subsequently to their present extensive quarters in Tremont Street.

THE NEW MUSICAL INSTRUMENTS.

EOLIAN HARP ORGANS

COMBINING THE SACRED TONES OF

A CHURCH ORGAN

WITH THE EFFECTS OF

A STRING ORCHESTRA.

THESE wonderful Instruments surpass all the different kinds of American Organs and Harmoniums previously introduced, and have been especially designed for home use. They are quite easy to play, the touch being very light and the blowing not at all fatiguing. The stops are well arranged, and can be easily drawn in and out. Any description of music can be performed upon the Instrument, and altogether the EOLIAN HARP ORGANS supply a home with a musical companion, the equal of which, at so small an expense, is impossible to find. Manufactured by the Mason & Hamlin Organ and Piano Company.

PRICE £36.

Complete, with Eleven Stops,

EXPRESSIVE KNEE SWELL, AND FULL ORGAN COMBINATION STOP.

Dimensions: Height, 5 ft. ; Length, 4 ft. 11 in. ; Depth, 1 ft. 11 in.
Weight, 172 lbs. (In packing case, 322 lbs.)

May be obtained of all Musicsellers, and of the Wholesale Agents,

METZLER & CO., 42, Great Marlborough Street, London, W.

Fig. 26. London agents for Mason & Hamlin were at one time Metzler. Here is a notice from "The American Organ Journal" of about 1890 concerning their "Eolian Harp" church organ with the peculiar ability to mislead many into thinking they were listening to a string orchestra...

The firm of Mason Bros. (Daniel G. and Lowell, sen.), book and music book publishers, were at this time doing an extensive business, and Henry Mason became associated with them. They published the music of their father, Dr. Lowell Mason, and the works of many famous authers, such as James Parton, Fanny Fern, &c. In 1863 Mason Bros. opened a house a 7, Mercer Street, New York, in a small third story [sic] back room, where in addition to their publishing business, they acted as agents for Mason & Hamlin, while that firm acted in the same capacity for Mason Bros. in Boston. Business rapidly increasing, they removed in 1865 to the second floor of 596, Broadway, where they had a floor space of 50ft. by 200ft., equally divided between the publishing and organ departments.

In 1868 a stock company was formed called the Mason & Hamlin Organ Co., and the Mason Bros., Daniel G. Lowell, jun., and Dr. William became members thereof. It is useless to speak of their success, as it is patent to the world. The stock paid an annual average dividend of fifteen per cent, which speaks for itself. The Mason & Hamlin Co. were the first to make the square cabinet organ with the full round tone that captivated the public: hence their great success. In 1882 the name was changed to the Mason & Hamlin Organ and Piano Co., which is its present title.

To sum up, in the language of one who knew him best, Mr. Mason was a man of 'fine business talents, great executive ability, and remarkable capacity for attention to details. He was an able financier, and possessed that iron will and unflinching firmness of purpose so characteristic of his family. He knew no such thing as failure; had a dogged determination to succeed, and did succeed in everything he undertook. He was always on time, precise and methodical. Honesty and generosity, perhaps, were his most prominent traits. Of a very sensitive nature, he was large hearted and affectionate; a loving husband and a judicious father.'

In 1857, he married Helen Augusta Palmer, who survives him, together with four sons, Edward P., Allan G., Henry Lowell, and Daniel G., two of whom, Edward P. and Henry Lowell, are associated in the business, and will continue it as heretofore.

Another equally important figure died the following year. Again *Musical Opinion* provides the story in its October 1891 issue:

An old time Brattleborough [sic] manufacturer has recently passed away in the death of Mr. Edwin P. Carpenter, of the Carpenter Organ Company. Mr. Carpenter was a native of Guilford, born on the old Carpenter homestead in that town on June 13, 1819. He came of a historic colonial and revolutionary stock. His [grand]father was Benjamin Carpenter, a Vermont pioneer, a field officer of the revolution, a participant in the battle of Bennington, a founder and framer of the constitution of the state, and its lieutenant governor in 1779. Cyprus, the youngest son of Benjamin Carpenter, was the father of Mr. E. P. Carpenter. He was a hard working farmer, and his son followed that occupation until he removed to Brattleborough in 1850, and bought a half interest in the organ making business of Messrs. Jones & Burdett [sic], taking the place of Mr. Jones, and the firm becoming Messrs. Burdett & Carpenter. In the course of time, Jacob Estey took an interest in the business, and later on, Mr. Carpenter sold his interests to Isaac Hines. Soon after this, in the year 1858, Mr. Carpenter removed to the west, and after a short time became again engaged in the organ business. He finally settled in Mendota, Ill., and here for a long term of years he devoted himself with success to the manufacture of cabinet organs. Two years ago, Mr. Carpenter returned to Brattleborough with his wife, and became the mechanical superintendent of the E. P. Carpenter Organ Company, holding that position until he reluctantly resigned it a short time ago. In his personal life and character, Mr. Carpenter was above reproach. He was a man of large mental endowment, a wide reader, holding himself always in control and winning and retaining the respect and good will of his workmen to an unusual degree.

His son, E. P. Carpenter, jnr, was chairman of the judges at the 1893 World's Columbian Exposition and awarded the highest medal for reed organs to Story & Clark who promptly capitalised on the honour to the full, proclaiming themselves 'pre-eminently the most progressive organ building firm in the world.' What it is to suffer from modesty'.

Thomas

Canadian Organs.

Made by British Labour
in Britain's Premier Colony.

Two Manual Organ

with Pedals.

As endorsed by Sir Frederick Bridge.

Manuals and Pedals in accordance with the
rules of the Royal College of Organists.

Sufficient knee room for pedalling, allowing
performer to sit upright.

Radiating and Concave or Parallel Pedals.

Folding Foot Blowers and Side Blower.

For Home or Church use.

Send for Particulars to Sole Importer :

Chas. E. Cartman,

49, Avondale Road,

Southport.

Fig. 27. External hand lever or conventional but foldaway pedals provided blowing for this Thomas Canadian Organ advertised in May of 1913. The text tells us that it was available with RCO radiating pedal board or straight, parallel pedals

To return, though, to obituary notices, since they tell us so much about people and events which contemporary historians have otherwise overlooked, those makers of reed organs who worked above the 49th parallel were naturally no less exempt from the call to join the Great Majority. That same periodical recorded in November 1916:

KARN ORGAN COMPANY

We regret to have to record the death of Mr. D. W. Karn, which took place at Toronto on September 19th.

Mr Karn was the original founder of the Karn Organ Company in 1867, later incorporated as the D. W. Karn Co., Ltd., in 1898, † and in 1900 the present title was adopted on amalgamation with the Morris Co. of Listowel.* Starting as a manufacturer in a small way, he was never content unless each succeeding year brought with it development and advancement. And advancement came only to be retarded more than once by the ill-luck which nearly every business man has experienced. Fire destroyed the result of years of labour upon more than one occasion. Mr. Karn was born in the township of North Oxford in February, 1843, a Canadian of the second generation, and passed through all the vicissitudes of bush life and eventually cleared his own farm of timber. He bought a melodion with the first forty dollars he ever earned. As a young man he studied music and taught singing school. He married and

† D. W. Karn Limited, 188 Yonge Street, Toronto, Ontario, Canada.

* Morris Piano Co. Limited, Listowel, Ontario, Canada. Piano makers, est. 1892.

remained on the farm until 1869; then, moving to Woodstock, joined a Mr. Miller, who was constructing about one cabinet organ per week. In 1872 he bought out Mr. Miller. He then put in small steam power and machinery. Then he purchased the block at the corner of Gordon and Dundas Streets, added yearly until it became one of the largest factories in Canada. In 1897 the pipe organ business was commenced and in 1900 player- pianos. On establishing the English agency in 1886 they received an order for 3,500 organs, the largest order for reed organs ever given in the world. Although an extremely busy man, Mr. Karn found time to lend his services to the problems of municipal government and has filled all positions, including that of mayor. The end was rather sudden. He had not been ill for more than a week or ten days.

Mrs. Karn preceded him to the great Unknown about two or three years ago.

A comparatively late starter in the world of reed organs, but nevertheless an important one, was W. W. Putnam, and his passing was not until after the end of World War I. From *Musical Opinion* of February 1919:

Mr. William Wallace Putnam, founder of the W. W. Putnam Company, organ and stool manufacturers of Staunton, Virginia, U.S.A., died recently at the age of fifty-eight. He was one of the best known organ builders in the States. He learned his trade at the Estey factory and a number of years ago started the concern which bears his name. The business of the W. W. Putnam Company will be continued under the management of T. C. Good.

It was not all doom and gloom within the pages of the leading trade journals, though, and *Musical Opinion* for June 1904 reports on one of the biggest deals of the era - a takeover which must have been viewed by contemporary businessmen as radical in the extreme:

New Plans for the Mason & Hamlin Co.

One of the largest deals made for years in the piano business of America has resulted in the securing of the business and factories of the Mason & Hamlin Co. of Boston, Mass., by the Cable Piano Co. of Chicago. This invasion of the eastern field by a western concern is something that Chicagoans and westerners ought to be proud of. The Cable Co. is not only the wealthiest concern of its kind in the world, but stands to day the world's greatest manufacturers of piano and organs. While the Cable Co. has already, through years of experience and effort, acquired an enviable position in the piano and organ business in America and had extended their business abroad, the control of the Mason & Hamlin output puts them in a place by themselves. There is now directly under control of this immense corporation, with its millions of capital and its millions of resources, the Mason & Hamlin piano, the Conover piano (which has won a high position in the trade), the Cable, Kingsbury and Wellington pianos. With splendidly selling commercial instruments, with a first class piano in the Conover, all crowned with an artistic leader, with the Mason & Hamlin (which has won a place among the few artistic pianofortes of national renown that are strictly of the highest possible grade of manufacture), the Cable Co. is in an impregnable position. The deal also gives the Cable Co. control of the world renowned Mason & Hamlin organs as well, with which they now run their own popular Chicago Cottage organs. Through the acquisition of the Mason & Hamlin interests, they now have possibilities for developing a pipe organ department, an industry which has greatly increased in importance in the last few years. They will also be able to meet orders for large reed organs, as this type of instrument is covered by the Mason & Hamlin Liszt organ. Finally, they will now also manufacture pipe organs, making a complete line of the greatest magnitude. - *Chicago Journal.*

One wonders who wrote that. It must either have been a very sycophantic reporter on the *Chicago Journal* or, more probably, a Cable Co press officer. At all events it makes turgid reading.

Royalty, even if it was a bit far removed from the shores within which one was domiciled, was always good for a news story. And so, in *Musical Opinion* for November 1889 we read:

Plate 20. Patented in 1914, the Orthotonophonium was invented by Arthur von Oettingen and offered a microtonal octave of 53 notes. A small number of these strange instruments was made by Schiedmayer of Stuttgart and featured a return to the very early harmonium style of full-width foot treadles (Staatliches Institut für Musikforschung, Preussischer Kulturbesitz Musikinstrumenten- Museum, Berlin)

Plate 21. Portable harmonium Model 26, by R F Stevens Ltd, Kentish Town, London. Made 1923. 4 octaves, C-C, 49 notes. One set of reeds. One knee swell. Suitcase style. Case of oak and plyboard. Closes up into a box with a leather handle on the top |picture below|. Celluloid keys. It is believed that only three of this style were ever made. Picture shows organ opened up for playing. Case number 24130. Sold by R W Pentland, Edinburgh (from the collection of Phil and Pam Fluke)

65

To the Queen of Italy the Bell Organ Co. have just had the honour of selling one of their full pedal organs (College of Organists' scale), with pipe top, style 600. The instrument has been dispatched to the palance at Monza, near Milan, the organ being for Queen Marguerite's own use.

Strictly speaking, this was a British-built instrument but it was a variant of the instrument designed and produced in Guelph, Ontario, by the Bell parent. This is made clear from another new item from March, 1901:

The Bell Organ and Piano Co. (the London branch is on the Holborn Viaduct) are controlling the Bellolian, the invention of Mr. Charles Warren, whose name is prominent in London patent annals, and who for years has made a study of pneumatics as applied to organs. We are informed that the instrument is attachable to any reed organ, and by means of the invention the keys are worked automatically as the perforated music unfolds. The most striking feature of the invention is claimed to be its simplicity; thus whilst the idea is an improvement on other arrangements of the kind, the cost of construction is much less. Mr. Warren intends to reside in Guelph in order to superintend its manufacture.

And so the makers came and went, but all left behind them their own individual contribution to the progress of the instrument. The cardboard-fan which was called vox humana came from the inventive genius of the Estey house as we have seen. A contemporary newspaper report recounted the tale of a young lady possessed of but partial understanding of the American organ and of this stop in particular, who apparently said that she was very fond of the sound of the 'nux vomica'. Many who were subjected to its gross use and misuse with sinus-toned reed organs may well consider that she got it right first time.

On the same subject, the fan tremulant, this time wind-driven, was a feature of the Aeolian Orchestrelle (in which, one has to admit, it sounded not all that unpleasant) and the late Bruce Angrave used to refer to this as 'the waffle stop'.

A matter which concerned many users of the American organ in Europe was compass. While European instruments were invariably C to C, the greater majority of American instruments were F to F. Early in the 1870s, Estey's first British agent (before Metzler took them on) was Breavington & Sons, and they successfully urged Estey to produce a number of C to C instruments. They were, however, discontinued after a short while because, apparently, the makers had problems with the tuning and voicing of the lowest seven extra notes required. The F to F compass had indeed some followers this side of the Atlantic, particularly those involved in congregational-singing accompaniment where the opportunity to play the bass line in octaves was thought better. Curiously, contemporary correspondents believed that the C to C compass would be 'shorter' and that the 'loss' of the six lowest notes would be detrimental. Those who put forward such beliefs had obviously not understood the problem although, in fairness, there was much confusion over the matter, in particular as to where the break between the halves of the keyboard would actually come - between E and F or B and C.

Some of the larger instruments such as those made by Needham and Estey did indeed employ the C to C scale, in the main because that was the scale of the traditional pipe organ; but the smaller, domestic style of organ made in America persisted in F to F until a surprisingly late date. Henry Mason of Mason & Hamlin wrote in 1897:

In all reed organs which consist of 8ft., 4ft., or 2ft. reeds, we most decidedly prefer the FF scale; in all organs containing 16ft. set throughout, we prefer the CC scale... In fact, the F scale is the distinctive feature of the small American organ, and a feature which has been adopted and adhered to by reason of its practicability and efficaciousness.

The matter dragged on for a long while and it was not until the turn of the century that American makers offered models in a choice of scales. Many manufacturers actually made a selling feature of the FF scale, for example A. B. Chase proclaimed all over its catalogues 'All Chase organs are to the F scale'.

In another direction, those American-made organs which incorporated a pedal board (and, in consequence, an alternative means of blowing such as by handle or motor) were as mentioned in chapter 3, still using the archaic straight pedal board as late at the first decade of this century. In Britain, the Royal College of Organists had drawn up its commendable specification for the

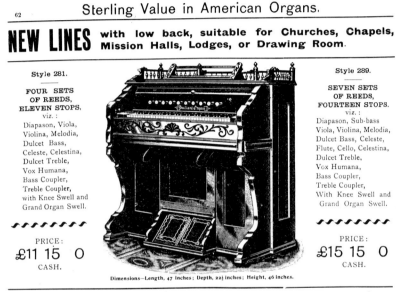

Fig. 28. Packard organs from turn-of-the-century trade catalogue

67

radiating and concave pedal board as early as 1881.

The question of technical improvements as compared to musical advances in the reed organ inspired a certain Arthur Wales to write to the *American Art Journal*. His letter was published and then subsequently republished in *Musical Opinion* for October 1889. What he had to say was interesting:

All attempts to enlarge the reed organ have damaged the quantity of tone in proportion as the reed-board and cells (or windchest) has been built too large and solid to respond sympathetically to the vibrations of the reeds. The United States Patent Office is well supplied with worthless patents aiming to produce large and ponderous reed organ windchests, of such complex construction that they would either crack or split by shrinkage, or smother the vibrations of the reeds and deaden their tone. Every conceivable invention to remove objections and allow of the production of large reed organs has been studied out, patented, and manufactured, and what is the result? Only a reed organ. The mechanical obstacles have been mostly overcome, but the quality of tone lost by the massing together of the many sets of reeds, boards, and cells has never been recovered, and never will.

There is a strong suspicion that Mr Wales had managed to hit a very important nail squarely on the head.

The United States spawned a very great number of reed-organ makers. As Harvey Roehl said in his preface to Whiting's *Estey Reed Organs on Parade*, in the 1880s there were probably 250 companies engaged in making reed organs in America. It took no vast amount of capital to be in this business, so therefore many of these firms were small and obscure and have long since been forgotten.

In 1892, there were 171 makers in the United States who between them employed 4,202 workers and held 305 US patents. The total capital invested was $3,922,338 and the value of total production was $6,136,472. The wages paid accounted for $2,142,539 - an average of slightly under $510 per worker per annum.

In terms of musical capability, the upper echelon of American makers produced extremely fine instruments. Within this corpus lie the products of Vocalion (later Aeolian), late nineteenth century Story & Clark, Estey, Mason & Hamlin, and earlier age Prince. Many other instruments, though, were musically cumbersome and uninspired, matching their roughly made cases, many of which were mass-produced along packing-case lines and merely held together with glue and nails.

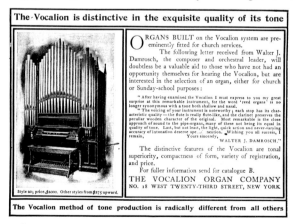

Fig. 29. The Vocalion Organ Company achieved considerable success with its tonally superior reed organs. Again the extensive pipework seen in this 1899 advertisement from "Munsey's Magazine" is pure imitation (courtesy of Mr William H. Edgerton)

CHAPTER 5

How the Reed Organ Works

THE HARMONIUM

There are three elements in the construction of the harmonium: the reed pan containing the reeds; the keyboard and player controls; and the wind department or bellows. The first of these, the reed pan, is often mistakenly called the sound-board. American manufacturers in particular, used the term when speaking of both pressure harmoniums and suction or American organs. The term, obviously translated from the piano-making industry, has no true significance in the case of the reed organ since any resonance imparted to the sound produced by the reed is nothing to do with the board to which the reeds are affixed.

The second component, the keyboard assembly, comprises the manual or finger keys and the various stop or register controls as well as mechanically operated features such as expression, swell and coupler. Generally, all these controls, whether mechanical features or directly involving sets of reeds, are termed 'stops' and they are almost always controlled by push-pull stop-knobs or draw-stops mounted or otherwise contained in a horizontal row along a narrow vertical stop-rail or stop-jamb placed behind the keys and beyond that traditionally, if unwisely, named keyboard feature called 'the thumper' against which the keys rest when not depressed.

The third component, the wind department or bellows, is almost always placed below the reed pan (often called the building table) and is so arranged that the alternating depression of the two foot pedals (more properly treadles) moves two bellows units which, in the case of the harmonium, operate as feeders to compress atmospheric air into a reservoir. Starting from the organ table (a horizontal board upon which the instrument is built up), all that is beneath it is termed 'the wind department' and all that above 'the organ proper'. There is, however, one proviso, and that is that the organ proper consists solely of all the music-making mechanism and sundry parts, *not* the casework which, as the illustrations show, can extend considerably above the music-making parts.

With the simple harmonium, the wind department comprises four parts: the feeders (operated by the foot treadles), the chimneys or wind-trunks, the windchest and the reservoir; the whole forming what is described as a horizontal pressure bellows.

To play the harmonium, air is compressed by feeders which are generally wedge-shaped in section and are attached on their upper faces to a horizontal wooden cross-board which, because of its position, is called the 'middle board'. Each of the lower, movable boards of the feeders is provided with a row of large holes across which is stretched a strip of leather tensioned with a small spring. This is a flap valve so that air can only pass one way into the feeder; as the feeder closes and compresses the air, the flap valve shuts tightly over the openings. Inside each feeder (or occasionally attached to the outside) is a Y-shaped spring called, because of its shape, a 'gull spring', which

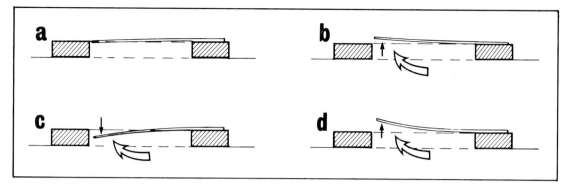

Fig. 30. The principle of the free reed as applied to the concertina, accordeon, harmonica, seraphine, harmonium and American organ. A shows a section of the reed at rest. At B air is pressing on the reed to escape, so lifting the thin flexible metal strip. At C the elasticity of the strip causes it to spring back and the cycle repeats at D. The speed at which this vibration occurs determines the pitch of the sound produced: the heavier and large the reed, the slower the frequency and the lower the note while the lighter, thinner and smaller reed will vibrate at a much faster rate, so producing a higher sound. In early times, and for obvious reasons, this form of reed was referred to as a *vibrator* and sometimes simply as a *spring*. To avoid making the reed physically too large for practical use, the flexible tongue could be weighted (usually by a marked thickening) so as to allow a relatively small reed to produce a low pitch. This can be seen in Fig. 32

keeps the feeder normally extended. These springs ensure a prompt return after each compression cycle.

Once the air is compressed, it has to be conveyed into the windchest and this is done through upright rectangular channels called 'chimneys'. In some instruments, the chimneys are separated and placed one at each end, in others there is one broad chimney in the front.

The chimneys convey the compressed air from the feeders into the windchest - a transverse box extending the width of the instrument, in the centre of which is a large opening leading into the reservoir bellows underneath. The opening is provided with a movable lid or pallet, the expression pallet, which can close it off. The reservoir is attached to the underside of this board and has collapsible sides; these folding sides, called 'ribs', allowing the reservoir to expand downwards as wind is forced into it. The air inside the reservoir is compressed by means of coiled or spiral 'bedsprings' which press up under it.

In normal use, the feeders compress air into the windchest, the reservoir distending to maintain a quantity of air at pressure so that, when there are any irregularities in pedalling, these are 'ironed out' by the additional spring-loaded reservoir. When the 'expression' stop is selected, the pallet closes off the reservoir so that the foot pedals directly pump wind into the chest. Deprived of the evening-out effect of the reservoir, it now becomes possible to impart expression into the music being played by careful use of the foot treadles.

To enable the feeders to move open and closed, their lower or movable boards are connected to the ends of levers called 'cross-bars' or 'rockers' whose opposite ends are linked directly with the foot treadles. Pressure downwards on a treadle thus moves the feeder up, compressing air into the windchest and reservoir.

The top board of the windchest, called the 'bellows-board' or 'pallet-board', closes it off so that air cannot escape. However, set in a line across this top board is a number of rectangular openings of varying lengths, equal in number to the keys of the keyboard. Screwed over each of these slits is a vibrator or reed tuned to the correct pitch for the note which it represents. Each reed in its slot is provided with an airtight pallet which prevents the air passing through the reed

70

until such time as the pallet is opened by the movement of a key on the keyboard above.

With the simple harmonium with a single row of reeds, this is virtually all that will be found inside the organ. However, it is usual to have more than one row of reeds and to divide the set of reeds into a top, treble. portion and a bottom, bass, section. With this configuration, the bellows-board is divided into two sometimes unequal portions, and the chimneys which lead from the feeders feed wind into each side.

The upper surface of the bellows-board is partitioned off across the width of the instrument, ie parallel to the keyboard, so as to provide a number of long shallow compartments, one for each pallet. Each of these pallets is so arranged that when a key in the keyboard is depressed, the pallet is opened and air admitted to the reed. This is the reed pan or sound-board which may have, arranged by the reed slots, small cavities or cells built around each reed and open at the front. The shape of these little chambers has a considerable effect on the sound produced by the reed, and a skilled reed-organ designer will indeed 'voice' his stops by the form of these cavities.

All the open ends of these chambers form a straight line and they are closed off by a hinged, felt-covered strip called a 'mute'. A second chamber may be arranged outside the cavities with their mute strip, and this chamber itself may have its open side covered with a hinged shade or occasionally a fixed section with a hinged extension. Control of these mutes and shades is from the draw-stop knobs which may also open primary wind-admission pallets within the windchest. There are many different systems of stop-knob operation; the sketch shows a few of the more common designs.

The operation of the draw-stop is to allow a part of a set of reeds to speak, usually the treble

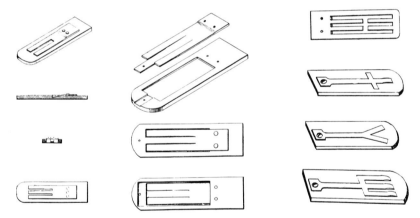

Fig. 31. There were many attempts to improve the sound of the early reeds, often by multiplying the vibrating elements. Here are just two, the left and central sketches being from the April 1884 patent drawings of James Baillie Hamilton, then of Boston, Massachusetts. He called his bifurcated reeds "unison bars". On the right are the drawings from the May 1884 patent of Merritt Gally, then of New York City. His words in his preamble to the specification are interesting in that they point to a sophisticated grasp of the principles of acoustics. The methods he describes, though, appear to refer only to his own early trials: "It is a well known fact that it is a difficult matter to increase the volume and power of any stop of a reed organ by a multiplication of unison reeds for any given note; as, unless the tongues of the several unison reeds are made to vibrate exactly on the same beat the tone is not augmented but made defective by the interference of vibrations. To obviate these defects it is a custom to tie together the tongues of two or more reeds by means of yokes or staples to complet them to vibrate together. This system however introduces difficulties in manufacture and also in the tuning and voicing of the reeds, as soldering would injure the temper of the reed tongues... The weight of the yokes is also a retarding element which must be counteracted by making the tongues too thin for producing 'body' of tone"

and the bass. Mention has been made of the way some organ builders applied a multiplicity of stop-knobs to their organs as a sales aid, Cornish & Co actually going so far as to have a stop knob for each octave (see page 13). When a draw-stop knob is pulled out, the action is to admit wind from the reservoir into a section of the organ.

There is a number of ways in which this can be done, the commonest being to provide a square metal plate with a spring and a hinge. This plate is hinged along one side parallel with the rod of the draw-stop. Beneath the metal plate there is a 'pitman' - a wooden, or occasionally brass, push-rod. When this rod is depressed, it opens a pallet in the organ and admits wind to a particular section. This is achieved using a wooden lever pivoted in the stop rod so that as the stop is drawn, this rod pushes down on the metal plate. The action of the expression stop is actually the reverse of this, the expression pallet being closed by the drawing out of the knob. The detail of this mechanism differs widely from maker to maker.

The reeds themselves comprise thin strips of brass rivetted to a rectangular brass plate containing a hole only fractionally larger than the reed. This brass vibrator was originally secured with one rivet, but it was found that after a while the rivet could work loose, allow the reed to slip fractionally sideways and thus produce a nasty buzzing or clatter. Initially makers tried using square-section rivets, but finally came down in favour of two rivets closely spaced in the end.

Harmonium reeds are relatively simple brass housings (see Fig. 32) and are held in place by a small woodscrew at each end. American organ reeds have housings which are hollowed-out on the underside to aid promptness of speech and the reed tongues are curved and sometimes slightly

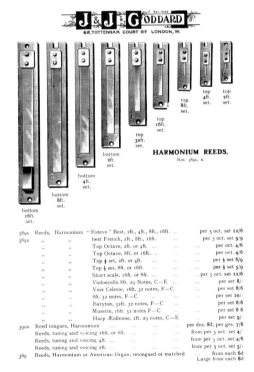

389A	Reeds, Harmonium "Esteve" Best, 2ft., 4ft., 8ft., 16ft. ...	per 5 oct. set 12/6
389B	,, ,, best French, 2ft., 8ft., 16ft.	per 5 oct. set 9/9
	,, ,, Top Octave, 2ft. or 4ft. ...	per oct. 4/6
	,, ,, Top Octave, 8ft. or 16ft. ...	per oct. 4/6
	,, ,, Top ½ set, 2ft. or 4ft. ...	per ½ set 6/9
	,, ,, Top ½ set, 8ft. or 16ft. ...	per ½ set 5/9
	,, ,, Short scale, 16ft. or 8ft. ...	per 5 oct. set 12/6
	,, ,, Violoncello 8ft. 29 Notes, C—E ...	per set 8/-
	,, ,, Voix Celeste, 16ft. 32 notes, F—C	per set 8/6
	,, ,, 8ft. 32 notes, F—C	per set 10/-
	,, ,, Baryton, 32ft. 32 notes, F—C	per set 8/6
	,, ,, Musette, 16ft. 32 notes F—C	per set 8 6
	,, ,, Harp Æolienne, 2ft. 29 notes, C—E	per set 9/-
390B	Reed tongues, Harmonium ...	per doz. 8d, per grs. 7/6
	Reeds, tuning and voicing 16ft. or 8ft. ...	from per 5 oct. set 4/
	Reeds, tuning and voicing 4ft. ...	from per 5 oct. set 4/6
	Reeds, tuning and voicing 2ft. ...	from per 5 oct. set 5/-
389	Reeds, Harmonium or American Organ, retongued or matched	from each 6d / Large from each 8d

Fig. 32. From the c.1914 trade catalogue of piano sundries suppliers J. & J. Goddard (est. 1842) comes this interesting page on harmonium reeds. The prices make interesting reading. Compare this with Fig. 47 (courtesy of Mr Tony Morgan)

twisted. Rather than secure these with woodscrews, the reeds have one rounded end and are installed by sliding them into a tightly-fitting slot in the reed cell as shown in Fig. 49.

The compass of the harmonium is generally from CC to C in alt (C - c3), covering 61 notes or 5 full octaves, that is from the C below the bass stave to the second C above the treble. Each row of reeds is generally divided into bass and treble compartments of $2\frac{1}{2}$ octaves each, the treble commencing on F in the first space of the treble stave. Each of these compartments is controlled by a separate draw-stop so that in an instrument with 4 rows of reeds, the reed compartments would total 8 in number - 4 bass and 4 treble - of 3 different pitches, namely unison 8ft, octave 4ft and double octave 16ft.

A study of the illustrations will show how the reed rows are set out in the organ and it will be apparent that the instrument is divisible by a spanwise line in front of which there is one section of the instrument and behind which there is another. For this reason it is common to refer to the front organ and to the back organ as two separate divisions. The front bass and treble rows comprise the diapason of 8ft pitch together with the bourdon of 16ft. In all organ practice, these are the foundation stops and they form the front organ. The back organ is allocated the solo stops such as the oboe (treble) 8ft and bassoon (bass) 16ft and the principal 4ft. The stops in the back organ are contained within a swell box which is also divided into fortes corresponding with the bass and the treble divisions of the registers. These fortes are controlled by hinged boards beneath the keyboard which can be moved by the knees; for this reason they are called knee-swells. A second knee-board has the ability to open up every register and so provide full organ.

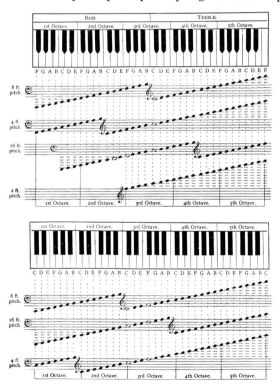

Fig. 33. Comparison of the F-F and C-C scales as used in harmoniums and American organs (courtesy of Mr F. H. Miller)

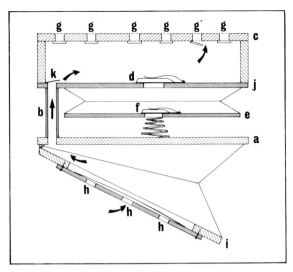

Fig. 34. The bellows of the harmonium seen in section. A = middle board to which are attached side by side the two feeders; B = wind trunk or chimney; C = upper board of windchest; D = expression pallet; E = bottom board of wind reservoir; F = spill pallet to relieve excess pressure and opened by a screw or other projection on the upper surface of board A; G = stop valves covering openings which lead to the reed pan, one valve shown open; H = air inlet holes bored in detachable board with a leather flap valve secured across the inside; I = bottom or movable board of the feeders; J = bottom board of windchest; K = leather flap valve

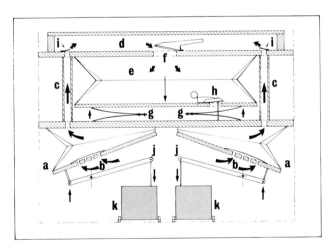

Fig. 35. Front elevation of the harmonium bellows. A = two feeders which, when at rest, are open and full of air; B = non-return flap valves so that as the feeder is lifted, the air inside increases in pressure and presses the valve shut, allowing the air to be compressed and pass upwards into the windchest; C = wind trunks or chimneys; D = windchest; E = air pressure reservoir; F = valve which allows wind to pass into reservoir and which, by its intentional closure, serves as the *expression* stop; G = springs to apply closing pressure to wind reservoir (may be coiled upholstery-type springs or gull-shaped as drawn here); H = excess pressure spill valve (compare with Fig. 38); I = flap valves to accept wind from feeders into windchest; J = pivoted linkage system to operate feeders from foot treadles; K = foot treadles

There are also more mechanical functions to be found in the harmonium. Among the earliest of these was the 'sourdine' which dates back almost to the earliest of harmoniums. This device, virtually obsolete by the turn of the century, restricted the amount of air to the organ by a special pallet which controlled its admission to the reeds so that they spoke very softly. It is interesting to note that, unlike the pipes of a pipe organ, reeds can be made to sound over a wide range of wind pressures; the reeds of a Mustel organ, for example, are voiced to speak across a pressure range of from 1mm to 180 mm of water-gauge.

Another of these quite early devices was the *prolongment* - the arrangement whereby selected notes could be sustained rather like a pedal- point after the fingers have left the keys (see page 18). In operation, the lower octave of the keyboard was provided with hooks or latches protruding

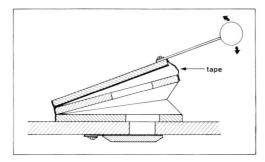

Fig. 36. The harmonium tremulant is in the form of a device to provide pulsing wind pressure inside the windchest. This is usually mounted somewhere on the upper windchest board. The pneumatic motor has in its top board a large opening covered by a hinged, leather-faced board carrying a weight. The movement of this board is limited by a check tape. When the pallet on the underside of the tremulant motor is opened by a stop knob, and as pressure mounts in the chest, the weighted closing board is lifted. The sudden venting of pressure causes the pneumatic motor to shut, pulling the weighted closing board down again. When properly adjusted by moving the weight along its arm, the cycle is repeated rapidly and imparts a wavering effect to the sound of the reeds.

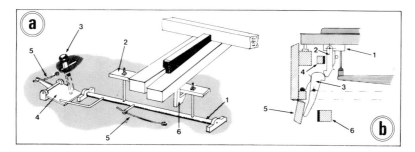

Fig. 37. The prolongment system was made in several styles. The Mustel system is shown at (A) on the left. 1 = pivoted iron roller; 2 = strip of wood supported on adjustable stand-offs from the roller; 3 = prolongment selection lever; 4 = hinged platform; 5 = wire springs; 6 = wooden hook screwed to the underside of each key subjected to the action of the prolongment. In operation, when prolongment is selected, each key depressed pushes the spring-loaded strip (2) to allow the hook to locate under it. This action releases any other key already hooked down. A second system, seen at (B), each key is provided with a hinged catch, 2, pivoted to a block, 1, fixed under each key and loaded by a wire spring at its rear. A movable jack, 3, has a matching notch and a spring. There are two padded rails, 4 and 6, which extend the length of the prolongment attachment. This system is brought on by moving the rail 5 so that catch 3 can be put in the right position to be caught by the catch 2. This system differs from (A) in that any key or number of keys selected, can be held down. A knee lever can be applied to press forward the bar 5 to disengage the jacks not already held in prolongment so that other keys can be played in the ordinary way without affecting those already held down until finally released by the operation of rail 4. This system was the basis of the full-compass prolongment used by Schiedmayer in the Hlavac-Harmonium

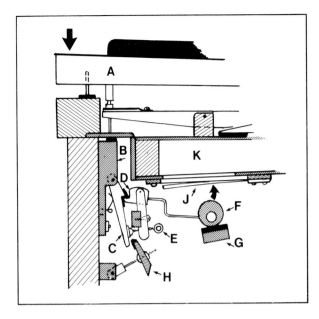

Fig. 38. The percussion action was also made in various forms but was restricted to the harmonium. As the key A is pressed, the plunger also pushes down the sliding carrier B and with it the jack C. A leather covered notch in the jack now engages the toe of the hammer butt D which then rises and strikes the reed J with the felt-covered hammer F. G is a rest-rail upon which the hammer falls back. The escapement is formed by adjusting the set-off E. The action is selected and cancelled by the operation of a drawstop which raises the padded rail H, so pressing back the jacks so that they are clear of the hammer butts D. The percussion action acts upon the front set of diapason reeds and is adjusted so that it strikes them at the instant compressed air is admitted to them so as to provide a *percussive* sound and ensure prompt speaking. The percussion is the only harmonium stop to be affected by the force applied to the keyboard key and, when properly adjusted, can be used for playing without the use of wind

beneath each key. When the prolongment was selected, a spring-loaded rail moved into such a position parallel to and under these keys that, when a key was depressed, its hook caught under the rail and was prevented from lifting when the player's finger was removed from it. When a second key was pressed down, the latch beneath it pushed the rail back, so releasing the previous key and at the same time itself becoming latched down.

A novel addition was the provision of percussion (see page 27). With this stop drawn, a piano-like escapement action was brought into operation and struck the reed with a small felt-covered hammer. It acted upon the reeds of the diapason the instant air was admitted to them, and produced

Fig. 39. The grand jeu is also only found in the harmonium: the similar affect achieved with the American organ is by different means and is quite different. Behind each hinged platform which controls the registers or stops runs a pivoted iron roller having along its length a number of arms which rest lightly on top of the hinged platforms. The *grand jeu* stop, however, seen here as number 2, has its arm under the hinged platform. When the *grand jeu* stop 2 is drawn, the roller is turned so that every stop which is intended to come under the influence of the *grand jeu* is selected regardless of the position of its own stop knob

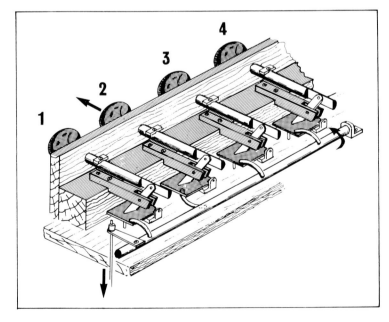

two results. First was a distinctive yet agreeably soft percussion sound of the same pitch as the reed which was struck. Second was the benefit that by starting the reed in its vibrations by mechanical means, more prompt speech was produced.

An additional mechanism, which was still in use by Humphreys and others in the early part of this century, was Dawes's melody attachment by the use of which it was possible to make the air or treble part stand out. When selected, and when used in conjunction with certain playing stops, prominence was given to the air by shutting off all the notes below it. The system was also adapted to the bass as a pedal substitute, but in this case it was the lowest note which was accentuated.

Among the most useful of these extras are those devices which couple keyboards or octaves, modify sound or extend the normal capabilities of the performer. The coupler, for example, comes in two principle forms: the octave coupler perfected by Samuel Howard and which can operate either in the treble or the bass, and the manual coupler which will unite the two manuals of a large harmonium, or the pedals and one or more manual. The most common system comprises the pivoted board with the cranked rods as shown in the sketch. Another type is the movable wedge which passes between the two manuals. Again the accompanying sketch shows these arrangements.

There is another type of coupler which, although made for the American organ, was equally feasible for the use with the harmonium - the so-called 'super-octave coupler' made to Jenkinson's patent and which performed a very interesting function based on the inherent shortcomings of the normal coupler (see page 39). Jenkinson's device was largely replaced by the introduction of 2ft registers as well as 4ft ones, so that the coupler effect could be achieved with a full additional register rather than a mechanical contrivance.

Then there are the keyboard-controlled and keyboard-controlling effects among which figure prominently 'double expression' and 'double touch'. The former (see page 33) is a pneumatic balance in the wind reservoir for exactly maintaining an equal pressure of wind by means of gradation. As used in the harmonium and American organ, double touch was one of the inventions perfected (but not originated) by an enterprising English professor of music, Augustus Tamplin. This was

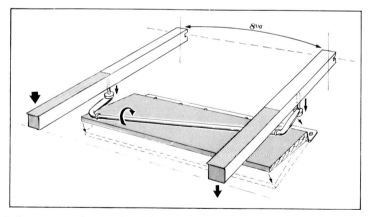

Fig. 40. The practical octave coupler, produced in several styles since its invention by Samuel Howard, operates by the use of a series of cranked iron levers, each of the same length and arranged so that the depression of a key results in the automatic depression of another key one octave higher. In practice, the levers are nested together on a hinged board. When the coupler is selected, the board is moved into position so the levers engage with studs fixed beneath individual keys

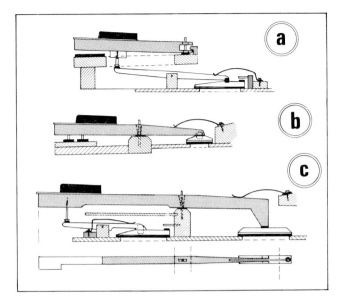

Fig. 41. Three of the most common harmonium keyboard actions. The back-hung key, seen at A, is the simplest and cheapest, requiring a very short key. Each key is pivoted on a peg at the rear and all are held into place by shaped wooden strip called the back-catch which must be removed before any key can be taken out. The centrally-pivoted key, B, is suitable for small harmoniums with only one or two full rows of reeds. As with A, the pallet is fixed to the end of the pivoted beam with a leather strip and held normally shut with a spring. Style C, which is virtually a combination of A and B, is usually found on larger harmoniums and features a centre-hung key. As the key is depressed, both pallets open simultaneously

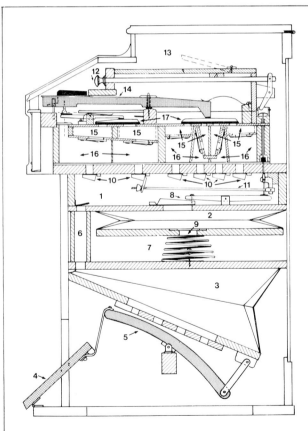

Fig. 42. Section through a six-register harmonium. 1 = windchest; 2 = reservoir; 3 = feeder; 4 = foot treadle; 5 = rocking lever; 6 = wind-trunk or chimney; 7 = reservoir pressure spring; 8 = expression pallet operated by lever and push-rod down through back of action and controlled by stop-knob 12; 9 = exhaust pallet for spill valve; 10 = stop valves and action, each being provided with a linkage, 11; 12 = drawstop; 13 = swell or forte hinged flap; 14 = key; 15 = reed cells, those under the front portion of the key being called the front organ, those at the rear being the back organ; 16 = reed pan with central divider to separate front organ from the back organ; 17 = pallets for front organ and back organ

able to give prominence or accentuation to certain parts by causing the back organ stops to speak sooner than those of the front, the latter being brought into play by the expedient of deeper pressure of the key.

Tremolo is a feature almost as old as the practical harmonium itself. To begin with, it drew its effect - that of imparting a wavering to the sound - by varying the normally constant pressure of wind in a far more rapid manner than was possible by the use of expression stops. The effect was achieved in the same manner as in pipe organs and, in particular, street organs of French origin - Gavioli in particular used the system in his small portative instruments. The device consisted of a pallet valve with a spring-loaded or counterbalanced arm with a weight on it, so that it would open and close the main windway chimney in the treble part of the harmonium windchest. While this was a satisfactory way of doing the job, it was prone to falling out of adjustment and its vibrating motion was often difficult to start up. It was the American-organ fraternity that perfected the rotating paddle which interfered with the sound as it passed from the reed chamber to the outside of the organ. Some of these paddles were very effective and they usually were far more prompt both in responding to the 'select on' command and then stopping after the stop was pushed in again.

All these additions to the harmonium served as means whereby the flexibility of the instrument might be enhanced. As Milne wrote in 1930, there is little doubt that, as a musical instrument, the harmonium has far more power of expression than its rival the American organ, and of the two is often preferred by those who understand the correct use of the expression stop.

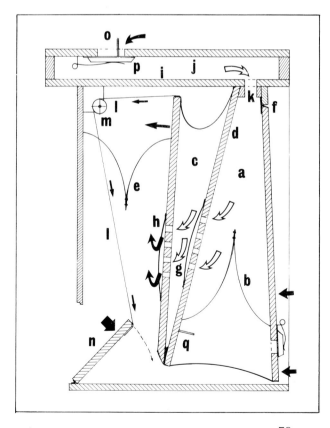

Fig. 43. Suction bellows for the American organ. A = exhaust reservoir which, when at rest, is held fully open by internal springs B; C = twin exhausters which, when at rest, lie against the middle board, D, under the pressure of external springs E; F = hinged back board to exhaust reservoir; G and H are flap valves; I = bellows board; J = air chamber connected to the suction reservoir by the airway K; The upper part of the air chamber is formed by the cavity board in which the reeds are placed together with pallets and stop action; O is the pitman depressed by the keyboard key which opens pallet P and lets the suction act upon the reeds; L = webbing strap connected to foot treadle N at the lower end, passing over roller M at the top and secured to the movable board of the exhauster C. The system operates by drawing out the air within the action, causing the back board of the exhaust reservoir to close up. If there is too much suction without air being admitted by the playing of notes, inner peg Q pushes open the external pallet on the hinged exhaust reservoir back board

THE AMERICAN ORGAN

Whereas the harmonium operates by wind pressure built up in a bellows reservoir, the American organ operates on the suction system. There is still a 'bellows assembly', but its use is the exact opposite of that previously described. And instead of a wind reservoir, there is a vacuum reservoir or accumulator. Besides this fundamental variation, there are several others. First is the fact that the effects achieved on the harmonium by the 'expression' and 'sourdine' cannot apply with the suction organ. Second is the fact that by far the greater number of earlier instruments are built with the F to F compass - 61 notes or 5 full octaves extending from FFF to F3, with each row divided into two generally unequal sections.

The illustration highlights the main parts of the American organ and, with a knowledge of the harmonium as a starting point, the operation should readily be understood.

While the suction bellows appear externally similar to the bellows of the harmonium, they are in fact quite different in operation. There may also be aids to 'pumping' (the slang term in parts of America for these instruments is 'pump organ' usually prefaced today with the description 'old Victorian') such as a hand lever worked by an assistant or an electric motor unit. These aids are needed where there is a pedal-organ option.

According to organ-building practice, the compass of a pedal keyboard for a 5-octave C to C instrument is 32 notes, from CCC (16ft) to G. However, the majority of pedal keyboards extend just 30 notes, from CCC to F.

Originally, pedal boards were straight, with parallel and level toe keys. The disadvantages of

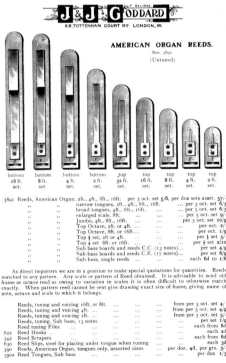

Fig. 44. American organ reeds from J. & J. Goddard's trade catalogue of c.1914 show that each is of the same width and body thickness, only the length and proportions of the tongue differing. The thickening of the bass reeds is clearly seen here. For the techniques of voicing, see the reed drawing in Appendix 2

Plate 22. Portable harmonium Model 25, by R F Stevens Ltd, Kentish Town, London. Made 1928. 4 octaves, C-C, one set of reeds. Case of oak and ash, side sections fold down with clips for carrying. Cast iron coffin handles which cost 2½d when new. Keys covered with celluloid. Picture |left| shows organ closed for transport. Case number 25556. Sold by R W Pentland, Edinburgh (from the collection of Phil and Pam Fluke)

Plate 23. Portable harmonium Model 55 made in June, 1945, by R F Stevens Ltd, Kelly Street, Kentish Town, London. 4 octaves, C-C, two sets of reeds. Manufactured for the Admiralty for use on board ship. Instrument tropicalised. 2 knee swells, the right one operating on the 8ft, the left one operating the second set of reeds, there being no stops. Back set = 8ft 49 notes; front set 4ft 49 notes; total 98 reeds. The oak case has brass screws. Foot pedals tuck up inside, then legs fold in and under; the back comes up and clips to the front. Case number 29419. Sold by Stevens direct to Admiralty for HM ships (from the collection of Phil and Pam Fluke)

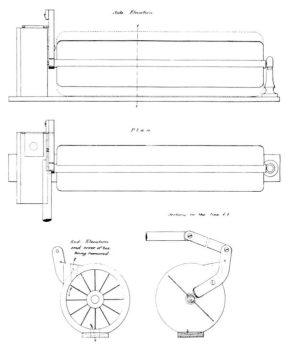

Fig. 45. James Harrison's 1885 patent drawing for his improved vox humana stop for American organs. The action, which required very little suction power to set into motion, included a positive mechanical brake lever, seen in the lower right hand corner, so that as soon as the drawstop action was cancelled, the rotating turbine and its two-bladed fan stopped instantly

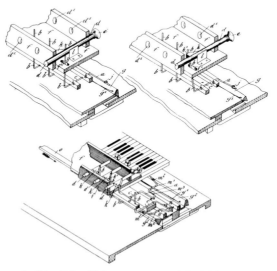

Fig. 46. The Birmingham organ-builder John Holt was renowned for high- quality reed organs and in 1885 was granted a patent for an improved, simplified stop action for American organs and harmoniums. Here is his patent drawing. The operation of the cams and the cranked rods is easy to follow

82

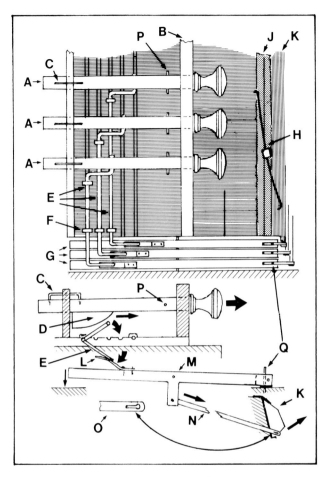

Fig. 47. A common form of American organ stop action as drawn and favoured by Milne. A are drawstops which pass through the front stop rail B and are prevented from rotating by wire staples C which pass through slots in the rear stop rail. The travel of the drawstop is limited by cross pin P. Each drawstop mounts a cam, D, which engages with a cranked iron rod, E, which is mounted on a stop action board and allowed to pivot in felt-bushed staple bearings, F. The ends of the cranked iron rods E engage with compensating springs L on arms pivoted at M and which are located by pins Q at their front ends. As the arm moves, so rod N pushes open the mute K. It is secured by a keyhole slot as shown at O. Since the action operates by suction, no great force is required to open the felt-faced mute K which is held normally closed by a wire torsion spring H and hinged with a strip of leather J

this - a feature which, incidentally, one still finds today on Japanese-made electronic organs - are easy to see. As the seated performer attempts to reach the alternate extremities of the pedal board, so his feet have to stretch and pivot further. It was in an attempt to remedy this situation that in 1881 the Royal College of Organists instituted their specification for the concave radiating pedal board in which the keyboard had a radius more or less equal to that of the player's legs from knee to ankle.

After this, virtually every organ made in Britain, both pipe and reed, where they were provided with a pedal board, conformed to this design. But, as mentioned in chapter 3, many European and the American makers ignored this recommendation and their pedal reed organs did not sell well in Britain. Mannborg's magnificent 21-stop three-manual exhibition combined American organ, harmonium and pipe organ built for the Paris Exposition of 1900 featured a perfectly straight 30-note pedal board although the coupler toe stops were arranged in a concave row. Even the Mustel Model 7, with its eleven rows of reeds, expression on each of its two manuals and a host of advanced features, maintained a straight 30-note pedal board in the 1910 catalogue. Estey, in its London leaflet of around 1910-12, announced its 175 guinea Estey Two Manual Practice Organ with 30-note pedal board and, although this was concave, it was not radiating.

SELF-PLAYING ORGANS

The self-playing reed organ, the history of which is recorded in chapter 8, is a simple adaptation of the normal instrument. It may be of the pressure type (Aeolian Grand, Wilcox & White Symphony, etc) or it can be suction (e.g. Aeolian Orchestrelle). In all cases the player action may be mechanical (as on the Nyström Reform-Orgel) or pneumatic, as on the Orchestrelle. For information on player organs, their design and operation as well as the principles of pneumatic action see Ord-Hume: *Pianola*.

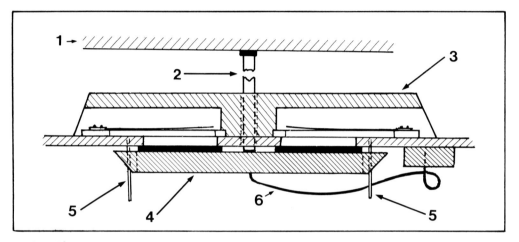

Fig. 48. American organ pallets. 1 = key; 2 = plunger or pitman; 3 = cavity board; 4 = pallet; 5 = steady pins to guide the pallet; 6 = spring

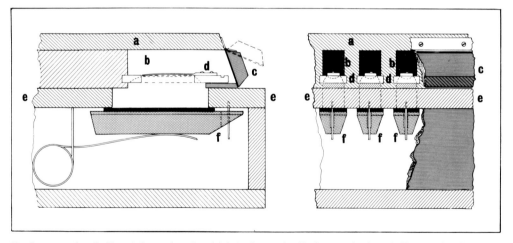

Fig. 49. Cross section (left) and front elevation (right) of a reed cell. A = cavity board; B = reed cell; C = mute; D = reed; E = soundboard; F = leather-faced pallet held closed by spring and guided by one or more steady-pins

CHAPTER 6

The Social History of
the Reed Organ

It would be wrong to consider the manufacturing of reed organs as substantially different from that of any other aspect of the musical-instrument industry except in two very particular ways. First is the social aspect in that it provided a low-cost instrument capable of expression and tonal modification suited to the needs of the ordinary person. And second, it played a major part in the development of the precision woodworking industry since by the mid-1870s highly sophisticated machinery had been developed for machining timber to hitherto unheard of production tolerances.

In the same way that building Paxton's Crystal Palace demanded new techniques in woodworking and machinery, shaping and boring of reed pans and other parts of the organ called for high-speed wood mills which could rout out recessed reed cells and form the complex shapes of mutes and swell shutters. In terms of precision woodworking machinery and tools, what highly specialised demands had been initiated by the piano industry became supplemented by the equally specialised demands of the reed-organ builder.

As far as price was concerned, the harmonium was cheap. A single-manual harmonium with one or one and a half rows of reeds could cost as little as 6 guineas in the middle of the nineteenth century. Second-hand instruments were even cheaper. At this time, depending on quality, a piano was anything up to three times the cost of an organ, being priced at between £15 and £20 (in January 1905 the north London manufacturers Grover & Grover offered to the trade pianos to retail from 14 guineas - and offered 'hire system terms' to the trade). And although the piano enjoyed an untarnished popularity in the minds of people as regards value and quality, it had the disadvantage of being very large and heavy. The reed organ was both light in weight and generally smaller than the upright pianoforte of the Victorian age.

Despite all this, the reed organ in its various forms was not viewed with the same degree of respectability as the piano. Even the poor-grade Victorian wall-climber upright piano was accorded more respect. The reed organ was the thing you bought when you couldn't afford 18 guineas or so for a real musical instrument. Amidst all the snobbery and insensitivity of the early Victorian age, reed organs proliferated almost like an anti-social disease as something not very nice, but unlikely to go away. Aided by the newly introduced instalment plan (known now as hire purchase), you might own an impressive piece of musical furniture from one of the cheaper makers such as Thompson of Govan, Glasgow, for little more than 5s a week. There were instruments considerably more costly, some of the most expensive emanating from the factory of Mustel in France; in 1909, for example, it was announced that organ students and organists alike would be delighted to know that a cheaper one-manual organ had been produced and this cost a mere 100 guineas! Just a few years earlier, in 1903, the Hillier Piano & Organ Co of London had produced their 'Crown' model with two full sets of reeds at £16. This was cased in American walnut with a mirror underneath the canopy. The 'Chancel' model with four full sets of reeds and sixteen stops cost £34. And in 1891, Murdoch & Co in London had on view a sample of the 'reed-pipe' organ allegedly manufactured by Lyon & Healy of Chicago. With single manual, seven full sets of reeds and seventeen stops, price ranged from 60 guineas upwards. The tone was produced from reeds mounted in cells of varying lengths 'according to the depth or the character of the tone required'. Although a true reed organ, it featured pipe resonators and, to highlight its imitation of pipe-like tones, it had an imitation pipe top to the case.

For the small working-class home where pretentions were limited by reality, the reed organ was acceptable in every respect and, in times more godly than ours today, there was a certain added benefit in owning an instrument which could be used to play religious music with some of the timbre of the chapel organ. Indeed, ownership of a harmonium could be justified to the piano-conscious snob on the grounds of its being a devotional instrument. Remember that hymns were very frequently sung, not just on Sundays, also that many of the popular pieces of drawing-room music tended towards the languorous and the bathetic. The early reed organ thus found instant acceptance with a very large sector of the public.

Besides domestic use, reed organs had a genuine market with the smaller churches, chapels and religious communities. The French magazine *Le Catholique* reported in the summer of 1907 that more than 1,000 American organs were purchased every year by the French communities of monks and of nuns who settled abroad and in the colonies. The report singled out the Isle of Wight, saying that 'almost all the establishments' there 'have one or more American organs in their chapels or music rooms and these were ordered for the most part through London agents'.

A trade columnist writing in *Musical Opinion* for June 1905, encapsulates the whole aspect of the harmonium in the following:

> The time of the portable organ has come again and this little instrument is once more in great demand in the north. On Sunday evenings its strains float away from street corners of our northern cities and on fine afternoons and evenings they rise above interested groups of holiday makers at Southport, Blackpool, New Brighton, Redcar, Scarborough and other watering places. The uses to which the instrument is being put differ widely. On the Sunday evenings and occasionally on other evenings the portable organ - by which of course is also meant the portable harmonium - is being much used at outdoor religious mission services. The number of outdoor services of this kind now being carried on in the north is surprising, and of late years the number has increased greatly. At most of these outdoor gatherings music is made a feature of the proceedings: in many cases members of church choirs assist and solos are usually sung. A small organ or harmonium is generally used to sustain the voices and to impart its own feature of instrumental music to the proceedings as an attraction. The value of this feature, in the estimation of those who carry on the services, is very great. It is astonishing what an effect the sounds of some simple air played on a reed organ or harmonium on a Sunday evening has on the loiterers in the streets of a large northern town. These people are arrested by the sounds: they draw near the instrument and stand and listen. When one air has been played or a song has been sung, they stand on waiting patiently for more.
>
> At the seaside the instrument is also used by Pierrots and by members of the cult of burnt cork, banjo and bones to sustain their voices in the solo and chorus work with which they charm the holiday makers. Some of these seaside minstrels I am aware use pianos for this purpose; but most of the professional regulars prefer the organ, and with good cause. The reed tone of a small and well made harmonium has more body and power than the softer string tone of a piano when played in the open air at the seaside. The brazen tone endures longer and carries further than string tone, though it does seem to

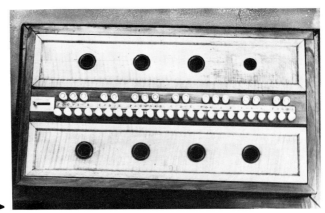

◄ ►
Plate 24. Button melodeon or lap-organ made c.1840 by Abraham Prescott, Concord, New Hampshire, USA. Compass of 3⅓ octaves (F-A). Instrument is played by the depression of buttons laid out in keyboard arrangement |see above|. The stand is almost certainly not original but is nevertheless old (from the collection of Robert E Lloyd)

►
Plate 25. Combined piano and reed organ made by Timothy Gilbert of 406 Washington Street, Boston, Massachusetts. He and Jonas Chickering were both trained as cabinet-makers at John Osborn's piano manufactory shop in Boston. The brothers Timothy and Lemanuel Gilbert were early makers of pianos in the States and between 1841 and the late 'fifties, were awarded a number of patents, exhibiting pianos at the Great Exhibition of 1851 in London. The organ-piano was introduced in 1847 to the designs of Obed Mitchell Coleman, holder of a US patent dated 17th April, 1844 (British Patent No 10,341, 10-10-1844). Instrument here has 6½ octaves, F-A compass (courtesy of the Smithsonian Institution, Washington, DC)

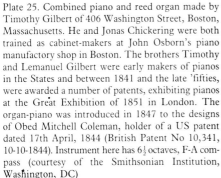

◄
Plate 26. The square piano form of melodeon enjoyed significant popularity in the United States in the formative years. The style emulated both the piano and contemporary American furniture with the over-heavy appearance and solid, chunky legs. This melodeon was made by Austin & Dearborn of Concord, New Hampshire, c.1848-52. 5 octaves, F-E compass (courtesy of the Smithsonian Institution, Washington, DC)

be wonderfully mellowed by the strong sea breeze. So the small organ is very popular with the minstrels in these seaside entertainments. The use of the organ for this purpose demonstrates a fact which ought to help the sale of them very materially,- this is the suitability of the organ or harmonium for playing lively music. One hears the most light and vivacious measures imaginable played on some of these seaside organs, and very well the music sounds.

Organs are again being used for these outdoor purposes and will be wanted for such entertainments for the next four months... The outdoor mission work alluded to is growing; this means that the number of sites or stations at which preaching is carried on is increasing.

Aside from the outdoor missions, the legitimate church has been a regular user of the reed organ since its inception. An official report of the state of psalmody in the Church of Scotland was issued in the summer of 1907. This revealed that it comprised 1,414 congregations. The church contained 362 pipe organs, 324 American organs, 291 harmoniums and 129 unspecified types of 'organ'.

The market for reed organs was virtually the same in the United States, where many of the provincial chapels relied exclusively on the reed organ for music. As patrons of music, the Russians were second only to Germany. The musical instrument trade with Russia was thus immensely important. As an indication of this, in 1908 a consular report from Moscow recorded imports of 428 grand pianos, 2,681 upright pianos, 31 organs (not portable, presumably church organs), and 947 organs of the portable variety, meaning harmoniums and American organs. In the first eight months of 1909, 620 organs described as of a portable nature were imported. World War I disturbed that trade, but an interesting insight to the Russian market is contained in *Musical Opinion* of November 1917:

Musical Instruments for Russia

Although no business can be done at present because of the war, this fact has not prevented the American Consul at Riga from reporting on the Russian market for musical instruments. The demand in normal times for pianos and other musical instruments has always been fairly important in the Riga consular district of Russia. The inhabitants are fond of music, and pianos are found in the homes of all persons of sufficient means. Violins, mandolins, guitars, and other stringed instruments are also numerous. The phonograph has been growing rapidly in popularity in recent years. There are also a few player-pianos in use...

Melodions, or small organs, are also popular, especially in the country districts. Many of them are of American manufacture, the prices ranging from £14 to £52. Some of these instruments are made in Russia, but they are generally small and cheap, selling as low as £8... Mouth-organs are very popular in Russia, but apparently few are made there, the bulk of the supply having been imported from Germany and Austria. Mouth-organs are the favourite instrument of the Russian soldiers.

The situation of the reed-organ trade was expressed in a series of interviews with American manufacturers published in Chicago's *The Indicator* and reproduced in *Musical Opinion* of March 1899. Under the heading 'The Reed Organ Trade is Growing', this eulogy asserts that rumours of declining sales in the organ world are not just wrong but that the truth is that the things are selling better than ever'. It savours something of the self-fulfilling prophecy.

It is hard to tell what has given rise to the impression that the trade in organs is slowly but surely falling off: but there has been more or less talk of this kind. The idea that the cheap piano might possibly bring about such a result may have had something to do with the matter. If it has, or if the idea that because so many organ makers have gone into the manufacture of pianos the organ has begun to lose its importance, the sooner that impression is wiped out the better.

P. J. Healy of Lyon & Healy was reported as saying:

I see no sign of the organ passing away entirely. They will always be used on their own account. The low priced pianos have affected and will continue to materially affect the organ trade. But... the organ will always be used on its own account, because it is easier to learn to play upon than the piano and because it is not affected by transportation and does not require tuning as does the piano.

H. D. Cable of the Chicago Cottage Organ Co said:

The reed organ is undoubtedly the best instrument for farmers and the average citizen of medium means... There are still very many who are not situated so they can buy a piano, and the organ is always within the reach of the masses.

Fig. 50. From an undated but c.1900 Sears Roebuck mail order catalogue quoted in "Michel's Organ Atlas" comes this notice showing a Beckwith organ with a Chicago fallboard address. Beckwith was Sears' own stencil brand and organs were made by others until 1903 when Sears set up the Beckwith Organ Co at Chestnut and 29th Street, Louisville, Kentucky

H. C. Dickson of the Hamilton Organ Co added:

> There is no doubt that the cheap piano has hurt the organ business to some extent and will continue to do so. [However] the general demand for organs is increasing.

E. H. Story of Story & Clark Co said:

> My belief is that the organ trade is only yet in its infancy, and is on the increase and not by any means falling off. There is a certain field the organ can alone fill; at least, until some new instrument possessing all the good qualities of the organ, with improvements in it, comes to take its place. But now, for churches, chapels, lodges, and in the homes of the medium classes, the organ is the one and only instrument.

The final word went to George P. Bent who, with characteristic ebullience, is on record as having said:

> Will the organ stay with us? Oh, yes, yet a while. Why? 'The poor ye have always with you'. I might answer, because the organ is the instrument for the farmer and class of people who can't or won't buy the piano. Yes, the trade is dying out in the cities, but not in the country. The organ is not going to leave us. Cheap pianos will never drive the organ out of the field. No matter how cheap you make a piano, you can get up an organ for one third of the money.

Commendable though the spirit behind these remarks may have been, the simple fact was that cheap reed organs became the instrument's own worst enemy. On both sides of the Atlantic, the trade became increasingly aware of the problem, yet still a largely untutored public and an avaricious trade sustained the output of the cheapjack organ builders. In 1905, the Chicago *Indicator* wrote:

> The cheap organ is not a satisfying instrument,- it is a makeshift; its great attractiveness is in the price; it is bought only by persons who want a musical instrument for appearance's sake, by the poor and by those whose musical sense is not fully developed. To the class of people that buy for appearance's or fashion's sake, the piano - and the dealer's arguments in its favour - will appeal finally..., thus leaving only the poor and the unmusical to become purchasers of the inferior goods... It must be owned that low priced organs have lowered the public's appreciation of organ values, and that the misapprehension afloat is an obstacle of serious consequence...

Against this, the same newspaper was also able to justify the quality reed organ, saying:

> The populace is learning the distinguishing characteristics of good organ tone, so that fairly good prices for high grade reed organs are not impossible to obtain. The American organ manufacturers [meaning makers in the United States - Arthur Ord-Hume], on the whole, can take a complacent view of the trade outlook, both domestic and foreign.

Along with this was the sharp dichotomy found in quality of workmanship in American organs. At this particular time there was a popular saying 'a German toy is often better finished than an American organ', which seems to have arisen because some makers used unseasoned or improperly seasoned timber for their instruments. On top of this, poor finish of metal parts and nickel plated fittings which corroded after a few months had to be contended with. The quality of these organs, which very rapidly began to give trouble, was compared with that of the pianos made by certain reputable London makers who asserted that no instrument should be sold until it had been in store for six months during which time it was to be tuned and maintained regularly. The majority of cheaper American organs - and a number of the better-priced ones - were literally nailed together, and joints were glued for strength when better-class makers would apply proper furniture practices such as dowelling, proper jointing and screwing. Reed chests were glued so that servicing was virtually impossible without major work, and synthetic material was used for the keys so that sunlight discoloured them and normal piano-key ivory rejuvenating techniques would not work on them. Felts were of the poorest commercial quality, leather was equally bad and bellows contained more cardboard than hide. The coming of rubberised cloth, used in piano-player and player-piano work, was a godsend to cheap builders and was often used in the wrong places.

By comparison, the early makers excelled in making first-rate cabinets for their wares. Seraphines in tasteful cases were a very far and different cry from the gawdy, top-heavy and grandiose cases which came to be associated with the American organ in later years. These things did their best to gain acceptability by visible overwhelming, by serving not just as a musical instrument but in doubling for the mantleshelf, the mantleshelf mirror, the cupboard, and a variety of similar random contemporary domestic necessities. If the better-class music-lovers of the seraphine age accepted the appearance of the instrument but were put off by the untutored sound and demeaned pedigree of the thing, then those of a later age, while finding the American organ more musically acceptable, were dismayed at its appearance.

The top-quality instruments were astoundingly well made with the highest possible standard of workmanship combined with obvious investment in specialised precision woodworking machinery. An Estey or Mason & Hamlin organ, for example, can be taken apart with a screwdriver. Certain others were dependent on the hammer, chisel and saw for dismantling.

In matters of taste, too, the American-made organ suffered.

Throughout the history of the poor-man's keyboard instrument on the one hand and the decidedly middle-class piano on the other, there had been periodic attempts at uniting the two. Besides doing this physically, as in the case of Whomes & Sons' Orgapian, unison in playing the two instruments together was also to be encouraged. If the reed organ had striven in certain quarters to join forces with the instrument it allegedly displaced, then it also in a small way proved beneficial to the market for the piano. Reverting to the columnist in the June 1905 edition of *Musical Opinion*:

> I may say that the use of pianos and harmoniums together... is becoming very common in the north. In many homes of the middle classes organs or harmoniums are now to be found as well as pianos, and the organs are played with the pianofortes. In Sunday schools, again, the use of a piano and a harmonium is a common thing and is becoming more so, owing to the commendation of this practice by inspectors of schools within the last few years... dealers need to take steps to inform the public of the great advantage, from the musical point of view, of being able to use the two instruments together.

Which, of course, is all very well so long as both instruments remain more or less on tonal conjunction. The unreliability of this in actual practice is the reason why the many combined piano-harmonium instruments met with limited market success. While the reeds virtually never went out of tune, the pitch of the piano did and the part iron frames of the cheaper grade of piano ensured that this was so. Piano tuners were never short of work, nor surprises, in their profession.

R. F. Stevens in north London was one of the many reed-organ builders who identified the potential market for an instrument small enough to be played with the piano by one player. In 1905 he introduced a pair of small 5- octave harmoniums built to be placed under the fall of the pianoforte, so that the pianist could still make use of the piano pedals yet instantly move slightly to one side to change over to the second instrument. The scale was C to C and they were also fitted with an expression stop. Another man who had the same goal was reed-organ maker George Taylor of 39 Leroy Street, London, who in 1907 patented an American-organ attachment which he fitted under the fall of a piano. The organ could be played alone or in conjunction with the piano, or the piano played on its own. Taylor said he could incorporate as many stops as desired.

All these were, however, attempts to secure a goal already achieved - and quite neatly, too - more than a dozen years earlier by Thomas Dawkins. With a partner named Manns, he was granted British Patent No 16,411 in 1893 for a reed organ attachment for the ordinary upright piano. Called the 'Clarion', it offered three octaves of reeds, F to F, tuned to concert pitch, and could be built virtually entirely within the piano case, only the single pedal protruding. A tremolo was fitted as standard. In 1910, London viewed the combined piano and reed organ factored by Breitkopf & Haertel. This looked, says the report in *Musical Opinion* for December that year, like an ordinary upright piano save for the row of stops over the keyboard and the provision of pedals for supplying wind. The division of the keyboard was at middle C.

Camouflaging the reed organ to look like a piano was all very well, yet if the harmonium was not quite the thing to admit to owning, some surprisingly important people went in for them at various times. Apart from the composers who wrote for them (and thereby presumably played them fairly well), Richard Wagner was a devotee. He owned one made by Burger of Bayreuth, and it survived at least until 1909 when it was said to be owned by 'a gentleman of Cologne'.

But, despite the prestige instruments of the musical world, the reed organ was here to stay. With this growing popularity of the American organ and of the piano - the two instruments enjoying a somewhat symbiotic relationship, with the piano often at one end of the social spectrum and the reed organ at the other, although this was not always the case - the expanding market itself sired new developments. In March 1902, the Pianoforte, Organ and Harmonium Tuners' and Repairers' Association came into being at Liverpool, the object being to improve the technical skill of both tuners and repairers. At that time, there was a tendency for anybody out of work to masquerade as a piano tuner and engineer, and these people were responsible both for ruining many good pianos and organs and for countless complaints.

As the reed-organ market expanded, it naturally forced repercussions on other older traditional aspects of the musical-instrument industry. Initially, the seraphine and harmonium robbed from the piano industry by expanding the overall market for keyboard players and by selling into homes which could not afford a piano. The harmonium with its improvements over the primitive seraphine killed off the latter. Then it, itself, suffered at the feet of the American organ. And finally this in turn suffered, first from the cheap piano as described later, then from the much later breed of high-quality self-playing reed organs such as the Aeolian Orchestrelle.

The harmonium industry really began to feel the pinch around the end of the 1880s, and nowhere more than in Germany. Production was cut as the mini-recession of the age spread its tentacles into the harmonium industry. It seemed that what money was available was being spent on American organs rather than locally made harmoniums. At a time when American market protectionism was the prime talking point in the industry - the Americans wanted to increase import duty to 40 per cent - the Leipzig correspondent to *Musical Opinion* of 22 May 1890 wrote:

> There is... an admirable opportunity now open for Germany to adopt retaliatory measures'. Why is not a forty per cent., *ad valorem*, duty on American organs clamoured for in the Reichstag? Simply because the German people are sensible enough to see that, if the harmonium trade of Germany is being driven to the wall by the competition of American organs, it is because the harmonium makers are behind the age, and do not give their instrument such an attractive exterior as the Yankees provide.

Almost exactly a year later, on 25 May 1891, the same correspondent wrote:

> According to various reports which have come to hand, the manufacture of harmoniums in Germany is looking up again, notwithstanding the keen competition of the American organ. The two largest factories in South Germany, in which harmonium reeds are made, are so full of orders that none will be accepted

for delivery before the autumn. Indeed, it has been rumoured that reeds have been imported from America, but these are probably only as required for the manufacture of American organs, an industry which has lately been introduced into the Fatherland.

Indeed, the Leipzig firm of Gebrüder Hug began making American organs that summer and prided itself in being able to turn out an instrument at a lower price than the American product. And yet, at the German Exhibition held in London that June, it was a large manual and pedal Estey organ which was used to illustrate a lecture on the Oberammergau Passion Play. The indignity was forced upon the Germans by economics: the instrument came from London Estey dealers Hodge & Essex.

A similar state of affairs existed in France. *Musical Opinion* reported in September 1903:

> The French harmonium manufacturers are complaining sadly of the competition created by the American organs. In some of the leading retail dealers' shops in Paris and the large provincial towns, the once popular 'sacred' instrument has entirely disappeared. There seems to be now only a demand for portable harmoniums, which are mainly used by street musicians.

Ownership of a decorative musical instrument did wonders for the market in places where such preferences held sway. A Berlin journalist was moved to write early in 1905 that:

> the people of the U.S. of America are truly by no means the 'most cultured music lovers' of the world, but they are certainly the best customers of the musical instrument manufacturers. From sixty to seventy thousand pianofortes and cabinet organs are annually sold in the United States, and many firms in 'musical Germany' would be thankful for less culture and more ready sales among their own countrymen.

The mass market for reed organs in Britain was, though, experiencing a surprise challenge from the very instrument it set out to usurp - the piano. The mass-production of low-cost (and often inferior) cottage pianos threatened the sensibilities of a consumer who still had the nagging feeling that, ornateness apart, the reed organ was truly the poor man's pianoforte. As early as October, 1904, a writer commented that 'organs used to sell well among the iron workers of Stafford; but, since the cottage pianos have been obtainable at fourteen to sixteen pounds, pianofortes have been preferred.'

But changes were afoot. The combined reed organ and piano was experiencing another of its periodic and short-lived revivals as the coming of the kinematograph created new markets. To quote *Musical Opinion* of wartime March 1915:

Endsleigh Organs and Harmoniums

Messrs James Humphreys, of 35, Drummond Street, Euston Square, N.W., continue to be so busy that orders have commenced to overlap one another. They enjoy an excellent colonial business for organs and harmoniums, and this has kept up remarkably well since the outbreak of war. Another department which is flourishing is the fitting of their organ attachment to ordinary pianos. The demand for these instruments is greatly on the increase, owing to the fact that they are so extensively used in picture theatres. Fitted with various suitable devices, these instruments can accompany any picture appropriately, giving any effects necessary to make the reel a success. For more years than we would like to admit we have known Messrs. James Humphreys, and we always look forward to spending a pleasant half hour in the factory talking over old times.

World War I was a traumatic experience for the British, both as regards the selling of instruments and the conflicting loyalties which it generated. By the early part of 1915, the losses of British lives in the battlefields of France dominated every aspect of life in the British Isles. So often the news that yet another life had been 'given', or that a man had 'fallen', concealed the horrific truth that such lives were neither 'given' nor laid down, but taken in awful, bloody circumstances. The anti-German feelings which this evoked killed at one stroke the market for German instruments. Those who had made a successful business out of the importing and selling of German pianos and organs lost that trade overnight. And when Julius Blüthner was awarded the Royal Warrant for supplying pianofortes to the royal family in 1915, there was a massive outcry. The presentation of a petition representing the 20,000 members of the pianoforte and organ-building industry who had gone to fight for their country - many of whom never returned - demanded immediate action. The Lord Chamberlain rightly and very quickly acted to revoke that honour and re-assign it to John Broadwood & Sons.

The British musical-instrument trade now depended almost solely on the output of British manufacturers, depleted in staff as they were due to the conscription of all able-bodied men to serve the war effort. On the one hand, British makers strongly promoted their wares as made by British hands while on the other their production was dramatically cut. *Musical Opinion* reported, with somewhat ill-concealed dismay, that women were now working in musical instrument factories, adding that, although there were a few exceptions, no woman aspired to the higher masculine skills such as piano-tuning. The only source of instruments to supplement the diminishing output of British industry was from across the Atlantic, for Canadian and American makers were now the only 'foreign' suppliers whose products the British public would buy: importers of Canadian organs emphasised strongly that their goods were made within the British Empire by British subjects.

Then came a cruel blow when the president of the Board of Trade, Walter Runciman, issued a proclamation to the effect that as from 27 March 1916, musical instruments of all sorts 'including pianolas [sic] and other similar instruments and accessories' would be prohibited. Gramophones, records, components, kits and materials were to be subject to the issue of licences by the Board of Trade and these would 'not in general be issued except where evidence is forthcoming that the goods were either (a) actually *en route* for the United Kingdom at the date of this notice or (b) paid for at that date.' The industry was up in arms at what it saw as a thoroughly ill-conceived move, and it was pointed out that if the ban was sustained, even when it was finally lifted it would take several years to rebuild the trade after the war. Runciman was unmoved and the ban, although not totally enforced for the supply of what was termed 'essential raw materials necessary to preserving the industry', bit hard. The musical instrument industry retrenched still further.

Staffed by elderly and often infirm workers who were otherwise unfit to serve their country, the industry suffered a progressive run down which the post-war years did not immediately remedy. There had been few if any apprentices, few elder craftsmen to tutor them, too many bereavements both at management level and on the shop floor and too steady a slow down of retail trade to bring about any hope of an overnight resumption of work in 1918. The slow recovery which Britain made at the end of hostilities combined with a continuing public reticence at buying anything German meant that the piano and organ industry stayed becalmed for a long, long while.

What resurgence did take place was directed towards the player-piano and the new-fangled wireless set and gramophone. The hey-day of the reed organ, so strongly in demand at the outset of World War I, was over, and what remained was a steady call for quality practice organs at one end of the market spectrum, and small chapel organs at the other. The great days of harmoniums in working class homes had departed, and somehow seemed so far back in time as to be memories bordering on the realm of history.

Since the earliest days of the instrument, American organ manufacturers had exhibited a bullish approach to the British market. Perhaps it was the first time that the British man-in-the-street

◄
Plate 27. Pressure reed organ by George A Prince & Co of Buffalo, New York, c.1860-65. 5 octaves, C-C compass. The bellows feeders are pumped using stirrups, a feature of several of Prince's models. This survivor is at The Franklin House, Launceston, Tasmania, and is owned by the National Trust of Australia

►

Plate 28. Single manual American organ by Clough & Warren of Detroit, Michigan, c.1880. 5 octave F-F compass with keyboard break at G sharp/A. 14 stops: diapason 8ft, viola 4ft, viola dolce, gemshorn 2ft, sub bass 16ft, coupler, forte, vox humana, cremona, cello 16ft, vox angelet 8ft, celeste, flute 4ft, melodia 8ft. Total number of reeds 229. 2 knee levers for full organ and swell. Unusual is the provision of 2ft reeds in the bass and a reedy 16ft in the treble. The diapason 8ft rank is equipped with Scribner Tubes - acoustically-tuned resonating chambers for each reed cell named after the inventor. Scribner's Tubes were an approach towards the evolution of the Vocalion tone ranks as used by Aeolian (from the collection of Phil and Pam Fluke)

◄
Plate 29. Flat top American organ by George Woods & Co, Boston,USA. Date 26th March, 1873. 5 octaves, compass F-F, 31 bass, 30 treble. $2\frac{1}{2}$ sets of reeds plus 13 note sub bass, total 165 reeds. 9 stops, 1 fretted knee board for full organ. Walnut case. Top cover encloses the whole of the upper part of the organ, including the fretted front. Ivory keys. Top 13 of the 8ft reeds and top 22 of the 4ft row each have their own pallets opened by stickers which pass down through holes to the reeds. Case number 19558. Sold by W A Boucher, Shrewsbury, Ludlow, Leominster (from the collection of Phil and Pam Fluke)

Fig. 51. Story & Clark turned a disaster into a business promotion when the great Tabernacle Street fire in London destroyed its new warehouse. This double-page advertisement appeared in "Musical Opinion" for July 1894

had been exposed to the brash transatlantic sales and promotion techniques to which we are now so thoroughly accustomed. Looking back one can see that the American methods of advertising, even in the refined form adopted by British agents, served as a forerunner of the great age of player piano promotions which largely took over the market created and nurtured by the reed organ. Indeed, the reed organ was arguably the first of what we would today all the consumer durables. The world was moving inexorably forward. What had happened, though, was that the needs of the market - even its locale - had changed and makers were forced to investigate and exploit fresh markets. And the richest market was India.

Discussing the potential piano and organ trades in that territory, *Musical Opinion* said in February, 1913:

> The demand exists in all parts... Harmoniums, solid polished oak case 16 stops, $4\frac{1}{2}$ rows of broad tempered reeds, octave couplers, foot and hand blowers, for church use, best English make, - R[upee]s 650... Portable mission organs, 3 and 4 octaves compass, compact, durable and excellent tone, Rs. 55, 65, 75, 85, 113, 135, 150 and 225... Folding box harmoniums, best French make, with six stops, Rs. 130, 140, 170 and 200... Best Paris made folding box harmoniums, used extensively for Hindustani music, with tubular metal wind trunks, two complete rows best reeds, compass $3\frac{1}{2}$ cotaves, Rs. 130 and 140... In portable instruments that close up into a small space there is a huge trade to be done.

By exporting the reed organ to India, that market was cultivated rapidly and as demand increased, inevitably it was not long before India started up its own reed-organ industry concentrating on the small, portable type of harmonium.

Meanwhile, as might be expected, the *mid-Atlantic* style of American organ still had its few devotees. An enthusiast, apparently organless, wrote to *Musical Opinion* in July of 1919 desirous of making his own American organ. Even at that date, in spite of the fact that the instrument had been so recently a trade mainstay, the editor's response was not all that encouraging:

Building an American Organ

Some years ago there was published by Messrs. Ward, Lock & Co. 'Amateur Work', in monthly parts, containing a series of illustrated articles on American organ building. There is also in volume 63 of The English Mechanic (332, Strand, London) a series of illustrated articles on 'How to Make an American Organ.' I believe you can obtain either of these books, though I cannot say what volume of 'Amateur Work' the articles by Thos. L. Wimmeth are in. Doubtless an enquiry would bring you the information promptly.

But with the waning of the reed-organ industry, it is interesting to revert to the early days when the visual and tonal excellence of the American-made instruments and the expanding market in Britain created sufficient incentive to develop this country as a selling platform. This, in fact, was not always a straightforward job; the problem lay in getting the products of the American organ factories to British shores. The only way was by sea and this, even up to the time of World War I, was an extremely hazardous operation. Between 1864 and 1869, for example, Lloyd's Registers give a world shipping loss of 100,000 sailing ships. In 1856 alone, 1,153 vessels were lost round the British coasts; and in one day of a great gale in 1859, 195 ships foundered. Another 298 ships were lost in the terrible November of 1893.

The sea was thus a great barrier to transatlantic trade and many valuable cargoes went to the bottom, or were plundered by the Cornish wreckers. As far as musical instruments were concerned, sea-water immersion invariably meant the cargo was rendered useless and fit only for firewood. Many were the long, cold winter evenings sustained by the warmth of a fire of ships' timbers and reed organs dredged from the reefs.

Typical of this type of catastrophy and an early victim in the organ cargo business was the three-masted barque *River Lune* laden with mixed cargo, including a consignment of American organs. It was 27 July 1879 when she allegedly suffered navigational error through a faulty chronometer, and ran aground on the Scillies in fog at night. The ship, eleven years old, heeled over and sank at the stern in twenty feet of water just ten minutes later. The crew got off, returned the next day for their belongings, and left this handsome ship to the ravages of the sea; she broke up nine days later. Most of the cargo was gone in a day, scavenged by folk from near and far; the organs on board disappeared. In those days before radio and telephones, it is often extraordinary how rapidly news of a wreck travelled; and with lifeboatmen and wreckers not infrequently in the same family, it was often a case of saving life and then beating the insurance surveyor by ensuring that there was nothing left to survey.

In December 1901, the one-time tea clipper *Glenbervie* launched in 1866, struck the Manacles - one of the most dreaded reefs off Cornwall east of the Lizard promontory - en route from Britain to the St Lawrence river in Canada. Her cargo of some 1,200 barrels of spirits was salvaged, to the dismay of the plunderers. However, a consignment of grand pianos on board was ruined.

On 18 April 1910 the *Minnehaha* struck on Scilly Rock on her way from New York to Tilbury. Sailing slowly because of thick fog, she was salvaged only after lightening her burden, and a valuable cargo of brand-new American cars, pianos and American organs had been jettisoned. It must have been an odd sight to see crates of organs bobbing about in the sea; the pianos would probably have accompanied the cars and gone straight to the bottom thanks to their iron frames.

Reed organs, containing so much wood, tended to burn well; a feature not overlooked across the years since they left their manufacturers, new, highly polished and steeped in varnish. They have been incinerated in great piles as their usefulness became superseded, and many a Guy Fawkes bonfire has been built around a neglected and unwanted instrument. This tendency to inflammability, has meant that next to the hazards of getting instruments from overseas to these shores was the ever-present risk of fire in warehousing and storage. The fact that piano and organ manufacturing itself was a fire hazard to all concerned only served to compound the risk of loss or damage by fire in any city where buildings and stores were huddled together in largely archaic surroundings. One had not only to be ever-mindful of the risks run in one's own premises, but had to trust that owners of other, neighbouring businesses were equally careful.

And so it was not by their own fault, but probably that of a neighbour, that Storey & Clark contributed with their almost new five-floor premises to one of the biggest and spectacular fires in the metropolitan area of London - at Tabernacle Street, Finsbury, in 1894. The street, a major centre for the cabinet-making industry and interspersed with the warehouses of merchants and other flammable industries, had over the years made its own singular contribution to London's fire losses and the payout of insurance companies.

The day in question, 21 June, was a Thursday, and the thirty-third anniversary of one of the most famous of London's post-1666 conflagrations - the great Tooley Street burnup in which the legendary James Braidwood, Superintendent of the London Fire Brigade, lost his life. It was ten minutes past nine in the evening when the alarm was raised that the building of merchants Angus & Co at Nos 66-68 was showing a strong light from the fourth floor. Very quickly there was no doubt that it was fire and, despite the rapid turnout of steamers from the London Fire Brigade and the pumping of thousands of gallons of water, the blaze, fed by huge stocks of merchandise, quickly engulfed all five floors.

Suddenly there was a gigantic rush of flame which spread not only to the furniture store of Harris, Lebus & Co next door, but flashed across the narrow street to the warehouse opposite. All the efforts of the brigades were powerless to check the fire which burst into a rope works and then into Storey & Clark's organ factory and warehouse. By ten o'clock, nine buildings on the eastern side of the street and five on the other were ablaze from top to bottom. Virtually every fire engine in London was now diverted to Tabernacle Street, leaving the City unprotected in the event of any other fire breaking out. By midnight, forty steamers were deployed around the area as, with twenty buildings now ablaze, London was illuminated as with a setting sun. The organs with their thin wood construction, were reduced to ashes in moments in a glare which was visible forty miles away. So serious was the blaze that all Finsbury and Shoreditch looked at grave risk from the flames, for the narrow streets were no protection. As wall after wall collapsed, the flames increased in intensity.

When finally the blaze was brought under control, some thirty buildings had been wholly or partly destroyed, but the large mass of ruins was to smoke and smoulder for ten more days. The total loss was £600,000, a large portion of which was not covered by insurance. Of Storey & Clark's two buildings and the seventy cases of brand-new dismantled instruments worth £1,000 which had been delivered only the previous day, nothing remained save two massive gaunt walls which had to be pulled down by twenty men. The following issue of *Musical Opinion* carried that company's famous double-page spread advertisement. On the left side it announced, boldly and accurately, that all the stock was gone, while on the right it announced a move into temporary premises and the immediate shipping of fresh stocks of the latest models from Chicago.

Making pianos and organs involved machinery, driven in later years by steam engine, and glue which had to be kept heated night and day. There was thus an ever-present risk of fire from within the factory through a carelessly damped stove, a stray spark catching the inevitable piles of wood shavings and timber stock, or a chimney fire. Many piano-makers' premises were burned, and many more than once. Just before three o'clock in the morning of 21 March 1906, Erskine Road in Primrose Hill, north London, was the scene of a huge blaze which practically destroyed reed-organ makers J. Malcolm & Co. Damage was put at £9,000 - not a lot by today's standards, but a considerable insurance loss in those days. Malcolm rebuilt on the site and in the interim took adjacant premises where work was soon in hand again. Barely five months later, precisely the same thing happened again, fire breaking out at 4.30 on a Saturday morning and again the building was virtually destroyed.

For many reasons, then, the reed organ and its industry played a significant part of everyday life, either by sweetness (sometimes harshness) of sound, by beauty and decoration - or by stark tragedy and disaster.

CHAPTER 7

Music for the Reed Organ

While all the technical development was taking place in improving, altering or just plain enhancing the appearance of the instrument, there was another factor to be considered, namely the matter of suitable music for the reed organ.

Way back in the late 1830s, collections of music for the seraphine had been produced. These emerged more as an aid to encouraging the sale of instruments to people who could not understand that they might *adapt* their own organ or piano pieces for the new instrument than as a serious exercise in adapting keyboard music to the potential of an instrument which could sustain its tones. Naturally, it was religious music such as hymns which formed the mainstay of such collections and these were very popular. All through the Victorian era, arrangements of popular songs, patriotic melodies and the inevitable drawing-room ballad were published for the reed organ. What was missing, however, was the composition expressly penned to take into account, and take advantage of, its capabilities.

As far as serious musicians were concerned, the harmonium was, as we have seen, not an instrument to be mentioned in polite circles. And so it would have remained save for the fact that the harmonium began to earn entries in the encyclopedias of music. It was probably this one move which drove home to people who should not have needed such blatant incentive the fact that the harmonium, while rather cheap and not as nice and refined as a piano or cabinet pipe organ, was out there in the big wide world and people wanted to play music on it.

The very first tentative reed-organ olive branches from the high echelons of the music world came almost grudgingly. Several serious musicians - Berlioz, Karg-Elert, Schoenberg, Strauss among others - either wrote eulogies on the merits of the instrument or composed music especially for it, but this move did not at once gain the approbation of the stuffy surroundings of the Victorian music scene. It was, however, a move in the right direction. And soon the harmonium came to be accepted outside the working classes and the chapels in the valleys and on the moors.

The seraphine and the harmonium brought to a far wider range of people the ability in performance of the pipe organ in that it could sustain its tones. However, the instrument could be no substitute for the pipe organ and in any case organ music proper was too complicated to play on it. While later examples were perfectly capable of performing this type of music and had an attack and rapidity of speech almost the same as a pipe organ, it was indentified quite early on that the instrument warranted a repertoire of its own.

So it was that these albums of tunes specially arranged for the harmonium and, in increasing instances, especially composed for it, came to appear on the market. Soon every music shop in the land sold albums of voluntaries, hymn tunes and sacred music arranged for the reed organ. Many publishers of this type of music capitalised on the fact that, unlike the piano, there was scope for providing instruction in how to play the harmonium. For this reason, a number of the music books which appeared around the middle of the last century and, indeed, right up to the turn of the century, also incorporated harmonium and American organ tutors which, in addition to basic fingering and elementary notes on reading music, also taught how to pedal, how to use the stops and how to interpret music. Style and lucidity varied greatly among these Victorian tutors, but their numbers give some idea of the great potential of this market which was anticipated by their publishers.

Reed organ writer Ernest Ward Lowry commented on the style of music suited to the American organ in his column in *Musical Opinion* of March 1905:

> Many folk still regard the suction organ as merely an improved harmonium, and hold that only sacred or slow music can be rendered (with accordion like solemnity) upon it with advantage. That the exact reverse is true can be proved by trying the two hundred compositions - not voluntaries - contained in Metzler's 'American Organ Journal', edited by J. Munro Coward, which now runs to thirty- five volumes, and is moreover 'still running'.

The flood of special compositions, some quite good, but still many others of a rather indifferent nature, had begun. The harmonium and now the American organ followed in the footsteps of the baryton and the saxophone: they had become accepted as musical instruments by virtue of having music written specially for them.

When the harmonium reached the Indian sub-continent and it was discovered that varying conditions of temperature had little effect on the tuning of the instrument, India took to the instrument like the proverbial duck to water. While this had an obviously unfortunate effect on the nation's native musical traditions, it created a whole new industry of manufacturers and, of course, music publishing. Fétis's successor at the Brussels Conservatory of Brussels, François Auguste Gevaert (1828-1908), listed in his library the title of a harmonium tutor 'printed in Hindustani and in the musical notation of Bengal (Harmaniyamsutra), Calcutta, 1874'.

Besides the entrepreneurs and harmonium enthusiasts - such as the London organist J. W. Elliott who was one of a number who produced a quantity of albums of arrangements, there was a growing following amongst quality musicians including composers as, accepted as a musical instrument, the harmonium rapidly attained the status of a folk instrument and was thus increasingly viewed as a worthwhile medium for 'good' music. To this end, Charles Gounod wrote six fugues for the instrument while opus 1 of Saint-Saëns consists of Three Pieces for Harmonium and his opus 8 is Six Duets for Harmonium and Pianoforte while his opus 13 is an Elevation for Harmonium.

Dvořák saw the potential in chamber music and composed some bagatelles in 1878 for harmonium, two violins and 'cello. Franck, in 1862, wrote a *quasi marcia*, and in 1863 Five Pieces and also Forty-four Short Pieces for the instrument. In 1871 he followed with an Offertoire on a Breton Air for harmonium, in 1873 a harmonium arrangement of his organ work, Prelude, Fugue and Variation (op 18), and in 1889-90, under the title of *L'Organiste*, fifty-nine harmonium pieces. Reger made a number of arrangements for harmonium of his own songs and those of others, while Lefebure-Wely identified the high hopes for the harmonium and wrote for it.

Karg-Elert toured as a recitalist with an instrument called the 'Kunst- Harmonium' (perhaps best translated as 'artistic harmonium') and wrote for it a sonata, an important passacaglia, and a large number of smaller works, and also compiled a work (in German), called *The Art of Registration for the Harmonium*. Strauss used the instrument in his ballet *Schlagobers*, where it provides a nocturne as background for a violin solo. But it was Percy Grainger who, while playing his harmonium one day and discovering a cyphering C, turned adversity to advantage and wrote a witty if lengthy piece around that unintentional note, calling it 'The Immovable Do' [doh].

Plate 30. Style 84 Boudoir American organ made by J Estey & Co, Brattleboro, Vermont. Date 1881. 5 octaves, compass F-F, 31 bass, 30 treble. 3 sets of reeds plus 13 note sub bass, total 196 reeds. 2 knee swells. Ebonised walnut case with carved designs highlighted in gilt. A highly unusual, fanciful cabinet. Ivory keys. Case number 119037. Sold by Locke & Son, Mendelssohn House, 36 Great Ducie Street, Manchester (from the collection of Phil and Pam Fluke)

Plate 31. Flat top organ by Jacob Estey & Co, Brattleboro, Vermont. Date 1883. Style 122. 5 octaves C to C, 28 bass, 33 treble plus 30 note flat pedal board. 3 full sets of reeds plus 30 notes pedal, totalling 213. 15 stops including four kick-down stops (pedal coupler, pedal forte, grand swell and grand organ). Mahogany case with one-piece fretted back. Split, folding lid, ivory keys and hand pumping device. Case number 131707. An unusual example of an 1880s American-made organ with a pedal board and only one manual manual plus a C-C compass. Case number 131707. Sold by Joseph Riley, 25 Constitution Hill, Birmingham (from the collection of Phil and Pam Fluke)

Several eminent writers on orchestration extending from Berlioz (1844) to Widor (1904), have treated the instrument with great respect. The former dealt with the harmonium at length in his *Treatise of Instrumentation* and the latter gave it consideration in his *New Treatise of Instrumentation*.

From the later seventies onwards, the harmonium's value and widening popularity in the Victorian home was also recognised by the song composer who often supplied an optional harmonium accompaniment - called an 'obbligato', presumably because it was not obligatory (Scholes) - to the pianoforte accompaniment.

The harmonium in its popular form was not an easy instrument to play in spite of claims to the contrary. This was partly due to the division and, in the case of the sub-bass, triple partitioning of the single keyboard. The reason for this was that in an instrument which had more than one row of reeds, it was common practice to 'divide' the stops, which meant that a whole sequential scale of pitches could not be selected just by the drawing of one stop-knob, but required each half of the row to be selected, one at the right for the upper half, one at the left for the lower half. Now this facility was provided so that, in organs with several registers and several pitches, a melody could be played with the right hand on, say, an 8ft and a 4ft register, while the accompaniment was played on just an 8ft pitch. The 16ft sub-bass normally covered only the lowest octave of reeds. The skilled player could take advantage of these three portions of the single keyboard and, with practice, avoid the catastrophic musical effects of one hand straying into the domain of the other, or a bass note suddenly rising into the accompaniment or vice-versa. For most players, though, it was all a bit too much and either they didn't care, or they just drew out everything and hoped for the best.

Another problem was that three or more stop-knobs would be used to control one rank of reeds; in a divided keyboard this could even be up six or more. The rank, acted on by a serious of various mutes or shades, could be induced to produce a choice of marginally different voices depending which knob was drawn. Out of one rank of reeds, for example, you could find the following pairs: diapason (bass) - principle (treble); diapason dolce (bass) - vox angelica (treble); viola (bass) - melodio (treble); the names chosen for these tones being often fanciful. The problem was multipled when octave couplers were used, because from the same row of reeds might be induced two or more so-called 4ft tones.

The short answer was that unless there was a multiplicity of rows of reeds, and those rows were of different styles, it was very difficult to induce a variety of tone colours from the harmonium or American organ. While this was quite possible with the larger and more expensive instruments, the single or one-and-a-half row models were not very musical and, once the primary stop was drawn, the effect of the other mutes was automatically negated since the primary stop would perforce have to affect all the mutes. From this it can be adduced that the seraphine and other instruments of that class were not particularly musical, offering no more than a single scale of pitches. We are told in many contemporary references that the Seraphine produced a 'harsh' tone. Ernest Ward Lowry's words from *Musical Opinion* of March 1905, comment on the tonal differences between harmonium and American organ playing:

> The suction force, being always under the direct control of the player, forms a foot touch as sympathetic and more easily controlled than the expression stop of the harmonium, while rendering blowing much less of a physical labour, which latter advantage is much appreciated by ladies. Suction tone is sweeter, purer, rounder, less reedy, and at very close range almost as powerful as that of the forced bellows, but does not carry so far or support a large number of voices so well. Suction reeds, being arched and twisted, admit of far less lateral vibration, and consequently give a purer and more distinct fundamental note with less admixture of overtones. A dissonance, such as the chord of the diminished seventh, which would be painful on the harmonium (owing to the whirring of its upper partial harmonics), is much more bearable on the suction organ.

The same writer looked to the musical value of the confusingly-named *vox humana* stops, the American organ's confusingly termed version of the tremulant stop found on harmoniums and pipe organs.

> A sane man can only once be caught with a cardboard fan, from which 'a perfect imitation of the vox humana of pipes' is promised; while a 'vacuum viola' (*Anglice*, a half lifted mute) is also a trap which can only once be set.

As for the reed organ/harmonium, the following table shows to which group - right, left or centre - the stops belong. Assuming that the keyboard is vertical to the page, bass half at the top, treble at the bottom, the letters S and M show which are sounding stops, and which are purely mechanical features.

[1] One set of reeds: three stops

forte = M
expression = M
forte = M

[2] One set of reeds: five stops

forte = M
sourdine = M
expression = M
tremolo = M
forte = M

[3] One and a half sets of reeds: eight stops

forte = M
sourdine = M
cor anglais = S
expression = M
flute = S
celeste = S
tremolo = M
forte = M

forte = M
sourdine = M
bourdon = S
cor anglais = S
grand jeu = M

[4] Two and a half sets of reeds: eleven stops
expression = M
flute = S
celeste = S
clarionet = S
tremolo = M
forte = M

forte = M
bassoon = S
clarion = S
bourdon = S
cor anglais = S

[5] Four sets of reeds: twelve stops
grand jeu = M
expression = M
flute = S
clarionet = S
fife = S
oboe = S
forte = M

forte = M
sourdine = M
vox humana = S
bassoon = S
clarion = S
bourdon = S
cor anglais = S
percussion = M
double expression = M

[6] Five and a half sets of reeds, two manuals: twenty stops
grand jeu = M
manual coupler = M
expression = M
percussion = M
flute = S
clarionet = S
fife = S
oboe = S
celeste = ·S
dolce = S
forte = M

[7] Seven sets of reeds: eighteen stops

forte = M
harp eolienne = S
bassoon = S
clarion = S
bourdon = S
cor anglais = S
percussion = M
grand jeu = M
expression = M
percussion = M
flute = S
clarionet = S
fife = S
oboe = S
musette = S
celeste = S
baryton = S
forte = M

This table only sets out seven sizes of instrument, yet the principles which it demonstrates apply throughout the reed-organ family. An awareness of this is necessary if the performer is to get the best out of an instrument.

For what purpose was the harmonium originally conceived? This is a good question and one which is hard to identify. Initially, it must have been viewed as a replacement for the more expensive and more bulky pipe organ and thus with some aspirations towards a devotional purpose, but its proportions and style of finish suggest that the early examples must have been produced for domestic consumption. With the arrival of the American organ came an unhealthy pandering to an excess of non-musical fancy woodwork with the Victorian parlour in mind. The major manufacturers certainly made models for church use, and reed organs such as the larger products of the better makers were eminently suited to small-church application, several makers (John Holt in Britain and Thomas in Canada for example) making high-quality organists' practice reed organs which featured appointments in many respects similar to the pipe organ.

A difficulty with the small harmonium in church use is that its thinnish tones do not carry. While in an empty church there is every opportunity to hear the instrument, when the building is filled with sound-absorbing people and, perhaps, they are singing, the sound has a remarkable ability to diminish. In the tiny cobble-floored fourteenth century of Sibbo in southern Finland, the music is provided by a two-manual Mannborg harmonium and, with a full congregation, even this is barely up to the task. So, while the harmonium was certainly a cheap and visually acceptable substitute for the organ in a small church, it was generally too close to the ground for its sound to carry adequately. The pipe organ scored here by having its pipework above the heads of the congregation and thus in clear air; the harmonium had to cope with legs and coats, pews and drapes.

The world of minstrels, missions and travelling preachers nevertheless owes the harmonium, and the portable version in particular, an immense debt of gratitude for, without it, it would be a task of superhuman proportions to bring music to the masses or to the worshippers, whichever may have been the greater.

Music for the harmonium demanded skill, not just to cope with the bellows which required continual pumping from the foot treadles, but care in registration and playing. When 'expression' was selected, considerable technique was needed to get the best effect from the direct wind supply. Mention has already been made of the difficulty of using a coupler and literally running out of treble notes in a crucial part of the music. There were other expression features to; there were increasing numbers of mechanical aids to performance - knee swells, ankle boards calling for foot-pivoting while pedalling; playing aids such as 'prolongment' to be used at the correct moment; shades, shutters, swells, mutes and stops to operate. Small wonder that many American organ owners preferred to draw out a handful of stop knobs and then play, leaving all else well alone.

The developed reed organ, except in the hands of a musician, was in that respect the precursor of today's hi-fi or video recorder; most users just did not know how to use it to fullest advantage. Those extra features which served initially to clinch a sale were so often ignored and forgotten.

Programme of Carl Rosa Opera Company's Theatre Royal, Drury Lane, performance of Goring Thomas's four-act opera "Esmeralda" on 27th November 1883

CHAPTER 8

The Development of
Self-Playing Reed Organs

The harmonium came into existence at a time when mechanical musical instruments were quite commonplace. It was not unusual to have a church organ which either played entirely by means of pinned wooden barrels and did not have a keyboard at all, or which could be played either by hand or by mechanical means. References abound in the first half of the last century to 'Barrel and Finger Organs', so much so that when an ordinary instrument was advertised or referred to, it was commonly described as a 'finger organ'. The inference was that an instrument which could only be played in one way, ie either by hand or by barrel, was in some way incomplete; it was only half an instrument.

Not unnaturally, the harmonium arriving in the middle of this era of duality was faced with having to set about mechanising itself into an expected unity as quickly as possible. Barrel-operated harmoniums enjoyed only a small following though, and the majority of these were made in France by Gavioli and his contemporaries. The smaller harmonium-type automatic street instrument did, however, proliferate, but is outside the scope of the present work.

It was not until the advent of perforated music that matters began to change. Thibouville-Lamy in Paris produced a number of keyless but quite large harmoniums which were played by cardboard books like a fair organ. Although this invention has long been claimed for Gavioli, perforated and folded books of punched cardboard predated Gavioli's invention both in Germany and America. Then, with the perfection of perforated paper rolls, inspired by the diminutive organette and suitably enlarged to match the compass of a keyboard instrument, came a whole flurry of automatic instruments which were increasingly musical, culminating in the Aeolian Orchestrelle and the Mustel Concertal, probably the finest player reed organs in the world.

On the way to that perfection, though, there were devices such as Nyström's Reform-Orgel - a harmonium which, while provided with a normal keyboard, might also be played mechanically by clamping a perforated cardboard disc onto the side of the casework and turning a handle, and Debain's Antiphonel, a key-top player using music represented as steel-studded wooden boards (called *planchettes*) and devised to play either the pianoforte or the harmonium. The first of these was build in Sweden and used the same type of cardboard music as perfected by Ehrlich in Leipzig for the Ariston organette. In fact, all Nyström's music discs bore the legend 'Ehrlich's Patents'. In Leipzig, Ehrlich himself made a self-playing harmonium working from discs, only these were fixed horizontally on top of the harmonium case.

The Aeolian Orchestrelle was by far the most popular brand of perforated-paper-roll-operated player organ. It was made in huge numbers and very many survive to this day. There were numerous

Fig. 52. Kimball's Self-Playing Organ was introduced by London agents Marples. This notice appeared in "Musical Opinion" for June 1899

other brands or makes, a one-time close runner being Wilcox & White's Symphony. Estey made player reed instruments as did Mustel in France, Malcolm and Maxfield in London, Schiedmayer in Germany and Bell in Canada, to name but a few. Perforated paper rolls were used to play a variety of instruments from pipe organs and orchestrions through to pianos and piano-orchestrions. The instrument which is best known today, however, was the product of one of the biggest piano and organ-making combines in the world - the free reed organ of a construction basically no different from that of the normal American organ.

The very first player reed organ was the small organette which was played using perforated metal or card discs, or zigzag-folded perforated cardboard books of music like the majority of fairground organs. These date in general from the 1870s although the principle was demonstrated, without too much success, on an experimental organ shown at the Great Exhibition in London in 1851. By the mid-1880s, the instrument had reached a high degree of perfection and market acceptance throughout America, Germany and Great Britain. Organettes proliferated and their large numbers brought cheap music to many who could not afford music of any other kind, least of all the much more expensive Swiss-style musical box.

As we have already seen, the basic reed organ had gained public acceptance in both America and France from a much earlier date. It was, however, the French who discovered that if instead of blowing the reeds by admitting wind at pressure to them, finer tones could be produced by sucking air through them using a suction bellows. But like so many good ideas, the French inventor did not capitalise on this invention and it was not until much later that the self-same technology was made in America and organs which sucked their reeds instead of blowing them were dubbed 'American organs'. This terminology was a little unfortunate for it was picked up all over the world and the genus 'American organ' was made in France, Germany, Great Britain and just about every other country that had a musical instrument industry. It tended to backfire at a later stage where a preference for British-made or European-made instruments existed. American organs did not necessarily come from America!

Significantly, there were very few British-made contenders in this specialised market, perhaps the best-known being the Maxfield organ. This was patented in 1896 and models cost up to £25. The instrument was the product of one of London's numerous manufacturers of reed organs, harmoniums and piano-players. It used music rolls which were narrow by comparison with others - a mere 5½in wide - and was altogether a small instrument having only 31 of its 61-note keyboard notes playable from the roll.

Another was the Phoneon introduced in the early summer of 1898 by Malcolm & Co and retailed in London by Murdoch & Co of 91 Farringdon Road. *Musical Opinion* said, in May that year:

> The instrument is a large American organ, playable either by the manual or by the use of perforated rolls. However, we think even a good performer would prefer to use the automatic arrangement, and thus devote his time to the marks of expression, &c. Phrasing he need not attend to, as the use of the perforated rolls arranges this matter.
>
> Music can be started at will; for directly the player touches the pedals a wind motor is set in motion, this apparatus in turn revolving the perforated tunes. Messrs. Malcolm & Co. have been working at their invention for a long time and have succeeded in placing the retail price of the instrument at 36gns.
>
> The Phoneon we saw was over 6ft. high and contained two full sets, many stops (including one with which to arrange the *tempo*), and two swells.

There were several other makes and makers, including the Orpheus introduced in Britain during 1902 by the Clark Apollo Co, but these instruments are seldom encountered today. This is a pity because the later models which tried so unsuccessfully to capture the market dominated by American products and those of Aeolian in particular were, generally, of superior quality. It was the old story, for these models came in too late, at a time when demand was no longer expanding but had begun to contract.

One of these models was the Mustel Concertal produced in Paris by the famed Mustel company. This was one of the finest of all player reed organs, for a number of reasons. First it featured a tonal basis which was far more colourfully and artistically established than that of the single-manual Orchestrelles. Secondly, the keyboard was truly divided between left-hand and right-hand stops (unlike the Orchestrelle which is purely divided in half with two draw stops to operate on each full rank of reeds). And thirdly, it had the highly developed Mustel system of control using locking knee-swells almost as *sforzando* pedals, and combining the prolongment stop for bass notes and the foundation setting of the organ into two small treadle cheeks which could be operated by the twist of the foot while pedalling. Significantly, so good was the Mustel that it was taken as the basis of the Schiedmayer Scheola, a high-quality German contender for the market which did not sell in large quantities, and those almost entirely in Germany. It was designed by two former Mustel apprentices.

Another maker was Estey, which produced a range of very high-quality reed organs. This company made fullest use possible of the tonal opportunities of reeds and resonating chambers in its instruments. But all this is away from the story which developed from the first attempts to incorporate the technology of the simple little organette into a keyboard reed organ.

There is some evidence to suggest that the first free-reed instrument to be fitted with a perforated-card playing pneumatic action was an Estey instrument modified by John McTammany in 1876. This was the culmination of experiments which began with a mechanism devised by him in about 1868 for the automatic playing of organ, his patent was filed on 7 September 1876. But the first serious attempts to produce such an instrument were made when McTammany, in 1880, modified the Taber reed organ to take his player action. During the following year, he similarly modified organs made by Taylor & Farley. By 1882, both these companies were defunct, and McTammany became associated with the Munroe Organ Reed Co as a result of which that company's large reed organ called the Orchestrone was offered with McTammany player action in 1885-6.

In Worcester, Massachusetts, the reed-organ makers Mason & Risch were in production with

Baillie-Hamilton's English-designed reed organ called the Vocalion. Introduced in America shortly before 1890, it was characterised by its tones which were produced by voicing its reeds in a special way and placing each one in a specially-shaped chamber or 'qualifying tube' after the manner discussed by Helmholtz in his studies and researches into sound. During the 1890s, Mason & Risch changed its name to the Vocalion Organ Co.

By this time, the seeds had been sown for the formation of the Aeolian Co. The history of the subsequent success of the Aeolian instruments is a long and involved one, but through it shines the personality of one man - William Barnes Tremaine. Born in 1840, he entered the family piano business of Tremaine Brothers in 1868. When two inventors Newman R. Marshman of New York City and Mason J. Matthews of Boston, Massachusetts, perfected the little reed instrument which they called the orguinette in 1878, Tremaine set up the Mechanical Orguinette Co to produce and market the instrument. It sold by the thousand. Later, The 'Celestina' was also introduced with considerable success. This was an enlarged variant of the first 'orguinette'.

It was against this background that, in 1883, the first Aeolian organ was produced. It was built for the company by the Munroe Organ Reed Co (which had been established in Worcester, Massachusetts, in 1860), the basic style being the 1050 which played 46-note music rolls. But it was an inauspicious beginning was plagued with troubles stemming not just from production problems, but marketing inexperience and under-capitalisation.

The Aeolian Organ Co was founded in 1887 at the township of Aeolian, in New Jersey. With the Aeolian organ in production, Tremaine played a masterful stroke. Both Orguinette and Celestina relied on two associated products for the production of their music - the perforated paper rolls made by the Boston-based Automatic Music Paper Co, and the actual organ reeds produced by the Munroe Organ Reed Co. Thus in 1888, Tremaine acquired all the patents and stock in trade of the Automatic Music Paper Co and formed the Aeolian Organ & Music Co to manufacture automatic organs and music rolls. Four years later, he completed the integration of the new company by purchasing all the patents owned by the Munroe Organ Reed Co. He now controlled all the prerequisites of success. This coincided with the introduction of the first player-piano, the *Aeriol* of 1895.

Tremaine's son, Harry Barnes, was born in Brooklyn in 1866. Thirty-two years later, he assumed command of The Aeolian Company as its president. His great triumph was to defeat the prophets of doom and launch the Pianola piano-player. In 1903, he united under the Aeolian Co all the piano and organ plants which had been supplying components for some years. Among these was the Vocalion Organ Co which supplied Aeolian with built-up sets of reeds, called tone-ranks, for the player organs. Some of these were made to Vocalion patents by the A. B. Chase company which had been formed in 1875 to build reed organs and was later to be controlled by Aeolian. Since the original Vocalion was an English invention, it is an interesting thought that the very qualities we ascribe to the Aeolian Orchestrelle, making it one of the finest of all player reed organs in the world, are truly British in origin. Aeolian now advertised that it operated manufacturing plants in Aeolian, Meriden and Worcester. Its prestigious offices were at Aeolian Buildings, 362 Fifth Avenue and 34th Street, New York City.

Harry B. Tremaine's vast empire was without doubt the largest manufactory of both reed organs and player pianos the world has ever known. True, its arch rival the American Piano Co, founded much later, was larger, but they only built pianos. With a $15.5million capitalisation, Aeolian rode the crest of the success wave through to the depression of the late 1920s and early 1930s and, by a quirk of fate, suffered its worst setback from its British subsidiary which went into liquidation in the 1930s, owing its parent a vast sum of money.

Plate 32. Four octave C to C compass one-row Estey harmonium. These very small chapel Esteys had a lusty voice yet even so were readily drowned by even a modest congregation and certainly not suitable for other than small churches. Preserved in partial playing order in Christ Church (Anglican) at Longford, near Launceston, Tasmania. Not recorded in Clark & Johnson's book "Pipe Organs of Tasmania" which, despite its title, refers to other church instruments (Author)

Plate 33. Smith Imperial Connoisseur 17-stop American organ, c.1887 made in Massachusetts. $5\frac{1}{2}$ octaves F-C compass with the break at G/C, total 326 reeds. The singularly ornate case is in cherrywood with gilded ornamentation. "The mechanism... is very elaborate," said the makers in their 1885 catalogue. "There is probably no piano-forte in existence whose interior works cost so much as the works of the Connoisseur." An unconventional feature is that the reed playing action is arranged vertically behind the decorative fronts of the louvred swell shutters visible either side of the central music desk. Also notable is the unusual stop action in which the mutes are opened using catgut strings. The tone of the organ reeds is modified by means of a sheet of zinc which lies across the action just below the key fall. Another novel feature is that this fall slides out from under the stop rail to close off the keyboard but leave the stops exposed (from the collection of Phil and Pam Fluke)

111

But to return to the 1890s, these were the years of success for Aeolian and the company introduced an improved style of player reed organ - the Model 1500, again using a 46-note roll. Models now in production ranged from the small $75 Princess Aeolian, the 1250 at $300 and the 1450 at $350 through to the large 58-note Aeolian Grand with an almost piano-size case at $750. By 1897, the company was also selling a model called the Aeolian Orchestrelle - the very first Orchestrelle model - at a staggering $1,500. The Orchestrelle was certainly introduced as a top or luxury-market artefact. So impressed was the German emperor Wilhelm II with the Orchestrelle that he ordered one to be placed in the saloon of his private yacht.

Within the short space of a year or so, the 58-note Orchestrelle was, along with the Aeolian Grand, the undoubted leader in the field of self- playing large-compass reed organs. Later, there were others, in particular the Mustel Concertal in France and the German variant, Schiedmayer's 61-note Scheola. These were more expensive and of higher specification and quality, but they did not sell in anywhere near such numbers as the Aeolian products.

By the turn of the century, the Aeolian Co decided to unify their brand names and so the name 'Grand' which was used for the harmonium-type blown Aeolian 58-note organ was replaced by the name 'Orchestrelle', and henceforth both blown harmonium instruments and sucked American-organ models shared the same name.

Around this time, there was another short-lived competitor in the London market for self-playing reed organs. This was the Wallis Auto-Organ advertised for sale in 1898 at a price of £60. *Musical Opinion* for January 1898 reported:

> The Auto-organ is in reality a new American organ, for the sale of which Messrs. Wallis (Lim.) have secured the sole agency. The instrument is a novelty, for it may be played upon in the ordinary manner; or, if desired, the perforated rolls of tunes can be inserted,- in which case the music is produced by simply pedalling. Upon a recent inspection of the invention, Batiste's 'Offertoire' was 'rolled off' for our edification. Light and shade can be duly attended to, for the pedallist cannot but observe the marks of expression,- they being marked upon the rotating, perforated slips. The organ which we examined had two full sets of reeds, but Messrs. Wallis & Son intend to introduce a sub-bass, in addition.

One of the earliest importers of automatic musical instruments into London was George Whight. He began business in 1886 at 143 Holborn Bars, and between 1893 and 1896 he traded solely as a musical instrument manufacturer and importer at 225 Regent Street. George Whight stocked

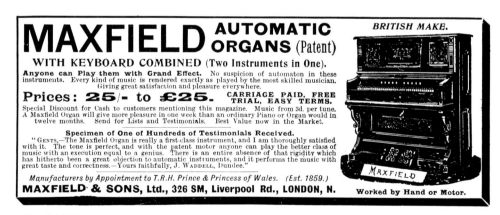

Fig. 53. Maxfield also made a range of automatic organs as seen in this notice from "The Royal" magazine of 1905

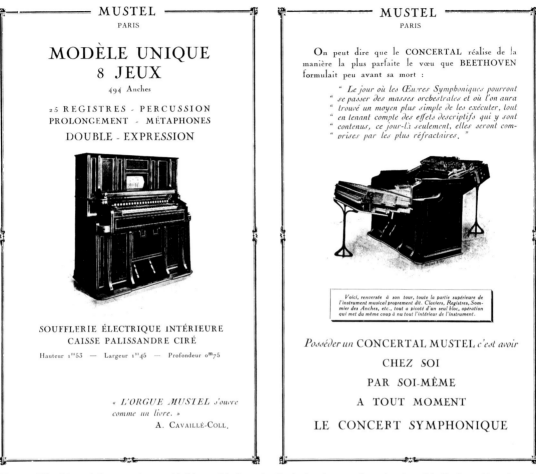

MUSTEL
PARIS

MODÈLE UNIQUE
8 JEUX
494 Anches

25 REGISTRES - PERCUSSION
PROLONGEMENT - MÉTAPHONES
DOUBLE - EXPRESSION

SOUFFLERIE ÉLECTRIQUE INTÉRIEURE
CAISSE PALISSANDRE CIRÉ

Hauteur 1ᵐ53 — Largeur 1ᵐ45 — Profondeur 0ᵐ75

« L'ORGUE MUSTEL s'ouvre
comme un livre. »
A. CAVAILLÉ-COLL.

MUSTEL
PARIS

On peut dire que le CONCERTAL réalise de la
manière la plus parfaite le vœu que BEETHOVEN
formulait peu avant sa mort :

" Le jour où les Œuvres Symphoniques pourront
" se passer des masses orchestrales et où l'on aura
" trouvé un moyen plus simple de les exécuter, tout
" en tenant compte des effets descriptifs qui y sont
" contenus, ce jour-là seulement, elles seront com-
" prises par les plus réfractaires. "

Voici, renversée à son tour, toute la partie supérieure de
l'instrument musical proprement dit. Claviers, Registres, Som-
mier des Anches, etc., tout a pivoté d'un seul bloc, opération
qui met du même coup à nu tout l'intérieur de l'instrument.

Posséder un CONCERTAL MUSTEL *c'est avoir*

CHEZ SOI

PAR SOI-MÊME

A TOUT MOMENT

LE CONCERT SYMPHONIQUE

Fig. 54. The Mustel Concertal was a highly sophisticated roll-playing harmonium developed in Paris and hand-made in small quantities. Like all Mustel harmoniums, the instrument could be opened up for easy service as seen on the right above

the first Aeolian player organs in the late 1890s. Prior to that he handled Wilcox & White products; in *Musical Opinion* for 1 September 1888, we read: 'Messrs. G. Whight & Co., of Holborn Bars, have secured the sole agency for the Wilcox & White organs.' The following month, Whight was advertising 'The Victolian Organ - plays Music of every description without the performer being a musician'. This cost 17 guineas. Here Whight gave his address as 225 Regent Street, suggesting that these were for a while additional premises to those in Holborn, and described himself as 'sole importers of the Victolian and Aeolian'. The true manufacturer of the Victolian might have remained unknown were it not for an American advertisement where the identical instrument is described as the Aeolian 'Princess'. An unusual feature of the Princess/Victolian is the arrangement of the music roll; it is horizontal. Because of this, it had been thought that it was a Wilcox & White product, in particular as in *Musical Opinion*, for 1 November that same year, Whight advertised: 'Wilcox and White genuine American Organs Are Unsurpassed in Quality of Tone, Rapidity of Action, Ease of Operation, Elegance of Design, Durability, and General Excellence.'

At this time, Wilcox & White of Meriden, Connecticut, had yet to devise their Symphony player organ and were making ordinary manually played instruments. This company was a true pioneer in many ways and was later to use the same action principles which it used in the Symphony in its refreshingly different Angelus player pianos. The first Wilcox & White Symphony appeared late in the 1880s and was to remain in production until the very early years of this century. But even though it was a well-made instrument, it never gained the popularity of its Aeolian rival. An unusual mutant of the Angelus pneumatic action was the Angelus Symphony - a piano-player which incorporated several ranks of reeds. With this instrument, the operator could perform either reed organ or piano, or both together just by selecting the stops on the player. These were at one time very popular and there are still a few to be found, although it assumes that the correct tuning of organ and piano will remain in perfect harmony.

To return to George Whight's London business, this prospered and soon he was handling only Aeolian organs having, one assumes, dropped the earlier Wilcox & White agency. By December 1889, he was advertising the self-playing Tonsyreno: 'This Unique and Wonderful Instrument renders any and every description of Music in the most Charming and Orchestral style, rivalling the most skilled Musicians.' Capable of being played by hand or by perforated paper roll, this 46-note organ retailed 'from 41 Guineas'.

In 1899, the newly founded Orchestrelle Co, British subsidiary of the Aeolian Co in New York, bought out George Whight's business. The new management was totally dedicated to Aeolian products and the takeover was masterminded by H. B. Tremaine. He became president of the new concern, the sales manager being O. Sundstrom. While the change was taking place, A. J. Mason, a senior New York executive, came over to London. The main thrust of the business at this time was to be the new Pianola piano-player. Later, the business was renamed the Aeolian Company Ltd. Initially, the Orchestrelle Co ran the premises at 225 Regent Street with the old Whight wholesale warehouse at 51 Farringdon Road. Until the end of 1908, there were assembly facilities for imported kits of parts and, later, the manufacture of pianos at Elm Street and Britannia Street off the Grays Inn Road. The Orchestrelle Co moved into 135/137 New Bond Street, better known as the Aeolian Hall, and established a large construction and assembly factory at Silverdale Road, Hayes, Middlesex. George Whight had traded well and, on his death in 1906, he was worth nearly £40,000 - a considerable sum of money in those days. He lived at 13 Wood Lane in Highgate, north London.

There were thus quite a few makes of pneumatic player organ on the British and American markets, but in terms of popularity, as already mentioned, the outright leader was the Aeolian Orchestrelle. Produced in the United States, by a process of shipping knocked-down components for assembly in England, it was also made at Aeolian's British factory at Hayes. This marque appeared in at least sixteen styles and sizes between the close of the last century and about 1920.

It was around 1903 that Aeolian introduced the first Solo Orchestrelle into Britain. This instrument, while having only one keyboard like any other Orchestrelle, allowed two-manual playing in that it was possible to play the melody on one set of stops while the counter melody or accompaniment was played on another. To permit this very sophisticated feature, the self-playing part of the organ was in effect two instruments, each controlled by different openings in the tracker bar. The openings, increased from 58 to 116, were alternately assigned to different halves of the organ. To make the instrument play, special 116-note music rolls were used and the tracker bar used two staggered rows of small holes the upper row of which could be isolated from the lower, so allowing a separate stop registration for each row and two-manual musical interpretation. Alternatively, the two rows of openings could be pneumatically connected in reverse (to reverse

▲Plate 34. Single manual chapel style American organ made by W Doherty & Co, Clinton, Ontario, Canada. Date 1889. 5 octaves, compass F-F, 31 bass, 30 treble notes. 4 sets of reeds plus 13 note sub bass, total 263 reeds. 2 knee swells, each with a stop mounted thereon and edged with metal. Case of burr veneer all over, cylinder fall made up from slats of wood veneered over. 4 candle stands on top. Fretted front, top and back which is also pierced. Celluloid keys. Case number 11429. Sold by Archibald Ramsden Ltd (from the collection of Phil and Pam Fluke)

▲Plate 35. Two-manual American organ by W Bell & Co, Guelph, Ontario, Canada. Date c.1890. 5 octaves, compass F-F, 28 bass, 33 treble. 3 full sets of 61 notes, three half sets of 33 notes, one half set of 28 notes and a 13 note sub-bass, total 323 reeds. 18 stops, 2 knee swells. Octave coupler, manual coupler. Case of walnut with design picked out in burr veneer, decorated with fretwork music stand and matching side panels. Candle stands extending from each cheek, celluloid keys and separate hand pumping system. Case number 29161 (from the collection of Phil and Pam Fluke)

115

the stop setting), or united so that normal 58-note rolls could be used. The mechanics of the Solo Orchestrelle were employed in a number of styles from thence onwards, Model F being both the largest and the first. By around 1909, the company was producing models such as the more compact XY and XW with two-manual player layout.

It seems that although production of music rolls for both the 58-note and 116-note Orchestrelles continued at least as late as October 1921 (the latest catalogue I have seen), production of reed organs was discontinued around the time of World War I.

The technique of the Orchestrelle was used as early as 1900 in the operation of a pipe organ as distinct from the free-reed Orchestrelle, and Aeolian made a large number of residence player pipe organs. These too could play both 58 and 116-note rolls and, in fact, all the 116-note rolls are labelled 'Aeolian Pipe Organ' although they are perfectly suitable for the solo-equipped reed-playing Orchestrelle.

The first of these instruments to be seen in Britain was described by the London musical magazine *Musical Opinion* for February 1904, although the correspondent does not seem too certain of his ground and has some shakey ideas about how electric motors operate:

> There is now on view at the Orchestrelle Co.'s rooms a handsome large two manual pipe organ (built by this firm at Garwood, New Jersey), playable by means of perforated paper rolls. Special '116 note' music - on which there are two separate rows of holes - is used, the topmost series of which causes the swell organ to play, whilst the bottom set of perforations acts on the great organ. An electric pneumatic action is used. On one key-board a solo can be performed, an accompaniment being possible by the paper rolls acting on the other manual; or the positions concerning the melody and accompaniment may be reversed. In an adjoining room there is erected an echo organ, the music from which is obtained from the key-board of the two-manual instrument. An electric motor is utilized for blowing, the current from which passes through chloride into three separate accumulators. Of course, if an automatic rendition be not desired, the organ can be played in the ordinary manner. Certainly, all interested in the 'king of instruments' should visit Aeolian Hall, New Bond Street.

By 1905, Aeolian in America was advertising the Aeolienne, a keyboardless console for playing pipe-organ rolls. This was not the same as the Aeolian pipe organ's remote console. All Aeolian's pipe organs, incidentally, were made at their plant at Garwood in New Jersey. And although the Aeolian pipe organ is related to the Orchestrelle and while both play the same rolls (with the exception of the Duo-Art pipe organ with its 17in-wide music rolls), the actions are, not surprisingly, quite different.

An interesting and late development came just before World War II by which time Aeolian had long since merged with the Skinner Organ Co in America. In January 1938, the Hammond Corporation, already earning a reputation for its electronic organs, manufactured a small batch of pneumatically sensed roll-playing models. Known as the Home Model B-A or Aeolian-Hammond player organ, the player units were manufactured in Boston, Massachusetts, by the Aeolian-Skinner Co. The music rolls looked like normal Aeolian pipe organ rolls and were the same width, but in fact had 120 tracker openings spaced at 12 to the inch.

The Orchestrelle Co prospered and in 1912 became The Orchestrelle Co Ltd, a company set up to acquire the entire capital of the Orchestrelle Companys in various parts of the world. At the beginning of 1914 this new company submitted its first annual report which showed a net profit of £34,000; it paid a 5 per cent dividend on its ordinary shares. The consolidated accounts revealed a profit of £79,000 - an increase of £12,300 - and a total accumulated surplus of £162,000 pushed the company into the position of a very attractive investment proposition. A contemporary writer commented: 'These figures are a satisfactory index of the way in which the player-piano

◄
Plate 36. Two-manual and pedal American organ by Bell Organ & Piano Co, Ltd, Guelph, Ontario, Canada. Dated 2nd April 1896. 5 octaves, compass C-C, 24 bass, 37 treble, plus 30 note flat pedal board. 4 full sets of reeds comprising 61 notes, one half set of 24 notes, two half sets of 37, two sets of 30 pedal notes, total 463 reeds. 23 stops in staggered rows. 2 knee swells. Kick-down couplers: swell to pedal, forte to swell, octave, great to pedal, forte to pedal. Octave coupler, manual coupler. Walnut case with burr veneer shapes. Detachable top with 17 dummy patterned pipes in decorative frame. Pedal board is retractable. Overall height 9ft. Case number 77107 (from the collection of Phil and Pam Fluke)

◄
Plate 37. Mirror-back American organ made in May, 1898 by Bell Organ & Piano Co, Guelph, Canada. 5 octaves, compass F-F, 28 bass, 33 treble, $2\frac{1}{2}$ sets of reeds plus 13 note sub bass, total 168 reeds. 2 knee swells. Keyboard break at G sharp/A. Walnut case with heat-embossed decoration and carving. Balustraded mirror back, central mirror. Two half candle stands and one extending from each cheek. Celluloid keys. Case number 80717. The provision of organ cases with mirrors was an innovation which first appeared around 1895 - there were one or two earlier examples, but not large-scale productions. Shelves, music racks, vase stands and other dust-collectors sprang upwards to give hatstand-like stature over the melodeon of the early days (from the collection of Phil and Pam Fluke)

trade has been developing lately.' War, just around the corner, was about to alter all that. The final name change came as 1917 drew to a close. From October forward, The Orchestrelle Co Ltd would be known as the Aeolian Company Ltd. The management remained unaltered.

Aeolian made its last player reed organs around 1918, although they were still selling from stock at least as late as 1920. An era, though, was past, and the harmonium and American organ receded into oblivion; all that remained was the expanding interest in small folding chapel organs. The industry had moved, it seemed, to India, as the wireless and gramophone became firmly entrenched. Music would never be made in the home again in the way that it had been for so many years.

"Musical Opinion", March 1902

CHAPTER 9

Other Free-Reed Musical Instruments

The range of free-reed musical instruments was both large and worldwide, with prices to suit all pockets; for the simple reed was the means of bringing music to the masses. In 1892, an enterprising American patented an automatic reed bugle within which a circular plate of reeds was mounted. By blowing into the mouthpiece and pulling a trigger, this plate was indexed one note at a time. The arrangement of the reeds around the plate could be selected to play a number of tunes. The musical spinning top which hummed a serene chord as it rotated was another application of the free reed. And each time the top was spun, a different chord was produced.

These were the rather peripheral uses of the free reed, though, and the most popular instruments were accorded considerable respect by their devotees. The free reed was dominant around the middle of the last century, for this was the era of the concertina. The instrument had enjoyed a ready following from the middle of the nineteenth century, and by the late 1850s it had become popular amongst the masses. Concertina contests were staged and even Lord Balfour (1848-1930), Britain's prime minister between 1902 and 1906, was, at least into his middle life, an ardent performer. With friends he enjoyed playing choruses from his favourite composer, Handel, upon whose music and life he was an authority. Particularly in the Midlands and north of England, concertina bands were a popular diversion in the early years of this century. They were frowned upon by serious musicians who thought them something of a joke, but the fact remained that the concertina, its music and its players appealed to a larger sector of the population - and was more readily available and attainable - than the somewhat distant world of the majority of serious music.

To most people today, the instrument which is played by pushing the ends together and pulling them out is either an accordion or a concertina - or even just the old musichall 'squeezebox'. The variety of instruments within this class is nevertheless extremely large, encompassing melodeons, button melodeons, accordions, button accordions and piano accordions, bandoneons, concertinas (in a variety of styles and types) and so on. Even the name 'accordion', like the name 'melodion', was spelled in different ways as 'accordeon', thus adding to the confusion. The evolution of the concertina and development of the piano-accordion represents a study almost as large as that of this present work; it is one which has yet to be done.

But by far the most popular of the portable free reed instruments was the mouth organ or, for a better class of consumption, the harmonica. A large number of makers once existed and whole villages in Germany thrived on the harmonica industry, one of them being Trossingen. Mouth organs appeared in a huge variety of styles and tunings, at prices from a few pence up to figures which could rival a small harmonium. Effects and gimmicks also prevailed, as did accessories such as bells and even drums and sound-amplifying horns.

As an example of the other and more transient forms of the free reed in musical instruments, in February 1886, the London musical instrument manufacturers and dealers Beare & Son of 34 Rathbone Place, Oxford Street, announced a brand new instrument, the Voixophone.

> The latest musical novelty (just patented). The tone of this charming little instrument is produced by the novel mode of *breathing gently* through a tube acting on reeds, by which every shade of expression and phrasing may be obtained. It has a piano keyboard of three and a quarter octaves, is quite portable (being only 3½ lbs. in weight), and is quite unsurpassed as a Solo Instrument for Melodies, with Pianoforte Accompaniment, Songs, Waltzes, &c., also for Conductors of Choral Societies, Professors of Singing, &c. It may also be used as a Digitorium for both hands. Price £3.3s.

Further detail was supplied the following month by *Musical Opinion* which advised that:

> The peculiarity in the wind supply is that it is produced by the aid of a rubber tube inserted in the mouth of the performer. It will be readily be understood that, the mouth being the bellows of the instrument, degrees of light and shade can be produced to almost any degree. It is claimed that, when played in conjunction with the pianoforte, the effect produced is very pleasing.

The musical scene in London was considered of particular importance in the world of new inventions and every product was quickly brought to the capital to test the market. In the early summer of 1909, J. F. Kalbe of Berlin showed, through their London representative Max Rink, a newly patented reed organ called the Arietta, described as a 'portable auto-organ', 'auto' meaning, as in auto-harp, that a musical-fingering guide was used in playing it. The Arietta comprised two box-like components mounted side by side on a base-board. That on the left was a concertina-type bellows which could be moved up and down by the hand suitably placed under a restraining strap and was provided with five stops, numbered one to five, which produced bass notes, and five more stops (more properly called 'buttons') which produced 2-note chords. Described as 'nearly chromatic', the twenty-one notes for the right hand were represented as long brass bars beneath which could be slid the specially prepared music instruction sheet. The retail price was 'forty shillings or less'.

There was also the range of mechanical musical instruments which used free reeds. Cylinder musical boxes were made which featured celeste-effect reed-organ accompaniments; these were often referred to as 'flutina' or 'voix celeste' boxes. Disc-playing musical boxes, such as the giant Fortuna, also had a built-in harmonium of accompaniment reeds. The Amabile was a clockwork organette which played free reeds by means of a circular tune-sheet. A vast range of organettes was produced, mainly in Germany, which played from discs, cardboard strips, paper rolls and even zigzag-folded cardboard books of music like a fairground organ. A harmonium was made in Sweden which could be played either by hand or using a perforated cardboard disc. The variety of these instruments, which were comparatively very cheap, was enormous and the numbers made were likewise huge.

The organette deserves a whole separate study of its own, but in these pages can only be referred to in passing. Suffice it to say that its proliferation went hand in hand with many significant experiments into the tonal abilities of the small reed in a mechanical instrument. Different materials were used, and various ways of amplifying or otherwise modifying the sound; it emerged as a completely new kind of harmonium.

That the harmonium was both lighter and cheaper than the pipe organ, did not escape the manufacturers of street barrel organs. A whole new industry sprang up making tiny portable

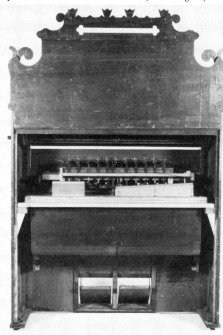

◀ Plate 38. Turn-of-the-century Mason & Hamlin "parlor reed organ" |left| and |below| the simplicity of the mechanism seen from behind (courtesy of the Smithsonian Institution, Washington, DC)

◀ Plate 39. Original photograph of a two-manual and flat pedal C-C compass Dominion American organ found by the author in the remains of a derelict harmonium factory. Transfer beneath the staggered rows of stops reads: "Forsyth Bros Sole Agts for the United Kingdom". The Forsyth business was established in 1857 at 126/128 Deansgate, Manchester.

▲ Plate 40. Indian table harmonium, maker unknown. Post war. $3\frac{1}{2}$ octaves, compass C-G, 44 notes. 2 sets of reeds, total 88 reeds. Case of light stained wood with small mirror in fold-back keyboard fall. Keys covered with white mother-of-pearl. Stop knobs have decorated black and white plastic fronts (from the collection of Phil and Pam Fluke)

harmoniums which played their music from pinned wooden barrels. With high-pressure wind and loudly voiced steel reeds, some of these instruments were veritable tours de force on the streets of London and Paris, both cities where they were made.

The Jew's (or Jaw's) Harp and, later, the mouth organ, were once as popular with schoolboys as the hoop, the bat and ball, the conker on a string. Great was the skill demonstrated by a good reed-twanger, and great was the oral dexterity of many a youthful mouth-organ performer.

The free reed thus played a clear part in the lives of very many people for almost 150 years - the life span of the mouth organ and concertina-type instruments. Portable, easy to play and loud enough to be used to accompany dancing and drinking, these were the fun instruments which people carried around with them. Troops went to war with their harmonicas and concertinas, sailors sang shanties to them, and lonely souls expressed their innermost feelings through these very personal instruments of music. Sadly, they have no modern counterpart as the once-popular art of making music has been usurped, for many, by the technology of the personal stereo and in-head music.

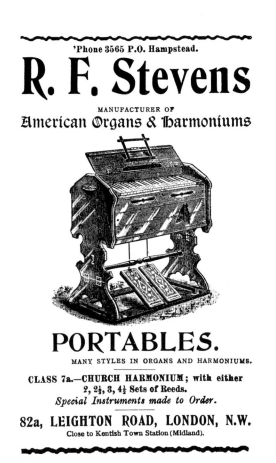

"Musical Opinion", June 1911

"Das Harmonium" (W. Riehm, Berlin), 1897

CHAPTER 10

Index of Makers of Reed Organs

Many were the names given to keyboard reed instruments in the early days of what was to become known almost universally as the harmonium. The actual name 'harmonium' was the creation of Alexandre Debain and followed lengthy experimentation in both name and instrument by many creators in several countries. Singular among these was Green whose selected name for the instrument - seraphine or the 'Royal Seraphine', as it became more commonly known - enjoyed early popularity.

While the term 'seraphine' did indeed get into the early musical instrument dictionaries, it was ultimately replaced by Debain's 'harmonium' as the generic term for instrument of the type. There were others, though. In the United States, these keyboard reed organs were styled 'melodeons', similar to the German 'melodion' (as with the word 'accordeon/accordion', so the spelling of 'melodeon' differed). The Scandinavians called them 'organharmoniums', sometimes spelled with a hyphen. Other terms which turn up in these early times include 'harmoni-chord' and 'harmoni-flutes'.

The instrument, as we have seen, gained in popularity so quickly that there was a truly enormous number of manufacturers throughout the world. To list all these would be pointless and impossible. What has been done is to mention as many as possible of those whose work was either innovative or seminal as well as those whose work is most frequently found in Britain, Europe and the United States today.

A study of establishment dates suggests that there were four definable peak periods in the manufacture of reed organs. The early 1840s saw the foundation of a number of early reed-organ businesses, while one can detect a second expansion in the period 1870 to c.1886. After a brief slow-down around the turn of the century, more businesses were set up in the decade or so up to the outbreak of World War I. There was also a mild boost in the early 1930s when as a direct result of the depression, piano manufacturers experienced a rough time as many small churches and chapels displayed renewed interest in the cheap harmonium or American-organ type of instrument.

A word on nomenclature; as we have already seen, the harmonium was known in the United States as the melodeon and in Germany it was sometimes, but not invariably, referred to as the melodion. Again, although a church-organ maker was just that, early directories often used the term 'organ-builder' or 'organ maker' to embrace both makers of reed organs and church-organ maker. This has caused confusion in the search through early directories, particularly in Germany where the title *Harmoniumbauer* is not always used to identify the reed-organ maker.

As regards sources, wherever possible, dates and address are given; where no dates are available, a floruit date (fl) is offered based on directory entries or a date on a known instrument. Unfortunately, some previous published sources have been found to be unreliable, including the *Reed Organ Atlas* by the late N. E. Michel which contains abbreviated information which suffers from inadequate checking prior to printing. While I have been able to corroborate certain of the information and have accordingly made use of it, a great deal has had to be dismissed due to incompleteness or established error. Even Alfred Dolge's two classic works on American piano makers has not proved absolutely reliable. For more accurate data there has, therefore, been no alternative to the lengthy process of consulting directories and contemporary advertisements, the former being extremely difficult to check as far as the United States is concerned.

Many were the agents and distributors for reed organs and quite often these people put their own names on the instrument. Leading provincial retailers in Britain such as Van Gruisen of Liverpool, as well as many London distributors such as Ivory of Holborn, did just this. It is thus imperative that a clear line be drawn between significant distributors (meaning importers) and pure merchants. It is hoped that the majority of the latter have been weeded out. Likewise, manufacturers and suppliers of components have been omitted since they did not make named organs.

The reader is recommended to use this chapter as more than just a casual reference section: it contains much historical data and thus is included in the historical reading. While the accuracy of the material which follows is as great as possible, the author would be delighted to receive additions or corrections at any time.

Abbey, J. 79 boulevard du Montparnasse, Paris 6e, France. Established in 1828 as E. & J. Abbey. Maker of harmoniums. By 1909 listed as 'Successors to E. & J. Abbey' with factory at 12 rue de la Chancellerie, Versailles.

Abeille Leon. 125 rue Thomas, Marseille, France. Established in 1888. Organ and harmonium builder who also distributed barrel organs and orchestrions as well as undertaking barrel-pinning work. Products distributed through Pierre Méritan of 144 rue Terrusse.

Abel & Sherman. Milwaukee, Wisconsin, USA. Makers of melodeons in 1866; also traded as Odenbrett, Abler & Co fl.1875; not listed 1884.

Abler & Co, Odenbrett. Milwaukee, Wisconsin, USA. Melodeon makers, fl.1870-80. See also under Abel & Sherman. Not listed 1884.

Acadia Organ Co. Bridgetown, Nova Scotia, Canada. Makers of American organs who appear to have been in business c.1880. Founder was Leander Miller who subsequently opened piano and organ agency, fl.1909.

Adamson, A. An inventor who, at the Musical and Ecclesiastical Exhibition held in London in 1892, showed an 'Automatic Tonic Sol-Fa Harmonium for teaching in class, the instrument showing to the player and pupil the Sol-fa name of each note struck in relation to any pre-arranged tonic.'

Adler Organ Co. Louisville, Kentucky, USA. Fl.1903 as makers of American organs under the brand name 'Loreto'. Not listed 1909.

Aeolian Co. New York, USA. Founded by William B. Tremaine who was born in 1840 and joined the firm of piano makers Tremaine Brothers in 1868. When Mason J. Matthews brought out his orguinette, Tremaine formed the Mechanical Orguinette Co in 1878 and sold these

instruments by their thousands, later on adding the improved Celestina organette. In 1883 the first Aeolian reed organ was brought out. In 1888, he acquired the patents and stock in trade of the Automatic Music Paper Co of Boston, forming the Aeolian Organ & Music Company to manufacture automatic organs and music rolls. In 1892 he bought all the patents owned by the Munroe Organ Reed Co of Worcester, which was involved with the Vocalion Organ Co, and in 1895 produced the Aeriol self-playing piano. It fell to William's son, Harry B. Tremaine, born in Brooklyn in the year 1866, to make the quantum jump for Aeolian. In 1898 he took over as president of the Aeolian Co. Aeolian thus went from strength to strength and became one of the most significant piano manufacturers in the world, particularly in the field of player pianos in the Aeolian marque of Pianola, and player reed organs in the marque Orchestrelle. William B. Tremaine died in 1907. In 1888 the Aeolian Organ & Music Co advertised itself as 'Successors to the Mechanical Orguinette Co and the Automatic Music Paper Co' with its offices and wareroom at 831, Broadway between 12th and 13th Streets. The factory at that time was situated on the corner of Tremont and Cambridge Streets in Meriden, Connecticut. For all their achievements, Aeolian never produced a simple American organ - only roll-playing instruments which nevertheless marked the high point in the development of the reed organ. Initially, tone-ranks for Aeolian organs were made by Vocalion [qv] at Worcester, Massachusetts. It can thus be said that the tonal capabilities of the Aeolian Orchestrelle owe a great deal to the direct development of the work of the Scotsman, Baillie-Hamilton, who built the first Vocalion organs in London in the 1870s. See

Baillie-Hamilton, Hamilton Vocalion Organ Manufacturing Co, Vocalion Organ Co, and William Hill.

Aggio, Fratelli. Via Saccarelli, Turin, Italy. Harmonium makers and restorers listed in 1909 directories.

Aggio, Luigi e Cesare. Rivoli, Italy. Maker of harmoniums and reed organs, listed in 1930 directories.

Akermans & Lunds Orgelfabriks Aktiebolaget. Sibyllegatan 10, Stockholm, Sweden. Established in 1860 for the manufacture of harmoniums.

Aktb. A. G. Rålins Orgel- och Pianofabrik. *see* Rålins Orgel- och Pianofabrik.

Aktb. Skandinavska Orgel- och Pianofabriken. *see* Skandinavska Orgel- och Pianofabriken.

Alberdi. Paseo de Gracia 126, Barcelona, Spain. Fl.1890-95. Makers of harmoniums. Distributed by Astort y Astragues at Paseo de Gracia 38 (fl.1909) who absorbed the Alberdi business.

Alexandre, Père & Fils. 10, Boulevard Bonne-Nouvelle [1829-54]; 39 rue Meslay [1855-95]; 81 Rue Lafayette, Paris 9e, France. Factory in Ivry-sur-Seine, rue Victor Hugo. Famed makers of harmoniums. Founded in 1829 by Jacob Alexandre, a maker of accordeons, who died c.1876. In 1834, he exhibited a small organ with two sets of reeds. Built a combined piano and harmonium now in the Kunsthistorisches Museum, Vienna. This employed an Érard 7-octave piano (A2 to a'''') and a 5-octave harmonium (C to c''''). There were two manuals plus pedals and the instrument is signed: 'Alexandre, Père et Fils, Paris/Piano d'Érard'. His son, Édouard Alexandre, made many seminal improvements to the reed organ which were patented throughout the world from 1854 onwards, and to the Alexandres goes credit for the invention of the Expression in the form adopted by the majority of makers. Alexandre also purchased the patent rights of Louis Martin [qv], inventor of the percussion action. The firm consistently won many medals for superior quality instruments, the most significant being the Medal of Honour at the French Exhibition of 1855. Soon after this, they established a large new factory at Ivry. Edouard's wife, Charlotte Dreyfus, was a well-known performer on the harmonium. *The Musical Times* for 1 November 1860 contained an extensive article by Hector Berlioz in praise of the Melodium Organ by Alexandre. The company was subsequently severely injured by the arrival of the American organ which was invented by one of its own craftsmen in 1835. Alexandre's lack of interest in this invention was to be regretted in subsequent years for although the company made a few examples it was not pursued and harmoniums were continued, while the invention was taken to Mason & Hamlin [qv] who are generally thought to have been the first to make an American organ on a production basis. In 1859, the then London agents Chappell & Co of 49 & 50 New Bond Street, advertised 'The New Alexandre Harmonium for The Drawing-Room' which was made to a new patent.

Later the agents were Metzler Ltd of 42 Great Marlborough Street. Édouard Alexandre died in Paris on 9 March 1888. See also:

Alexandre, Père et File (G. Fortin, successor). 81 rue Lafayette, Paris, Maker of reed organs, fl.1930.

Alleger & Co, H. W. Washington, New Jersey, USA. Founded in 1869 by Hiram W. Alleger. Makers of American organs and, later, pianos. When pianos were in great demand, the organ business was hived off as Alleger, Bowlby & Ed. Plotts with a factory at East Washington and Railroad Avenue (1879). Brand names manufactured included Acme, Star (for the Star Parlor Organ Co). Also manufactured for Daniel B. Beatty (qv).

Allin, Otto, B. 65 Købmagerg, Copenhagen, Denmark. Makers of harmoniums, fl.1930.

Allison & Co., Arthur. Leighton Road, and 10 Charlton King's Road, Kentish Town, London. Founded in 1840 for the manufacture of harmoniums and pianos. Few harmoniums made as business quickly concentrated on the piano.

Allmensinder Piano & Organ Co. Ann Arbor, Michigan, USA. Founded in 1869 by Daniel F. Allmendinger. Restyled as the Ann Arbor Organ Co (qv) in 1888.

Alloway, W. & R. 35-36 Foley Street, Great Portland Street, London. Piano manufacturers who factored reed organs made in Leipzig by M. Hofberg [qv] c.1905. By 1909 restyled as Berkhardt & Sons at the same address.

Alm, N. O. Boden, Län Norrbotten, Sweden. An organist who, in 1869, set up in business as a distributor for pianos and organs. Although his name appeared on instruments he factored, he was not a maker, Fl.1909.

Ambridge & Son. Piano Works, Fountayne Road, Broad Lane, South Tottenham, London; wholesale showrooms at 67 Wells Street, Oxford Street. Est. 1890. In 1905 advertised catalogues of Needham organs. Sole agents (1914) for Carpenter organs.

American Express Co. 10 James Street, Liverpool, Lancashire. Agent for Foley & Williams Manufacturing Co's (qv) 'Peerless Organs' who advertised in 1902: 'After January 1st, 1902, send all Orders and Enquiries for Catalogues and Prices to our Forwarding Agents, American Express Co.'

Anderson, K. A. Kammakaregatan 27, Stockholm, Sweden. Maker of harmoniums, fl.1909. Possibly the same as:

Andersson Eftr, K. A. 39 Hagag, Stockholm, Sweden. Maker of harmoniums and reed organs listed in 1930 directories.

Andresen & Co, John P. Ringkjöbing, Denmark. Makers of harmoniums, fl.1930.

Andresen & Co, P. Langesgade 10, Aalborg, Denmark. Founded c.1912 as makers of harmoniums. By 1930 listed at 56 Alg., Aalborg.

Angelus Piano & Organ Co. *see* Wilcox & White.

Angster es Fia, Jozsef: Mariengasse 35 and Josefgasse 30, Pecs (Fünfkirchen), Hungary. Established in 1867 for the manufacture of organs and harmoniums. In 1909 run by Josef, Emil and Oskar Angster, sons of Jozsef.

Ann Arbor Organ Co. Ann Arbor, Michigan, USA. Claimed to have been established in 1869; other sources give 1872. The former is probably the date of the formation of Daniel Allmendinger's business, and the later one that of the successors, the Allmendinger Piano & Organ Co (qv). The name of Allmendinger was changed to the Ann Arbor Organ Co in 1888. The earliest London agent was Henry Klein of 84 Oxford Street. In 1902, the products were distributed in England by Story & Clark and Kaim & Sohn Ltd of 67 Berners Street, London. Ann Arbor Co finally acquired the name and goodwill of Story & Clark (qv) in the summer of 1901.

Anneessens et File, Charles. rue du Nord, Halluin, Belgium. Established in 1865 as a builder of harmoniums. The business comprised a number of branches set up by various members of the family, the earliest probably being that of Oscar Anneessens-Veranneman who was in business in Courtrai (29 rue Conscience) in 1837 and was thus the earliest Belgian maker of reed organs. A branch was opened by his son Charles in Menin in 1865. The descendants were in business as:

Anneessens-Marinis, O. 10 Boulevard Philippe-d'Alsace, Courtrai, Belgium. Makers of harmoniums, fl.1930.

Anstradd, Gottrfried. 19 Bafvernsgrand, Uppsala, Sweden. Maker of harmoniums, fl.1930.

Apollo Reed Organ Works. 13 Islington, Liverpool, Lancashire. Makers of the Apollo Pedal Reed Organ introduced in 1913 to offer home practice for organists and students of the pipe organ - two manuals and pedals. Two models were available, Model A at £60 and a better specification, Model B, at £80. The London agents were The Vincent Music Co Ltd, 60 Berners Street. The Apollo company was an offshoot of Rushworth & Dreaper, established in 1828 at the same address and also 21 Basnett Street.

Arnold, Heinrich. Rheinstr 29, Darmstadt, Germany. Makers of pianos and harmoniums, fl.1940.

August & Co. Ritterstr 76, Berlin SW, Germany. Manufacturer of 'Kosmos' harmoniums, fl.1903.

Austin, Charles. Concord, New Hampshire, USA. Charles Austin was an early maker of melodeons in this early centre of American reed-organ construction, apparently in business c.1844. Later the business was styled Austin & Dearborn for a while, after which it was known as Charles E. Austin into the present century.

Auto-Organ Co. 39 Blenheim Road, Upper Holloway, London. Makers of a self-playing reed organ in 1900 which sold for 36 guineas.

Bacher, Euge.. Schulstr 15, Schorndorf, Württemberg, Germany. Maker of harmoniums, fl.1940.

Bachrodt Nachfolger, R. Leipzig, Germany. Reed-organ builder, fl.1900, not listed 1909.

Baillie-Hamilton, John Buchanan. Scottish inventor born 20 January 1837, the son of Gerard Baillie-Hamilton of the 7th Fusiliers. He was a man of some wealth who devoted himself to inventing improvements to the reed organ. In collaboration with John Farmer (qv) and with the assistance of Hermann Smith (qv), he devised an instrument called 'The Vocalion'. Farmer is is generally considered to have been the inventor of the Vocalion principle; the first patent is accorded to him and dated 13 November 1872. The original idea, though, was apparently the notion of Hermann Smith who later accused Hamilton of appropriating his invention. Baillie-Hamilton and John Farmer were granted a patent on reed organs and upon his manner of the voicing of reeds. He described this, with illustrations to the Royal Institution on 21 May 1875, having demonstrated it successfully at Harrow on 23 March 1875. Soon afterwards it was demonstrated at Westminster Abbey and other places. The success of the Vocalion was in its tone, described as 'much better and rounder' than the then harsh tone which characterised the majority of reed organs. Grove's *Dictionary* (first edition) described the Vocalion as:

An 'organ' or instrument of the free-reed kind. The first patent was taken out in 1872 by John Farmer of Harrow for a combination of reed with string or wire - either as a continuation of the reed or as a coil fastened to the back thereof - and was succeeded by many more... The first attempts gave a beautiful and very peculiar quality of sound, but by degrees the combination of reed and string, from which this proceeded, had to be given up, for practical and commercial reasons, and the instrument now exhibited is virtually a harmonium with broad reeds, giving great rigidity of action and therefore purity of tone, and large channels, and acted on by high pressure of wind - not suction. A main peculiarity of the vocalion is that the reeds are placed above the pallets and below the slides, and that though the sliding 'plug' of three reeds is only the width of the groove, the cavities are more than twice as wide. This is expressed in Mr. Hamilton's latest patent (U.S.A., 1884) as the 'combination of pallets, soundboard, and reeds with cavity-boards, one above the other, the lower one containing the nostrils and the upper one the mouths, and an intermediate controlling slide.

In spite of the involvement of John Farmer, Baillie-Hamilton's co-inventor and assistant was described as being Hermann Smith, a corset maker whose business was in the Marble Arch area close to where the father of Sir Henry Wood traded in the sale of mechanical toys. In Baillie-Hamilton's later days in London he was befriended by Sir Henry Wood who used to take him to his home in Elsworthy Road, north London, to meet and dine with his guests. Hermann Smith was a frequent contributor to *The English Mechanic* in the 1870s and was thus well-versed in practical organ matters. Smith lived at England's Lane, close to the home of Sir Henry Wood, and is believed to have died around 1914. A Baillie-Hamilton Vocalion was shown at the Inventions Exhibition of 1885 and was described as being 6ft square and standing on a somewhat larger pedestal which contained the bellows and windchest. It was provided with great, swell and choir manuals, two stops in the pedals and three in each manual plus three extra ones of lighter quality called 'complementary'. The instrument was built by Hill, the pipe-organ builders, but seems not to have been produced in large quantities and in the late 1870s Baillie-Hamilton took his invention to the United States, where he dropped the hyphen in his name. His 1884 British patent for 'unison-bar' reeds gives his address as 'at present of Boston, Massachusetts'. Here he is thought to have worked with Mason & Hamlin (qv) in the development of the Vocalion, but apparently parted after a disagreement regarding the construction of the instrument. He then went to Canada where, with Canada's then leading pipe-organ builder C. S. Warren, he worked for about two years developing the so-called 'Canadian Vocalion'. An agreement was entered into with Mason & Risch (qv) to handle the entire sales in Canada, and the name which appeared on the instrument was the 'Canadian Vocalion, manufactured by S. R. Warren & Son'. Soon after this, Hamilton and Warren came to London with the idea of raising capital for further development but poor sales prevented this. In 1886 Hamilton went back to the United States and there managed to finance a fresh company to proceed (see Hamilton Vocalion Organ Manufacturing Co). In 1919, Arthur Clayton (qv) wrote in *Musical Opinion*: 'Acting as an expert and voicer for Mr. Hamilton for a number of years, I carried out many experiments, and during that time we were able to determine many points regarding free reeds. I have several times reversed the reeds of an American organ and put them on pressure wind and the results were most satisfactory, the tone being much bigger and more characteristic.' Regarding Baillie-Hamilton's Vocalion organs built by the organ builders William Hill, Philip de Soyre wrote to *Musical Opinion* on 18 November 1902: 'The tones produced by the reeds appeared to me to be very pipe-like: but the cost of a small instrument with three or four stops on each manual seemed to me to be prohibitive, when compared with that of a small two-manual organ possessing far greater power.' It seems that Hamilton returned to England later and was, around 1926, living in Berkeley Street, Portman Square, from which address he invented and patented an idea for a combined piano and reed organ in which the windchest was formed from the soundboard of the piano itself. The reed organ component was placed above the hammers and

strings. See also under Hamilton Vocalion Organ Co, Smith, Vocalion, Mason & Risch, and Wedlake.

Baker & Co, Ltd, G. F. Leeke Street Corner, King's Cross Road, London. Repairers and suppliers of components for reed organs, fl.1914-29.

Baldwin & Co, D. H. 142-144 West Fourth Street, Cincinnati, USA. Music teacher Dwight H. Baldwin founded a music store in 1862 when he was aged forty. Eleven years later he was making pianos and reed organs, a move accelerated by the acquisition in 1889 of the Hamilton Organ Co of Chicago (qv). Brand names included Monarch, Baldwin and Valley Gem.

Baldwin, W. T. 131 Stapleton Road, Bristol. Founded in 1886 for the manufacture of American organs and harmoniums. The business did not survive the World War I.

Ball, Beavon & Co. 31 Aldermanbury, London. Wholesalers, manufacturers and importers of musical instruments, who first advertised in December 1889 as handling harmoniums and American organs.

Balthasar-Florence, H. Rue Dewez 12, Namur, Belgium. Est. after 1918 as maker of harmoniums and American organs.

Baranoff, J. S. Dorf Alexandrowskoje, Schlusselburg-Prospect 1, St Petersburg, Russia. Manufacturer of harmoniums, fl.1906.

Barckholl, Carl. Salem, Ohio, USA. Church organ maker who was also a maker of melodeons, fl.1870.

Barnett Samuel & Sons. 32 & 34 Worship Street, Finsbury, London; also at 127/135 Shepperton Road, north London. Established 1832. Musical instruments importers and wholesalers. In 1909 advertised as agents for organs made by the Cable Co, Chicago (qv). Manager of the business at that time was Nelson Dingley.

Barry, Edward. Soho Square, London. Granted a provisional British Patent no 1607 on 17 July 1855 for a transposing piano, organ or seraphine. 'I insert in the body of each instrument five or more notes or sounds above the number of keys in the keyboard, whether higher or lower in pitch, as may be desired, and by a mechanical contrivance I cause the keys to act upon different notes or sounds in the body of the instrument, thereby raising or lowering the pitch of the entire instrument at pleasure, and obtaining what I have before termed the transposition effect.'

Bartunek, Adolf. 496 Tylova tr, Kutna Hora, Czechoslovakia. Makers of harmoniums, fl.1930.

Barz, R. Bismarckstr 36, Kircheim, Teck, Germany. Maker of harmoniums, fl.1940.

Bauer, Gilbert L. Ogle Street, London. One of the earliest makers of harmoniums with pedal boards of twenty-four notes. Floruit second half of the nineteenth century. By the turn of the century the business was listed as Bauer & Co at 34 Kings Road, St Pancras. Not listed 1909. The business ultimately came under the control of Edmund Barnes, JP, member of the London School Board (later to become the LCC), who also controlled pianomakers Muir Smith & Co after the failure of the founder. King Hall in his Novello primer *The Harmonium* [no date but apparently c.1880] comments: 'A very high pitch of excellence... has been attained by a clever and ingenious English manufacturer, Gilbert L. Bauer, whose instruments are remarkable for the simplicity of their mechanism, and the variety of *timbres* of the various registers.' Learned his trade in France and employed mostly French workers. Gilbert Bauer was the son-in-law of piano-maker John Brinsmead and was the father of the pianists Harold and Ethel Bauer. Harold, born at New Malden, Surrey, on 28 April 1873, became a noted performer and a Debussy exponent. He later settled in America where he finished his career, dying in Miami, Florida, on 12 March 1951.

Baynton & Co, J. 23 Bayford Street, Mare Street, Hackney, London. '(Near London Fields Station, G.E.R.) Manufacturers of Harmoniums and Harmonium Pans (or Sound Boards). Makers of the New Portable Harmonium.' Advertised in 1880; by 1883 was advertising as makers of 'American organs and Jordan's transposing Harmonium'.

Bazin, James Amiraux. Canton, Massachusetts, USA. The Bazin family were of French Huguenot origin and came from St Aubin in Jersey, Channel Islands. Emigrating to the United States in 1778, they eventually settled in Boston, Massachusetts where James was born in or about 1798. He began making elbow melodeons and is said to have produced sliding brass reed pitch pipes, a mouth organ in 1828, a reed lap organ in 1833, an accordeon in 1835 and other instruments. An early maker of free-reed instruments in the United States who was granted US Patents in 1842 and 1853 for reed organ improvements.

Beasant. 17 Portugal Street, Lincoln's Inn (until 1865), then 11 Kirby Street, Hatton Garden, London. Advertised in May, 1865 *Musical Times*: 'Beasant's £3.10s. Portable Harmoniums have full-sized keys, large vibrators, superior tone, hand and foot blowers. Harmoniums with two rows of keys and pedals, best quality, prices low.'

Beatty, Daniel F. Railroad Avenue and Beatty Street, Washington, New Jersey, USA. Established c.1868 as makers and mass-merchandisers of American organs. These were offered on hire purchase (then known as 'the instalment plan') and were manufactured to a rock-bottom price. Among the companies used to supply instruments was Alleger (qv). The factory was destroyed by fire in 1881, large new one opened the following year. Bankruptcy about two years later with enormous loss to creditors said to be due to marketing very cheap organs and making insufficient return on capital to settle debts. In 1884 the business was restructured and became the Beatty Organ & Piano Co; two years later it was sold to the Beethoven Piano & Organ Co. In 1889 was taken over by the Needham Piano & Organ Co (qv).

Beaucourt, H. 4 place de la Reconnaissance, Monplaisir, near Lyon, France. Maker of organs and harmoniums with factory in Halluin (Nord). Fl.1909. At the 1862 International Exhibition staged in London, showed an 'organ-harmonium'.

Beckwith Organ Co. Chestnut and 29th Street, Louisville, Kentucky, USA. Founded in 1903 for the manufacture of reed organs expressly for distributors Sears, Roebuck Co. Beckwith was a Sears brand name and prior to this date instruments with this name were made by several makers, among them Ann Arbor (qv).

Bedwell & Son. Cecilia House, Cambridge, England. Established in 1868. Traded as this name to c.1900, then as G. C. Bedwell Ltd. Makers of pipe organs who also made harmoniums.

Bell, Joseph. Gillygate, York, Yorkshire. Cabinet maker Joseph Bell was apprenticed to organ builder R. Posthill. He began making harmoniums, barrel and church organs in Petergate, York, in 1847. At the 1862 London International Exhibition he showed 'an harmonium with wood reeds and pedals, two octaves; also an instrument containing bassoon, oboe, and clarinet, in the shape of a violoncello, with two rows of keys and wood reeds'. No further details. In the years that followed, he worked at 22 Feasegate and then at 28 Swinegate. Ultimately he became a factor of musical instruments and retained two premises, 14 Stonegate and 28 Swinegate. He was dead by 1909 when the business was run by his widow, Sarah Bell, and described as banjo manufacturer, piano and organ and sundries retailer.

Bell Organ & Piano Co. Carden and MacDonnell Street, Guelph, Ontario, Canada. Established in 1864. Founders were the Scottish-born brothers William and Robert Bell as makers of melodeons. Later made American organs and also the Bellolian available both as a player organ and as a player action for keyboard instruments. Branch in Ottawa. The first London representative was Henry Hannington (qv). In 1888, Hannington and Charles Warren bought the business and ran it successfully. *Musical Opinion* reported in March 1901:

> The Bell Organ and Piano Co. (the London branch is on the Holborn Viaduct) are controlling the Bellolian, the invention of Mr. Charles Warren, whose name is prominent in London patent annals, and who for years has made a study of pneumatics as applied to organs. We are informed that the instrument is attachable to any reed organ, and my means of the invention the keys are worked automatically as the perforated music unfolds. The most striking feature of the invention is claimed to be its simplicity; thus whilst the idea is an improvement on other arrangements of the kind, the cost of construction is much less. Mr. Warren intends to reside in Guelph in order to superintend its manufacture.

BELL ORGAN.

The "CHOIR" Model.

WALNUT CASEWORK.   FIVE OCTAVES.

Height - 4ft 4in.	Nett Weight 217lbs.
Width - - 4ft.	Weight boxed 360 ,,
Depth - 1ft. 11in.	Cubic meas. - 42ft.

PANELLED AND POLISHED AT BACK.

The following Actions are fitted.

Action No. 92.

11 Stops, Knee Swell and Grand Organ contains 4 Sets (107) Reeds.

Bass.—Pipe-Diapason, 8ft. Pitch ; Dulcet, Soft on Pipe-Diapason ; Sub-Bass, 16ft. Pitch ; (alternative stop :—Viola, 4ft. Pitch) ; Bass Coupler : Forte ; Vox Humana.

Treble.—Pipe-Diapason, 8ft. Pitch ; Dulciana, Soft on Pipe-Diapason ; Celeste, 8ft. Pitch ; Echo, Soft on Celeste ; Treble Coupler.

Action No. 95.

16 Stops, Knee Swell and Grand Organ Contains 7 Sets (216) Reeds.

Bass.—Viola, 4ft. Pitch ; Dolce (Soft), 4ft. Pitch ; Diapason, 8ft. Pitch ; Dulcet (Soft), 8ft. Pitch ; Bourdon, 16ft. Pitch ; Bass Coupler.

Treble.—Flute, 4ft. Pitch ; Melodia, 8ft. Pitch ; Dulciana (Soft), 8ft. Pitch ; Celeste, 8ft Pitch ; Echo (Soft), 8ft. Pitch ; Euphone, 16ft. Pitch ; Cremona (Soft), 16ft. Pitch ; Treble Coupler ; Forte ; Vox Humana,

Action No. 98.

17 Stops, Knee Swell and Grand Organ. Contains 9 Sets (272 Reeds)

Bass—Bourdon Bass, 16ft Pitch ; Viola, 4ft. Pitch ; Diapason, 8ft. Pitch ; Dulcet, Soft on Diapason ; Violetta, 2ft. Pitch ; Harp Æolian, 2ft. Pitch ; Bass Coupler ; Forte ; Vox Humana.

Treble.—Flute, 4ft. Pitch ; Celeste, 8ft. Pitch ; Echo, Soft on Celeste ; Melodia, 8ft. Pitch ; Dulciana, Soft on Melodia ; Euphone. 16ft. Pitch ; Cremona, Soft on Euphone ; Treble Coupler.

(The Harp Æolian Stop is of quite a new quality, and is beautifully voiced.)

The Bell·Piano & Organ Co., Ltd.,

BARTHOLOMEW ROAD, KENTISH TOWN, LONDON, N.W. 5.

Trade leaflet, c.1920

By 1890, the directors were W. J. Bell and a Mr Alexander. The Bellolian was said to have had 11 sets of reeds and 18 stops and retailed at 80 guineas. In the summer of 1890, the British arm of the business became a limited liability company, the London director being Mr Jenkinson of superoctave-coupler fame at High Holborn (see Jenkinson & Co). In that year the company celebrated ten years of trading in Europe and also the sale of their fifty-thousandth organ. London office was the Bell Organ & Piano Co, 58 Holborn Viaduct. By 1913 was called the Bell Piano & Organ Co. and the address was 49 Holborn Viaduct with premises in Pratt Street, Camden Town. In that year the business advertised the Bell 'Students' model, an instrument with a pedal klavier. 'Each stop draws a complete Row of Reeds'. At the end of 1915, the company moved office and showroom under one roof at 109 Bartholomew Road, Kentish Town, the manager being H. A. Grimsdick. In 1928 the company ceased making both pianos and organs. It seems that the D. W. Karn organisation of Toronto (qv) took over the Bell name for organs after that. As for the London end, by 1929 the business, while retaining the same name, was owned by the Piano & Gramophone Co Ltd. At that time player pianos were the main stock in trade, although reed organ making was still listed in directories. See also Samuel Howard.

Benda, Hermann. 7 Sorge, Gera, Reuss, Germany. Described as a reed organ and harmonium maker, fl.1930.

Bendzko, F. Hinter Rossgarten 14, Königsberg, Prussia, Germany. Maker of harmoniums, fl.1940.

Benson, A. Hessleholm, Sweden. Maker of harmoniums and reed organs who was in business between 1890 and 1930.

Bent, George P. 81 Jackson Street, Chicago, Illinois, also at 1304 St Louis Avenue, Kansas City, Missouri, USA. George Payne Bent set out in business in 1870 making sewing machines, adding reed organs later. The business was then known as 'makers of the Crown Sewing Machines & Organs'. By 1880, the company had a factory at 211 Wabash Avenue, Chicago. Later at 281-9 Wabash Avenue and subsequently at Washington Boulevard and Sangamon Street in Chicago. Maker of 'Crown Organs'. A major producer of American organs in the late 1880s.

Benvenuti, Carlo. San Giovanni in Croce (Cremona), Italy. A maker of harmoniums, fl.1909.

Berger, Ed. Förstereistr 52, Dresden, Germany. Described as a maker of harmoniums, fl.1909.

Berggreb & Bengzon. Seffle, Sweden. Makers of harmoniums, fl.1909.

Berkhardt & Sons. *see* Alloway, W. & R.

Berliner Harmonium-fabrik, GmbH. Alexandrinenstr 22, Berlin, Germany. Maker of harmoniums for schools. Business founded in 1902, unlisted by 1909.

Bernhardt, Gebrüder. Gambach, Hessen, Germany. Maker of harmoniums, fl.1909.

Berntsen, Anton. Founded a business in 1901 at Örstedsgade 19, Vejle, Denmark, as a harmonium manufacturer. By 1909 was listed at 19 Jorstedsgatan, Vejle.

Bertran, Miguel. 70 calle de Torrijos, Gracia-Barcelona, Spain. Makers of reed organs, fl. 1930.

Bertz, Gottlob. Wernerstr 25, Ludwigsburg, Germany. Maker of harmoniums, fl.1940.

Berutti, Luigo. 180 bis, Strada Casale, Turin, Italy. Maker of harmoniums and reed organs listed in 1930 directories.

Bettex, Friedrich. Steinsfurt Kr, Heidelberg, Germany. Maker of harmoniums and reed organs, fl.1930.

Beversluis, P. Dordrecht, Holland. At the International Exhibition staged in London in 1862, this maker showed 'semi-melodiums'. No further details.

Beyer, L. M. Bielefelder Str 46, Brackwede, Germany. Maker of harmoniums, fl.1940.

Bilde, Ch. 3 Avenue de Chambery, Annecy, France. Established in 1892. Maker of reed organs. At the 1900 Paris Exhibition, he showed in the historic section a small 5-octave instrument of 8ft pitch reeds made prior to 1825. The instrument was fitted with an octave coupler - a device claimed to be an American and later invention. Paris address in 1920 was 17 rue de Lancry. Fl.1930.

Billhorn Brothers Organ Co. 207 North Wells Street, Chicago, Illinois, USA. Established in 1885 by Peter Philip Billhorn. At various addresses in and around Chicago. Makers of folding harmoniums, fl.1930.

Biswas & Sons. 5 Lower Chitpore Road, Calcutta, India. Manufacturers of harmoniums, fl.1930.

Blackwell, Jonathan Caldwell. Granted provisional protection under British Patent No 1016 of 10 December 1862 for 'the obtainment of "a perfect double action without the use of two sets of vibrators" in an instrument having free vibrating tongues or reeds'. No drawings were published.

Blaker, A. 20 Whitfield Street, Tottenham Court Road, London. Maker of portable harmoniums, fl.1914.

Blankenstein & Co Ltd. 135 Finsbury Pavement, London. Agents for Miller organs, fl.1914.

Bliss American Organ Co. Bridgeport, Connecticut, USA. The UK branch was set up in summer 1885 operated by Major Herrick at 264 Oxford Street, London. Showed a 7-octave organ. No further references located.

Boca, G. Via S. Chiara 43, Turin, Italy. Listed in directories as a harmonium builder, fl.1909.

Bock, A. 41a Southampton Road, Gospel Oak, London. A builder of harmoniums who in 1905 advised he could offer the trade an oak-cased cheap instrument having seven stops and one row of reeds for £7. At the same time, William Thomson (qv) of Govan in Scotland was offering the trade cheap lines to retail at £8 10s.

Boehmer, Ottilie. 153 Balls Pond Road, Islington, Middlesex. In 1886 was granted British Patent No 5521 for a combined pianoforte and harmonium or American organ devised in conjunction with pianomaker Ferdinand Thurmer of Meissen in Germany (est. in 1834). This appears to have been Thurmer's only attempt at making reed organs.

Bokums, Bräli. 24 Jürmalas ielā, Liepaja, Latvia. Harmonium maker, fl.1930.

Bongardt, Friedrich. 44a Gasstr, Barmen, Germany. Maker of harmoniums and reed organs, fl.1930. See also under Brüning & Bongardt. May be related to:

Bongardt & Herfurth, Harmoniumfabrik. Loher Str 23, Barmen, Wuppertal, Germany. Harmonium maker, fl.1940.

Bonnel, G. 5 avenue de l'Opera, Paris, France. Manufacturer of harmoniums and American organs, fl.1920.

Boosey & Ching. 24 Holles Street, London. At the 1862 International Exhibition staged in London, showed 'six harmoniums - two with pedals, one having self-blowing machine'. Described as being Evans (qv) harmoniums, the 'organ harmonium' was said to have 2 rows of keys and 2⅓ octaves of pedals offering 32ft and 16 ft pitches. The upper manual played on the swell organ, and the lower was the great. There were 11 sets of reeds and full couplers (pedal to great, swell to great, etc). The instruments in this exhibition were in cases designed by Hugh Stanus of the Sheffield School of Art. Regarding Evans, the catalogue noted:

> These instruments, first introduced by Mr. Evans in 1843, were brought prominently before the public in 1859, when Messrs. Boosey undertook the full development of the plans Mr. Evans had so successfully designed. Since that period, they have rapidly increased in popularity, and have been the means of dissipating the prejudice which formerly existed against the harmonium. Quickness of 'speech', flute-like quality of tone, and a great combination of delicacy and power of expression are some of the characteristics of the English harmonium. Very beautiful effects may be produced by the combination of the harmonium with the pianoforte and chamber stringed instruments, so as to form a miniature orchestra capable of rendering the highest class of chamber music.

Boosey & Ching also manufactured Case's Patent Concertinas. Later became known as Boosey & Sons.

Boosey & Sons. *see* Boosey & Ching; Evans.

Bork, H. 56a Crogsland Road, Chalk Farm Station, London. Maker of American organs who advertised in a very small way c.1902. *Musical Opinion* for December 1902 carried the note: 'Mr. H. Bork, American organ manufacturer, has experienced a couple of busy months. He has had many repeat orders, and has been pleased with visits from former customers. Mr. Bork lately showed us a testimonial he had received from a country dealer to whom he had supplied an eleven stop instrument for use in a church in his neighbourhood.'

Bosanquet, R. H. M. London professor of music and theoretician who was an exponent of the enharmonic organ. He had an instrument made for him by Jennings (qv) in 1872-3 which featured a keyboard of 84 fundamental notes in 7 rows to provide 53 microtones to the octave. Similiar to Orthotonophonium by Schiedmayer (see text reference) and an instrument by Kewitsch (qv). See also Brown, Colin.

Bourguignon-Boonants et Fils. 59 rue du Moulin, Grammont, Belgium. Makers of harmoniums, fl.1930.

Boyd, Ltd. 19 Holborn Bars, London. Established by 1903 as makers of the Boyd piano-player. Introduced a range of American organs. Branches at 183 High Road, Kilburn; 167 High Road, Ilford; and 322 Barking, East Ham. Factory at Warwick Gardens, Harringay, north London. Also made several models of player piano including the unusual 'Pistonola' and 'Terpretor'. As late as 1929 the business was described in directories as 'makers of harmoniums and reed organs'.

Braendle, Friedrich. 25 Poststr, Stuttgart-Untertürkheim, Germany. Maker of harmoniums and reed organs, fl.1930.

Branz E. Cia. 21 via S. Martino, Trento, Italy. Maker of harmoniums and reed organs listed in 1930 directories. Described as 'Armonium a mano' maker.

Brattleboro Organ Co. (Brattleboro Organ & Piano Co). Brattleboro, Vermont, USA. Established 1867 as the Brattleboro Melodeon Company by Silas M. Waite and J. J. Estey, son of Jacob Estey (see Estey Organ Co). Not listed in 1903. Showed reed organs at the Music Trades Exhibition in London, June 1901, when one exhibit was described as 'in a very compact and handsome case'.

Brauner & Cie, Wilhelm. Mahr, Neustadt, Czechoslovakia. W. E. Brauner founded the business in 1881. Makers of harmoniums, fl.1930.

Breitkopf & Haertel. 54 Great Marlborough Street, London. Best known as music publishers, they were the London agents (fl.1914) for Mannborg (qv) harmoniums.

Bressani, Giovanni. Bolzaneto, Italy. Organ and harmonium builder fl.1909.

Bridgeport Organ Co. Spruce Street and Howard Avenue, Bridgeport, Connecticut, USA. Managed by T. J. Patterson (qv). Established in 1877. English office originally at 246 Harrow Road, London, but later at 78 Finsbury Pavement. Advertised as makers of 'The cheapest high class organs in the Trade'. In February 1902 a notice appeared in *Musical Opinion* stating that the Bridgeport organs were the first to use the Jenkinson Superoctave Coupler and that 'all now use it'. In 1905 advertised 'single and two manual American organs' in which connection they were 'The first firm to adopt Jenkinson's Coupler'. In 1911 advertised also as 'British house for Mittag Berlin Pianos, Mittag Acme Player Pianos, Bridgeport Pianos and Organs'.

Broberg & Co. Amal, Sweden. Makers of organs and harmoniums, fl.1909.

Brooklyn Piano Co. *see* Green & Savage.

Brooman, Richard Archibald. London. Although Brooman is always associated with inventions in free reed instruments, he was merely the agent for the true patentee. The matter in question is British Patent No 2066 of 27 August 1860, described as a communication from Joseph Poole Pirsson for 'Improvements in melodions [sic] and similar keyed musical instruments' - a novel system whereby the depth of touch controlled a variable number of reeds so that registration could be achieved by the distance by which each key was pressed down. Described as a 'Trylodeon', each key had 'two, three, or more reeds connected with it, all of which are of the same musical note or letter, but of progressive degrees of loudness... Each reed has its own separate valve or pallet fitted with springs... so that when the key is predded down to its fullest extent, all of the reeds will be made to sound, and if pressed to a less distance, only two will sound, while if touched but slightly, one only will be heard'. No examples of the Trylodeon are known to survive.

Brown, Colin. Glasgow, Scotland. Manufactured an enharmonic reed organ which he called the 'Voice Harmonium' and which was built to the design of one Henry Poole.

Broz, Josef. 29 Spalena ul, Prague, Czechoslovakia. Maker of harmoniums, fl.1930.

Brüning & Bongardt. 29 Gemarker Ufer, Barmen, Germany. The name seen on harmoniums and reed organs; Brüning & Bongardt were, however, only wholesalers and distributors, fl.1930. See also Friedrich Bongardt.

Buffet, Candide. Paris, France. Leon Pinet claims that Buffet was the inventor of the accordion in 1827. Buffet's instrument was apparently a help to Grenié (qv) in the development of his *orgue expressif*.

Burdett & Carpenter. Chicago, Illinois, USA. Early makers of American organs. See also:

Burdett Organ Co. Sedgwick Street, Chicago, Illinois, USA. Established in 1866 by Riley Burdett. During the 1870s, Burdett was involved in lengthy litigation with Jacob Estey concerning an alleged patent infringement (see S. H. Jones & Co, also Estey Organ Co). In 1889 the business was at Erie, Pennsylvania. Ceased trading as such by 1909 in which year the Burdett Piano Co is listed in Monroeville, Ohio. Michel says that the Edna Organ Co of Monroeville took over Burdett but it seems more likely that Burdett acquired Edna as a piano factory. The former Burdett factory in Chicago was taken over by Newman Brothers Co. (qv) until destroyed in the great Chicago fire. In 1902 William Thompson of Glasgow, Scotland, [q.v.] advertised as sole UK agents.

"Neue Musik Zeitung", Cologne, February 1885

Burger, Hermann. Kurze Str 6 and Kirchstr 6, Leutzsch-Leipzig, Germany. Established in 1873. Operated by Paul Hörügel and Wilhelm O. Jürgens as a branch of M. Hörügel (qv). The business, originally in Bayreuth, and there until c.1903 at Wilhelmstr 4, was entrenched in Leipzig by 1909 and still operating in 1930.

Burkhardt, G. E. Hamburg 5, Germany. Manufacturer of cheap harmoniums, fl.1885.

Buschmann's Instrumentenbau. Barmbeck, Hamburger Str: 173, Hamburg, Germany. Established in 1805; operated in 1909 by Gustav Adolf Buschmann. Makers of pianos and reed organs.

Bussell, H. 11 Westmoreland Street, Dublin, Ireland. Manufacturer who showed pianos and harmoniums in the 1865 Dublin Exhibition.

Busson, Constant. 166 Boulevard Voltaire (1883); 17 rue de France (1892), Paris, France. Established in 1835 as a piano manufacturer. At the 1862 International Exhibition staged in London, showed 'accordions and harmoni-flutes'. Also made barrel organs and miniature reed organs.

Cable Co, The. 240 Wabash Avenue, Chicago, Illinois, USA. Established in 1881 as makers of pianos and American organs. In 1904, acquired Mason & Hamlin Co (qv) of Boston Massachusetts to form one of the biggest organ and piano manufacturing combines in the world at that date. In 1903, it was said that the factory capacity was 18,000 American organs a year: three years later it was stated as being 24,000. Most famous brand name for organs was Chicago Cottage; brand names of pianos included Conover, Cable, Kingsbury and Wellington, the first-named being significant as a first-class instrument.

Cadby, Charles. London manufacturer of pianofortes and harmoniums who showed at the 1862 International Exhibition in London. Charles Cadby began his Patent Piano Manufactory in 1839 at 21 Alfred Street, Bedford Street. In 1848 it was at 33½ Liquorpond Street; by 1851 at No 37; by 1853 at Nos 38 and 39; by 1863 at 33, 38 and 39 Liquorpond Street; in 1867 at Little Tothill Street, Little Gray's Inn Lane; in 1869 as Charles Cadby & Co, it was at West Kensington New Pianoforte Works, 'Near Addison Road Station'; by 1879 it was Charles Cadby & Co, Hammersmith Road. Cadby made several

◀ Plate 41. Table harmonium by R R Vadi Vala, Bombay, India. Date 23-2-49. 3 octaves, compass C-C. 2 sets of reeds, total 74 reeds. 4 stops: engage coupler, select front row of reeds, select back row of reeds, open 2nd vent for front row. Stained light wood case. Keys have tortoiseshell fronts and mother-of- pearl tops, green for naturals, brown for accidentals (from the collection of Phil and Pam Fluke)

◀ ▲ Plate 42. Johan Petter Nyström's Reform-Orgel, a single-row 5-octave F-F suction organ built in Karlstad, Sweden, was unusual in that it could also be played mechanically using perforated card-board discs of the type used on the Ehrlich Ariston organette. In this form, the organ could only play 28 notes of its compass of 61 notes. The disc measures $13\frac{3}{4}$ inches in diameter. Models were made with up to two full rows of reeds and three kneeboards controlling full organ and swells. See the complete description in "The Music Box", Vol 8, 1977, p 2 (by courtesy of Bill Lindwall and Sven Forsell)

improvements to the pianoforte, among them his patented suspended and tensioned soundboard.

Calame, Robert V. Salto Oriental, Uruguay. Makers of pianos and harmoniums, fl.1909.

Camp, G. 106 Euston Road, London. Advertised in *The Musical Times* for July 1865: 'G. Camp's Superior Harmoniums in polished mahogany case, 5 stops £7.7s; in walnut, 7 stops £8.8s.'

Campton & Co. Burbage, Hinckley, Leicestershire. Retailed Rodolphe harmoniums in 1860. The 4-octave model with one set of reeds was 6 gns in oak or £7 in rosewood; up to 5 octaves, 5 sets of reeds and 16 stops was 40 gns in oak and £41 in rosewood.

Čápek, Karl. 47 Dolní Předměstí, Polička, Czechoslovakia. Established in 1874 at Obere Vorstadt 165 by Friedrich Čápek; fl.1909. Karl succeeded him, fl.1930. Makers of harmoniums.

Carhart & Needham. 97, 99, 101 East 23rd Street, New York, USA. Established in 1850, the business formed originally by James Carhart in 1846 to manufacture reed organs made on his suction principle devised while he was in the employ of George Prince (qv). Made a large variety of instruments.

Carpenter Co. 40 Elliot Street, Brattleboro, Vermont, USA. Established in 1850 by Edwin P. Carpenter, a native of Guilford, born 13 June 1819. He came of a historic colonial and revolutionary stock. His grandfather was Benjamin Carpenter, a Vermont pioneer who was a field officer of the Revolution, a participant in the battle of Bennington, a founder and framer of the constitution of the state, and its lieutenant governor in 1779. Cyprus, the youngest son of Benjamin Carpenter, was his father. He moved to Brattleboro in 1850 and bought a half interest in the organ-making business of Messrs. S. H. Jones & Co (qv); when the partnership was dissolved later the same year, the firm became Burditt & Carpenter, Burditt later changing his name to Burdett. Ultimately, Jacob Estey (see Estey Organ Co) took an interest in the business and later Carpenter sold his share to Isaac Hines. Soon after this, in 1858, Carpenter moved west, and after a short time became again engaged in the organ business as the Carpenter Organ Co. Carpenter settled in Mendota, Illinois, and manufactured cabinet organs. In 1889 he returned to Brattleboro and became mechanical superintendent of the E. P. Carpenter organ company. He died in summer 1891. His son, E. P. Carpenter, jnr, was chairman of the judges at the 1893 World's Columbian Exposition where he awarded the highest medal for reed organs to Story & Clark. See also:

Carpenter, E. P. 40 Elliot Street, Brattleboro, Vermont, USA. Reed organ manufacturers. Originally established in 1850 in Worcester, Massachusette, the company published the following notice on 1 March 1885: 'The E. P. Carpenter Co. beg leave to announce to Patrons and Friends their Removal from Worcester, Mass., to Brattleboro', Vt. In short, we have returned to our old home - Brattleboro' is the birthplace of the founder of this Company'. In 1886 advertised organs 'with Divided Coupler - 26 Gns.' *Musical Opinion* for August 1898, reported: 'The E. P. Carpenter Co. announce the retirement from their corporation of Mr. W. C. Carpenter, and his resignation as general manager and travelling representative. The company have secured the services of Mr. B. H. Mitchell, who will hereafter represent them.' In 1898, Murdoch & Co (Lim) of 91 and 93 Farringdon Road, London, E.C. advertised as stocking 'the complete range' of Carpenter organs at prices from 23 gns. to 250 gns. Murdoch had handled this make of reed organ since 1885. By the early part of the century the agency had been taken over by the London office of Julius Heinrich Zimmermann (qv) of Leipzig at 4 Wells Street, Oxford Street. In 1914, Ambridge & Son (qv) advertised themselves as 'sole agents'.

Cartman, Charles E. Rosslyn Lodge, Crumpsall, Manchester; having moved to this address in 1904 when he became sole agent for Thomas Organs (see Thomas Organ & Piano Co). By 1913, when he was advertising the Thomas two-manual organ, he was at 49 Avondale Road, Southport, and, two years later, at 18 Saunders Street, Southport. See also Bell.

Casa, Aset. 4 Mayor, Madrid, Spain. Maker of reed organs, fl.1930.

Casper, Franz. Reinickendorferstr 37B, Berlin, Germany. A maker of harmoniums listed as in business in 1903.

Cassini. 1 Finsbury Road, Wood Green, London. Advertised in *The Musical Times*, October 1864: 'The cheapest house in the trade at which to purchase. Mahogany 3 stop instruments in walnut cases 7 guineas each. The trade and shippers supplied.'

Cesarani. Paris, France. Early manufacturer of good quality harmoniums in France. Distributed in London by Charles Kelly (qv).

Chaperon, A. 31 bis, Rue Victor-Masse, Paris, France. Claimed to have been established in 1832 and successor to A. Debain (qv). Maker of reed organs, fl.1930.

Chappell & Co. 50 New Bond Street, London. Established in 1812. At the 1862 International Exhibition staged in London, showed 'patent' pianofortes and harmoniums, with and without pedals.

Chase & Co, A. B. 86 Fifth Avenue, Norwalk, Ohio, USA. Office at 19 Whittlesey Avenue, factory at Newton Street. Makers of 'Parlor and Chapel Organs'. Founded by Alvin B. Chase, made its first reed organ on 4 July 1876. Chase himself was not to live to see the growth of his company, for he died in 1877 and Calvin Whitney assumed control. Whitney was born at Townsend, Ohio, on 25 September 1846, and died on 6 June 1909. An astute man with what Alfred Dolge described as 'lofty ideals', he was among the first to take the player piano seriously;

in 1905, the company produced the Aristano grand player-piano - one of the very first grands so equipped. The Chase company was granted its charter on 1 September 1875, erected its first building January 1876 with a capacity of twenty-five organs a week, completed its first organ that July and demand exceeded capacity by January 1880. That June additional buildings were opened, doubling capacity to fifty organs a week. Success was short-lived: on 3 September 1880 the entire works was destroyed by fire. Loss was $60,000. By the following January new brick buildings were completed with a capacity of seventy-five organs a week. By July 1883 yet bigger premises were erected and the capacity increased to 6,000 a year. In September 1885 the company also began making pianos and that December increased its capital stock to $200,000. An innovative company in many ways, in received a patent in January 1879 for mouseproof protection on organs. In January 1885 it was one of the first to fit the vox humana to all organs and that July introduced an organ in a piano-style case. All organs were made to F scale. At the 1885 New Orleans World's Exposition the firm received the two highest awards of merit. Makers also of the Duplex piano-playing apparatus, c.1909.

Chicago Cottage Organ Co. Wabash Avenue, Chicago, USA. Established in 1880 by Herman D. Cable who was born at Walton, New York, on 1 June 1849 and spent his early days on a farm. In 1880 he formed a partnership with organ builder F. R. Wolfinger and founded the Wolfinger Organ Co; this led to the Chicago Cottage Organ Co. In 1890 he acquired the business of Conover Brothers of New York, piano manufacturers. This gave him the valuable assistance of one of America's most eminent piano constructors, J. Frank Conover. As the business grew, he called on his brothers - former school teacher Hobart M. Cable and Fayette Shepherd Cable - to assist. Herman D. Cable became president, but his 'exceedingly nervous temperament' (Dolge) plus his insistence on involving himself with every detail of the business, brought him to a premature end at his Evanston, Chicago, home on 2 March 1899. Officially his death was due to pneumonia. He was fifty years of age. The business continued, but the name was changed to the Cable Company in December 1900 with F. S. Cable serving as president until 1903. In that year he left to form the Cable-Nelson Co of Chicago with factories making pianos in Cableton, Michigan. The Cable Company was then run by F. S. Shaw and grew to produce player-pianos and become one of the great bastions of America's piano industry. Chicago Cottage Organs were distributed in Britain by sole UK agents Barnett Samuel & Sons, 32-36 Worship Street, London, 1899-1914.

Chidley, Rock. 135 High Holborn, London. At the 1862 International Exhibition staged in London, Chidley showed harmoniums and concertinas. Chidley was a nephew of Sir Charles Wheatstone (qv), inventor of the 'Symphonium' which is considered to be the prototype of the mouth-blown free-reed instrument which was the forerunner of the mouth-organ - the harmonica.

Chisei e Decio Figlio, Giuseppe. Pratovecchio, Arezzo, Italy. Established in 1837 as makers of harmoniums. Still in business in 1909. Also styled as Giuseppe Chisei & Figlio.

Christensen, N. C. Thisted, Denmark. Harmonium and organ builder, fl.1909.

Christophe & Étienne, H. 97 rue de Charonne, Paris 11e, France. Established in 1861. Early makers of quality harmoniums. By 1909 the business was run by Noel Chaperon. In 1914 the UK agent was Wallis & Son Ltd, 133-135 Euston Road, London. See also:

Christophe et Étienne, Rodolphe Fils, Cottino, A. Debain (A. Chaperon, successor). 31 bis, rue Victor-Masse, Paris, France. Maker of reed organs, fl.1930.

Chute & Butler. Peru, Indiana, USA. Makers of pianos and American organs established in 1901 at La Fontaine, Indiana. Brand name Piolian. Operated by H. E. Chute; fl.1909 but unlisted 1912.

City Harmonium Works, C. S. N. Swamy & Son. Nr. Jaganmoham Palace, Mysore, India. Harmonium makers, fl.1930.

Clarabella Organ Co. Worcester, Massachusetts, USA. Makers of American organs. Brand name was the Clarabella and models included the Tudor and the Kings. The UK agent was J. A. Matthews of 9 North Place, Cheltenham, Gloucestershire. Fl.1885-1900, not listed 1909. In 1898, George A. Gray & Co. of Rathbone Place, Oxford Street, advertised as 'sole London agents'.

Clark Apollo Co. Ltd. 67 Berners Street, London. Makers of the Apollo self-playing attachment for pianos and also the Orpheus self-playing organ.

Clark & Rich. Chicago, Illinois, USA. Melville Clark was born in Oneida County, New York, and served an apprenticeship as a piano and organ tuner. Rapidly gaining proficiency in reed voicing and organ construction, he formed a business in Californa making high-grade organs. This was a success but the market too limited, so in 1877 he sold out his interest and, after a short stay in Quincy, Illinois, began making organs under the name of Clark & Rich in 1880. The identity of Rich remains unknown. Four years later, he teamed up with H. L. Story as Story & Clark (qv), later his interest in devising player piano actions caused him to leave in 1900 and start up his own piano busines. His achievements in piano-playing mechanisms were numerous and significant to the development of the instrument.

Clarry, W. W. 23 Hertford Drive, Liscard, Cheshire. Established in 1875 as maker of organs and reed organs. Agent for W. Doherty of Clinton, Ontario (qv). By 1914, address listed as 'Strathcona', 23 Hertford Drive in Liscard.

Clayton, Arthur. 25 Whitehall Parade, Archway Tavern,

London. A reed-organ voicer who advertised in 1898 that he specialised in 'enlarging' or altering the pitch of harmoniums and reed organs. He was in business before 1890 and moved to this address in the summer of 1898 to open a piano, sheet music and small goods shop. See under Baillie-Hamilton.

Claus Fils, F. 96 rue Ange-Blaize, Rennes, France. Maker of reed organs, fl.1930.

Clementi & Co. *see* Hewitt.

Clough & Warren Co. 213 Woodward Avenue, Detroit, Michigan, USA. Established in 1850 as William P. Blakeman, melodeon makers. In 1854 was known as A. A. Simmons & Co and, by 1889, as Simmons & Whitney. By 1868 was styled Simmons, Clough & Co, then the Simmons & Clough Organ Co until 1874 when the name Clough & Warren was used for the piano and reed-organ makers formed by one-time Estey employees, the brothers George P. and Joseph A. Warren, who joined the firm c.1872. After a massive fire in 1899, the business was rebuilt and by 1903 also had branches in Adrian and Monroe but the manufactory remained in Detroit. Organs

fitted with what the makers termed 'qualifying tubes', better known as Scribner's tubes - wood box chimneys through which the air passed on its way to the reeds. The business went bankrupt c.1911 but was reorganised just before World War I. Sole UK agent, fl.1885-1914, was Chappell Ltd., 50 New Bond Street, London.

Collard & Collard. *see* Hewitt.

Collet, A. 14 rue Jules-Dalou, Malakoff, France. Maker of reed organs, fl.1930.

Collino e Cia, Vittoria. 11 via S. Francis de Paolo, Turin, Italy. Maker of harmoniums and reed organs who was listed in 1930 directories.

Collins & Co. Mare Street, Hackney, London. Established in 1882 by C. H. Collins. Under this name until 1900, then as the Collins Organ & Piano Co. On the retirement of Collins early in 1902, a new company was formed called the Imperial Organ & Piano Co. [q.v.] to take over the business. The factory, advertised as 'steam works', was at 45/47 Ellingfort Road off Mare Street. It is possible that the name was changed due to the existence

"Young Ladies Magazine", 1888

of another business of a similar name, that of J. H. Collins & Co at 52 Tollington Park, north London, which was run by John Hoar Collins and acted as agents for H. Lubitz of Berlin. This Collins was established in 1896. C. H. Collins was apprenticed to a London reed-organ maker before going to America to gain further experience. His first address was Mare Street off the Hackney Road, then Goldsmith Row, after which he moved to Ellingfort Road from where he finally retired in 1902, settling in Birchington, Kent.

Columbian Piano & Organ Co. Wabash Avenue, Chicago, Illinois, USA; sometime at Grand Crossing, Illinois. Melodeon makers in business pre-1898, later pianos and American organs, brand name 'Columbian'.

Corneglio, G. Caselle Torinese, Italy. Maker of harmoniums, fl.1909.

Cornish & Co. Hornbaker Street, Washington, New Jersey, USA. Established in 1879 by Joseph B. Cornish who died in 1910. His son, Johnston Cornish assumed control of the business. Unusually for reed organ makers, Cornish sold direct to the customer, so maintaining low prices. Unlike Beatty (qv), Cornish turned out reasonably well-made instruments and was said to be the only Washington maker who consistently showed a profit on sales. Made as many as 10,000 reed organs a year at the peak of production (c.1901) and was to claim that a quarter of a million Cornish organs were in use during the early part of this century. The London office was at Memorial Hall, Farringdon Street, Ludgate Circus; but in 1904 moved to 67 Farringdon Road. Was also sometime at 6 Fleet Lane. The business survived the World War I, but disappeared c.1920.

Cottiau, P. F. J. Paris, France. At the 1862 London International Exhibition showed reeds for 'organ-harmoniums and accordions'.

Cottino. 119 rue de Montreuil, Paris 11e, France. Established in 1863. Makers of quality harmoniums. By 1909 was run by Cheval. Handled in UK by Weekes & Co, 14 Hanover Street, London. By 1920, was described as 'R. Francois Successor' and advertised 'L'America système français perfectionne'.

Couty & Line. Paris, France. Showed transposing two-manual harmonium in 1878 Paris Exhibition and won a Silver Medal. A maker called Richard showed transposing harmoniums in 1867; by 1875, he and Couty had joined forces as Couty & Richard, Paris. Unlisted in 1903.

Cramer & Co Ltd, J. B. Castle Road, Kentish Town, London. Moved to 139 New Bond Street by 1914. See also Mason & Hamlin.

Crane & Sons Ltd. Scotland Road and Church Street, Liverpool, with branches also in other privincial towns including Wrexham, Birmingham, Dublin, Belfast and Manchester. In 1899 set up in London at 149 Oxford Street. Concertina makers. At that time, held agency for

Doherty (qv) organs. In 1902 advertised the 'sole agency for Christophe & Etienne harmoniums' (qv) from 10 to 300 guineas.

Crawford, F. 17 The Broadway, Eltham, London. Crawford moved to this address from earlier location in March 1900. By 1914 he was at 41 Heavitree Road, Plumstead, London. Maker of reed organs.

Croger, Richard. Croger's Warehouse, 184 Whitechapel Road, London. Maker of portable and normal harmoniums, fl.1842. Single manual 3-stop in rosewood case £12 10s; 10-stop £27; one stop £9. In 1860 he advertised a portable, collapsible harmonium in travelling case for seven guineas: one of the earliest to make such an instrument. Later concentrated as a piano and musicseller with additional premises at 140 Mile End Road. The Whitechapel Road store was closed early in 1894. Croger died in the autumn of 1895 and the business continued under the management of his son. It was listed in 1909 directories but was gone by 1914.

Croger, Thomas. 4 Hertford Cottages, Hertford-road, Kingsland, London. Musical instrument factors who advertised in 1859:

> 'Harmonium Notes and Keyboards. These instruments are an excellent substitute for the Organ. Any persons wishing to fit one up according to their own taste, can be supplied with a set of notes ready tuned, of the best make. 5 Octaves, chromatic, for 30s.; a set of keys (best quality, well seasoned, that will not twist), fitted on to the frame, for 40s.'

Also advertised 6-guinea harmoniums, portable harmoniums, etc. In 1860, advertised as 'Thomas Croger, Musical Instrument Manufacturer and Importer, 483, Oxford Street, four doors east of Museum Street, London (W.C.)' and pictured the Organine, a portable harmonium 'with piano keyboard' and three stops. Probably purely factors and not actual manufacturers of harmoniums. In *The Musical Times* for 1 December 1862, the following notice appeared:

> Emma C. Croger (Widow of the late Thomas Croger), 483, Oxford-street, sole manufacturer of the New Patent Aeolian Harps and Metallic Harmonicons, begs most respectfully to state that she still continues to supply musical instruments, and materials of every description in the music trade, on the lowest possible terms. Price lists post-free on application. Post-Office Orders to be made payable to Emma C. Croger, at the High Holborn money-order office.

Crown Organs. Brand name of instruments made by George Bent (qv) in Chicago. Slogan was: 'The one with the Crown on top'. Sole agents in Britain were Sir Herbert Marshall & Sons Ltd.

Cullun, Charles Frederick. 108 Euston Road, London. Was granted British Patent No 5043 of 23 April 1885 for a piano combined with a harmonium or American organ or both. No further details. A member of the Cullum family was associated with Imperial Organ & Piano Co. [q.v.].

Cuonzo, Vincenzo. Bitonto, Italy. Maker of harmoniums and reed organs listed in 1930 directories.

Dale, Daniel. The Dale name is closely associated with the early London piano manufacturing scene. Daniel Dale snr opened his business is 1835 at 6 Surrey Grove, Old Kent Road; but he is only listed as having been there two years. His name has been seen on a seraphine. A second Daniel Dale, possibly a son, was in business between 1850 and 1874, opening first at 143 Albany Road, London; then at 3 Albany Road (1855),; 368 Albany Road (1863), changing the name to D. Dale & Son at this address in 1871. By 1872, however, the business was Samuel Dale. Daniel Dale is associated with the manufacture of harmoniums. Much earlier (1791-1809) a Joseph Dale was in business at 19 Cornhill as a piano manufacturer and music seller and from 1836-7, a Thomas Dale was making pianos at 2 Devonshire Square, Bishopsgate. It is uncertain whether Joseph or Thomas were in any way connected with reed organs.

D'Almaine & Co Ltd, T. 91 Finsbury Pavement, London. Established in 1785 and described as 'Oldest Organ House in England'. Makers of reed organs. Made pedal practice organ with two manuals advertised in 1913 at 35 guineas. On Thursday, 19 June 1913, the entire stock of the company was auctioned by Fryett, White & Co in preparation for the demolition of the lease-expired premises. D'Almaine meanwhile moved to a West End showroom at 244 Tottenham Court Road.

Darley & Robinson. Oshawa, Ontario, Canada. *See* Dominion Piano & Organ Co.

Dawes, William. 2 Ridge Terrace, Leeds, with manufacturing premises at Bagby Mills, 56 Wade Lane. An engineer who invented several improvements to pianofortes and harmoniums. In 1868 he patented a compensating frame for pianos to counteract the effects of temperature variations on the tuning (British Patent No 3299, 28 October). He is best remembered, however, for the so-called 'melody attachment' for the seraphine and harmonium, patented on 15 June 1864, No 1477. This was intended for pipe organs or pianos as well as reed organs. Dawes also patented a 'pedal bass' effect for the instrument which was developed from the melody attachment. It appears originally to have been introduced as a 'pedal substitute' and to have been contrived with the assistance of Archibald Ramsden (qv). He also took out a patent for a complex multi-feeder blowing system for producing wind or vacuum at various pressures for harmoniums and American organs (patented 15 October 1873). He was also some time at 2 Kingston Grove, Leeds.

Dawkins & Co. 17 Charterhouse Street, Holborn Circus, London; later moved to 205-7 City Road. Established in 1780. Musical-instrument makers and distributors who were also makers of reed organs. Published catalogues of harmoniums in 1851 and 1856. In 1894, advertised the 'Clarion' attachment for pianos whereby a reed organ accompaniment could be built entirely within the case of an ordinary upright pianoforte. Used three octaves of reeds forming one rank tuned to concert pitch and extending from F above middle C to F. There was also a tremolo stop. This was the invention of Frederick Mann and Robert Adolphus Mann of High Street, Colchester. Essex, who, together with Thomas Dawkins, were granted British Patent No 16,411 on 13 September 1892. The device was fitted in the top of the piano case and connected to the keys by stickers. A foot-operated bellows unit was placed under the treble end of the keyboard. 'The Price of the Clarion is very moderate' stated the advertisements. (See also Robinson; Henry Ivory for similar devices.) Dawkins handled a number of American organs and in 1914 had agency for Hillstrom organs made in Indiana. By 1930 the business was restyled Herbert Dawkins & Co Ltd, based at Old Sessions House, Farringdon Road. Here it operated and advertised as importer for French harmoniums and reed organs.

Day & Myers. 37 Poultry, London. John Day was granted British Patent No 4080 on 14 November 1816 for a cabinet pianoforte with a 'frame of musical glasses' (described in Harding). Francis Day was granted British Patent No 5802 on 19 June 1829 in conjunction with August Munch for a seraphine stop comprising small boxes to modify the sound. Day probably worked with Clementi where he would have met Green (qv). With Myers (qv) he produced a very early keyboard reed organ which he called the Seraphine and a version which was styled the Aeolophon. In March of 1836 advertised the Aeolophon and Seraphine and also the 'grand Double Aeolophon' under the heading 'by His Majesty's Royal Letters Patent'. The Myers patent was 8164 of 1839. See also Myers & Storer.

Debain, Alexandre François. 15 rue Vivienne, Paris, France. Born in Paris in 1809, he trained as a cabinet maker. In 1825, having completed his apprenticeship, he worked in several piano factories and attained the position of foreman. In 1834 he began his own factory in Paris, invented several musical instruments and devoted a great deal of time and effort to perfecting his Antiphonel key-top piano and organ-playing mechanism which was ultimately produced in a number of forms and styles. To Debain goes the credit for inventing the name 'harmonium' in 1834 and he subsequently became a manufacturer of these instruments on a large scale. Among his inventions was the so-called 'Clavi-harmonium', patented in 1846, which was a combined piano and harmonium and the precursor of numerous similar mutations throughout the years to come. At the 1862 International Exhibition staged in London, showed 'harmonichords'. Debain died on 3 December, 1877 and his business was absorbed into that of Rodolphe as Maison Rodolphe Fils & Debain réunies at 15 rue de Chaligny, the factory being at Nogent-sur-Seine. Ultimately this business was in turn taken over by the old-established firm of harmonium-builders, Christophe et Étienne (variously described as having been founded in 1862 and 1832) as Christophe H. & Étienne, Rodolphe Fils, A. Debain, Cottino (Anciens Etablissements réunies). The London agents advertised in 1860 from Debain's Warehouse, 43 Watling Street, Cheapside, London. Debain also had premises at 357 Oxford Street, London, c.1870.

Debierre, Louis-François. Born in Nantes 18 July 1842. His father was a cabinet maker and Louis-François learned the trade. He was then apprenticed to organ builder Henri Thibault, one-time foreman to the house of Daublaine-Callinet and later the house of Ducrequet, at 146 rue de Vaugirard. After two years, Louis-François left to take up piano making and worked with Debain making *orgues expressifs* and harmoniums. The business, said to have been founded in 1862, much later became known as Debierre (Glotton, G, successors), at 35 rue Saint-André, Nantes, France. Maker of reed organs, fl.1930.

Deighton, R. H. 24 & 25, Charlotte Terrace, Copenhagen Street, Barnsbury, London. Established in 1860 as manufacturer of pianoforte, harmonium and organ keys.

De Lil, Albert. 101 rue Theodore-Verhaegen, Brussels, Belgium. Maker of harmoniums and reed organs fl.1930.

Delmotte & Fils, Th. 26 chaussée de Lille, Tournai, Belgium. Established in 1840 and among the earliest of the Belgian harmonium builders.

Deutsch-Amerikanische Orgel-Harmoniumfabrik, R. Metzner. Lauchstädler Strasse 38-42, Leipzig-Plag Germany. Established in 1902 for the manufacture of reed organs. By 1909 was listed at Mühlenstr 38/42, Leipzig-Plagwitz.

Deutschmann, Jakob. Wienstr 39, Vienna, Austria. Fl.1849-83. Exhibited a 'melodium' at the 1851 Great Exhibition in London where he described himself as 'manufacturer'. An early apprentice of his was Peter Titz (qv).

Dieckmann, F. Baerwald-Str 60, Berlin, Germany. Maker of harmoniums, fl.1903-9.

Dienst, E. Eisenacher Str 10/12, Leipzig-Gohlis, Germany. Established in 1871 by Edouard and Johannes Dienst to act as main agent and importer/distributor for instruments including harmoniums and American organs. Was agent for instruments by Wilcox & White (qv) in 1890.

Dinse, Gebrüder. Dresdener Str 12, Berlin, Germany. Established in 1839 as harmonium manufacturers. In 1909 operated by O. & P. Dinse.

Doherty & Co, W. Clinton, Ontario, Canada. Established in 1875. Makers of pianos and reed organs. Factory destroyed by fire in 1898; the replacement covered twenty acres and was equipped with a 225hp steam engine. By 1908 was re-styled the Doherty Piano & Organ Co. In 1920, the business was acquired by the Sherlock-Manning Organ Co. (qv) but retained the Doherty name for the product. European representative in 1901 was W. W. Clarry (qv) whose address, in 1889, was 6 Beaconsfield Street, Princes Road, Liverpool. By 1901, he was at 14 Westmoreland Road, Liscard, Cheshire. By 1909, he was described as a reed-organ maker in his own right.

Dominion Piano & Organ Co Ltd. Bowmanville, Ontario, Canada. Established in 1872 at Oshawa as Darley & Robinson and within two years was known as the Oshawa Organ & Melodeon Manufacturing Co. Makers of Dominion reed organs and pianos. Sole agents (1914) Forsyth Brothers Ltd, 122-4 Deansgate, Manchester. By 1898 was known as the Dominion Organ & Piano Co.

Dourte, Juan. Bilbao-Begona, Spain. Maker of reed organs, fl.1930.

Duffield, William H. Gloucester House, 108 Leighton Road, London, Established in 1881 as a maker of harmoniums. By 1888 was describing his business as that of a 'harmonium and American organ maker'. In 1898 was reported to have exported 'various models' to India, South and West Africa, also Tasmania. In 1914 directories is listed as a supplier of parts including reed pans as well as a reed organ maker. Not listed 1925.

Dumont & Lelièvre. Les Andelys, Eure, France. Also known as L. Dumont Fils. Established in 1857. May be connected with F. G. Dumont, 'facteur d'orgues et de serinettes a Mirecourt, No. 36, Department des Vosges', an inscription seen on a serinette. Dumont & Lelièvre were makers of organs and harmoniums under the name Mediophone, first introduced in 1889. Awarded a silver medal at the Paris Exposition of 1889 for a harmonium-type instrument called the Claviphone. Also showed a church harmonium with pedals called the Choriphone. Fl.1930. In 1889, under the name Dumont & Lelièvre, patented an improvement to the harmonium called the 'Harmoniphrase'. The business still functioned in 1930 as:

Dumont & Cie. Rue Dumont, Les Andelys, Eure, France. Successors to Dumont, Lelièvre & Cie.

Durand. 177 route d'Espagne, Bordeaux, France. Maker of harmoniums, fl.1909.

Dyer & Hughes. Foxcroft, Maine, USA. Established in 1866 as makers of American organs and organ actions for other manufacturers.

Earhuff, John G. 161 Superior Street, Chicago, USA. Founded in 1876 by John G. and G. A. Earhuff. A maker of American organs who, in the 1880s, was described as a major producer, having an output of 3,600 organs per year by 1897. Manufactured under the brand name Peerless. Subsequently moved to St Paul. Appears to have ceased trading c.1903.

Eason, Alexander. 217-219 Kentish Town Road,

London. Harmonium maker who was awarded a gold medal at the 1871 International Exhibition. An instrument is reported as being of extremely small proportions, the dimensions being 40½in across, 14in from front to back and just 30in high.

Eastern Harmonium Factory. 11 Colootola Street, Calcutta, India. Harmonium makers, fl.1930.

Edna Piano & Organ Co. Monroeville, Ohio, USA. Established in 1886. Believed acquired by Burdett Organ Co (qv) in 1906 to become the Burdett Piano Co. Out of business by 1909.

Eesti Klaveirivabrik a/s 'Astron'. 16 Kalda t., Tartu, Estonia. Makers of reed organs, fl. 1930.

Effner, Robert. Blumenstr 77, Berlin, Germany. Maker of harmoniums and reed organs. In 1903-9 run by Frau Ww. Pauline Effner and Robert Effner.

Ehrlich, Frederick Ernst Paul. Leipzig, Germany. A leading pioneer in the design and manufacture of mechanical musical instruments. His work in the field of the organette, particularly the mass-produced Ariston, is legendary. In July 1890 he was granted a German patent for a self-playing harmonium playing Ariston-type cardboard discs. These were clamped horizontally on the top of the harmonium case. Nyström in Sweden (qv) used Ariston-type music on his Reform-Orgel player harmonium. By the late 1890s, the business name was changed from Paul Ehrlich & Co to Fabrik Leipziger Musikwerke; in 1904 it became Neue Leipziger-Musikwerke A. Buff-Hedinger at Herloss-sohnstr 1-4, Leipzig-Gohlis.

Eichler, Max. Lobauer Str 36, Gorlitz, Germany. Established in 1861 as a builder of harmoniums, fl.1909.

Elfstrom, C. Ljungby, Sweden. Maker of 'organharmoniums', fl.1909.

Emmer, Wilhelm, GmbH. 19 Seydelstr 20, Berlin, Germany. Run by Fraulein Emmer Ahrens (by 1909) as agent and handler of pianos and harmoniums. Established in 1870. It is likely that Wilhelm was the reed-organ maker and his widow continued the business on his death. By 1930, the business was styled Wilhelm Emmer, GmbH, makers of reed organs.

Enderby & Son. 11 Church Street, Boston, Lincolnshire. Edward Enderby founded his organ-building business in 1867. By 1909 he had been joined by his son in the manufacture and factoring of pianos, organs and other musical instruments. He appears to have made some harmoniums in the early part of his business career.

Endsleigh Organs. *see* Humphreys & Son, James.

Eriksen, L. 2 Bragernaes Torv., Drammen, Norway. A harmonium maker who is listed in directories for 1930.

Eriksson, A. Kage, Sweden. Builder of 'organharmoniums', fl.1909.

Eriksson, E. Gefle, Sweden. Organ and harmonium-builder, fl.1909.

Erste Productiv-Genossenschaft der Harmonium-

Macher Wien's. Hartmannsgasse Nr 15, Vienna, Austria. Established in 1884 by Josef Strizik at this address; by 1912 was at V Hartmannsgasse 10. Makers of harmoniums and American organs.

Eschenbach, Bernard. A tax collector from Kønigshoven in the duché of Cleves, who, in 1814, conceived a free reed instrument which he called an 'organo-violine'. His cousin was the piano and organ maker Johann Caspar Schlimbach who in 1810 made a free-reed keyboard instrument with metal reeds and developed from the Jew's harp.

Essig & Co. Mitlerre Georgstr 4, Leipzig-Gohlis, Germany. Established in 1902, not listed 1909. Makers of harmoniums.

Estadella, Cayetano. 58, calle de Martinex de la Rose, Barcelona, Spain. Maker of reed organs, fl.1930.

Estey & Green. *see* S. H. Jones & Co.

Estey Organ Co. Birge Street, Brattleboro, Vermont, USA. Originally formed out of S. H. Jones & Co (qv) which itself was established in 1846 as J. Estey & Co founded by Jacob Estey and Julius J. Estey. Also had branches in Atlanta (Georgia) and Boston (Massachusetts).

JACOB ESTEY & CO.,

MANUFACTURERS OF

The Cottage Organ,

Admitted by all to be the best instrument of the kind made in the world. Also the

HARMONIC ORGAN, &C.,

With Patent Bass Dampers, Harmonic Attachment and Manual Sub-Bass Improvements, found in instruments of no other makers.

The Vocal Tremulo,

Will be found *only* in our instruments. It is considered by all leading Artists the most beautiful, and far surpassing all other improvements ever added to a reed instrument.

Send for Circular.

Brattleboro, - - - - Vermont.

Directory advertisement, 1866

Prolific makers of high-quality American organs. Jacob Estey was born in Hinsdale, New Hampshire, 30 September 1814, to poor farming parents. At the age of four he was working on a farm. At the age of thirteen, he ran away after mistreatment and went to Worcester where he became apprenticed in a plumbing business and graduated from a manual labour academy. Returning to Hinsdale in 1834 to attend his father's funeral, he decided to invest all his $200 capital in a Brattleboro', Vermont, plumbing venture. This he successfully ran until 1855. During part of this time, an area of a building he owned was rented out to a melodeon builder, Edwin B. Carpenter, whom he was later to join in a partnership which ultimately led to the formation of the J. Estey reed-organ business. Jacob Estey died 15 April 1900, active in the business to the very end. His partner, Levi Knight Fuller, was born at East Westmoreland, New Hampshire, 24 February 1841, of a German mother and Welsh father. Skilled initially in printing, he joined Estey in 1860 as an engineer. He married Estey's daughter Abby and ultimately ended up as governor of Vermont. After Jacob's death, the business was continued by his son Julius along with his two sons, Jacob Gray Estey and Julius Harry Estey. For more than ten years, the company was involved in litigation over an alleged patent infringement with a former founding partner in the old company, Riley Burdett, who by then had his own American-organ business (see Burdett Organ Co). The case was one of the major legal battles of nineteenth century America; Estey was the victor after the Supreme Court reversed a former decision made by a circuit judge. By October 1890, a quarter of a million organs had been produced; ironically, it was to take more than sixty years to double that figure. In February 1917, *Musical Opinion* recorded that:

> The Estey Organ factory at Brattleborough [sic], Vermont, U.S.A. has recently seen the completion of its 400,000th organ constructed by this well known firm. A full page advertisement in 'The Music Trades Indicator' of Chicago gives an illustration of this instrument leaving the factory on a motor lorry, with the proud legend to the effect that it is No. 400,000 emblazoned on the packing case. The organ was en route for New York, and the entire journey of 196 miles was made by motor lorry.

The business prospered even in the face of declining interest in the reed organ, and managed to survive into the 1950s, the last reed organ being made in the mid-'fifties. In 1961, the business finally became Estey Electronics, Inc. During its existence, it made around half a million reed organs and around 3,500 pipe organs under the guidance of five generations of the Estey family. The London agency was originally Hodge & Essex of 42 Holborn Viaduct (qv) who exhibited Estey organs at the International Exhibition, Crystal Palace, in April 1884.

Finally, though, this name was changed to the Estey Organ Co (Hodge & Essex), 12 Rathbone Place, Oxford Street. Still in business at that address as late as 1929. Patterson Sons & Co were sole agents for Scotland, and Thompson & Shackell for south Wales. See also Haskell, William E; also Howard, Samuel.

Europa-Musikinstrumenten-Ges. 109 Gumpendorfer Str, Vienna, Austria. Musical-instrument wholesalers and distributors who handled harmoniums, fl.1930.

Evans, Wardle Eastland. London. A noted mid-nineteenth century maker of harmoniums. Born in Cheltenham, Gloucestershire, and originally working there, he became a most skilled inventor and craftsman who did a great deal for the harmonium in England. Made double-manual instruments which enjoyed a vogue among amateur organists. Made a small reed instrument which he called the 'orchestrina-di-camera' which forestalled the tonal capabilities of the later American organ in that it could imitate the tone of the flute, oboe, clarinet, bassoon and French horn. This was a typical example of his skill in reed voicing. Inventor of a harmonium expression stop. He died aged seventy-four years in May or June 1884 as the result of a stroke. He had been negotiating the sale of his patent at the time. The business was originally at 2b Market-place, Great Portland Street (c.1866) but later moved to Marylebone Road. In 1860, *The Musical Times* carried an advertisement for: 'Evan's Improved Patent English Harmoniums, manufactured exclusively by Boosey & Sons, Holles Street, London, under the personal superintendence of Mr. W. E. Evans'. There follows testimonials from Sterndale Bennett, W. T. Best, M. W. Balfe and Alfred Mellow. Prices are from 10 to 44 guineas 'with single row of keys', and from 45 to 100 guineas 'with two rows of keys'. A notice in *The Illustrated London News* for 11 August 1860 mentions the Evans Harmonium manufactured by Boosey & Son, adding 'with/without percussion action. 2 octaves and one third of German pedal reeds plus self-acting wind apparatus. 10 to 140 gns. Mr Evans in attendance to demonstrate.' A notice in *The Musical Times* for July 1864 suggests either that the Boosey tie-up had been terminated, or that Evans kept a separate line going. It says: 'Evan's English Harmonium.- The Cottage Harmonium... 7 gns. The School Harmonium... Manufactured solely at 2b, Market Row [sic], Great Portland Street.' Immediately under this is a notice reading: 'The Cottage, or Six-Guinea Harmonium has a soft, agreeable quality of tone.. Boosey & Sons. Boosey's English Harmoniums, by Evans and other makers. An immense variety, new and secondhand, a greatly reduced prices...' Was this a stock-clearing exercise? See also Boosey & Ching.

Excelsior Company. Exhibited harmoniums at the Music Trades Fair, London, June 1901. No further details.

Fabbrica Italiana Pianoforti. 55 via Moretta, Turin, Italy. Maker of harmoniums and reed organs listed in 1930 directories.

Faber, Homo. 375 South Robey Street, Chicago, Illinois, USA. Makers of folding harmoniums, fl.1930.

Fabránek, Frantisek. Rájac, Czechoslovakia. Harmonium maker, fl.1930.

Fabrik Leipziger Musikwerke vorm. Paul Ehrlich & Co, Aktiengellschaft zu Leipzig-Gohlis. Möckernsche Strasse 30b-30d, Leipzig, Germany. Established in 1877 and directed by Paul Ehrlich. Formerly styled as the Paul Ehrlich Co, co-inventors of the disc-playing musical box as well as a very wide range of small reed organs and organettes. As well as making mechanical musical instruments, the business advertised in 1903 directories as makers of salon organs, small church organs with pipes and harmoniums.

Farley, John A. Born in Concord, Massachusetts, USA, an early centre for the development of the American reed organ. With John G. Pierson and M. M. Morse, he began business as a melodeon maker - one of the earliest in the States. Early instruments were elbow-blown, 4-octave fully chromatic lap organs with two rows of buttons, one for naturals, the other for sharps and flats. This was the ruling style and similar to those made by Prescott (qv). In 1852, the business became Pierson & Loring, later becoming Loring & Blake (qv). Farley was in business briefly as Farley & Pearson (believed to be the same as John G. Pierson) at Worcester, Massachusetts, before setting up in business as Taylor & Farley (qv).

Farmer, John. Harrow, Middlesex. Inventor of the Vocalion. See Baillie-Hamilton.

Farrand & Votey Organ Co. 12th Street and Grand Trunk Railway, Detroit, Chicago and New York, USA. Established in 1884. The Detroit Organ Co was formed as a co-operative by a number of skilled organ builders in 1881, but was not destined to survive and, in 1883, a prominent music dealer C. J. Whitney and E. S. Votey, a practical organ builder, bought the business and formed the Whitney Organ Co. In the same year (Dolge), W. R. Farrand joined the company and the name was changed to the Farrand & Votey Co. It began making church organs in 1888 and shortly afterwards acquired the Roosevelt Organ Co formed by New Yorker Frank Roosevelt. It was a high prize winner at the Chicago Exposition of 1893. Later it became the Farrand Co and the birthplace of the Pianola piano-player; hence it was one of the seeds from which grew the Aeolian Co. Reed organs were an early and extensive product and the London company was the Farrand Organ Co at 24 Denman Street. At the London Music Trades Exhibition held in June 1901, Farrand showed three Farrand & Votey reed organs among them a roll-playing model called 'The Olympia'. In November 1901, the company moved to newly-built premises at 44 Great Marlborough Street managed by D. Wood. By 1914, the business was at 14 Miller Street, N.W. The importance of the British market to the company was such that import restrictions during World War I were the final blow to a declining business and bankruptcy ensued in 1915.

Favre, J. Lyon, Rhône, France. At the 1862 International Exhibition staged in London, showed harmonichords.

Fidler, J. 56 Burton Street, London. Advertised in *The Musical Times* in July 1864 as a harmonium manufacturer. Stated to make instruments from £5, 'ditto with pedals and 16ft. tone from £8.10s' in which case he must have been quite an early maker of instruments provided with a pedal board.

Fiedler, A.G, Gustav. 17 Sedanstr, Leipzig, Germany. Established in 1871 by Gustav Fiedler for the manufacture of harmoniums and reed organs; fl.1930 as Gustav Fiedler A.G.

Fischer, Karl J., J. Ph. Palmstr 21, Schorndorf, Württemberg, Germany. Maker of harmoniums, fl.1940.

Fittler, Sandor. 20 Hatar ut., Budapest-Pesterzsebet, Hungary. Maker of harmoniums, fl.1930.

Foley & Williams Manufacturing Co. 46 Jackson Buildings, Chicago, Illinois, USA. Also at 121-123 5th Street West, Cincinnati, Ohio. Initially made sewing machines but later introduced bicycles and reed organs. Ultimately (after 1898) concentrated on reed organs. Maker of Peerless brand name organs, a name also used by Earhuff (qv). Owned the Moore Organ Co (qv) and also handled Tonk music stools. Late in 1898 the Chicago factory was burned down, but was subsequently rebuilt. Initially had London warerooms at 12 Southwark Bridge Road. After 1 January 1902, the products were distributed in England by a business called American Express Co (qv).

Förster, August. Georgswalde, Czechoslovakia. Makers of harmoniums, fl.1930. Also at Albertstrasse 14, Löbau, Saxony, Germany. In 1940, advertised as having been in business for eighty years. Dolge gives date of foundation at Löbau as 1859. In 1940, factory still in Georgswalde, Sudetenland.

Förster & Nikolaus. 5 Butzbacher Str, Lich, Oberhessen, Germany. Established in 1842 as makers of harmoniums and reed organs; fl.1930.

Fort Wayne Organ Co. Fort Wayne, Indiana, USA. Founded in 1871 by Isaac T. Packard, makers of the Packard organ. By 1899 the name was changed to the Packard Organ Co (qv). The London agency was reported to have been 'transferred' to Ellis Parr (qv) in February 1889. Who the first agent was is unknown. After Parr retired, the agency went to E. Hirsch & Co (qv). See also Loring & Blake Organ Co.

Fortin, G. *see* Alexandre Père et Fils.

Foster & Thayer. Winchester, New Hampshire, USA. Foster was an early maker of lap melodeons in America, his first being produced around 1831. Joined in partnership by Albert Thayer c.1842, but relationship short lived. At various times known as J. & E. Foster (with his brother Ephraim) and Foster & Felt with a partner Charles Felt. A Foster was still making reed organs well into the 1860s.

Francois, R. *see* Cottino.

Friedrich & Schulze. Siemeringstrasse 30, Leipzig-Lindenau, Germany. Makers of harmoniums and American organs, fl.1903.

Frohlich, Ernst. Dragsdorf über Zeitz, Germany. Maker of harmoniums, fl.1940.

Fummo, A. Naples, Italy. Exhibited at the 1862 London International Exhibition a 'piano-melodium with two rows of keys' as well as a 'vertical melodium'.

Gaboriaud, R. (successor to Richard et Cie). Etrépagny, France. Established in 1875. Maker of reed organs, fl.1930.

Galanti Bros. New York, USA. Makers of player piano with accordeon in glass case, coin-freed. Example in Bellm Collection, Florida.

Gally, Merritt. 25 East 14 Street, New York City, USA. A talented inventor of organettes and small reed organs who applied a knowledge of acoustics and physics to the design of novel shapes for harmonium reeds in order to try to increase the 'body' and power of their tone. He was granted British Patent No 7708 of 14 May 1884 for this invention, one month after Baillie-Hamilton patented a somewhat similar idea with his 'unison bar' reeds.

Galvan, Egidio. 100c Vittorio Emanuele III, Borgo di Valsugana, Italy. Maker of harmoniums and reed organs listed in 1930 directories.

Garnier, Marcel. 16 rue Ernest-Cresson, Paris, France. Maker of reed organs, fl.1930.

Gavioli et Cie, Société. Founded in Paris at 2 avenue de Taillebourg by Ludovic Gavioli. Manufactured street organ, show organs and many mechanical processes for their construction and playing. Prior to his well-documented application of zigzag-folded punched cardboard music and his invention of the book-playing mechanism for instruments, Gavioli produced barrel-and-finger harmoniums played either by hand in the normal manner or by turning a handle while pedalling. Significantly, and contrary to widely-held beliefs, Gavioli was not the first to produce punched cardboard folded 'book' music: this was a Leipzig product by Ehrlich and Pietschmann. Gavioli, however, was the first to apply it to a large concert or dance organ.

Gebhardt, J. 1 rue Madame, Paris (1920); 239 rue de Paris, Clamart, France. There is an advertisement for a 'B' Gebhardt at this address. Maker of reed organs specialising in portable harmoniums under the brand name 'Aeoliphone'. Fl.1920-30.

Gedge, William Edward. 11 Wellington Street, Strand, London. Patent agent who, on 14 March 1861, was granted British Patent No 628 for 'improvements to Melodiorgues' using two different wind pressures and conical bellows. The invention was attributed to one Bertrand Feuga of Toulouse in France. Instruments made and advertised as to 'Gedge's Patent'. Not to be confused with sundries dealer Gedge & Co of 90-92, St. John's Street, Clerkenwell Road who operated early in this century.

Geng, Jun, Robert. St Georgen, Blumenstr 14, Freiburg-im-Breisgau, Germany. Maker of harmoniums, fl.1940.

Gilbert (Successor to Rousseau Alexandre). 113 rue de Vaugirard, Paris, France. Established in 1855 for the manufacture of harmoniums, still in business in 1930. No detail on Rousseau Alexandre but unlikely to be related to Jacob Alexandre (qv).

Gildersleeve & Co. 26 Angel Hill, Bury St Edmunds, Suffolk. Maker of reed organs, fl. 1895-1909.

Gilmour, James. Glasgow, Scotland. Described as a 'manufacturer', Gilmour was granted British Patent No 1750 on 13 July 1864 for improvements to harmoniums. His patent covered the provision of an 'improved swell' and 'more refined tone' and a means of obtaining 'a greater and more effective variety of sound.' The swell-box had four or more openings which could be opened at will to provide a gradation of sound volume.

Glassl, Egyd. 13 Weingasse, Komotau, Czechoslovakia. Makers of harmoniums, fl.1930.

Glotton, G. *see* Debierre.

Godby, Williams. 19 Wynell Road, Forest Hill, south London. Described 1909 as a maker of harmoniums.

Godefroid-Vossaert, B. 23 rue d'Eyne, Audenarde, Belgium. Maker of reed organs, fl.1930.

Goderich Organ Co. Goderich, Ontario, Canada. Established in 1889. Operated by Alexander Saunders. Reed organ makers. Brand name was Mascot.

Goodman & Frisbie. *see* Whitaker & Frisbie.

Graf, Hermann. Nordstr 2, Augustusburg (Erzgeb), Germany. Began as a maker of harmoniums and reed organs in 1908, fl.1930.

Graham & Sons, Walter. Moon Street, Theberton Street, Upper Street, London. Established in 1882, maker of harmoniums and American organs. In 1904 the business was mentioned in an advertisement as 'Walter Graham's Organ & Harmonium Factory' and a notice referred to Graham's 'steam works'. Listed 1909, gone by 1914.

Green, John. 28 Norfolk Street, Strand, London (c.1815-20); 33 Soho Square, (c.1820-48). Composer, music agent, music seller and publisher. Inventor and sole manufacturer of the Royal Seraphine. Advertised at various times as agent for 'Logier's Patent Chiroplast, &c.', 'proprietor of Maelzel's Metronome and the Royal Kent Bugle' (1825) and, in 1839, as a Seraphine Maker. He was thus also a musical-instrument dealer and Langwill lists a number of wind instruments bearing his name including a Charles Pace 3-valve trumpet and a 12-key bassoon marked 'Selected by J. Green, 33, Soho Square, London'. John Green had been a traveller for Clementi when he decided to leave and develop on his own account. According to a Mr Peters who was sometime in the employment of Messrs Broadwood, piano makers, and had been one of Green's pupils, Green obtained his reeds for the seraphine from the piano maker Gunther (see Gunther & Horwood) while Bevington & Son, the pipe-organ builders, made the cases. Green's job was to assemble the pieces. Green is said to have invented his instrument in 1834 (Marcuse, p738) or 1833 (Grove's *Dictionary*, 1st ed; also Sachs' *Real-Lexikon*) or 1831 (Grove's *Dictionary*, 5th ed). King Hall states that the seraphine was not invented by Green and refers incorrectly to the oldest traceable patent as being that of 20 July 1839 granted to Myers and Storer (qv). In fact Green was granted British Patent No 7154 of 27 July 1836, for 'forming musical-instruments in which continuous sounds are produced from strings, wires or springs'. Green's invention became what he termed his 'Royal' Seraphine. Samuel Wesley was engaged to provide weekly performances on the seraphine in his shop. He sold a number of these instruments over the years at the staggering sum of 40 guineas each. The wind department of the seraphine was a dead-weighted bellows as with a pipe organ, and this gave a uniform pressure. There was also a swell effect produced by the opening of a shutter fitted to the box over the reeds. Green's seraphine was rendered obsolete by the greatly improved design of W. E. Evans's 'Organo Harmonica' invented in 1841. Green's stock in trade was offered for sale by Puttick & Simpson during 1848, 1849 and 1850.

Green & Savage. The Brooklyn Piano Co, North-West gate, York Road, Cattle Market, London N. Established in 1876 by George Green and Charles Savage, both former employees of The London Pianoforte Co. Began as makers of harmoniums but by 1890 they were also making pianos. Made a limited number of combined pianos and harmoniums under their brand-name 'Brooklyn'. After the death of the founders, the business was continued by their foreman, a man called Smith.

Grenié, Gabriel-Joseph. Born Bordeaux, France, 1756; died Paris 3 September 1837, aged eighty-one years. A musical amateur who became fascinated by the musical properties of vibrating reeds. As early as 1790, he built a free-reed instrument of two octaves. By 1810, he had built his first *orgue expressif* which was the true forerunner of the seraphine (England) and the harmonium (France). He built both reed organs and pipe organs on this principle. In his letters-patent of that year he referred to the earlier works in this direction of Erard and Vogler, but claimed his greatest inspiration had come from Dom Bedos de Celles's *L'Art du Facteur d'orgues* (1766-78). The term *orgue expressif* has remained in use for the instrument more or less ever since. One of his pupils was Theodore-Achille Müller (qv) who made significant improvements to the instrument.

Grob & Co, J. M. Leipzig-Eutritzsch, Germany. Johann Matthäus Grob was an early inventor and distributor of organettes and harmoniums. He was involved with Ehrlich

(qv) in the perfection of reed organs. He died on 17 October, 1891 and his business was taken over by Ludwig Hupfeld.

Groeneveld J. & A. 51-70 Koestraat, Schoonhoven, Holland. A distributor of musical instruments, harmoniums and American organs, fl.1930. Name seen on organ fallboard.

Grover, J. 26 Peter Street, Hackney Road, London. Organ builder, fl.1859, who also built harmoniums. Almost certainly connected with:

Grover & Wood. 62 Glengall Road, Old Kent Road, London. Fl. to 1900; not listed subsequently. Grover & Grover Ltd at South Road, New Southgate, were well known and early piano makers, established in 1830.

Gschwind, J. G. (Erste Wurtt. Reparaturanstalt Harmonium- u. Piano-Fabrik). Lindenschurstr 45, Stuttgart, Germany. Established in 1858. Formerly known as Pross, Gschwind & Co (qv). Manufacturers of harmoniums. By 1909 run by Lucie Gschwind.

Gunther & Horwood. Camden Town, London. Early British makers of seraphines and harmoniums, fl c.1820-50. John Henry Anthony Gunther was a piano maker operating between 1819 and 1878 at 27 Tottenham Street. He was granted British Patent No 5673 of 10 July 1828, for improvements to pianofortes. Robert Gunther was at 31 Little Queen Street, Holborn, in 1820. In 1823, Gunther & Horwood was formed at this address. By 1839, Henry Gunther is listed at 6 High Street, Camden Town and in 1840 at 6 and 7 High Street, Camden Town. The existence of a seraphine in the church at Longford, Tasmania, marked 'Gunther & Horwood, Camden Town' suggests that a form of partnership existed at the time of the High Street address as well as the Holborn one. It was Gunther who made the reeds for John Green's 'Royal Seraphine' probably either because he was already making seraphines or he became a manufacturer in his own right as a result of his work for Green. See also Green, also Hewitt.

Hamilton Organ Co. Henry Street & 85, 14th Street, Chicago, Illinois, USA. Established in 1890. Absorbed by D. H. Baldwin & Co (qv) in 1889 and by 1909 was at 257 Wabash Avenue making pianos as well as reed organs. Brand name for organs was the Monarch. In 1914, British agents were Waddington & Sons, 42-46 Stonegate, York.

Hamilton Vocalion Organ Manufacturing Co. Worcester, Massachusetts, USA. When Baillie-Hamilton (qv) failed to make a success of his Vocalion reed organ in Britain, he went to America. 'Musical Opinion' for May 1886 reports:

> Baillie Hamilton has started a stock company at Worcester, United States, for the manufacture and sale of the Vocalion. The company is called the Hamilton Vocalion Organ Manufacturing Co., and has a fully paid up capital of £40,000. Mr. Munroe, of organ reed

◀ Plate 43. Early Wilcox & White Symphony player reed organ c.1890. 6 octaves, F- F compass. Oak case surmounted by dummy pipes with carved crest and swags. Two carved figures of monks at each side (one missing) suggesting chapel use. 22 draw stops. While in later models the player mechanism operated 58 notes, this example of the early products worked on 44 notes, the compass being an abbreviated C to C, less the first two sharps. One knee swell. The key fall is a sliding desk-type lid which slots in under the dummy pipework top (courtesy of Christie's South Kensington)

▲

Plate 44. Wilcox & White 58-note Symphony roll-playing reed organ. 5 octaves F- F compass. Although the makers were virtually opposite the factory where Aeolian made its player reed organs, the Symphony, while always in a stylish walnut case, was an inferior instrument. It was produced in a variety of styles yet did not have the tonal range of the Aeolian Orchestrelle. Like the early Aeolian Grand pressure player organs, the Symphony used one large harmonium- type reed chest mounted vertically with the action work at the rear. The music- rolls played differed from Aeolian's: they were marginally wider although the pitch of the holes was the same. (Author's picture, courtesy of William Edgerton, Darien, Connecticut)

◀ Plate 45. Story & Clark Orpheus suction player reed organ. Two sets of reeds, C-C 61-note keyboard compass with the break at C/C sharp. Plays 58 notes from a special Story & Clark music roll. Non-standard operating system and a clockwork roll-drive motor make this a most unusual small instrument. See full description in "The Music Box", Volume 9, 1980, p 306 (courtesy of Nicholas J A Simons)

fame, is a member of the corporation. The claim for the Vocalion organ is that it will occupy a distinct field of its own in the organ trade, and will possibly take the place of the more expensive church organs. Various sizes are shortly to be placed before the trade.

Soon after this, the Munroe Organ Reed Co established a London agency with Erhardt & Co at 38 Brooke Street, Holborn. In 1887, the Hamilton Vocalion Co was in financial difficulties with Archibald Ramsden (qv) and Baillie-Hamilton listed as creditors in respect of royalties on their patents. The fact that Hermann Smith (qv) once worked for Ramsden at his New Bond Street musical-instrument business, establishes that the Vocalion as manufactured in America and adopted, in modified form, by Aeolian, was indeed a British invention. See also Hill, William.

Hands, C. W. Harpur Street, Bedford. Described as an organ builder who also handled pianos and harmoniums. Name seen on instruments but no certainty that he actually manufactured reed organs.

Hannington, Henry. Henry Hannington was born at Stockwell in London and was a talented musical performer before the age of sixteen. He decided, however, to take up piano making and joined Neumeyer, rapidly gaining promotion on the sales side. Before he was twenty, he became London representative for the Bell Organ Co. Soon afterwards he accepted an offer to join the Smith Organ Co and he alone was responsible for building up the Smith business in Britain, ultimately becoming a partner. On one occasion he netted a cash order from a retailer for 180 Smith organs worth almost £3,000. Around 1901 his health began to fail and he moved to smaller premises at 11 St James's Square where he was helped by his sister and brother. On 13 February 1904, following a short illness brought on by over-exertion at a Crystal Palace trade show, he died at the early age of thirty-nine years. Henceforth the business was carried on by his brother and sister as:

Hannington & Co, Albert. 39 East Street, Manchester Square, London Agent for Smith American Organ Co (qv) following the death of Henry Harrington (qv).

Hansen & Son, F. Raadhusstraeds 8, Nyköbing, Denmark. Makers of harmoniums, fl.1909.

Hardt, Walter. Thomasiusstr 17, Leipzig, Germany. Began business in 1891 as a maker of harmoniums.

Harland, Alfred Joseph. 76 East Road, City Road, London, also 106 Wenlock Street, New North Road, Hoxton, London. Began in 1879 as a piano maker. *Musical Opinion* for October 1904 reported that: 'Mr. A. J. Harland... claims to have produced the lightest portable harmonium ever made.- the weight is 18 lbs. For use in foreign countries, the keys are rivetted and the bellows leather is treated so as to resist the ravages of insects.' Listed in 1925, unlisted by 1929.

Harmoniumbau, GmbH. 21 Mathilderstr, Ludwigsburg, Germany. Makers of harmoniums and reed organs, fl.1930.

Harnmona Co. Blenheim, Massachusetts, USA. Makers of reed organs. Unlisted but name recorded on one organ. No dates.

Harrison & Harrison. *see* Woods & Co.

Harrison, James. 168 Drummond Street, Hampstead Road, London. Described as 'organ small work maker' for the firm of Thomas Harrison & Son (established in 1830) of that address. Inventor of the practical 'blade wheel' rotating-fan vox humana mechanism for reed organs. Although Estey (qv) built an instrument with one at an earlier date, that was propelled mechanically by a third pedal. Later pneumatic models used control valves to work the motor, adding to complexity and creating the problem that the fan took some time to get up to speed and likewise to come to a halt. Harrison used bellows' wind to turn the fan motor. He was granted British Patent No 8476 of 13 July 1885, for this invention.

Haskell, William E. In 1905 'invented a method of preventing the outward bulging of the membranes of small bellows or pneumatics, such as are used in organs. Heretofore it was a common occurrence in such bellows that, when the internal air pressure exceeded the external, the membrane was blown outwardly and the folds projected beyond the base and movable board of the bellows, thus interfering with the proper movement of adjacent pneumatics'. He assigned the rights in this invention to the Estey Organ Co (*Musical Opinion*, October 1905, p65).

Hattersley, William. Began his piano-making business in Regent Street, Westminster, in 1845; by 1850 was at 22 Great Smith Street as Wm. Hattersley & Son. In 1853, styled as Wm. Hattersley & Co, he was at 5 New Bridge Street, Vauxhall and the following year at 3 Darlington Place. His last listing was Wilton Place, Pimlico, in 1856. Also produced seraphines. His son, William P, continued in business as a factor of instruments in Sheffield, but is not thought to have manufactured instruments.

Heinrichsdorff, Otto. Poggenpfuhl 76, Danzig, Germany. Established in 1832 as maker of a pianos and harmoniums. Still producing harmoniums in 1910.

Helmholtz, Herman von. Eminent physiologist and physicist (1821-94) who was closely involved in the understanding of tone, tonality, acoustics and musical sound in general. His association with the reed organ centres on his two-manual enharmonic instrument built by Bosanquet (qv) and which had 53 micro-tones to the octave.

Henry, Justin. Orbev, France. Maker of harmoniums, fl.1930.

Hepworth Organs. *see* Jenkinson & Co.

Herngren, C. A. Lindköping, Sweden. Maker of 'organharmoniums' fl.1909.

Hewitt, Daniel Chandler. 6 High Street, Camden Town, London (1842-44); 16 Hanover Street, Hanover Square (1844). The Camden Town address had been that of Henry Gunther (qv), the probability being that Chandler worked for him in the manufacture of pianos and seraphines. Gunther cannot be traced after 1840. Hewitt devised various improvements to the seraphine, in particular the percussion action which he patented on 9 November 1844 (British Patent No 10,385). He was not the first inventor of such an action; see Martin; Kaufmann; Storer. The same Camden Town address appears also at the time of Hewitt's patent to have been one of the addresses of Clementi's successors, Collard & Collard (qv) who, in 1845, are listed at 26 Cheapside, 195 Tottenham Court Road and 6 High Street Camden Town.

Heyl, Gustav. Brühl 27 and Kirchstr 27, Borna-Leipzig, Germany. Established in 1828. Makers of harmoniums and pianos. In 1909 run by Gustav and Walter Heyl. Still in business 1930.

Hildebrandt, Hermann. 206a Rosslebener Str, Wiehe, Halle, Germany. Established in 1881 as makers of church organs and harmoniums, fl.1909. British agents for Hildebrandt reed organs was M. A. Witkowski, 12 Percy Street, London, W. [Witkowski also acted for Neugebauer, q.v.] Still in business in 1930.

Hill, R. S. Highland Park Station, Louisville, Kentucky, USA. Early American maker of reed organs who appears to have been in business c.1860-80.

Hill & Son, William. London. Church organ-builders who built a small number of reed organs to the Baillie-Hamilton (qv) Vocalion design. Fewer than a dozen instruments in all are thought to have been built; all were hand-made and differed in detail. Dates of manufacture vary between 1880 and c.1886. The voicing of the qualifying chambers around each reed was all individually done and was the direct precursor of the Vocalion Organ Co's tone ranks for the Orchestrelle by Aeolian (qv).

Hillier Organ Co. 288 York Road, Camden Road, London. Established in 1855; makers of pianos and organs. Founded by James Hillier who was born in Camden Town and served his apprenticeship as a piano maker to Charles Cadby of Liquorpond Street, London EC. Began making pianos himself at premises in King's Road, St Pancras (later expanded and renamed as the London Piano & Organ Co). In 1861 he turned his attention to harmoniums and later began making American organs. In 1879 bought a large plot of land in the old York Road cattle market and built a five-storyed factory there equipped with steam power. In November 1880, advertised

Steam Harmonium and American Organ Works - J. H., having carefully selected the latest and most improved Machinery at the Paris Exhibition, is now enabled to greatly improve, and at the same time greatly reduce many of the prices of his much admired

Instruments, and hopes to be able to meet the rapid demand of his patrons. Prices from 4 to 450 Gns.

At the 1878 Paris International Exhibition, he exhibited a very ornate instrument which he called an 'Orchestrophone', a 2-manualled reed organ with 25 stops controlling 13 sets of reeds, each apparently covering $2\frac{1}{2}$ octaves, together with 2 knee swells. The 'Illustrated Catalogue' published by Virtue, talked of James Hillier as a man 'who is held in high repute as an organ-builder', referred to it, somewhat disapprovingly, saying:

We have only to do with the Art employed to decorate the case, which is good, although somewhat over-elaborate. As a specimen of Art manufacture it is of great excellence, highly and carefully finished in all its parts. It will be a grand acquisition in some building of magnitude, where the music it creates can have its full sway.

Hillier made some very fine instruments at this relatively early epoch of the developed harmonium. He died in his sixty-seventh year on 18 March 1899 (obit *Musical Opinion* April 1899, p488). His two sons James and John continued in the business which was managed by his widow, Mrs E. S. Hillier, a sound business lady. Address sometimes shown as '288 York Road, Cattle Market'. Also known at this time as the Hillier Piano & Organ Co. In 1884, Hillier had secured the contract for the supply of harmoniums [and their repair] to the British government.

Hillstrom Organ Co. 2-28 Main Street, Chesterton, Indiana, USA. Established in 1900 as makers of American organs. President was O. W. Leeds. Agents in Britain were (1914) Dawkins & Co. (qv).

Hines & Co, I. see Jones & Co, S. H.

Hinkel, Ernst. 3 Hämpffergasse, Ulm a. d. Donau, Württemberg, Germany. Established in 1872 as a maker of harmoniums and reed organs. In 1909 claimed to be 'the largest harmonium maker in the european continent'. Still fl.1930.

Hinners & Albertsen. 341 Court Street, Pekin, Illinois, USA. Makers of melodeons and American organs. Founded prior to 1880 by John L. Hinners who, by 1881, was joined by one Fink, the name becoming Hinners, Fink & Co. A. J. Albertsen joined in 1885, the name changing to Hinners & Albertsen in 1899. In 1902 reformed as Hinners Organ Co at 125 Court Street, Pekin, under which name the business flourished until the early 1940s.

Hirsch & Co, E. 59-60-61 Hatton Garden, London. Established in 1885 by Emil Hirsch and F. S. Heiden-Heimer as makers of pianos and piano-players. Was also the London company for the Simplex Piano Player Co. Hirsch died suddenly on 23 December 1898, and Heiden-Heimer assumed ownership. Advertised as handling pianos by "Hyde and Himer" a play on the owner's name. Early this century, held the agency for the Packard organ made by Fort Wayne Organ Co (qv), presumably after first agent Ellis Parr had retired. Hirsch also handled the organs made by Springfield (qv). By 1911 was at 244 Tottenham Court Road with factory at 113 Cottenham Road, London N, (the one-time address of the Transposing Piano Co which had moved into its then-new factory in May of 1899). The anti-German feeling following the outbreak of the World War I inspired Heiden-Heimer to change his name to F. S. Hyde but, largely as a result of the war, Hyde's business was finally declared bankrupt and dissolved, April 1916.

Hissa, Jaakko. Lapua, Finland. Set up in business in 1890 as a distributor of harmoniums, American organs and kanteles (the Finnish folk harp).

Hodge & Essex. 42 Holborn Viaduct, London. Agents for Estey organs in 1884 showed at the International Exhibition at the Crystal Palace, Sydenham, on 23 April that year.

Hodges, Edward. Granted provisional protection under British Patent No 1276 of 20 May 1864 for a percussion action for a free reed instrument. Described as an

"Welt-Adressbuch", Leipzig, 1909

invention consisting of 'the introduction into harmoniums of jacks for the purpose of initiating vibration.' A jack was provided for every reed or tongue 'which is actuated or moved at the same time with the motion of the wind, by which the vibration when begun is to be continued. The jacks are similar to those used in the harpsichord.'

Hofberg, M. Klingenstr 22, Leipzig-Plagwitz. Established in 1891 for the manufacture of harmoniums and miniature harmoniums. In the early years of this century, the London agent was W. & R. Alloway (qv). By 1940 was at Breite Str 79.

Hoffmann, G. Schönhauser Allee 178, Berlin, Germany. Harmonium builder, fl.1903. Unlisted 1909.

Hoffmann, Benedict. Coselstr 102, Oberglogau, Schlesien, Germany. Established in 1850 for the manufacture of harmoniums. Fl.1909 as music seller, instrument maker and retailer.

Hofmann & Czerny, A-G. 174-180 Linzer Str, Vienna, Austria. Makers of harmoniums and American organs. Established in 1902 for the manufacture of orchestrions and the retailing of musical instruments, fl.1930.

Hollander, Gerge. Feuchtwangen, Germany. Established in 1885. Church organ and harmonium builder, fl.1909.

Holstebro Orgel-Harmoniumsfabrik K. Kamstrup. Holstebro, Denmark. Makers of harmoniums, fl.1930.

Holt, John W. Pioneer Works, 12 Station Road (1907-46) and Clarence Road, Harborne, Birmingham. Founded in 1876 by John Holt at 62 Upper Gough Street, Birmingham; was at 81 Latimer Street in 1890 and the following year at 176 Station Road. Makers of American organs and agents for same in 1909. On 30 October 1885 was granted British Patent No 13,069 for a reed organ stop action, his home address was shown as 141 High Street, Bordsley, Birmingham. At the musical instrument exhibition staged in the Agricultural Hall, Islington, in 1896, he showed a 4-manual reed organ just 32in wide so that it would pass through a normal doorway. In 1915 advertised the John Holt 'Pioneer' pedal reed organ, special student's model for 45 guineas. In 1916 he built and installed a 3-manual and pedal instrument in the Edinburgh War Hospital, which incorporated a 32ft pedal reed and a swell-horn diapason. Holt died aged eighty-three on 14 January 1932, from pneumonia after a short illness. He remained actively engaged in business until a few days before his death. *Musical Opinion* for February 1932 commented: 'The quality of his reed organs has been known for many years, and under the management of his son, Mr. John W. Holt, the same high standard of workmanship will be maintained.' The latter's son, Walter G, worked for Rushworth & Dreaper Ltd at 42-46 Whitechapel, Liverpool, until his delayed retirement in 1967 at the age of ninety-one. After the death of John W. in 1946, the business was closed down. While working for Rushworth & Dreaper, Walter G. designed their Apollo

reed organ which was built by Rushworth & Dreaper at their Apollo Organ Works. The original Holt organ was designed to conform with the Royal College of Organists' specifications as soon as they were issued in 1881. The Apollo, which sold for £190, was first introduced in 1911, built to the same standards. The Apollo remained in production up to the outbreak of World War I, later models being equipped with an electric suction motor so that a balanced swell-pedal could be introduced.

Horbiger, Aloysius. Atzgersdorf, Vienna, Austria. Exhibited at the 1862 London International Exhibition where he showed a 'vox humana' reed organ.

Horn, Max. Berliner Str 81a, Leipzig, Germany. Harmonium maker, fl.1940.

Hörügel, M. Kirchstr 6 and Kurze Str 6, Leipzig-Leutzsch, Germany. Established in 1893 (or 1894) for the manufacture of harmoniums and American organs. Operated by Paul Hörügel and Wilhelm O. Jürgens. By 1930, business was at 4 Kurze Str. In 1903, the *Zeitschrift für Musikinstrumentenbau* reported that Hörügel was the largest harmonium producer in Europe, a claim also made by Ernst Kinkel (qv). See also Burger.

Howard, Samuel. 2 & 4 Swan Street, (1897), 55 Market Street (1900-02), 78 King Street (1903-?), Manchester. A talented inventor of improvements to the American organ who was described (*Musical Opinion* 1898) as a prominent music dealer and professor. His first patent covered the octave coupler, British Pat. No 1600, 20 April 1878. This involved pivoting the keyboard key, not about the far end, as normal, but at its centre like that of a piano, enabling the end of the key to pull up on a coupler-rod when the coupler was selected. He then applied himself to the design and making of a system whereby the melody could be made to stand out from the accompaniment. His first Patent for such a method was No 4168 of 16 February 1897 which was improved upon in No 13,852 of 22 June 1898. The system which earned him recognition throughout the musical world, however, was that covered by Patent No 14,744 of 18 July 1899 and referred to a system which could emphasise either the highest or the lowest note of a melody or chord. Called Howard's 'Melody or Solo Organ', it was first demonstrated fitted to an Estey organ in London in 1898. The following year, on 11-14 April two concurrent live demonstrations were given, one every morning with an Estey at the Estey organ showroom of Hodge & Essex in Rathbone Place, and the other each afternoon with a Bell at the Holborn Viaduct showrooms of the Bell Organ & Piano Co. Was also fitted to a number of Thomas organs. In 1900, he applied for improvements under Patent No 405 of 8 January, but this was not completed. In 1901, Howard founded the Melody Organ Co Ltd. at 55 Market Street, Manchester with whom he shared the application for a further patent, No 12,658 of 21 June: this, too, was abandoned. In the autumn of 1902, he advertised a 'Patent Melodia

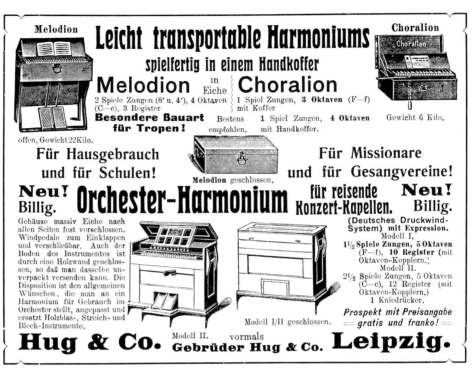

Melodion

Leicht transportable Harmoniums

spielfertig in einem Handkoffer

Choralion

Choralion

Melodion in Eiche { Choralion

2 Spiele Zungen (8' u. 4'), 4 Oktaven (C—c), 3 Register } 1 Spiel Zungen, 3 Oktaven (F—f) mit Koffer

Besondere Bauart Bestens **für Tropen!** empfohlen. 1 Spiel Zungen, **4 Oktaven** mit Handkoffer.

Gewicht 6 Kilo.

offen, Gewicht 22 Kilo.

Für Hausgebrauch und für Schulen!

Melodion geschlossen.

Für Missionare und für Gesangvereine!

Neu! Billig. # Orchester-Harmonium für reisende Konzert-Kapellen. **Neu!** Billig.

Gehäuse massiv Eiche nach allen Seiten fest verschlossen. Windpedale zum Einklappen und verschließbar. Auch der Boden des Instrumentes ist durch eine Holzwand geschlossen, so daß man dasselbe unverpackt versenden kann. Die Disposition ist den allgemeinen Wünschen, die man an ein Harmonium für Gebrauch im Orchester stellt, angepasst und ersetzt Holzblas-, Streich- und Blech-Instrumente.

(Deutsches Druckwind-System) mit **Expression.**
Modell I.
1½ **Spiele Zungen, 5 Oktaven** (F—f), **10 Register** (mit Oktaven-Kopplern.)
Modell II.
2½ Spiele Zungen, 5 Oktaven (C—c), **12 Register** (mit Oktaven-Kopplern.)
1 Kniedrücker.

Modell I/II geschlossen.

Prospekt mit Preisangabe
= *gratis und franko!* =

Hug & Co. Modell II. vormals Gebrüder Hug & Co. Leipzig.

Attachment' for pianos and organs. 'We can make them doubly interesting at a small cost by... producing a beautiful Reed Solo, with Accompaniment... Write direct to the Patentees and Manufacturers... Howards' [sic] Ltd., 1, Fountain Street, Manchester.' This would appear to have been a small reed organ equipped with the Melody attachment which could be applied to an existing organ or even a piano. See also Thomas Organ & Piano Co.

Howe Co, Hermann. Gr Frankfurter Str 44, Berlin, Germany. Established in 1875. Church organ builders who also made barrel organs and harmoniums. Operated, in 1909, by Max Howe. Also operated as an agent and distributor for musical instruments.

Hug & Co. (Gebrüder Hug & Co). Königstr 20, Leipzig, Germany. Established in 1885. Wide range of harmoniums including 'Orchester-Harmonium' in 1908.

Hüller & Stiegler. Delitzscherstrasse 144, Leipzig, Germany. The business of Hüller & Co was originally at Nürnberger Strasse 59, Leipzig. Makers of 4-octave, 49-key miniature harmoniums, fl.1909.

Humphreys Ltd, A. & E. Little Camden Street, King Street, Camden Town, London. Established in 1883. American-organ and piano makers. There is probably a family tie-up between this business and that of James Humphreys less than a mile away. Humphreys & Son, James: 198 Seymour Street, Oakley Square, London, N.W.

(1883); 35 Drummond Street, Euston Square, (1897). Established in 1867. Harmonium and American organ builders. Makers of the 'Endsleigh' reed organ. Advertised as the 'Cheapest House in London for Reeds' in 1883. Built a combined reed organ and piano with 58 stops catering for registers from 1ft to 32ft and totalling in excess of 1000 reeds. Subsequently patented a reed-organ attachment for pianos which *Musical Opinion* of March 1915 reported was in great demand 'owing to the fact that they are so extensively used in picture theatres'. By 1929 was listed at 459-463 Caledonian Road, London, N.7. Senior partner J. W. Humphreys died January 1932 - the same month as another significant reed organ-builder, John Holt (qv). His brother and his father had by then been in business for over fifty years. *Musical Opinion* for February 1932 said: 'During that long period no name in the trade has stood higher than theirs, and the death of Mr. J. W. Humphreys robs us of a life long friend who cannot be replaced. Mr. A. T. Humphreys will carry on the business in the same manner as before.' Another Humphreys, this time Charles Humphreys, had been in business in the same street: in 1902 he advertised from 16 Crawley Mews, Seymour Street, Euston Square: 'Bellows for Harmoniums and American Organs:- Est. 1883.'

Huttner, Eduard. Josephstr 31, Leipzig-Lindenae,

150

Germany. Established in 1908 for the manufacture of harmoniums and American organs. Later as Karl Stock (qv).

Ibach, Rudolph. Neuer Weg 40/42, Winklerstr 5/7 and Alter Markt 4, Barmen, Germany. Established in 1794 as a maker of pianos. Restyled Rud. Ibach Sohn c.1880 and produced of harmoniums until the late 1920s. Handled Estey agency for that part of Germany.

Iljin, N. J. Jew Smoljenskoje, Schlüsselburgsky 65, St Petersburg, Russia. Maker of harmoniums and American organ agent, fl.1909.

Imperial Organ & Piano Co Ltd. 45-47 Ellingfort Road, Mare Street, London. Formed early in 1902 to take over the Collins Organ & Piano Co. (qv) on the retirement of its founder. Advertised '(we) are actual manufacturers)'. Directors were H. J. Cullum, F. J. Best and H. E. Green (managing). In 1902 the company actually exported some instruments to North America - a 'coals to Newcastle' exercise'. In February 1919, the premises were destroyed in a £10,000 fire after which the business was moved to Perren Street, Rylands Road, Kentish Town, NW5. By 1930 it operated also at 45 King's Road, Camden Town but in 1937 advertisements refer to the Perren Street address. See also Collins & Co.

Ingalls & Eaton. Bristol, New Hampshire, USA. Established in 1842 as seraphine makers by Gustavus W. Ingalls and Cyrus W. Eaton.

Irrgang, Adam. 1 Theaterpl, Weimar, Germany. Makers of harmoniums and reed organs, fl.1930.

Ivory & Co, Henry A. 310a York Road, Euston Road, and 23 Holborn Viaduct, London, EC, also the Piano Steam Works, Wood Green, north London. Henry Ivory founded his piano-making business c.1860, initially as Ivory & Prangley, and ceased business in 1881. Referred in advertisements to being owners (or users) of 'Robinson's Patent', this being British Patent No 2907 of 17 July 1879, awarded to Joseph Robinson (qv) for a combined piano and reed organ. Indeed, Ivory did make a combined piano and harmonium using one keyboard. Illustrated in *Pictorial World* for 24 May 1879. (See also under Dawkins

A. & E. HUMPHREYS.

Price Lists *will be sent by post on application.*

Manufacturers of **American Organs** *and* **Harmoniums,**

LITTLE CAMDEN STREET, *Camden Town, London, N.W.*

Model 90.

One Full Set of Reeds (Five Octaves).
SEVEN STOPS:
Melodia,
Diapason,
Gamba,
Echo,
Vox Humana,
Bass Coupler,
Treble Coupler,
Crescendo Knee Swell
Height 5ft. 1½in.
    Length 3ft. 4in.
        Depth 1ft. 5in.
Bevelled Mirror and Marqueterie Panels.

"Musical Opinion", January 1904

for similar device). Also makers of the 'Orchestral Iron Piano'. After his death, Ivory's Wood Green factory was taken over by Barratt, the confectioners.

Jacobsen, J. Haderslev, Denmark. At the International Exhibition staged in London in 1862, showed an 'organ aeolodicon; aeolodicon with one stop' as well as an upright pianoforte. No further details are available.

Jacques, R. 51 rue Aug-Blanqui, Choisy-le-Roi, France. Maker of harmoniums, fl.1930.

Jahn & Sons, Julius. Josephinenstr 18, Dresden, Germany. Established in 1818 as organ builders. Early makers of harmoniums, fl.1909 (operated then by Julius and Johannes Jahn).

James & Son, Henry. Allerton Road, Stoke Newington (factory) and 15 Warwick Court, High Holborn, London (showroom). Established in 1878; still in business 1909. Makers of harmoniums.

Jansson, A. 10 St Nygt, Uddevalla, Sweden. Maker of harmoniums and reed organs listed in 1930 directories.

Japan Musical Instrument Factory. *see* Nihon Kakkiseizo Kabushik.

Jardine & Sons. East 39th Street, New York, USA. At this address in 1900, but by 1909 was no longer in business under this name. Manufacturer of pipe organs and harmoniums.

Jarrett, Richard William. Eleanor Road, London Fields, Hackney, London. Richard W. Jarrett began making harmoniums c.1880 and finally formed a partnership with John Goudge as Jarrett & Goudge, manufacturers and dealers in pianos, player pianos and reed organs. The address was London Wall, Moorgate Street, with three factories at The Triangle, Mare Street;

308 Mile End Road; and 401 Mare Street.

Jaulin, L. J. Paris, France. At the 1862 International Exhibition staged in London, showed a 'harmonichord.'

Jehmlich, Gebrüder. Grossenhainer Str 22, Dresden, Germany. Established in 1808. Makers of harmoniums. In 1909 was run by Bruno and Emil Jehmlich.

Jenkinson & Co. (Hepworth Organs). 45 Hampstead Road, London. Managed by Percy Mason. Founder Samuel Jenkinson, described as an organ builder, was granted British Patent No 3115 of 13 February 1894 for an attachment to reed organs whereby an extra octave of reeds could be played when the coupler was selected, so

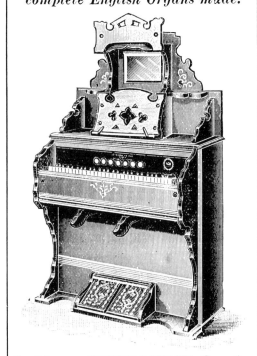

Jenkinson
ORGANS.

Don't forget that these are the only complete English Organs made.

Jenkinson SUPEROCTAVE Coupler
IS KNOWN, ENQUIRED FOR, AND USED THE WIDE WORLD OVER.

Castle Road, Kentish Town, London

"Musical Opinion", June 1902

ensuring that the top octave of the keyboard was truly coupled up to its highest note. This was Jenkinson's superoctave coupler which was actively promoted from 1897 onwards. Was first used by Bridgeport Organ Co (qv) which maker henceforth used it on all its instruments. Also subsequently taken up by a number of other makers of American organs. *Musical Opinion* for January 1898 said:

> The patentee of this invention has ingeniously placed an extra octave of reeds in a small box immediately under the key-board. By this means the coupler is a real affair, giving twelve additional notes (F sharp to F) above the normal F of the key-board. The ordinary coupler produces no extra power for the last octave, the reeds for the same being non-existent; but this invention of Mr. Jenkinson literally makes a five-octave organ into one of six octaves, and naturally brightens and amplifies the tone where and when it is most needed.

In *Musical Opinion* for February 1902, a correspondent who signed himself 'Free Reed' wrote:

> I repeat that the American organ is ill-balanced; that is why Jenkinson's superoctave coupler is so much in demand to supply the top octave which the organ lacks. The sub-bass is a monstrosity, because on the C it doubles the power of that note, whilst all the other notes are single; it is out of proportion and only supplies a bass to some chords, whilst leaving others without any.

An extensive article on Jenkinson's Coupler was published in *Musical Opinion*, January 1904.

Jennings, T. A. 127 Pentonville Road, north London. An early exponent of enharmonic reed organs. In 1876 created a harmonium of $4\frac{1}{2}$ octaves with microtonic scaling from between 24 and 84 tones per octave. See Bosanquet, Helmholtz, Kewitsch and Schiedmayer for similar instruments.

Jentsch, Reinhard. Gutenbergstr 5, Stettin, Germany. Maker of harmoniums, fl.1940.

Jewett & Hillyer. Granby, Connecticut, USA. Early manufacturer of reed organs. A 5-octave instrument called an 'Eoliphon' was made in 1832. Jewett's son was S. A. Jewett of the Jewett & Goodman Organ Co of 195 Ontario Street, Cleveland, Ohio. This business was founded in 1866 and was extant in 1885 when the Eoliphon came to light and was proclaimed the oldest 5-octave reed organ in America. The case was described as being built 'in the organ style from solid mahogany' and the original price was £40.

Johansson & Co, P. A. Sköfde, Sweden. Maker of harmoniums, fl.1909.

Jones & Company. 21 & 22 Bridge Street, Bristol, Gloucestershire. Factory at Broad Plain, Bristol.

Established in 1864. Makers of the 'Combination Orchestral Bristol Organs for Home, Church, or Mansion, from 6 G[uineas].' John Jones, trading as Jones & Co, was granted British Patent No 860 dated 7 July 1884, for 'combination organ and harmonium'. The instruments were unusual in that 'the American Exhaust System and the Harmonium or Pressure System [is incorporated] in the same instrument.' A second patent was granted to Jones on 7 April 1885 - No 4304. In June 1887, *Musical Opinion* recorded that one of the company's 'Chordalian' organs had been inspected. 'The two key-boards are supplied with distinct systems of wind, the upper having some excellent solo stops, while the lower manual combines the characteristics of the swell and great organs in power and effect.' Advertised as such in May 1885. In 1898 the business was taken over by Ernest Crichton, who had founded his business at 38 Regent Street, Clifton, Bristol, in 1866. He retained the 22 Bridge Street address. Opened another branch in Cheltenham in 1904. No longer manufactured instruments, but factored organs, pianos and talking machines.

Jones & Company, S. H. Brattleboro', Vermont, USA. Samuel H. Jones originally worked with Foster & Thayer (qv) making melodeons. When that partnership was dissolved in 1844 he worked on his own as a melodeon-maker. Two years later he moved to Brattleboro and, with John Woodbury and Riley Burditt (later Burdett), formed the partnership of S. H. Jones & Co in 1846 to make melodeons (harmoniums). In May of the following year, Burdett acquired Woodbury's interest and the business became known as Jones & Burditt. By 1850, the business employed ten men and turned out seventy-five instruments a year. In August that year, the partnership was dissolved, Edwin B. Carpenter joining Burdett and the business being styled Burditt & Carpenter. In January of 1852, Jacob Estey is thought to have bought Burditt's share of the business which now became E. B. Carpenter & Co. In May 1853, Isaac Hines, Jacob Estey and H. P. Green purchased the business and formed I. Hines & Co. By February of 1855, Estey & Green succeeded the Hines company and advertised as makers of 'The Perfect Melodeon'. In September 1857, the workshop was destroyed by fire. Estey & Green's new factory was completed in February 1858 and by that April twenty men were employed making ten instruments a week. Jacob Estey bought out H. P. Green in January 1863 and took over completely. Early in 1864 fire again destroyed part of the premises and in 1865 the business was reorganised as J. Estey & Co with shares held by Jacob Estey, Riley Burdett, Silas Waite and Joel Bullard. In April 1866, this partnership was dissolved and the business again reorganised as J. Estey & Co with two partners, his son Julius J. Estey, and his son-in-law, Levi K. Fuller. See Estey Organ Co for further details.

Jones & Sons, George. 350 Commercial Road, London.

George Jones was born in 1832 and at the age of 12 he began making concertina reed pans for Wheatstone (qv). Very soon he became a prominent maker of concertinas under his own name and others such as Wallis (qv). He became associated for a time with Boosey & Co (qv) for whom he made concertinas. In 1853, he began making harmonium reeds and then, four years later, complete harmoniums. He developed the first portable instrument for a Mr Turner of Cheapside. The demand for portable harmoniums, he wrote in 1911, was so great that he could not keep up with it or protect his design which he had to see copied and improved upon by Busson in Paris (qv). George Jones retired in 1899, leaving his two sons Arthur George and Harry Sidney to run the business under the new style of George Jones & Sons. The business, however, did not prosper, one of the sons selling out and emigrating. The father had to pay off the debts of the failed business in 1909. He outlived his sons and died in 1919.

Jorio, Fratelli Amedeo e Auguste. Giuliano di Roma, Italy. Makers of organs and harmoniums, fl.1909.

Jujiya Gakki-Ten. 2 Ginza Sanchome, Tokyo, Japan. Maker of harmoniums and reed organs; listed in 1930 directories.

Kailash Harmonium Works. Egerton Road, Delhi, India. Makers of harmoniums, fl.1930.

Kaland, Einar. Olaf Kyrres Gade 16, Bergen, Norway. Established in 1897 as a maker of organs and harmoniums. In 1909 operated by Fridthjaf Kaland. By 1930 was listed at 31 Vaskerelvsgade, Bergen.

Kalbe, J. F. Gipstrasse 13, Berlin, Germany. Established in 1840. Important makers of cheap accordions, concertinas and mouth organs who also produced a range of harmoniums. Trade mark was two anchors side by side. Run by Paul Kalbe and Ph. Katte jnr in 1909. Represented by Max Rink, 11 & 12 Bridgewater Street, Barbican, London; Ch. & J. Ullmann, Paris; Wm. R. Gratz Import Co, New York; and Paul Th. Gebhardt & Co, 16 Hopfenmarkt, Hamburg. Harmonium production appears to have ceased before 1885 when the business began to concentrate on the 'Imperial' brand accordions. In 1912, the business was acquired by Matth. Hohner of Trossingen, the Black Forest makers of mouth organs. Kampmann, Heinrich Emil: Carnapstr 48a, Elberfeld, Germany. Established in 1850. Maker of harmoniums and organs.

Kaps, Ernst. Seminarstr 20, Dresden, Germany. Showrooms at Prager Str, Eingang Waisenhausstr 14. Established in 1858. Described as manufacturers of pianos. Name also appeared on American organs and harmoniums, but possibly not an actual maker.

Karn & Co, D. W. 188 Yonge Street, Toronto, Ontario, Canada. Also at 532 Dundas Street, Woodstock, Ontario with additional branches at Winnipeg and also in Hamburg (Germany). The Hamburg business was founded in 1865 as a branch of the Canadian operation to distribute the Woodstock-made instruments and the address was 36 Grosse Theaterstr 34. The Canadian business was said to have been established in 1867 by Dennis W. Karn and John M. Miller as Miller & Karn. Used the name Woodstock Organ Co. After three years, Karn bought out Miller and re-styled as D. W. Karn & Co. In 1896, bought out the organ-manufacturing business of S. R. Warren of Toronto (qv). Makers of American organs and also the 'Pianauto' piano-playing attachment. In September 1908 *Musical Opinion* described the latest Karn organ as having a C to C compass, six full sets of reeds and to the left of the keyboard 'there is fitted the bassotenuto stop... which, when pressed, enables the player to sustain any one note within a certain compass; and when another tone is desired, the note formerly sounded is concluded'. Another re-invention of the prolongment'. Absorbed the business of Bell Organ & Piano Co (qv). London branch at 3 Newman Street. By 1910, business was the Karn-Morris Piano & Organ Co Ltd. In 1915, the London company was advertising: 'These World-famous organs are made in Canada. We are a British firm and all our instruments are made at our factories in Woodstock and Listowel.' Patriotism obviously dictated that the German connèction be forgotten. The Listowel address was that of the Morris Piano Co Ltd, itself established in 1892, which had been absorbed by Karn in 1909. After World War I, there were several changes of ownership culminating in bankruptcy in 1924 whereupon the assets were acquired by Sherlock-Manning (qv).

Karn, Leopold. Stuttgart, Germany. The Stuttgarter Pianoforte-Salon-orgel und Harmonium-Fabrik Leopold Karn was an early manufacturer which flourished in the 1870s but was untraceable by 1903.

Kás, Adalbert. Neugasse 25, Brünn, Mähren, Hungary. Organ and harmonium builder founded in 1896.

Kasriel, Les Petits-fils de Maurice. 6 rue Tolain, Paris 20e, France. Organ, harmonium and harmoniflute manufacturer established in 1839; fl.1930. At the 1862 International Exhibition staged in London in 1862, the business showed a 'flute-harmonium, harmoni-flutes [sic], &c' and was styled L. M. Kasriel. In the patent for a portable harmonium (see under Joseph Wallis & Son), the address is shown as M. Kasriel, 92 rue d'Angouleme, Paris.

Katholnig, Heinrich. Sigmund-Haffner-Gasse 16, Salzburg, Austria. Maker of harmoniums, fl.1940.

Katzer, Franz. Olmützer Str 57, Mährisch-Neustadt, Sudetenland, Germany. Maker of harmoniums, fl.1940.

Kauffmann, Johann Marcel. XV Robert-Hamerling-Gasse 30, Vienna, Austria. Established in 1877 for the manufacture of organs and harmoniums. A maker of some quality, fl.1912, no longer listed 1930. Was this the same as, or related to:

Kaufmann. Dresden, Germany. Inventor of a percussion action for harmoniums around early 1840s.

Kelly, Charles. 11 Charles Street, Middlesex Hospital, London. May have been connected with the Kelly of piano makers Kelly & Lion who traded at 8 Kensington High Street and 22 Nassau Street, Middlesex Hospital, (1851-5) and subsequently at 58 Baker Street. Importer of the Cesarini harmonium from 1860. Once commented that 'the only genuine Cesarini harmoniums have H. C. & E. round the margin of the name-plate: all others are imitations'. In the middle of the nineteenth century, Charles Kelly Snr operated a 'pianoforte bazaar' at this address. His contribution to the development of the harmonium is significant. He made first-rate instruments and supplied Queen Victoria and other members of the Royal Family as well as exhibiting them with success at the Paris Exhibition of 1867. Traded subsequently as:

Kelly & Co. 14 & 16 Mortimer Street, London. Origin uncertain, but may have been related to that of Kelly & Lion who were in business as piano makers at 8 Kensington High Street, London (1851-55) and then at 58 Baker Street (see entry for Charles Kelly, above). Advertised as 'Manufacturers, Auctioneers, and Valuers of Organs and Unmanufactured Stock' in 1885. In August 1890 advertised 'Prize Medal, Inventions, 1885', and 'Pianoforte, Harmonium, & American Organ Manufacturers to Her Majesty'. Sole importers of Hermann pianos. Fl.1884-1900, not listed by 1909. A single-row instrument bearing Kelly's name together with a transfer representing the 'prize medals' won, survives in the Church of St George at Arreton on the Isle of Wight.

Kemmler & Co, C. 26 Wigmore Street and 12 Gees Court, London. Established in 1884 as makers of harmoniums.

Kemp, Robert Alexander. 50 New Bond Street, London. Kemp was described as a musical instrument maker and was granted British Patent No 10,574 of 7 September 1885 for a combined reed organ and pianoforte. In a novel way, he employed the piano soundboard as an amplifier for the reed tones and also considered that the sound waves from the strings should 'impinge directly upon the soundboard and strings'.

Kerkhoff, Emile. 11 place Masui, Brussels, Belgium. By 1930 was at 17, place Masui, Brussells. Maker of harmoniums, established in 1905.

Kesho Ram & Sons. Brendroth Road, Lahore, India. Importers and wholesalers of harmoniums, fl.1930.

Kessels & Co. 57 Berners Street, London. Makers of reed organs and pianos, fl.1914.

Kewitsch, Johannes W. 35 Potsdamer Str 27b, Berlin, Germany. Established in 1878. Maker of harmoniums, fl.1909. In 1892 patented a harmonium having each key constructed on two levels, the front portion lower than the rear with the front half of the key tuned one syntonic comma higher than the back. This was to make it possible

◄

Plate 46. Story & Clark's Orpheus Grand player organ of the late 1890s. This 6- octave C-C compass organ employed a full 58-note player action and a clockwork roll-rewind motor which was wound up during playing. The instrument played special Orpheus rolls or the 58-note Angelus Symphony music. With the use of a spool-end adaptor, it was also possible to play Aeolian organ rolls. 15 stop knobs control registers and mechanics plus two knee swells. Single-hinged keyboard fall (courtesy of Christie's South Kensington)

►

Plate 47. The most popular models of the Aeolian Orchestrelle were the 58-note specimens, one of which is seen here. Other styles included the so-called "Solo" models which played from a single keyboard, but could use special 112- note "solo" rolls of the same type used in the Aeolian pipe organ. In this mode, the instrument performs as a two-manual organ, each row of tracker-bar openings controlling a separate part of the organ and with its own set of registers. Musically, these instruments represent a peak of player reed organ development (courtesy of Christie's, South Kensington)

◄

Plate 48. Aeolian Orchestrelle 58-note player organ. 5 octaves C-A. Fine, ornate fretted case. 19 stop knobs controlling registers and mechanics plus 2 knee swells. Note the characteristic multi-fold key-fall, here half open showing its strap hinges: most models used normal piano hinges for the three- section fall (courtesy of Christie's South Kensington)

to play pure thirds at will. Additionally, in 1889 built an enharmonic harmonium which was played successfully by Shohe Tanaka. This could be tuned to pure intervals and had twenty keys to the octave. See also Bosanquet, Helmholtz, Jennings and Schiedmayer for similar instruments.

Kimball Co, W. W. Jackson Boulevard, Wabash Avenue, Chicago, Illinois, USA. Established in 1857 by William Wallace Kimball; president Curtis N. Kimball. Makers of American organs as well as the Kimball player-piano. Was awarded 'highest honours' at the World's Fair, Chicago, 1893, for its organs and was the only musical-instrument exhibitor to receive three medals (but see also Story & Clark). At that time claimed average daily production of sixty organs and thirty pianos. London distributors up to World War I were R. M. Marples, originally at 7 Cripplegate Buildings. Wood Street, EC (c.1895), then at 153 Farringdon Road, EC. By 1914 it was Bertram Ison & Co, 662b Seven Sisters' Road, South Tottenham.

Kinnard Melodeons. Cleveland, Ohio, USA. Founded in 1857 as a maker of melodeons and, later, harmoniums. Subsequently known as Kinnard, Dreher & Co. Appears to have ceased c.1875.

Kirkman & White. 3 Soho Square, London. Joseph Kirkman, jnr, began his piano-manufacturing business at 67 Frith Street, Soho, in 1822 and moved to 3 Soho Square in 1831. During this time he was for a while in partnership with piano maker R. H. White, later to work on his own briefly. In the early 1840s, the partnership is again listed as producing a number of reed organs styled 'The Improved Seraphine'. In 1846, Joseph Grant Kirkman moved to 9 Dean Street and by 1848, White was at 56 Marchmont Street, Brunswick Square.

Kirscheisen, E. Bruno. Zöllnerstr 10, Dresden, Germany. Established in 1880 as builder of reed organs.

Klassmeyer, Friedrich. 22 Papenstr, Lemgo, Germany. Makers of harmoniums and reed organs, fl.1930.

Klein & Cie, Alphonse. Rouen, France. Alphonse Klein was making harmoniums before 1865 and was an early manufacturer of an instrument with a transposing keyboard. By 1909, the business was re-styled Klein Succr., Elilien Ledru at 20 rue Jeune d'Arc and it was no longer making instruments but advertised as a musical goods retailer and instrument repairer.

Klein & Co, Henry. 84 Oxford Street, London. Agent and wholesaler who secured the sole UK distributorship for Ann Arbor (qv) organs in February 1895. Six or seven styles were offered, one (Style 458) featuring seven sets of reeds and thirteen stops. Klein's name often appears on instruments as well as that of the actual maker.

Kleinjasper, Charles. Harmonium-maker with premises at 23 rue Caumartin, Paris (1876-95), then at 47 rue Notre-Dame de Lorette, Paris 9e. By the early twentieth century, manufacture had given way to retailing.

Knight & Son, W. H. 145 East Reach, also Corporation Street, Taunton, Somerset. Makers of 'cottage organ' style harmoniums also retailed pianos and other musical instruments. Fl.1892-1908.

Koefoed, H. P. Torvegade 10, Randers, Denmark. Established in 1876 as makers and importers of musical instruments including harmoniums and reed organs. By 1909 was listed as J. P. Koefoed as this address.

Koeppen, Paul. Friedrishstr 235, Berlin, Germany. Established in 1889. Makers of 'Koeppen's Normal-Harmonium'.

Köhler Ed, Fritz. Schloss Pretzsch (Elbe), Germany. Makers of harmoniums and reed organs, fl.1940.

Kolař, Bohumil. Stiftgasse 12, Brünn, Mähren, Hungary. Harmonium builder, fl.1909.

Konieczny, Alojzy (Kronieczny). Wegierska 32, Přzemysl, Austro-Hungary. Maker of harmoniums and reed organs in general, established in 1888, fl.1909.

Kotykiewicz, Teofil (Peter Titz Nachfolger). V Straussengasse 18, Vienna, Austria. (Successors to Peter Titz). Established in 1852 by Peter Titz (qv) who was born in 1823. After his death in 1873, the business was continued by his son-in-law Teofil Kotykiewicz (1849-1920) and he in turn was succeeded by his son of the same name, born 1880, died 1971. Makers of quality reed organs of both harmonium and American-organ type.

Kranzer, Johann. Ober Donaulange 41, Linz, Donau, Germany. Maker of harmoniums, fl.1940.

Kratochwil, Otto. 2a Baumschulenallee, Bonn, Germany. Makers of harmoniums and reed organs, fl.1930.

Krause, H. Karlstr 17, Berlin, Germany. Maker and repairer of harmoniums, fl.1903-9.

Krause, Theodore. Handelstr 19, Berlin, Germany. Director of music and professor who also designed reed organs, c.1903.

Krause, E. Stuttgart, Germany. Established in 1870, fl.1900, no trace by 1909. A harmonium maker.

Kristinehams Orgelfabrik. Kristinehamn, Sweden. Makers of the Alptona-Orglar harmonium. It is thought Nystrom (qv) was associated with this company.

Kröger, J. P. H. 20 Schulstr, Elmshorn, Germany. Manufacturer of harmoniums and reed organs, fl.1930.

Krumbholz, Paul. Zwotzen, Lasurstr 6, Gera, Germany. Maker of harmoniums, fl.1940.

Krzemiński, Josef. ul. Dabrowska, Bendzin, Russia. Harmonium maker fl.1909. Also agent for stringed instruments.

Kunkel, Wilhelm. Markplatz A21, Ottingen, Bayern, Germany. Maker of harmoniums, fl.1940.

Kuper, Adolf. 95 Breitenfelder Str, Leipzig-Gohlis, Germany. Began making harmoniums and American organs immediately after World War I and remained in business well into the mid 1930s.

Kyoyeki Shosha (The). 13-15 Takekawa-cho, Kyobashi-

Teofil Kotykiewicz

K. und k. Hof-Harmonium-Fabrikant [202

WIEN V.
Straussengasse 18.

Erstklassige Fabrikation
vom
kleinsten Harmonium bis zu den grössten Werken
mit beliebiger Disposition,
wie 3 Manuale, Pedal, Perkussion, grossem Prolongement, Prolongement-Automat, verschied. Koppelungen, Grandsourdine, Motorantrieb für das Gebläse und allen modernen Neuerungen.

Illustriertes Preisbuch frei.

"Welt-Adressbuch", Leipzig, 1903

ku, Tokyo, Japan. Maker of harmoniums and reed organs, listed in 1930 directories.

Labrousse, J. 41 rue du Temple, branch at 16 rue de Rivoli, Paris, France. Manufacturer of harmoniums, fl.1870-1900. In the 1909 directories, the addresses are shown as 14 [sic] and 51 rue de Rivoli and also 64 boulevard des Batignolles. By 1930, the business was styled G. Labrousse, harmonium maker, at 51 rue de Rivoli.

Lagerquist & Co. Norrgatan 22, Örebo, Sweden. Founded by Gustav Lagerquist in 1901, the business was unlisted in 1909 directories.

Lakeside Organs. *see* Tryber & Sweetland.

Lamberf, Vve. 79 rue de Bagnolet, Paris, France. Maker of harmoniums, fl.1930.

Larche, E. Place Saint-Sauveur, Dinan (1920); 27 rue Carnot, Dinan, France. Maker of harmoniums, fl.1930.

Laukhuff, Augustus. Weikersheim, Germany. Makers of harmoniums and reed organs, fl.1930.

Laurent, Constant. 85 High Street, Marylebone, London. Established in 1859, advertised in 1883 as 'Harmonium and Anglo-Organ Manufacturer; Repairing and Tuning executed promptly... Intending Purchasers are respectfully solicited to inspect my Instruments and Factory.'

Lawson & Co. 31 Fowler Street, South Shields, Durham. Henry Lawson founded his organ-building business before 1880 and around the turn of the century made harmoniums. Fl.1909.

Lee Organs. *see* W. H. Taylor & Co.

Lehmann & Co, Adolf. 49 Möllendorfstr, Berlin-Lichtenberg, Germany. Makers of harmoniums and reed organs, fl.1930.

Lehr & Co, Horace. Easton, Pennsylvania, USA. Established in 1890 for the manufacture of reed organs. Sole London agent was E. Hirsch & Co of Hatton Garden which advertised a new Lehr organ in October 1893: 'New Musical Invention; The Organ has seven octaves of Reeds, & looks exactly like an upright piano.'

Leonhardt & Co, M. 28 Sebastian Bachstr, Leipzig, Germany. Makers of harmoniums and reed organs, fl.1930.

Lidén & Olsson. Vara, Sweden. Makers of harmoniums, fl. early twentieth century.

Lídl & Velík. Moravský Krumlov, Czechoslovakia. Established in 1921. Shown as makers of harmoniums, fl.1930.

Liebig, Gustav.. 3 Schiessgrabenstr, Zeitz, Germany. Established in 1882 as makers of harmoniums. Specialised in 'coffer-organs India'. Fl.1930.

Ernst Erich Liebmann, Gera (Reuss)
Orgel-Harmonium-Fabrik.
Fabrikant des Harmonium-Spielapparates „Liebmannista".
Mit diesem Apparat kann jedermann ohne Notenkenntnis nach speziellem Liederbuch sofort 4 stimmig Harmonium spielen und zwar vermöge des verstellbaren Griffbretts in **12 verschiedenen Tonarten.**
═══ Ohne Konkurrenz! ═══

"Welt-Adressbuch", Leipzig, 1909

Liebmann, Ernst Erich. Hainstr 10, Gera, Reuss, Germany. Established in 1871. Makers of harmoniums, melodions and barrel organs. Manufactured a player mechanism for the harmonium which was called the 'Liebmannista' (patented in Germany DRGM 283302). The business was still operating in 1930.

Linard, Dr. Vienna, Austria. Designed and built a combined reed organ and piano in the case style of the latter. Featured a harmonium reed chest under the keyboard. The player could operate either piano or harmonium or both and could play a 'melody sostenuto with an organ or pianoforte accompaniment'. First seen in Britain at the offices of the International Music Publishing Syndicate, 1 Chiswell Street, Finsbury, London, in July 1890. Featured in *Musical Opinion* for August 1890. The instrument was called the Linardian (also referred to as 'Linardion'). That the instrument was short-lived is confirmed by an item in *Musical Opinion* for March 1894, which tells us that the February sale by auctioneers Puttick & Simpson included this self-same example. The paper commented: '...it was so costly in construction - some hundred and sixty pounds - that no more of the pattern are likely to be made'. See similar instruments under Debain, Whomes and Robinson.

Lindholm, O. Breitestr 431b (1903), Emilien-Str 9, (1909), Borna-b-Leipzig, Germany. The business was begun by Olof Lindholm in 1894. Harmonium and American organ manufacturer. In 1930 at 9, Breitestrasse.

Lindmark & Johnson. Dals Rostock, Sweden. Maker of harmoniums and reed organs listed in 1930 directories. Possible associated with:

Lindmark & Jonsson. Mellerud, Sweden. Maker of 'organharmoniums', fl.1909.

Ljungquist, S. Landvetter, Sweden. Maker of harmoniums and reed organs, listed in 1930 directories.

London Piano & Organ Co. *see* Hillier.

Loos, Josef. Seestadtl, Czechoslovakia. Makers of harmoniums, fl.1930.

Lopez, Eusebio. 2 calle Hurtado, Jaen, Spain. Maker of reed organs, fl.1930.

Loring & Blake Organ Co. 64 Southbridge Street (1868); Hammond Street (1875); Adams Block, Main and Southbridge Street (1885); 19 Union Street (1889), Worcester, Massachusetts, USA. Later moved to Toledo, Ohio. Initially known as Loring, Blake & Co. Still listed in 1900 directories but gone by 1909. Also known as the Taber Organ Co. Makers of the Palace organs. Distributed in Britain through the Palace Organ Depot, 62 Great Russell Street, London. See Farley, John A.

Louis, Lafayette. A Buffalo, USA, inventor who, according to Spillane, 'took out a patent in 1863 for a combination of the reed organ and piano after Coleman's methods, which had a short term of life'. No further details.

Luff & Son, George. 103 Great Russell Street, Bloomsbury, London. At the Great Exhibition of 1851, showed: 'Harmonium, an instrument played like the pianoforte or organ, claiming powerful tone and simplicity of construction'. The catalogue editors added a footnote to this entry, saying: 'The peculiar tone of the harmonium class of instruments is produced by metal springs set in motion by a stream of air'. George Luff began piano-making at this address in 1839 as George Luff & Co. However, as early as March, 1836, he advertised as 'Luff & Co' from 92 Great Russell Street. By 1861 was also at 7 Caroline Mews, Bedford Square.

Lyon & Healy. First opened factory in Ogden Avenue, Chicago, Illinois, USA. By 1909 had extensive premises

Plate 49. J & P Schiedmayer of Stuttgart manufactured a sophisticated two-manual player reed organ called the Scheola which featured an F-F compass. The instrument was clearly influenced by Mustel of Paris and it seems more than likely that, knowing the brothers Schiedmayer had a strong connection with Mustel - they were former apprentices - the main portion of this instrument was indeed brought in from Paris. The example seen here with an unusual style of upperwork to the case is owned by Werner Baus of Fuldatal and is contained in his private museum (courtesy of Werner Baus)

Plate 50. Another example of the Scheola is this one in a more typical case and which is preserved on exhibition today at the Museum of Musical Instruments in Berlin (Staatliches Institut für Musikforschung, Preussischer Kulturbesitz Musikinstrumenten-Museum, Berlin)

159

"Welt-Adressbuch", Leipzig, 1909

160

as 199-250 Wabash Avenue in that city. Established in 1864. Retailers of reed organs and a wide range of musical merchandise. In 1890, took over the Peloubet Organ Company (qv) and for a while continued manufacturing the Peloubet church organ which was a very large reed instrument.

Macchitella, Terigi. 2 via Pergola, Brindisi, Italy. Maker of harmoniums and reed organs listed in 1930 directories.

Macilius, Ant. 42 Vytauto g-ve, Marijampol, Latvia. Makers of harmoniums, fl.1930.

Maga, Ercole. 4 via Felice Cavallotti, Stradella, Italy. Maker of harmoniums and reed organs, listed in 1930 directories.

Magen. 3 rue des Augustins, Agen, France. Maker of harmoniums, fl.1920.

Maier & Co, Aloys. Friedrchstr 16, and Rittergasse 4, Fulda, Germany. Founded by Aloys Maier in 1846 for the manufacture of harmoniums. By 1909 run by the two sons Richard and Wilhelm. Also made automatic players for reed organs. Fl.1930.

Maiolo, Giovanni. Borgosesia, Italy. Maker of harmoniums and reed organs listed in 1930 directories.

Maisons Rodolphe Fils & Debain Réunies. 15 rue de Chaligny, Paris, 12e, France. Manufacturers of harmoniums and pianos est. 1848. Factory in Nogent-sur-Seine [Aube]. See also under Debain and Rodolphe.

Makisen Tehdasliike Osakoyhtio. Helyla, Sortavala, Finland. Established in 1881 for the manufacture of harmoniums. Also handled pianos and other instruments.

Malcolm & Co, John. Erskine Road, Regents Park Road, London. Established in 1891. Makers of reed organs and the Malcolm piano-player. In 1898 the company was so confident of the quality of its reed organs that it offered a six-year guarantee. It also urged customers to 'count the number of reeds, not the stops' when selecting an organ. It defined a 'row' of reeds in a five-octave organ as 60 in number, while a 'set' meant only half a row at 30 or 31 reeds. Although largely forgotten today, Malcolm was a significant maker as regards the quality of instruments. Output, though, seems to have been too small to have gained widespread respect. The Malcolm player organ was first produced c.1904 and was made to the pneumatic system devised by Frank Stone, a man who had gained his experience in the United States and was to die in tragic circumstances as a disillusioned man.

Malkin, E. 34 Spencer Hill, Wimbledon, London. Builder of reed organs. In 1932 advertised the 'Malkin' Patent Pedal 3-manual Reed Organ from £49. Also made pedal attachment for pianos and sold and hired Mustel organs and Celestas. Established after 1929. By 1937, address was 6 Malcolm Road, Wimbledon, SW.

Malleville. 142 avenue de Versailles, Paris, France. Maker and repairer of harmoniums, fl.1930.

Malvestio, Domenico e Figlio. 4 via Dietro Duomo, Padova, Italy. Makers of harmoniums and reed organs, listed in 1930 directories.

Mamontow, A. P. Wologda, Russia. Maker of harmoniums, fl.1909.

Mannborg, Theodore. Kornerplatz 3/4 (1894-1904); Angerstrasse 38, Leipzig-Lindenau, Germany. Karl Theodore Mannborg (1861-1930) had been apprenticed to Nyström in Sweden. In 1889, he opened up a workshop at Borna in Saxony for the manufacture of harmoniums. In 1894 he moved his manufactory to Leipzig. The business prospered and in 1904 the premises and site on Angerstrasse previously owned by the Komet-Musikwerke Bauer & Co, makers of the Komet disc-playing musical box, were acquired. New buildings were erected and Mannborg moved in during July 1904. Was a maker of quality harmoniums and American organs. Advertised as 'Erste und alteste Harmonium-Fabrik in Deutschland nach Saugwind-System' ('The first and oldest reed-organ factory in Germany to use the suction principle.'). Sole UK agents (1914) Breitkopf & Haertel (qv). Still operating in 1930 at this address.

Manning Organ Co. Rockport, Massachusetts, USA. In 1872, William H. Manning obtained a US patent for the manufacture of very cheap American organs which were dismountable without the use of tools. Claimed that the instrument could be taken apart in less than a minute without tools and cost half the normal price of an instrument. Manufacture began c.1873 but the business quickly entered financial difficulties and was sold off two years later. Manning himself opened a musical-instrument warehouse in Rockport retailing pianos and organs and this was still functioning, run by his son, in 1912.

Mariani, Antonio. Corso Garibaldi 77, Milan, Italy. A maker of harmoniums, fl.1909.

Maristany, Hijos de Romulo. 18 Plaza Cataluna, Barcelona, Spain. Established in 1870. Listed as harmonium-makers.

Marples & Son, R. M. A successful agent and distributor, Marples began in business in London in 1868 and became an agent for Feurich pianos and Kimball (qv) organs. Later also handled Putnam (qv) organs. Around 1895 his address was 7 Cripplegate Buildings, Wood Green, London, and later at 153 Farringdon Road. In 1909 was at 6/10 Clerkenwell Road, London. For a while around 1911, the business was styled as Stockwell, Marples & Co, Ltd, at this address and was heavily into talking machines. By 1913, the name had reverted and Marples, now dealing once more only in pianos and organs, claimed to have handled Putnam organs for eighteen years and had moved to Gwydir Chambers, 104 High Holborn. At this time he had dropped Kimball instruments.

Martin, Louis Pierre Alexandre. Sourdun, France. Highly important inventor who made significant improvements to the early French reed organ. For a while, Martin was a partner in the business of Jacob Alexandre (qv Alexandre, Père et Fils). In 1841 he devised what

MASON & HAMLIN
AMERICAN ORGANS.

WITH

THREE MANUALS and INDEPENDENT PEDAL ORGAN.

STYLE 1200.

Resonant case, with polished veneered panels ; moulded and carved front and ends ; folding fall-board, &c. Accompanied by VENEERED WALNUT BENCH.

Length, 6 ft. (with blow handle, 6 ft. 8 in.) Height, 4 ft. 7 in. Depth, 3 ft. 1 in. Weight, 650 lbs, (with Stool, in Packing Case, 1000 lbs.)

This Organ can be taken apart and passed through a space 2 ft. 8 in. wide. Directions for taking apart sent with each Organ.

Containing THREE MANUALS, COMPLETE PEDAL ORGAN OF THIRTY NOTES COMPASS & THIRTY-ONE STOPS.

SOLO ORGAN.
SERAPHONE, 8 ft.   SAXAPHONE, 8 ft.   BASSET HORN, 8 ft.   TRUMPET, 8 ft.   PICCOLO, 4 ft.   CLARION, 4 ft.

SWELL ORGAN.
DIAPASON, 8 ft.   MELODIA, 8 ft.   DULCET, 8 ft.   FLUTE, 4 ft.   VIOLA, 4 ft.   VIOLA DOLCE, 4 ft.

GREAT ORGAN.
CONTRA BASSO, 16 ft.   CORNO, 16 ft.   MUSETTE, 16 ft.   CLARABELLA, 8 ft.   ENGLISH HORN, 8 ft.
BASSOON, 8 ft.   HAUTBOY, 8 ft.   VOIX CÉLESTE, 8 ft.

PEDAL ORGAN.
SUB-BOURDON, 32 ft.   BOURDON, 16 ft.   BOURDON DOLCE, 16 ft.   VIOLONCELLO, 8 ft.

ACCESSORIES.
PEDAL COUPLER (Great to Pedals).   MIDDLE MANUAL COUPLER (Swell to Great).
UPPER MANUAL COUPLER (Solo to Great).   TREMULANT TO SOLO ORGAN.   FORTÉ TO SOLO ORGAN.
FORTÉ TO SWELL ORGAN.   FORTÉ TO GREAT ORGAN.

COMPOSITION PEDALS.
FULL ORGAN.   GREAT TO PEDALS.   SWELL TO GREAT.   SOLO TO GREAT.   PATENT COMBINATION
SWELL PEDAL.

"The American Organ Journal" Vol 2, nd

appears to have been the first percussion action for the harmonium which he patented in France in 1841 and 1845 (British Patent No 1842). Also invented the *prolongment* operated by a knee board and later transferred to the stop-jamb as a drawstop. The patents were adopted by Alexandre. Was also known as Martin de Provins.
Mason & Hamlin Co. 492-494 Boylston Street, Boston, Massachusetts, USA. Established in 1854. Also at 162 Broadway, Cambridgeport, Massachusetts, and 303 5th Avenue, New York. Founded by Henry Mason and

Emmons Hamlin who had made the important discovery of the techniques of voicing reeds. Hamlin perfected this and with Mason set out to produce a new musical instrument called an 'organ harmonium'. They soon developed, and are usually considered first makers of, what became known as the American or 'Cabinet' organ as distinct from the melodeon. In 1881 added the manufacture of pianos. Henry Mason's son, Edward P. Mason, born at Cambridge, Mass, in 1859, became president of the factory on the death of his father in May

1890. London agents (1885 on) were Metzler & Co, (qv). A most significant manufacturer whose instruments were built to a high standard in every respect. Also made pipe organs and pianos. In 1884 was the first American-organ maker to introduce black walnut (*betula lenta*) for organ cases. Earlier had introduced mountain mahogany also known as Canada or mahogany birch for organs. Early in 1904, the entire business was acquired by the Cable Piano Co of Chicago. By 1913, UK sales were being handled by J. B. Cramer & Co Ltd of Castle Road, Kentish Town, London, with West End showrooms at 139 New Bond Street.

Mason & Risch Vocalion Co. Jackson and Beacon Streets, Worcester, Massachusetts, USA. Established in 1889. The concept of the Vocalion is generally attributed to Baillie-Hamilton (qv). In reality it was the idea of Hermann Smith (qv) who sent a two-column letter to *Musical Opinion* in the early 1880s in which he claimed that Baillie-Hamilton had appropriated his ideas. The letter, was set into type, but never printed as it was considered by the editor to be potentially actionable. After the flurry of activity with the Vocalion in the 1870s and early 1880s, the concept was adopted by Mason & Risch who operated under the name Mason & Risch Vocalion Co until c.1901 then as Vocalion Organ Co. Ultimately, the Vocalion Co was making tone-ranks for the Aeolian player organ, the Orchestrelle, and when the business was finally absorbed by Aeolian, it was Vocalion technology which made the Orchestrelle what it was.

Matsumoto Gakki Goshi Kaisha. 5 Tsukishama, Nishinaka-dori Kuchome, Kyobashi-ku, Tokyo, Japan. Maker of harmoniums and reed organs; in business 1902 and still listed in 1930 directories.

Matthews, J. A. 9 North Place, Cheltenham, Gloucestershire. Described as the 'sole wholesale manager for Europe' for the Clarabella organ made in Worcester, Massachusetts; fl.1885. In August 1889, he advertised: 'New styles are just introduced, including the Grand Orchestral Organ, 45 gns. eleven sets of reeds and eighteen stops'. London agents at this time were R. Cocks & Co, of 6 New Burlington Street.

Matto, M. Petersburger Str 117, Dorpat (Jurjew), Finland. Established in 1891 for the manufacture of harmoniums and church organs.

Maxfield, Alfred. 326 Liverpool Road, north London. Described on his patents, the earliest dated 1887, as a mechanical engineer, Maxfield devised several variants of the organette and produced the 'Seraphone' which was similar in many ways to the 'Celestina'. Also built small reed organs and harmoniums which (in 1898) ranged in price from 25s to £25. Sole agents were John G. Murdoch & Co Ltd of 91 and 93 Farringdon Road. In later years became the Maxfield Player Piano Co and by 1918 the business was amalgamated with John Malcolm Co (qv) to produce player pianos.

Mayekawa Zenbei. 19 Minami Kyuhoji machi Higashiku, Osaka, Japan. Makers of harmoniums, fl.1902-09.

Mayer, Albert. 225 Szigeti Orszagut, Pecs, Hungary. Harmonium maker, fl.1930.

Mayer-Marix. 146 rue Montmartre and 46 Passage des Panoramas, Paris, France. Maker of reed organs who showed 'harmoniflutes' at the 1862 International Exhibition staged in London. Appears also to have been an agent for various musical instruments and this name also appears on French street barrel organs. Later the hyphen was dropped from the name.

Mead Ltd, A. C. 15 Foregate Street, Worcester, Worcestershire. Maker of harmoniums in business in 1930.

Meinl, Ernst. 124 Richard Wagnerstr, Graslitz, Czechoslovakia. Maker of harmoniums, fl.1930.

Meinschenk, Walter. Frauengasse 27, Altenburg, Thuringia, Germany. Maker of harmoniums, fl.1940.

Meinvere, Vve. 10 rue de la Tour, Malakoff, France. Harmonium builder, fl.1909.

Melzer, Josef. Rudni ul, Kutná Hora, Czechoslovakia. Makers of harmoniums, fl.1930.

Melody Organ Co Ltd. *see* Samuel Howard.

Mentasti & Figlio, Paolo. Via Torino (Casa Deambrosi), Casale Monferrato, Alessandria, Italy. Fl. before 1900 to after 1909.

Merhaul, Alfred. Petersteinweg 18, Leipzig, Germany. Established in 1868 to manufacture of harmoniums including the 'Sonorium Merhauts Patent-Orgelharmonium mit Doppelsystem'. Fl. 1909.

Mertel, Hans. 59 Neuhauserstr, Salzburg, Austria. Harmonium maker, fl.1930.

Metzler, George. Styled as Metzler & Co, by 1830 at 105 Wardour Street, Soho (1839); 37 Great Marlborough Street, Soho (1842); 35 Great Marlborough Street (1857); 38 Great Marlborough Street (1858); 16 Great

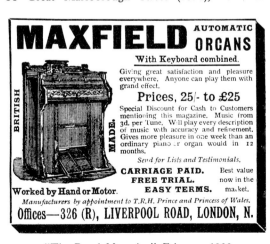
"The Royal Magazine", February 1900

Marlborough Street (additionally) (1863); 36 Great Marlborough Street (1864); 26 to 29 Great Marlborough Street (1869). George Metzler set up in business in 1781 as a maker of pianofortes and, later, seraphines. Became:

Metzler & Co Ltd. 42 Great Marlborough Street, London. Established in 1864. Stockists for Mason & Hamlin Co (qv). Also advertised the 'Eolian Harp Organ'.

Metzner, Richard. Mühlenstr 38/42, Leipzig-Plagwitz, Germany. Listed so in 1903 directories. Manufacturers of school harmoniums. In 1903 the company changed its name; see Deutsch-Amerikanische Orgel-Harmoniumfabrik R. Metzner. By 1909 the address was 40/42 Mühlenstr and by 1930 the business was operating as:

Metzner Nachf, Richard. Frohburg, Saxony, Germany. Makers of harmoniums and reed organs, fl.1930.

Miglia, Giuseppe. Caselle Torinse, Italy. Maker of harmoniums and reed organs listed in 1930 directories.

Miller, John M. 532 Dundas Street, Woodstock, Ontario, Canada. A reed-organ builder who formed a partnership with D. W. Karn (qv) as Miller & Karn c.1867 which lasted for three years until Karn bought out Miller.

Miller Organ Co. 8th and Maple Streets, Lebanon, Pennsylvania, USA. Founded by Adam B. Miller in 1873. Born 10 January 1848, c.1873 he made several reed organs. In 1874 a two-storey building was erected which, in 1883, was increased to four storeys. In 1886, pipe-organ building was started as well. There was a retail showroom at 738 Cumberland Street in Lebanon. Adam's son, Aaron H. Miller, joined the business c.1887 and retired c.1892. Around 1902-14, the London agents were Blankenstein & Co Ltd, 135 Finsbury Pavement, London (founded in 1881).

Minasi, C. 3 St James's Terrace, Kentish Town Road, London. Showed a harmonium at the 1862 International Exhibition staged in London. Mitropolsky, D. A: Nr 154, Bologoje, Russia. An early twentieth century maker and repairer of harmoniums.

Miwa Organ Manufacturing Company. Nagoya, Japan. Manufacturers of harmoniums, fl.1902-9.

Mohn Bros. 3 Lower Citpore Road, Calcutta, India. Harmonium makers, fl.1930.

Mola Gav, Giuseppe. 82 via Nizza, Turin, Italy. A manufacturer of harmoniums and reed organs who began work in 1862 and was still listed in 1930 directories.

Moller, Mathais Peter. Hagerstown, Maryland, USA. Established in 1880 as makers of church organs and cabinet reed organs, fl. 1909.

Montree, J. & R. Pentonville Road, King's Cross, London. Listed as a harmonium maker, fl.1900; no subsequent reference.

Moore Organ Co. 46 Jackson Buildings, Chicago, Illinois, USA. A major producer of American organs in the late 1880s. Business still in existence in 1909, but no longer in reed organs.

Moore & Moore. 59-61 New Oxford Street, London. Founded in 1838 by two brothers, John and Henry Moore, the sons of a Chipstead schoolmaster, and originally in Bishopsgate Street (once the residence of Sir Thomas Gresham). Started business as cabinet makers in Finsbury but later moved to making pianos. Became renowned musical instrument makers; there were also music theoreticians in the family. Moore's son, Henry Keatley Moore, was born 15 August 1846 and joined the business in 1869. In 1911 he invented the Indian harmonium with twenty-two notes to the octave and said to be the only instrument capable of accurately reproducing the Indian scale. The first example was shown to the Maharajas of Gwalior and Baroda when they visited England, and they immediately placed orders to be sent out to India. (*Musical Opinion*, February 1913, p378). The business was re-styled Moore & Moore Pianos Ltd, and in 1925 directories address is given as 57 New Oxford Street. By 1929 the company had moved to Albion House, 233 Tottenham Court Road. In January 1936, *Musical Opinion* noted the death of Ernest James Moore at the age of eighty-two, saying:

> It is close on thirty years since Messrs. Moore & Moore left the premises in Bishopsgate Street, migrating further west to New Oxford Street. Mr. Ernest retired about twenty-four years ago leaving the business in the hands of Mr. H. Keatley Moore and his son, Harry, who so ably looks after the interests of the firm in its present home in Tottenham Court Road. Mr. Keatley Moore, who has reached an advanced age, is now living in retirement. We believe the late Mr. Ernest Moore was, with Mr. Peet, one of the founders and the first secretary of the Wholesale Musical Instrument Manufacturers and Dealers Association (later in part becoming the Pianoforte Manufacturers Association), and was also interested in the work of the Provincial Music Trades Association.

Henry Keatley Moore died on 11 August 1937, just four days short of his ninety-first year.

Morel, E. 51 rue Franklin, Lyon, France. A maker of harmoniums, fl.1930.

Morhange, A. 38 rue Vivienne, Paris, France. Makers of harmoniums, fl.1920.

Moutrie, G. 22 Werrington Street, Oakley Square, London. Of Huguenot origin, Moutrie advertised as maker of harmoniums in January 1866. 'Five octaves in polished case 5 guineas. Seven stops, 8 guineas. Ten stop, 15 guineas.' With Collard, formed Collard & Moutrie at 50-52 Southampton Street, London, which later developed the 'Moutrie' piano-player. Moutrie's son, William Robert, had a business under his own name at 2 Jackson Road, Holloway, north London, where he sold pianos and reed-organs, fl.1909.

Müller, Emil. Friedhofstr 40/42 Werdau, Saxony,

Germany. Established in 1887. Also made the 'Harmonista', a self-playing apparatus for harmoniums. By 1930 was operating at 25 Pestalozzistr., Werdau.

Müller, J. T. Barensteiner Str 5, Dresden, Germany. Established in 1890. Makers of harmoniums and chord zithers, fl.1909.

Müller, Théodore Achille. France. A one-time apprentice to Grenié (qv), Müller was to make several significant improvement to the *orgue expressif*.

Mundul & Co. 3 Bow Road, Bazar Street, Calcutta, India. Makers of harmoniums, fl.1930.

Munroe Organ Reed Co. Worcester, Massachusetts, USA. Established in 1860 by William Munroe of Cambridge, Massachusetts. The business was devoted to the manufacture of organ reeds and was incorporated in 1869 with premises at Hermon Street, Worcester. By 1879 it was at 25 Union Street. Manufactured organettes for McTammany and Merrit Gally among others. As early as 1881, annual production of reeds reached four million which represented almost one-third of the alomost 100,000 organs produced in America in that year. The company was amalgamated into the Aeolian business in 1892. William Munroe tried to expedite the manufacture of reeds by dispensing with the method of attaching the tongues to their frames with separate reeds. Instead, he punched up two cheeks from the frame heel and squeezed the tongue into place between them. This invention was covered by US Patent No 73,114 of 7 January 1868. However, it seems that the European style of rivetted reeds, such as made by makers such as Esteve, were more popular with reed organ builders. Also as:

Munroe Organ Reed Co. London depot at 38 Brooke Street, Holborn. Fl.1890. Suppliers of reeds, cavity boards and sundries to the reed organ trade. Subsequently handled by C. Erhardt & Co Ltd at 36 Southwark Bridge Road (established in 1870).

Murdoch & Co, J. G. 91-93 Farringdon Road, London. Harmoniums, and American organs. In 1888 held sole agency for E. P. Carpenter's Angelus organs. At the beginning of 1894, handled Carpenter's piano-cased instrument which, at 48 guineas, embodied unusual features. With 7¼ octaves and five sets of reeds which were controlled by just six stops, the walnut-cased instrument had nickel fittings and a three-compartment top door. Most novel, though, was that 'unlike most American organs, the more vigorously a performer pedals, the louder the tone becomes, - hence knee swells are dispensed with' (*Musical Opinion*, February 1894). In 1898, Murdoch advertised the full range of reed organs by Malcolm (qv) at prices from 8 gns upwards, and what it claimed to be 'the finest organs ever manufactured' - the Peloubet (qv) Reed-Pipe Organ from 100 gns to 500 gns. Later also handled the British-made Angelus instruments.

Murphy, William. St John, St John County, New Brunswick, Canada. Described as a dealer in pianos and organs, devised a mechanical octave coupler of simple design (British Patent No 2261 of 16 February 1886).

Mussillon, E. 61 rue Hermite, Nancy, France. Maker of harmoniums, fl.1920.

Mustel & Cie. 46 Rue de Douai, Paris 9e, France. Founded in 1855 (or 1853) by Victor Mustel, the true inventor of the American organ principle and applied to the Mustel reed organs described by its manufacturers as 'the finest reed organ in the world'. The factory was at 48 rue Pernety, Paris 14e. Mustel organs were first

ORGUE A DOUBLE EXPRESSION.

NOUVEAU SYSTÈME, B^te S G D C.

MUSTEL FACTEUR,

42 rue de Malte, 42.

PARIS.

Trade notice, c.1855-6

introduced to the British market by Archibald Ramsden (qv). The London office was Mustel & Co, 80 Wigmore Street. At the 1862 International Exhibition staged in London, C. V. Mustel showed an 'organ-harmonium'. Victor Mustel died in Paris on 16 March 1919 in his seventy-eighth year. Business continued by his son, Alphonse. When Alphonse died in 1936, a lengthy tribute in *Musical Opinion* for that December told much about the company:

A death to be noted with more than usual interest occurred recently when Alphonse Mustel passed away at Cannes-Ecluse. He came of the line of inventors who gave us the best in keyboard reed instruments. - the first Victor, then Auguste and Charles, and lastly Alphonse. While the whole line was musical, Alphonse was distinguished as a virtuoso on and composer for the instrument with which the name Mustel will ever be associated. He was a pupil of Guilmant: and he wrote charming works which employed to the full the features of the organ which his forebears had brought to perfection. ... Victor, the founder of the line of reed organ makers, began life in a shipyard at Le Havre, and chance having thrown in his way one of the crude early accordions (it must have been within a few years of their invention in 1829), he felt impelled to set about improvements. Afterwards he worked for a while in various harmonium factories in Paris; but seeing no scope for his inventive genius in working for other men, he started to make harmoniums on his own account, and then followed a series of inventions and improvements which made his name famous among musicians and music lovers. Indeed, his fame and that of his sons and grandson was such that rival makers (if any there were) were foremost in their praise for Mustel. Makers in the States who also produced reed organs of high quality, admitted their inability to approach the beauty of the reed voicing. Mustel organs are known to have been almost wholly hand-made, and consequently could never be said to have been a commercial proposition. However, in the 'eighties and 'nineties, when the fame of the Mustel was at its height and reed organ recitals frequent, the agents in London placed an open order with Paris to take all that could be sent.

Between 1854 and the mid-1880s, the output of harmoniums did not exceed fifteen a year. Output increased sharply after that and by the opening of the new century, factory production was extensive. King Hall says of Mustel's harmoniums 'for exquisite blowing, for perfection in mechanism and workmanship, and for beauty of *timbres* of the registers individually, are, without doubt, unequalled.' In the closing months of 1898, Mustel's London agents, Henry Klein, showed a Mustel organ at their address 84 Oxford Street, which 'cost 400 guineas' (*Musical Opinion*, January 1899). Later the company was listed as:

Mustel. 16 avenue de Wagram, Paris, France. Maker of harmoniums and celestas, fl. at this address by 1930 and still in business there today as a radio and hi-fi store.

Myers, John Frederick, and Joseph Storer. The business of Myers & Storer commenced in 1837 and two years later the two partners were granted British Patent No 8164 of 20 July 1839 for 'improvements in the construction of... seraphines and to certain descriptions of organs'. Illustrated in the *Repertory of Arts*, vol 16 (new series), p193. See also Joseph Storer; Day & Myers.

Nagy, Josef. Strada Sfintilor 42, Bucharest, Rumania. Established in 1867 for the manufacture of pianos and harmoniums.

Nederlandische Orgelfabriek 'Worcester Reed Organ Works'. 185 Arnhemsche Weg, Amersfoort, Holland. Makers of American organs and harmoniums, fl.1930.

Needham Piano & Organ Co. 41 West 25th Street, New York, USA. Also with factory at Washington, New Jersey. Established 1847 (possibly 1846). Manufacturers of pianos American organs and the Paragon piano-player and player piano. Run by Edmund G. Hartman. See also Daniel F. Beatty.

Neef, G. Feuerthalen, Schaffhausen, Switzerland. At the 1862 International Exhibition in London showed a church harmonium. No further reference.

Neiss. Schlesien, Viehweg Muhle 90, Germany. In 1886 advertised as a manufacturer of harmoniums using the brand-name 'Caecilian' and priced from 90 Mks with seven registers to 225 Mks.

Neugebauer Nachf, C. Bell & Co. 27 Andreasstr 32, Aufg 3, Berlin, Germany. By 1930 was at 22 Blucherstr, Berlin. Established in 1878 as a piano manufacturer and also as the German branch of the Bell Organ & Piano Co. Managed in 1909, by G. Bell, A. Mattutat. H. Seelig, F Neumann, P. Schutz and G. Voight. London agent was M. A. Witkowski [q.v.].

Neumeyer, Ernst. 36 Gorlitzer Üfer 22, Berlin, Germany. Manufacturer of pianos. In 1885 advertised the 'Cantus Trancendentalis', a keyed reed instrument 'on the harmonium principle, with a peculiar tone character, sustaining apparatus, and a vibrating and modulating contrivance' which was the invention of Karl Hahn who also designed a concertina along new but now forgotten principles.

Neusser, Johann. 60 Mühlgasse, Neutitschein, Czechoslovakia. In 1930 was described as a maker of harmoniums.

Neusser, Karl. Oberthorstr 62, Neutitschein (Mähren), Austro-Hungary. Organ and reed-organ builder founded in 1827; still listed in 1909 directories.

New England Organ Co. 1297-9 Washington Street (1871-80); 632 Harrison Street (1881); 57 Washington Street (1883), Boston, Massachusetts, USA. Makers of American organs founded in 1866 as the Boston Organ Co at 6 Avery Street, Boston. Acquired the Smith American Organ Co. No longer listed after 1903.

New Haven Organ Company. New Haven, Connecticut, USA. Originally the New Haven Melodeon Co, established before 1860. Later re-named to produce American organs; fl. with this name in 1883. Sole UK agents Thomas Dawkins & Co, 17 Charterhouse Street, Holborn Circus, London.

Newman Brothers Co. Chicago Avenue West and Dix Street, Chicago, Illinois, USA. Makers of American organs who, although little remembered today, were major producers in the 1880s and, by 1902, claimed a capacity of 4000 organs a year. Established in 1880 by John Newman whose family went to Chicago from Sweden when he was thirteen, c.1863. John, with his two brothers Gustave and Charles, began organ manufacturing in the old Burdett factory, then at Sedgwick Street. Continued until the great Chicago fire which destroyed the Burdett factory, after which they continued at Fort Wayne. John

Newman died from consumption at the age of forty-two in October 1894. Robert Cocks & Co of New Burlington Street advertised in 1894 as sole importers for Newman American organs. Later the firm was re-styled as:

Newman Brothers Organ Co. 806-826 Dix Street, Chicago, Illinois, USA. Makers of reed organs listed as fl.1930.

Nicholls & Co, E. 118 Mile End Road, London. Advertised in 1880 as 'manufacturers of Good Cheap Harmoniums'.

Nicole Frères. Ely Place, London. One-time famous Swiss makers of musical boxes. After this company sold out to London dealer Brun, the company also sold harmoniums; but it is likely that, as with its musical boxes in later years, these were manufactured for it and sold as stencil-brands.

Nihon Kakkiseizo Kabushiki Kaisha (Japan Musical Instrument Factory). Hamamatsu, Japan. Manufacturers of pianos and harmoniums, fl.1902-9.

Nippon Gakki Seize Kabushiki Kaisha. 250 Nakazawa, Hamamatsu, Japan. A maker of harmoniums and reed organs listed in 1930 directories.

Nishikawa Torakichi. Hindecho 2 chome Nr 30, Yokohama, Japan. Makers of harmoniums, fl.1902-9.

Norling, Aug. Tradgardsgatan 15, Råå, Sweden. Established in 1898 for the manufacture of organs, pianos and harmoniums. In 1930 directories, the address is given as 15 Tradgaardsg, Sala, Sweden.

Nyström, C. G. Spelmannsgatan 17, Kristinehamn, Sweden. Established in 1875 for the manufacture of harmoniums. Made self-playing instruments which used a perforated card disc. See also Kristinehams Orgelfabrik.

Nyströme Orgel-und Piano-Fabrik, Aktiebolaget. Karlstad, Sweden. Founded in 1865. Manufactured the Nyströms Pianoharpa barrel-operated table piano. Also made harmoniums and pianos.

Oeckelen, Cornelis Jacobus van. Born in Breda, North Brabant, Holland, on 26 June 1798, died in New York, USA, 20 February 1865. The son of a clockmaker, Cornelis first distinguished himself in music by making a mechanical piano which would play twelve tunes. Always living on the verge of poverty, he took his family to Boston, USA, in 1855 where he made a number of free-reed instruments starting with the melodium lap-organ, the triolodeon, the night-melodeon and a variety of others, some of which were the subject of US Patents.

Oettingen, Arthur von. Dorpat, Leipzig, Germany. 1836-1920. Professor of Physics who contrived a quarter-tone enharmonic harmonium haveing a compass of 57 notes, each octave being divided into 53 notes. Patented in 1914 and built by Schiedmayer of Stuttgart, it was called the Orthotonophonium.

Okenfuss, Anton. Triester Str 47, Vienna X, Austria. Organ and harmonium-builder, fl.1909.

Olbrei, J. Jurjewstr 461, Reval, Estonia. Reed organ maker established in 1890. By 1930 the addressed was 6 Suur Tariu M, Tallin, Estonia.

Ono Gakki-Ten. 1 Tokiwa-cho, Kyobashi-ku, Tokyo, Japan. Maker of harmoniums and reed organs listed in 1930 directories.

Oor, J. (George Oor, Successor). 30 rue d'Arenberg, Brussells, Belgium. Established in 1850 as makers of harmoniums, fl.1930

Orchestra Spol Sro. 26 Jungmannova tr, Prague, Czechoslovakia. Makers of harmoniums, fl.1930.

Orchestrelle Co. *see* Aeolian; George Whight & Co.

Orean y Cia. 40 Ponzano, Madrid, Spain. Makers of reed organs, fl.1930.

Orntlich, Hans. Poststr 8/9, Reval, Russia. Established in 1896 for the manufacture of pianos and harmoniums.

Országh & Sohn, Alexander. Rákospalota-Ujfalú, Austro-Hungary. Maker of harmoniums, founded in 1861; managed in 1909 by Emerich and Ladislaus Orszagh.

Oshawa Organ & Melodeon Manufacturing Co. *see* Dominion.

Östlind & Almquist, Aktiebolaget. Esplanadgatan 125/126, Arvika, Sweden. Established in 1888 for the manufacture of pianos and harmoniums, fl.1909. Branches in Stockholm, Malmö and Gothenburg.

Ott, M. Launtal 13, Giengen, Brenz, Germany. Maker of harmoniums, fl.1940.

Packard Organ Co. Fort Wayne, Indiana, USA. Founded by expert reed-organ builder Isaac T. Packard in 1871. The family were English emigrants; Samuel Packard left his Sussex home in 1638 for the New World. Isaac Packard was born in 1817; his brother Edmund two years later. The two began making melodeons with their cousin Caleb, as Packard Brothers (Co) before 1839. Edmund moved to Hingham in Massachusetts in 1862 and effectively left the organ-building scene; his brother Isaac excelled in the craft. He was granted numerous patents for improvements to the instrument and set up a business in Chicago as Packard, Keith & Talbot. He left at the time of the great fire there in 1871, went to Fort Wayne, Indiana, and interested a number of industrialists in forming a company. The first premises were at the junction of Fairfield and Organ Avenue, the latter later being renamed Kinsmoor Avenue. By 1872 the very first Packard organs were being manufactured. The 1891 Packard 'Grand' was a piano-cased model very similar to the Aeolian Orchestrelle Style V, but its stops were mounted in rows in the decorative side panels above and outside the keyboard cheeks. Devised and patented a special design of reed cell in which there were two interconnected cells, one above the other, for each reed and each row of cells provided with a separate mute. Organs built with this feature, including a range of chapel-style instruments, were called the 'Humanola', a name subsequently used by others for piano-players. See also Fort Wayne Organ Co. London agents in 1889 were Ellis

Parr & Co and E. Hirsch (qv).

Pagnoulle, A. 53 rue Gallait, Brussels, Belgium. Harmonium wholesaler, fl.1930.

Pajkr & Co, Rudolf. Neu-Königgrätzer Str, Königgrätz, Austro-Hungary. Established in 1894 for the manufacture of harmoniums and American organs (instruments operating on pressure and suction were advertised). The factory was at this address and there were branches in Budapest (VIII Jozsef korut 15) and Vienna (VII Mariahilferstr 86). The business was run by Rudolf Pajkr. By 1930, the business was both re-named and relocated as Pajkr A Spol, Rudolf, at Velké Nám, Hradec Kralové, Czechoslovakia, also as Rud. Pajkr & Vomp, 25 Delej ucca (X), Budapest, Hungary.

Palace Organs. Worcester, Massachusetts, USA. Manufactured by Whitney & Currier of Quincy, Illinois, USA. Business begun by August H. Whitney c.1855 and later as the A. H. Whitney Organ Co. His sons Frank and J. W. were also in business separately manufacturing reed organs well into the 1880s. On the cessation of that business, the name Palace was taken up by Loring & Blake (qv), also Taber (qv). In 1901 London agents were J. Perino, Great Russell Street.

Pandharpurkar Bros, A. M. Dandia Bazaar, Baroda, India. Makers of harmoniums, fl.1930.

Parr & Co, Ellis. 16 Long Lane, Aldersgate, London. Musical instrument agent, distributor, inventor and patentee. In autumn 1888 moved to 99 Oxford Street and 1 & 2 Great Chapel Street. In December 1890 advertised as distributors of the Packard organ (qv) 'the best reed instrument in the world'. See also Packard Organ Co; E. Hirsch & Co.

Patterson, James T. Bridgeport, Connecticut, USA. Maker of American organs who advertised in 1889 with the slogan 'Takes the lead'. Later reformed as the Bridgeport Organ Co. (qv).

Paul & Sons. 2 Lower Chitpore Road, Calcutta, India. Makers of harmoniums, fl.1930.

Pearson, John G. 203 Main Street, Worcester, Massachusetts, USA. Reed organ builder who was in business around 1865-8 and who advertised as maker of 'seraphines, melophines and Aeolians'. The references in contemporary literature to John G. Pierson is considered to be a mis-spelling, for evidence suggests that both were one and the same man. Also sometime as Pearson & Loring as successors to Farley & Pearson; later Loring & Blake (qv). See also John A. Farley.

Peaseley, Aaron Merrill. Boston, Massachusetts, USA. Early American maker of reed organs who was granted a US Patent on 11 November, 1818 for 'an improvement in organs' in which he describes: 'substituting in place of the pipes usually called reed pipes a plate of metal or any other fit substance in which a number of holes of proper form, in each of which is fitted a piece of brass or any other elastic substance capable of vibrating so as

to produce a tone.' Pecchioni, Redento: Sissa (Parma), Italy. Harmonium and reed organ maker, fl.1909.

Peloubet Organ Co. New York, USA; also 26 and 32 Worship Street, London. Makers of 'Standard' American organs who advertised as such in 1886. In 1890, the business was taken over by Lyon & Healy (qv) who continued to manufacture the Peloubet church organ for a while. This was one of the largest reed organs in the world and one model, a 3-manual and pedal instrument, featured 36 stops and 1,948 reeds. Michel lists 'Peloubet, Charvier' as being in New York about 1812, also Peloubet & Pelton Co of New York. An Alex Peloubet is also listed for 1812 at 222 Greenwich Street, New York.

Penso, Victor. 24-6 Duke Street, Brushfield Street, Bishopsgate, London. A brief note in *Musical Opinion* for January 1898, says that 'In consequence of increased business... has moved to more convenient and larger premises at... This information infers, we think, that this gentleman is appreciated by the retailers who buy his pianos, American organs, stools and music cabinets'. Advertised as a pianoforte and organ manufacturer in 1902, and his work for a while around this period.

Perl, Bernhard. Waldheimer Str, Hartha, Saxony, Germany. Established in 1882 as a maker of piano-stools who also produced harmoniums.

Peter, Andr. Mühlbach-bei-Eger, Dux, Bohemia, Austro-Hungary. Established in 1877. Maker of harmoniums and reed organs. Still operating in 1930.

Petersen & Steenstrup. Store Kirkestraede 1, Copenhagen, Denmark. Established in 1839. 'First maker of harmoniums in Denmark', gained silver medal at Malmö, Stockholm and Paris exhibitions. Importer of American organs by Estey, Carpenter, Needham, Packard and Vocalion. By 1930, still described as makers of harmoniums, but address given as 28, Bredgade, Copenhagen.

Petitqueux-Hillard. Domaine de Biscaye, Lourdes, France. Maker of harmoniums, fl.1930.

Petrelli, Giovanni. Talamona, Italy. Maker of harmoniums and reed organs listed in both 1909 and 1930 directories.

Petrof, Anton. Neu-Königgrätzer Str (zur Stadt Brünn), Königgrätz, Bohemia, Austro-Hungary. Established in 1864. Operated by Anton and Marie Petrof in 1909. Piano factory at Temesvar, Hungary.

Piatrasranta, Flli. 4 via Sarzanese, Lucca, Italy. Maker of harmoniums and reed organs listed in 1930 directories.

Pichler, Francis. 162 Great Portland Street, Oxford Street, London. In 1862 advertised: 'Harmoniums and Pedal Harmoniums. - Manufacturer, inventor, and maker of the Prize Medal Instrument of 1851; also of the Cottage Harmonium. Originator of the Round-end Sharps, so extensively used in Pianofortes and Harmoniums'. In January 1863, repeated the same notice, adding 'Manufacturer to the late W. Wheatstone'. Although the addresses are different as are the dates, there is the possibility that he may be tied up with Wedlake (qv) and if the name has been confused with the 'Pilcher' [sic] who is alleged to have built the harmonium which replaced the Bevington Apollonicon which for a short while performed in the Colosseum in Regent's Park and, if it is, whether the instrument was in truth made by Wedlake. See under Pilcher. See also in Ord-Hume: *Barrel-Organ*.

Piedmont Mfg Co. High Point, North Carolina, USA. Reed organ maker, fl.1930.

Pilcher, W. 19: Stockbridge Terrace, Pimlico, London. Barrel organ and harmonium maker who is quoted as

"Harper's Weekly", 24th November 1866

having manufactured a large instrument to replace the Bevington Apollonicon erected in the Colosseum in Regents Park. See also Pichler.

Pittaluga e Figli. 17r via Gioffredo Mameli, Sampierdarena, Italy. Maker of harmoniums and reed organs listed in 1930 directories.

Pizenhoffer, Alois. Deveeser, Austro-Hungary. Harmonium builder and repairer, fl.1909.

Poirot Frères. Mirecourt, Vosges, France. Makers of mechanical organs and harmoniums c.1850-75 as well as orchestrion and showground organs.

Polacek, Vaclav. Rusinova tr, Rychnov, Czechoslovakia. Founded in 1905 as maker of harmoniums, fl.1930.

Popper & Co, GmbH. 14 Bitterfelder Str, Leipzig, Germany. Makers of self-playing harmoniums and reed organs, fl.1930. Also made orchestrion organs and a variety of mechanical musical instruments.

Porre, Diego. 3 piazzetta San Giuseppe, Brescia, Italy. Maker of harmoniums and reed organs listed in 1903 and 1930 directories.

Praeger, F. W. 77 Brook Street, Chorlton-upon-Medlock, Manchester. Harmonium wholesaler, fl.1930.

Prescott, A. Concord, New Hampshire, USA. Abraham Prescott was a maker of bass-viols who began work in Deerfield, New Hampshire, in 1809. In 1831 he opened a small shop in Concord where he acquired a button melodeon and decided to improve upon it. In 1836 he began manufacture, and in the following year won a silver medal at a local trade fair. Although little more than a lap-organ with buttons instead of keys, it was a significant instrument in the early history of the reed organ in America. Eventually, his firm now called the Prescott Organ Co, many reed organs were produced. Around 1885 the company began making pianos as well, the Prescott Piano Co of 181 North Main Street, Concord, being founded in 1886. It finally ceased trading in 1912. Concord was an early centre of American reed-organ activity.

Prince & Co, George A. Buffalo, New York, USA; also premises in Chicago (fl.1866). George Prince, son of a sea captain, was born on 17 February 1818 in Boston. Began making melodeons around 1846, becoming the most important manufacturer of reed organs in the United States during the middle of the nineteenth century. He was granted an American patent on 28 December 1846 and in 1866 advertised as 'The oldest establishment in the United States. Manufactory, corner of Niagara and Maryland Streets, Buffalo, N.Y. Over 40,000 now in use. Geo. A. Prince & Co's Melodeons and Automatic Organs... We now manufacture over Forty Different Styles of the Melodeon, Organ Melodeon, School Organ, Automatic Organ, &c.' In one style, bellows operation was by means of 'stirrups' upon which the player placed his feet. The business was still functioning by 1870.

Prince & Bacon. Buffalo, New York, USA. The brother

of George Prince (qv), Samuel N. Prince, and Charles E. Bacon formed a partnership in 1879 for the manufacture of reed organs as successors to the earlier business

Pritchard, Isaac. Sherfield English, Romsey, Southampton. Described as a music tuner, was granted British Patent No 7865 of 17 May 1884 for a combined pianoforte and harmonium. The latter instrument was placed under the keyboard of the piano and was controlled by a separate pedal and an on-off cut-out stop. Pitmans passed down through the piano keybed so that the harmonium keys could be operated from the piano keyboard.

Proctor & Son, Willian Charles. Wilson Place, Town Street, Bramley, Leeds. Maker of harmoniums, fl.1930.

Pross, Gschwing & Co. Stuttgart, Germany. Established in 1858. Exhibited harmoniums at the 1862 London International Exhibition, including a 2-manual model with 5 octaves, two manuals and 15 stops (£70), and another with 5½ octaves and 10 stops for £20. The exhibit was awarded a medal. See also Gschwind & Co.

Punter & Co, John William. 2 Old Market Street, Staple Hill, Bristol. Established in 1878. Makers of pianos and reed organs, fl.1909.

Putnam & Co, W. W. (Putnam Organ Co). Staunton, Virginia, USA. William Wallace Putnam gained experience in reed-organ building with Estey, Bell and Clough & Warren before starting up on his own in 1894. Became one of the best-known organ builders in the States. When he died in 1918 at the age of fifty-eight, the business was carried on under the management of T. C. Good. Sole agents for Europe were R. M. Marples & Son, 153 Farringdon Road, London. In 1902 advertised a new model called 'The Virginia' made in black walnut or golden oak with or without dummy pipe front and to retail from £14. Agents Marples also handled Kimball organs. By 1913, Marples had handled Putnam instruments for eighteen years, no longer advertised Kimball and had moved to Gwydir Chambers, 104 High Holborn, London.

Racelina, J. rue Gallieni, Tananarive, Madagascar. Described as a maker of harmoniums, fl. 1930.

Radice e Figli. 3 via Manzoni, Seveso S. Pietro, Italy. Maker of harmoniums and reed organs listed in 1930 directories.

Raith, Gustav. Charlottenburg 5, Fritschestr 68, Berlin, Germany. Maker of harmoniums, fl.1940.

Rålins Orgel-och Pianofabrik, Aktb. A. G. Amål, Sweden. Makers of reed organs listed as operating c.1930.

Ramsden Ltd, Archibald. 12 Park Row, Leeds, Lancashire; later with a London branch at 103 New Bond Street; fl.1909. Established in 1860. Originally a reed organ maker, Archibald Ramsden later became a piano and reed organ factor. Was a noted performer on the harmonium who in later years became an important musical-instrument retailer. He was the first to introduce the Mustel organ into Britain. Collaborated with William Dawes (qv) in the perfection of Dawes' Melody Attachment for Harmoniums which was patented in 1864. He appeared at a command performance before Queen Victoria around the late 1860s playing a harmonium fitted with Dawes' attachment; so pleased was the queen she apparently purchased the instrument. A correspondent in *Musical Opinion* of February 1937 writes: 'For his association with the reed organ, Archibald Ramsden deserves to be remembered. From his great tenacity of purpose and his long-lived business at Leeds, one may assume that he was a Yorkshireman: but of his coming into or going out of the world nothing seems to have been recorded'.

Rand & Co, John. 24a Cardington Street, Hampstead Road, London. Fl.1848-55. Piano manufacturers who advertised as 'makers of the Aeolian Attachment', a reed organ which could be incorporated with a piano. This was an early example of this concept.

Raska, Ignatz. Stramberggasse 595, Freiburg, Ostsudetenland, Germany. Maker of harmoniums, fl.1940.

Raygaert Frères. 27 rue Adam, Grammont, Belgium. Makers of harmoniums, fl.1930.

Raynard, S. A. 35 calle Tallers, Barcelona, Spain. Maker of reed organs, fl.1930.

Rechnagel, Leo. Fredensborg, Denmark. Builder of harmoniums who was listed in 1930 directories.

Reed & Sons, J. W. Handel Works, 32 Hanover Street, Islington, London. Established in 1868 as makers of harmoniums. By 1890 also making pianos. By 1914 were at 2a Elfort Street, Drayton Park. Not listed by 1925.

Reich, H. Weissenburgerstr 29, Berlin, Germany. Harmonium maker, fl.1903.

Remek, Jan. 13 Smečky, Prague, Czechoslovakia. Described as a maker of harmoniums, fl.1930.

Renner, Joseph. Regensburg, Germany. Name found on instruments, but Renner was an agent and not a maker. In 1885 advertised that he handled 'American harmoniums' from 150 to 1000 Marks and handled Peloubet and Dominion organs. Unlisted 1903.

Renner, Wilhelm. Gartenstr 22, Ludwigsburg, Germany. A maker of harmoniums, fl.1940.

Restagno Cav, Vincenzo. 90c. Vittorio Emanuele, Turin, Italy. A maker of harmoniums and reed organs listed in 1930 directories.

Reusch, L. 16 Seelowerstr, Berlin, Germany. Makers of harmoniums and reed organs, fl.1930.

Reynold & Co, J. 11 Lindsay Street, Calcutta, India. Makers of harmoniums, fl.1930

Richard et Cie, J. Etrépagny, Eure, France. See also Roger Gaboriaud.

Richart, Heinrich. Berlin, Germany. Harmonium builder. Established in 1874, fl.1900, gone by 1909.

Richartz, Heinrich. Hauptstr 159, Kommern, Germany. Established in 1890 as harmonium maker. By

E.A.ROETHINGER
STRASBOURG

L'HARMONIUM
DE QUALITÉ

"Musique Adresses Universel", 1930

1930 was H. Richartz Nachfolger [Successor], 159 Kölner Strasse.

Risberg, F. Stampgatan 6, Gothenburg, Sweden. Established before 1883 as a harmonium builder. By 1909 the business was operated as Johannes Risberg.

Rissmann, C. C. 32 Stader Chausee, Hannover, Germany. A maker of harmoniums and reed organs; fl.1930.

Ritz & Co, Louis. Catherinenhof, Holzbrucke 7/11, Hamburg, Germany. Established in 1875. Makers of the Ritz and Kaim brand harmoniums.

Rivoreda, F. 6 bis via Vittozzi, Turin, Italy. A maker of harmoniums and reed organs listed in 1930 directories.

Roberts, A. G. Laxon Street, Long Lane, Borough, London. Maker of harmoniums who advertised in 1880: 'Pedal Harmoniums, with one, two, or three Manuals, of any description and size, to order. - Bellows, Pans, and other Fittings supplied. - Established 1848.'

Robinson, Joseph. 28 Oxford Street, Swansea, Glamorgan, Wales. An inventor who was granted several British Patents for developments and improvements in combined pianos and reed organs, the first being No 2449 of 14 June 1876. The prime patent was No 2907 of 17 July 1879 for such a combination, which could be played as a unison instrument or as two solo instruments. It was employed by Ivory (qv). See Linard, Spence and Whomes for similar devices.

Rodeheaver Co, The. 218 South Wabash Avenue, Chicago, Illinois, USA. Maker of folding harmoniums, fl.1930.

Rodolphe, A. Paris, France. At the 1862 International Exhibition staged in London, showed an 'organ-harmonium'. See also:

Rodolphe Fils & Debain, Maison. Rue Chaligny 15, Paris 15, France. Makers of harmoniums, fl.1909 and described as 'Successors to Rodolphe Fils'. Established in

1848. See also Debain and Christophe & Étienne.

Roethinger, E.-A. 44 rue Jacques-Kable, Strasbourg, France. Maker of harmoniums, fl.1930.

Rossberg, Carl. 11 Neue Gasse, Dresden, Germany. A maker of harmoniums. May be the same as:

Rossber, C. Aug. Ziegelstr 2, Dresden, Germany. Harmonium maker; fl.1909. Unlisted in 1920.

Rothe & Schönbrodt (Roth & Schvenbrodt). Wolfgang 14, Eisenach, Germany. Established in 1895. Harmonium builders; fl.1909.

Rousseau, Alexandre. see Gilbert.

Roylance, Charles. 122a Drummond Street, London. A repairer of melodeons and harmoniums who went on to build and repair concertinas. In 1904 he was also advertising tuition classes for the concertina. By 1914 the business was styled C. & S. Roylance, 88 Seymour Street, London, NW.

Ruche & Fils, J. 19 rue Claudius-Pernet, Lyon-Montchat, France. Maker of harmoniums, fl.1930.

Rudert, G. Gross-Zschocker, Schleussiger Weg, Leipzig, Germany. Established in 1898 for the making of harmoniums and small organs. Run by Gustav Rudert in 1903. Not listed 1909.

Rushworth & Dreaper Ltd. see Apollo Reed Organ Works; John Holt.

Rutt & Cowing. London makers of reed organs 'suitable for congregational use' (c.1900). By 1909, Robert Spurden Rutt 'late of Rutt & Cowing' was in business on his own as a church organ builder at King Edward Road, Leyton, East London. Shortly after this, Rutt became a 'company' and, by 1914, was at Cedars Terrace, Leyton. Became a significant builder of church pipe organs. It seems that the cessation of business partnership with Bertram Cowing as Rutt & Cowing marked the end of the making of reed organs. (See *The Organ*, April, 1903.)

Ryrfeldt, C. J. Mellerud, Sweden. A maker of harmoniums and reed organs listed in 1930 directories.

Sakai Gakki-Ten. 6 Monzen-cho, Nakaku, Nagoya, Japan. Maker of harmoniums and reed organs listed in 1930 directories.

Saks, I. 2 I. Toe tan, Parnu, Estonia. A maker of reed organs, fl. 1930.

Sames Ltd, William. Mozart Works, Balsall Heath, Birmingham with showrooms at 8 Corporation Street. Established in 1855. Makers of pianos and American organs. Was originally styled J. Sames & Sons (c.1883). The founder was 'J' and the sons were William and Matthew. April 1884 a news item in *Musical Opinion* read: 'The partnership hitherto consisting between Messrs. William and Matthew Sames, in the business of harmonium and organ makers at Birmingham, has been dissolved by mutual consent. Mr. William Sames continues the business and will receive and pay all accounts'.

Samuel Barnett & Sons Ltd. 32/36 Worship Street,

171

London (factory at 127/135 Shepperton Road). Also styled as Barnett Samuel. Described as makers of harmoniums but also as agents for the Cable Organ Co. of Chicago.

Sato & Co, T. 360 Shimoyamate 7-chome, Kobe, Japan. Maker of harmoniums and reed organs listed in 1930 directories.

Sawyer, J. W. Beeston Organ Works, 21, Barton View, Beeston Hill, Leeds. Established in 1885 by John William Sawyer who built his factory in 1899. A most talented reed-organ maker and voicer who built 2-and 3-manual and pedal practice reed organs to a very high standard. His work, along with that of John Holt (qv), Spencer (qv) and Rushworth & Dreaper's Apollo (qv), stands supreme in the realm of the British reed organ. In 1905, advertised:

> The Ideal Organ: Have you seen or heard one of these beautiful instruments? If not, in order to save yourself lasting disappointment, you should enquire, and do so if you have any intention of purchasing an Organ. They are built on the model of an up-to-date Pipe Organ; are so far away in advance of any Reed Organ ever made in solid organ-like tone, thoroughness of workmanship throughout, usefulness and real practicability. The tone and variety of the larger instruments are astonishing, and the likeness to Pipe Organ effects simple startling.

In *Musical Opinion* in 1919, he was described as 'the late J. W. Sawyer' in a letter describing a 2-manual and pedal reed instrument he had built. A letter of similar date refers to his having built a 4-manual instrument with 'some seventy registers, pneumatic action and several wind pressures.' The business was still functioning in 1935 as J. W. Sawyer & Co.

Schaeffer, C. 397 Kingsland Road, London, NE. A notice in *Musical Opinion* for January 1899 refers to this man as a 'reed organ maker' and says that he has just moved to larger premises at this address. No further reference traced. See reference for Shaeffer.

Schaeufele, Ferd. 3 Weberstr, Esslingen, Germany. Makers of harmoniums and reed organs, fl.1930.

Scherzer, A. Solmsstr 10, Berlin, Germany. Maker of harmoniums, fl.1909.

Scheytt, C. G. Stuttgart, Germany. Fl.1900 as harmonium-builder. No further details.

Schiedmayer, J. & P. Neckarstr 12a and 12b, and Ulrichstr 1, 3 and 5, Stuttgart, Germany. Established in 1853. By 1897 restyled as Schiedmayer Pianofortefabrik. Manufacturers of harmoniums and American organs ('Druck-u. Saug-system') who exhibited at the 1862 London International Exhibition a whole range of instruments, including a 3-stop pipe-organ in a table and a number of harmoniums. Awarded the major medal at the 1854 Munich exhibition, and a bronze medal at the 1855 Paris Exposition. Produced the 'Hlaváč Konzert Harmonium' in 1897 which had $8\frac{1}{2}$ sets of reeds, 31

registers, percussion and 2 knee swells. Berlin agents were dealers and music publishers Carl Simon of Markgrafenstr 21. The factory survived World War II but while the business still operates today, the Neckarstrasse premises were derelict for many years. Author has a picture of the old buildings, taken from across the motorway which now cuts off the site, immediately prior to their demolition c.1981.

Schiedmayer & Soehne. Stuttgart, Germany. Factories at Neckarstr 14 and 16, also Urbanstr 27. Established in 1809 by Adolf and Hermann Schiedmayer. Appears to have operated with J. & P. Schiedmayer (qv), yet retained independence. Also exhibited at the 1862 London exhibition where they showed only pianos.

Schlimbach, Caspar. Königshofen, Germany. Born Bavaria 30 July 1777; died Königshofen 21 May 1861. Worked with Eisenbach, inventor of the Aeoline, one of the precursors of the harmonium (see reference in text). Maker of pianos and harmoniums who produced a number of combined instruments. One is preserved in the Deutsches Museum, Munich, and another, giraffe pattern, in the Germanisches Museum, Nuremberg.

Schlosser, Ludwig. Nieder-Ohmen, Hessen, Germany. Makers of harmoniums and reed organs, established in 1926; fl.1930.

Schmidt, W. Wettinstr 2, Borna, Leipzig, Germany. Maker of harmoniums, fl.1940.

Schóier, L. C. Nörregade 37, Odense, Denmark. Established in 1904 as manufacturer and restorer of harmoniums.

Schone & Bocchese. 13 p. Aspromonte, Milan, Italy. Harmonium and reed organ makers listed in 1930 directories.

Schulz, Gustav. Wiesenstr 9b, Frankfurt, Germany. Founded in 1898 as a harmonium and organ-builder. Still in business in 1930.

Schwab, Joseph. Gololoboka, Russia. Established in 1888 as a church organ and harmonium builder.

Schwabe & Ritter. 23 Spiegelstr, Zwickau, Germany. Makers of harmoniums and reed organs, fl.1930.

Schwarz, F. W. Überlingen, Germany. Makers of harmoniums and reed organs, fl.1930.

Schwarze, Ludwig. Anholt, Westfalia, Germany. Established in 1840. Maker of harmoniums, fl.1909.

Schwarzkopf, Carl. Ilshofen, Württemberg, Germany. Makers of harmoniums and reed organs, fl.1930. Possibly the same as:

Schwarzkopf, Karl. Friedrich-Hermann-Str 4, Metzingen, Württemberg, Germany. Maker of harmoniums, fl.1940.

Schwenkedel, Georg. 1 chemin du Cuivre, Strasbourg-Königshoffen, France. Maker of harmoniums, fl.1930.

Shaeffer, C. 27 Baxter Road, Essex Road, London. Advertised in May, 1898 as: 'American Organ & Portable Harmoniums - for cheap, reliable instruments, try C.

Shaeffer, Manufacturer'. Was this a mis-spelling of Schaeffer (qv)?

Shaw, M. L. 5/1 Dharamtala Street, Calcutta, India. Makers of harmoniums, fl.1930.

Sherlock-Manning Organ Co Ltd. London, Ontario, Canada. Founded in London, Ontario, 1902, by two former employees of William Doherty & Co, John F. Sherlock and Wilbur N. Manning. In 1920, acquired the assets of Doherty & Co (qv) upon the death of William Doherty and opened a branch factory in the old Doherty factory at Clinton, Ontario. By 1930 also operated a branch in Winnipeg, Manitoba.

Shinkichi Matsumoto. Tsukiji, Tokyo, Japan. Harmonium manufacturers in business in 1902 but unlisted in 1909.

Shipman & Shipman. Poynings Road, Junction Road, Kentish Town, London N. Established in 1877 as makers of harmoniums. By 1890 was also making pianos.

Shoninger Organ Co, B. New Haven, Connecticut, USA. Bernhardt Schoninger was born in Germany in 1828; went to America in 1841 where he Americanised his name and began making small melodeons in Woodbridge, Connecticut around 1850. He then moved to New Haven and in 1863 built a workshop at Kimberley Avenue. Two years later it burned down. His son, Simon B. Shoninger, acquired the business of Treat & Lindsley (see Whitaker & Frisbie).

Silberhorn, Ernst. Karlsvorstadt, Böblinger Str 197, Stuttgart, Germany. Established in 1877 for the manufacture of harmoniums, but by 1903 was concentrating on reed organ components and reeds in particular. Also made reeds for pipe-organ builders. Still in business in 1927.

Sindel, Heinrich. Krailsheim, Württemberg, Germany. Harmonium manufacturer founded in 1873; fl.1909.

Singer Organ Co. Chicago, Illinois, USA. A major producer of American organs in 1887. Later became the Singer Piano Co at 235 Wabash Avenue.

Singer, P. Peter. Salzburg, Austria. Inventor who, in 1839, demonstrated a new free-reed instrument called the Pansymphonikon or Polyharmonium.

Skandinavsko Orgel-och Pianofabriken, Aktb. 41, Mastersamuelsg, Stockholm, Sweden. Maker of harmoniums and reed organs listed in 1930 directories.

Slootmaekers Frères. 153 rue Masui, Schaerbeek, Brussels, Belgium. Established in 1905 as manufacturer of pianos and harmoniums. Still in business in 1930.

Smith American Organ Co. 531 Tremont Street, Boston, Massachusetts, USA. Branches at 817 Main Street, Kansas City, and 59 Holborn Viaduct, London. Established in 1852. Produced 112,000 instruments by 1885 at prices ranging from $50 to $1000. A wide range of F compass American organs one continuously stressed feature of which was their power. Makers of the 'Connoisseur' series of reed organs 'specially made for professional musicians' introduced around 1882 and said to be the the subject of 'no less than Seven Patents'. The makers stated that 'the mechanism of this instrument is very elaborate... There is probably no piano-forte in existence whose interior works cost so much as the works of the Connoisseur.' One novel feature of this instrument was that its reeds were mounted vertically instead of horizontally, a system said to have allowed more scope for orchestral effects. 'The... bellows are upright, and a sounding board extends from the foot to the top of the case, and upon this... the reeds are so placed that they are over and above the keyboard and directly in front of the player. This position... gives to their vibrations a deep, distinct, and almost startling resonance; the tone obtained being the maximum ever produced from reeds.' This principle was approached by other makers at a later date, most devising their own styles to get round the Smith patent. Was said to have been the first American organ imported into Britain. In November, 1880, the company advertised temporary UK offices at Sterndale House, Vere Road, Brighton, Sussex. Later (1884) the Smith American Organ Co was formed as a subsidiary business at 157 New Bond Street, London. From this address exhibited Smith American organs and Chickering pianos at the International Exhibition, Crystal Palace, in April, 1884. Subsequently opened retail showroom at 59 Holborn Viaduct but, by the summer of 1887, had decided to abandon the retail trade and concentrate its efforts in wholesaling from a West End warehouse. By 1899, was known as the Smith American Organ Co (Henry Hannington) of 84 Oxford Street, London. See separate entry under Henry Hannington. By 1914, the agency for Smith organs was held by Albert Hannington & Co of 39 East Street, Manchester Square, the business run by Henry Hannington's brother and sister. See also New England Organ Co.

Smith & Co, Edwin. 53 Darwen Street (factory at Mount Street), Blackburn, Lancashire. Established in 1879. Described as organ-builders, a major line in 1909 was organ blowers. In 1902, advertised as agents for Weaver Organ & Piano Co's (qv) American organs.

Smith Freeborn Co. Derby, Connecticut, USA. In business as piano and organ makers to c.1901, not in directories after 1908.

Smith, Hermann. 29 Shaftesbury Road, Hammersmith, Middlesex. The true inventor of the Vocalion organ (see Baillie-Hamilton). In addition he made various improvements to the harmonium including the design of a bellows and reservoir which was placed along the width of the instrument and hinged along the lower edge, so that it operated vertically very much like that of the American organ. He also devised keyboard and reed-chamber modifications which were covered by British Patent No 10,795 of 24 August, 1886.

Smith, James Henry. Granted British Patent No 1783

of 6 July 1865 for 'improvements to harmoniums', one aspect of this convoluted specification being 'the provision of separate feeder bellows and reservoir' [sic] to each register of reeds or bank of vibrators. Believed associated with:

Smith & Smith. 1 Chapel Mews, Chapel Street, Somers Town, London. Harmonium makers. Advertised in 1880 as 'from Cramer and Wood, American organ makers to the Trade; Bellows supplied to the Trade'.

Smyth, Ralph. Hampton Court, Middlesex. A retired Lieut.-Colonel of HM Indian Army who invented features for the reed organ. Granted British Patent No 541 of 25 February 1865 for 'improvements to organs and harmoniums', one aspect of which was the provision of so-called 'knee-action pedal boards' to enable the performer 'to sound the notes of the lower or bass octave independent of the action of his hands'. This appears to have been a form of coupler, selected initially by the drawing of a stop-knob and then brought in at will by a knee-board. Also Patent No 1895 of 20 July 1865.

Snell, Robert. Ball's Pond, London. At the Great Exhibition of 1851, exhibited a 'Seraphine, with bichromatic or double scale of notes, producing perfect harmony in every key, without the aid of temperament; the improvement effected by an octave of pedals, one being put down, corrects to scale for the key required'. Probably the father of:

Snell Brothers. 402a Essex Road, Balls Pond, north London. Established in 1864 as harmonium-makers. In 1864 advertised 'E. and W. Snell's Drawing-Room Harmonium... for sweetness of tone, rapidity of articulation, and general excellence'. Five octaves 3 stops cost 8 gns,; the School Model with 5 octaves was 5 gns. Address at this time was 19 Church Terrace, Kentish Town Road, and King Street North, Camden Town. By 1884 was styled Snell & Co (E & W Snell). In January that year, the business moved from King Street North, to 'more eligible and commodious premises' at 3, Colonnade Buildings, Holloway Road, London. In 1861 claimed to have invented the 'tirasse-tenuto' or Pedal Substitute stop for reed organs. This appears to have worked in the same way as the Mustel 'prolongment' stop which holds down any note in the lower octave until another is touched, and so on. At the end of 1895, Harry Snell took additional premises close by at 97 Duncombe Road, Upper Holloway, where he began making pianos in addition to reed organs. This appears to have been either a third brother or other relative since his year of establishment actually predates that of E. & W. Snell. At the end of 1901, Harry Snell moved again, this time to the 'Alberg' Piano Works, 7a Andrews Road, Mare, Street, Hackney. In January 1898, *Musical Opinion* carried an advertisement saying: 'Ed. Snell & Co. (late of Bayswater), makers of the 'Lieblich' and 'College' Pedal Reed Organs. As built for many of the leading Organists and Professors

throughout the Country. C.O. Scales. Perfect Home Practice. Wonderful Value. 54, Essex Road, Islington, London, N.' This is certainly the same company: the foundation date is shown as 1864. The same periodical stated in October 1898 that:

Messrs. Ed. Snell & Co. have removed to 383, Hornsey Road, at which place - trading under the new title of Snell Brothers - they intend to devote themselves more to the trade, and will be ready to build instruments to suit the needs of trade customers. The firm have lately made a special feature of three manual organs, to the construction of which they have given great attention. We know that their work is first class, and they tell us that 'the price is right'.

By 1902, the address was Nightingale Works, Hornsey Road. In summer 1904, Snell Brothers moved again, this time to 100 Blackstock Road, Finsbury Park. A correspondent in *Musical Opinion* writing in October 1935 commented:

E. & W. Snell [were] both men of high aims and making their 'box of tricks' in Little King Street North: at least that is what an acquaintance of mine dubbed the Snell organ, owing to an alleged lack of order in its arrangements. These two men continued to make reed organs and harmoniums in various parts of North London, but they seem to have had a hand-to-mouth existence.

Another writer in the same paper for June 1937 said: "I bought the last instrument they said they would ever make. That was, I believe, in 1907, and they were both then very old men. The instrument [has] a fine pipe-like tone, rapid action... two manuals and pedals..."

Sociedad Franco-Hispano-Americana Para la Construccion de Pianos y Armoniums. 31 Canuda, Barcelona, Spain. Makers of reed organs, fl.1930.

Socin, Fidel. Kaiserin-Elisabeth-str. 10 and 10a, Bozen, Tirol, Hungary. Established in 1870 as makers of accordeons, concertinas, bandoneons, and harmoniums. Managed in 1909 by Rudiger Socin. May be the same as:

Socin, Fidel. 10 via Regina Elena, Bolzano Novarese, Italy. Maker of harmoniums and reed organs listed in 1930 directories.

Solomon & Co, H. Houndsditch, London. Sole agents in Britain for Busson's harmoniflutes and flautinas, also harmoniums of Christophe & Etienne and Cesarini. Fl. second half of the nineteenth century.

Sora & Figlio, Giovanni. Mondolfo, Italy. Makers of harmoniums listed in 1909.

Sora, Don Cesare. Quinzano d'Oglio, Italy. Organ and harmonium-builder, fl.1909.

Sotyga. 17 Gliwicka, Katowice, Poland. Maker of harmoniums and Amercian organs, fl.1930.

Soubeiran, J. 5 rue Grignan, Marseille, France.

Manufacturer of harmoniums, fl.1920.

Spaeth, Gebr. Ennetach-Mengen, Germany. Makers of harmoniums and reed organs, fl.1930.

Spaethe, Wilhelm. Gera, Reuss, Germany. Established in 1859 as makers of pianos and reed organs. London office at 7, Victoria Avenue, Bishopsgate Street Without, London, EC.

Spang, Xavier. Syracuse, New York, USA. Early maker of melodeons in. Of German extraction, he was in business at 15 North Salina Street in 1852, then at no 245. In 1860, his workshop was at numbers 64 and 66 where he produced some forty different styles. In 1881 formed partnership as Spang & Mertens but this dissolved by 1886 when the address was 2-4 Noxon Street. On 9 November 1871 was badly injured when an organ fell on him. His son and partner, Rupert, died in 1915 at the age of seventy-eight.

Spence & Co. 219 Hyde Road, Manchester. Reed organ makers and importers. Appears to have been founded c.1914, but not to have survived World War I. The name is linked with the Annexe combined organ and piano, but it is uncertain whether Spence manufactured this or imported it.

Spencer, Arthur J. 96 Upper Brook Street, Chorlton-upon-Medlock, Manchester. Makers of the University reed organ with two and three manuals plus pedals. Appears to have begun business c.1914. Walter G. Spencer died in April of 1934 aged seventy-seven having developed a high reputation for the manufacture of quality reed organs at moderate price for which he had established a strong home and export market. After his death the business was continued by Charles F. Spencer,

Sprague, William. 7 Finsbury Pavement and 20 Little Moorfields, London. Sprague set up in business in 1847 making pianos and seraphines. In 1881 the business was at 87 Finsbury Pavement, but ceased in 1883, presumably on his death. An early and distinguished maker of reed organs in London.

Springfield Organ Co. Chicago, Illinois, USA. Makers of reed organs, fl.1902, not listed 1909. See also Hirsch & Co.

Stagg & Sons, James G. 56 Red Lion Street, Holborn, London. The business was established in 1867, and up to World War I the business operated as a major retailer of cheap, secondhand and surplus stocks of pianos, harmoniums and reed organs of all types. The business survived into the immediate post war years as a wholesaler and retailer, fl.1919.

Star Parlor Organ Co. Railroad Avenue, Washington, New Jersey, USA. Founded in 1969 for the manufacture of cheap American organs. Shared premises with Beatty (qv). Appears to have ceased trading c.1881.

Stather, Robert. 187 Seven Sisters Road, Finsbury Park, London. Established in 1870 as harmonium-maker and maker of American organs. By 1883 his address was 202 Liverpool Road, London. On one instrument formerly in Crockston Methodist Chapel, Bedford, a patent date of 1885 was found on the vox-humana together with the number 15042. This patent has not been discovered: if it is that of a British patent, it is one of a small batch which are listed as 'abandoned' by the Registrar of Patents in London. It might be an invention not by Stather but one for the use of which he paid for the rights such as an American invention. On the other hand, the number, which might not be that of a patent, may be just an instrument serial number. By 1914, Stather was making pianos and repairing reed organs, and in later years reverted to being a piano and organ dealer. In autumn 1932, he celebrated his ninetieth birthday and *Musical Opinion* of December that year referred to him as 'the oldest piano dealer in the British Isles'.

Steinmann & Vierdag (Firma). 79 Brinkstr, Enschede, Holland. Maker of harmoniums who was in business c.1921-30.

Steinmeyer & Co. Leipzig, Germany. Established in 1848; fl.1900, gone by 1909. This name is often found on cheap pianos whose sellers wish them to appear of expensive pedigree. Originally the name of a reed-organ maker, it was maliciously applied for many years afterwards as a means of enhancing the apparent worth of instruments. But see:

Steinmeyer & Co, G. F. Öettingen, Germany. Makers of harmoniums and reed organs, fl.1930. By 1940 was listed as:

Steinmeyer & Co, G. F. (Steinmeyer & Strebell). see Steinmeyer & Co.

Steirer GmbH, Franz. 3 Ühlandstr, Besigheim, Württemberg, Germany. Makers of harmoniums and reed organs, fl.1930. By 1940 was at Industriestr 11, Bieticheim, Württemberg.

Sterling Organ Co. Derby, Connecticut, USA. Established in 1860. Makers of reed organs.

Stevens, F. C. 7 Green Street, north London. Mid nineteenth-century harmonium-builder. Little known of his product, nor of his possible relationship with:

Stevens, R. F. 82a Leighton Road, Kentish Town, London. Established in 1869. Maker of harmoniums. In 1914 advertised as harmonium and organ maker, transposers, also bellows and pan maker. By 1929, address listed as 84a Leighton Road. A prolific maker of instruments in a wide variety of sizes and styles. *Musical Opinion* for May 1905 reported:

> The other evening Mr. R. F. Stevens showed us a couple of small five octave harmoniums for use in conjunction with pianos. The little instrument is placed under the fall of the pianoforte; and the pianist is free to utilise his pedals inasmuch as the small reed instrument is not placed too near them. The scale is C to C [sic] and there is an expression stop.

Stevens & Klock Organ Co. Marietta, Ohio, USA. Fl.1885 with this name. In 1892 was restructured as the Stevens Piano & Organ Co. Reed-organ makers.

Stock, Karl. 2 Herlossohnstr, Leipzig, Germany. Originally Edouard Hüttner (qv). A maker of cabinets for harmoniums who also made instruments and was listed as a maker in 1924-30 directories.

Stoltz, Eugene. 79 avenue de Breteuil, Paris 15e, France. Established in 1846 as a harmonium-maker. Still in business 1909.

Storer, Joseph. Stanhope Street, Mornington Crescent, London. Described as a maker of pianofortes at this address in 1846, he was also an early manufacturer of reed organs. Together with John Frederick Myers (qv), he was granted a patent (No 8164 of 20 July 1839) for improvements to the seraphine and, this time on his own, as No 11,261 of 27 June 1846. This marked him as an early patentee of a percussion action for harmoniums and included a transposition device whereby the keyboard could be shifted. Soon after this he moved to 26 Piccadilly,

London, and was at this address by the time of the Great Exhibition of 1851. Here he exhibited a 'percussion Aeolophon, with two sets of vibrators, one an octave higher than the other, with appropriate stops, intended as an economical substitute for an organ'. Storer described himself as 'patentee and manufacturer'.

Story & Clark Organ Co. 16th and Canal Street, Chicago, Illinois, USA. Makers of American organs who gained a 'first award' at the Chicago Exhibition of 1893 for organs. Business begun by Hampton L. Story born in Cambridge, Vermont, 17 July 1835. He took employment in a local music store but decided to form a piano-making business. With a partner named Powers, he began manufacturing the Story & Powers piano in 1862. This, observes Alfred Dolge, was probably the first piano factory in the State of Vermont. Although the business prospered, the field was too limited and when Jacob Estey of Estey Organ Co (qv) offered him the agency for Estey organs in the western states, Story shut down his Burlington, Vermont, business and established himself in Chicago. In 1868 he formed a partnership with Isaac N. Camp as Story & Camp, soon to become a major force in the piano and organ trade with premises in both Chicago and St Louis and controlling a large retail and wholesale trade throughout the entire West. He could, however, foresee the time when the West would be manufacturing its own instruments, and so he retired from Story & Camp and in 1884, along with his son Edward H. Story and Melville Clark, formed Story & Clark. The business, says Dolge, was a success from the start, and in 1888 the Story & Clark Organ Co was incorporated with E. H. Story, son of the founder, as president and Melville Clark vice-president. A factory was built in London in 1892, under the management of Charles Wagener, and the following year another in Berlin. Melville Clark left the business to form his own company as the Melville Clark Piano Co in 1900. (See also under Clark). The factory and warerooms in London were at 62-64 Tabernacle Street, but proved to be short-lived, for this was one of the many buildings totally destroyed in the giant Tabernacle Street fire on 21 June 1894. Temporary premises were obtained at 53 City Road, Finsbury, until the offices and warerooms could be re-established (as the Apollo Co) at 233 Tottenham Court Road by Oxford Street. In 1898 advertised as Story & Clark and F. Kaim & Sohn Piano and Organ Co Ltd at 67 Berners Street, Oxford Street, W. 'We are the largest combination of Manufacturers in existence, thereby saving 25 per cent. working expenses'. See also Clark. Straube's Harmoniumbau-anstalt: Schönebergerstr 27, Berlin, Germany. Established in 1869. In 1903 business run by Johannes and Karl Straube. By 1930 address was Garbenteicherstr 15, Lich, Oberhessen, Germany. Harmonium maker, fl.1940.

Sulzer, Leopold. Rötestr 65, Stuttgart, Germany.

R. F. STEVENS,

American Organ & Harmonium Manufacturer,

82a, LEIGHTON ROAD,
KENTISH TOWN, LONDON, N.W.

This Instrument can be fitted with Octave Coupler if desired at an extra cost of 2 Guineas.

CLASS 4.

HARMONIUM.

Contains 1 Set of Reeds, 5 Octaves, and 1 Set 3 Octaves. Eight Stops. Wind Indicator and Pinned Keys.

Especially manufactured for extreme climates, with Lock-up for Pedals, Solid Oak Case, Polished Dark, Brass Bound, Wood and Zinc Bottom, Solid Panel Back.

Length, 3 ft. 7 in.   Height, 2 ft. 10 in.   Depth, 1 ft. 5 in.

Price   -   -   £19.

PLAINER MODEL in Solid Oak Case, 1½ Sets of Reeds, 3 Stops.

Price   -   -   £14   14   0.

Trade leaflet, c.1920-30 (courtesy of the Fluke Collection)

Described as a maker of harmoniums, fl.1909.

Sundqvist, K. F. Sköfde, Sweden. Harmonium-builder, fl.1909.

Sundqvist & Co, Leon. Jacobsgatan 21, Örebo, Sweden. Makers of reed organs, fl.1905

Svensson, Alfred. 12 Lastmakaregatan, Stockholm, Sweden in 1890s, and by 1909 at Mäster Samuelsgatan 40, Stockholm. Established in 1894 as maker of reed organs.

Swamy & Son, C. S. N. *see* City Harmonium Works.

Taber Organ Co. Worcester, Massachusetts, USA. Former Loring & Blake (qv) employee William B. Taber took over the first Worcester Organ Co (qv) and renamed it c.1877. Manufactured American organs with the brand name Palace. Unlisted in 1903.

Tamplin, Augustus Lechmore. English professor of music. Inventor (but not patentee) of double-touch key action for the organ and harmonium c.1859. His invention was taken up by Evans (qv) on the harmoniums built under Evans' supervision by Boosey & Co. Tamplin was organist of St. James's Marylebone and died in 1889 (his obituary appears in *The Musical Times* for June, 1889). Organ-builder Henry Wedlake of Regent Park, London, knew both A. L. Tamplin and his father, 'the celebrated Dr. Tamplin'.

Tannhäuser Sächsisches Harmonium-werkstatten. Rittersgrün, Germany. Makers of harmoniums and reed organs, fl.1930.

Tansain Harmonium Works, The. Gujranwala, Punjab, India. Makers of harmoniums, fl.1930.

Taylor, G. 39 Leroy Street, Old Kent Road, London. Portable reed organs and attachments for piano and reed organs (1914). Business not listed by 1925. Possibly the same as the Taylor of Leicester mentioned in 1889 as being the inventor of a student's organ which took up less space that a piano.

Taylor & Co, W. H. 51 Mattison Road, Harringay, London. Agents and importers who, in November, 1905, advertised as distributors for 'Lee Organs, Boston, U.S.A.' No further details.

Taylor & Farley. Hermon Street, Worcester, Massachusetts, USA. The Taylor name is one of the earliest - also most prolific - in the annals of the American reed organ. At least seven makers with this name are known from as early as 1821 through to the last decade of the nineteenth century. The brothers Abraham and George were engaged in making melodeons and cabinet organs in 1829; other names are James B.; P. H.; C. R. Taylor & Co.; A. Taylor & Co (fl.1890); Charles Taylor (Milwaukee, Wisconsin, c.1877-8). Taylor & Farley, a partnership with John A. Farley (qv), began making instruments in 1830 and became one of the largest reed-organ makers in America during the first half of the last century. Later the business was absorbed into Loring & Blake (qv).

Tealdo, Antonio. 20 Settembre 18, Vicenza, Italy. Maker and repairer of harmoniums, fl.1909.

Teck-Harmoniumfabrik, GmbH. Löwenberg Schloss, Teck, Germany. Makers of harmoniums and reed organs, fl.1930. By 1940 was at Kircheim, Teck, Germany. Maker of harmoniums, fl.1940.

Thibouville-Lamy & Co, Jerome. 140 rue St Charles, Paris 15e, France, with factories at Grenelle, Mirecourt and La Couture. Founded in 1790. Manufacturers of musical instruments created by the acquisition of a large number of French manufacturers. The harmonium works was at 1 avenue Graillet, Mirecourt, Vosges. Made a variety of instruments including automatic harmoniums, harmonium-players and American organs. London branch at 10, Charterhouse Street, Holborn Circus, E. C.

Thiel & Tschiedel. Schmejkalplatz 2, Teplitz, Bohemia. Established in 1897 as harmonium-makers. By 1930 trading as Thiel & Sohn, 14 Schulg, Teplitz, by then Czechoslovakia.

Thomas, Ernest G. 66a Wellesley Road, Kentish Town, London NW. Makers of reed organs, fl.1904-9.

Thomas Organ & Piano Co. Woodstock, Ontario, Canada. Established in 1832 by Edward G. Thomas. Makers of reed organs described as 'Canada's favourites'. Factory size and capacity was doubled in 1904 and a considerable export business was carried out with New Zealand, Australia, the British East Indies, South Africa and many other parts of the world, not least the British Isles. Sole UK agents (1902) were Roenne & Co of 24-26 Shudehill, Manchester, but within a few years the agency had passed to Chas. E. Cartman whose address was Rosslyn Lodge, Crumpsall, Manchester (in 1905), 49 Avondale Road, Southport, Lancashire (in 1913) and 18 Saunders Street, Southport by 1915. At the Music Trades Exhibition held in Manchester in August that year (reports *Musical Opinion*), Cartman showed a Thomas's 'Diamond' model 'a new and elegant design, the case having a centre mirror and richly-carved side panels. This organ had eleven stops, including Howard's melody solo stops, by which a distinct solo effect can be obtained. An organ in Thomas's Ruby case (with a Chippendale gallery), an organ in the maker's Agate case and one in their Daisy case - all attractive designs enriched by choice carving - formed the collection'. In response to an enquiry, Cartman wrote in *Musical Opinion* for October 1904, that Howard's melody or solo stop had been supplied in 'quite a number' of Thomas organs sold in Britain, 'some of the organs containing as many as four solo stops, - i.e. on the 4ft. 8ft. and 16ft. stops in the treble and on the 16ft. in the bass'. He added: 'The effects produced by these solo stops are indeed very fine, thus obtaining from a one manual organ effects which as a rule are only to be had from a two manual [and] pedal organ.' In 1913 advertised the Two Manual Organ with Pedals for church or home use as 'Made by British Labour in Britain's Premier Colony'.

In 1915 advertised single and double manual organs for Church, Mission, Lodge or Home use, in particular the Chancel model 'with a Pipe Tone'. In 1922 advertised the Thomas Orchestral Reed Organ and, later, the Symphony. See also Samuel Howard.

Thomson, William. 'Beethoven House', 3-7 Govan Road, Glasgow. Established in 1888. Reed-organ maker with branches in Falkirk and Clydebank. In 1902 advertised as sole UK agents for Burdett organs. In 1905 advertised models from £8.10s upwards. By 1914, address shown as 5-7 Govan Road and the agencies held included sole UK Scotland and North of England for Weaver, Burdett, Ann Arbor and Miller.

Thulé, B. A. Kangasala, Finland. Established in 1843 for the manufacture of harmoniums; fl.1909.

Tidder & Sons, W. H. 228 Mile End Road, London. Makers of portable harmoniums and seraphines, advertising in 1898. In 1909 directories shown as William Henry Tidder & Son, 2a Whitehead Street, Cleveland Street, Mile End, makers of American organs, established in 1870. By 1914 was shown as American organ and portable harmonium maker. Business does not appear to have survived World War I.

Titz, Peter. Vienna, Austria. Titz was an apprentice with Jakob Deutschmann (qv) at Wienstr 39 in 1851 but began on his own account by 1852 as a maker of harmoniums until his death in 1873 whereupon the business was continued by his son-in-law as Theofil Kotykiewicz (qv) at Straussengasse 18.

Tofanelli, Emanuele. Via Umberto I 83/85, Viareggio (Lucca), Italy. Manufacturers of church organs and harmoniums, fl.1909.

Tomati & Cia. Corso Roma, Diano S. Pietro, Italy. Established in 1830 for the manufacture of harmoniums. A quite early Italian maker. By 1909 run by Battista Tomati.

Tonzaa et Houpin. 16 boulevard Saint-Germain, Paris, France. Maker of harmoniums, fl.1920.

Torkildsen, Bredrene. Aasen, Norway. Maker of reed organs, fl.1930.

Tosco, Giovanni. 16 via S. Dalmazzo, Turin, Italy. Maker of harmoniums and reed organs, listed in 1930 directories.

Trayser & Co, Ph. F. 100 Röthebulsstr, Stuttgart, Germany. Established in Leipzig 1848 by Philip Trayser who learned his trade in Paris with Alexandre (qv). Maker of quality harmoniums. Awarded medal of honour at the Munich exhibition, 1854. Exhibited at the 1862 London International Exhibition and awarded a medal. The business moved to Stuttgart after 1900. Was said to have used a special, secret metal for the making of reeds which he produced in octaves, each separate tongue being affixed to the plate. Trayser announced that he had ceased to manufacture harmoniums in the early part of 1905 (see *Musical Opinion*, March, 1905) having manufactured more than 35,000 organs. An American company, Trayser Melodeons & Organs of Indianopolis, Indiana, was set up in 1849 by Philip Trayser's brother Georg Wilhelm, also ex-Alexandre. According to Dolge, this subsequently became the Trayser Piano Co with an involvement with James S. and Benjamin Starr. George Trayser retired in 1878.

Treat & Lindsley. *see* Whitaker & Frisbie.

Trost, E. 263-4 Whitechapel Road, London. In 1863 advertised 'patent organ accordions, with stop, £3.5s.; 5 octave Harmoniums, in solid oak or mahogany (polished), £6.6s.; ditton, 10 stop, rosewood or walnut, £17.10s.'

Truchsess, Theodor. 22 Jesinger Str, Kircheim-Teck, Germany. Makers of harmoniums and reed organs, fl.1930.

Tryber & Sweetland (Lakeside Organs). Lake Street, Chicago, Illinois, USA. Founded in 1874. Listed as such in 1900 but by 1909 was listed only as Tryber Piano Co at 244 Lake Street. Was a major producer of American organs in the late 1880s.

Tschanun Frères. G. & A: 46 Grand Pré, Geneva, Switzerland. Maker of harmoniums; fl.1930.

Tubi, Dott. Graziano. Castello Sopra, al Caleotto, Lecca (Como), Italy. Maker of harmoniums est. 1860. By 1930, business was styled Tubi comm. dott Graziano.

Tuček, Jan. 210 Svatobarborská ulice, Kutná Hora, Czechoslovakia. Makers of harmoniums, fl.1930. Successor to Johannes Tuček, organ, harmonium and organ pipemaker of Kuttenberg, Bohemia, who began his business in 1869.

Tucker, W. B. 329 Euston Road, and 95 King Street, Chelsea, London. Maker of portable harmoniums; fl.1900-14.

Turconi Antigua Casa. 405 Rodriguez Pena, Buenos Aires, Argentine. Importers of reed organs and harmoniums; fl.1930.

Tyler Apparatus Co Ltd. 15 Gerrard Street, London. The only record of this company appears in an advertisement in *Musical Opinion* for February 1915 in which it promotes: 'All British Combination Instrument. Ideal for Theatres, cinematograph theatres, concert halls, parish halls, Etc.' which incorporated piano, reed organ, bells, zither, harp played 'from one keyboard. Played as an ordinary piano.' The instrument was called the Tyler Orchestral Grand and was priced at £95. No further information and it seems no examples survive.

Ullmann, Ch. & J. 11 rue de Faubourg Poissonnière, Paris 9e, France. Founded in 1881 by Charles and Jules Ullmann. Musical instruments of all sorts carried the Ullmann brand name but, rather like Thibouville-Lamy, were probably contracted from other manufacturers. Listed as harmonium makers.

Ullmann, Ludwig. Grosse Görschen-str 31, Berlin, Germany. Established in 1889. Agents for Needham organs. Advertised in 1909 that the previous year's production had been 17,000 harmoniums (American organs) and 3,000 pianos.

University Reed Organs. *see* A. J. Spencer.

Uxbridge Piano & Organ Co Ltd (Uxbridge Cabinet Organ Co). Uxbridge, Ontario, Canada. Makers of reed organs established before 1875 and still in business in 1909. Original name in parenthesis; restyled as entered for 1909 directories.

Vadi Vala, D. R. Bombay, India. Maker of harmoniums, fl.1949.

Vancouver Organ Co. 3425 Pt Grey Road, Vancouver, British Columbia, Canada. Makers of reed organs, fl.1930.

Végh, V. Károly. 63 Rákóczy út, Budapest, Hungary. Maker of reed organs and harmoniums, fl. 1930.

Veit, Antoni. Dzika 47, Warsaw, Poland. Barrel-organ and harmonium builder, fl.1909.

Venditi, Francesco. Cava de Tirreni, Italy. Maker of reed organs, fl.1930.

Veneri, Nestore. Sammarcello (Ancona), Italy. Maker of harmoniums who was in business in 1909.

Venkat & Co. 130 Mint Street, Madras, India. Makers of harmoniums, fl.1930.

Verhasselt-d'Outrelepont, F. Brussels, Belgium. Exhibited at the Great Exhibition of 1851 a 'patent harmonium melodium for churches. The same for drawing rooms. Patent double piano-harmonium capable of being separated at pleasure.'

Vermeulen Mart (Firma). 27 Voostr, Woerden, Holland. A maker of reed organs, fl.1930.

Vestre's Orgel-Fabrik. Ostnos pr. Aalesund, Norway. Manufacturer of pipe organs, American organs and harmoniums established in 1896, fl.1909.

Virot, Charles. 15 Seymour Street, Euston Square, London. Maker of harmoniums, fl.1880. Advertised reeds, fittings etc. Also repairer and tuner. Claimed to supply 'the cheapest reeds to be obtained in London.'

Vittino, Francesco. Centallo (Cuneo), Italy. Established in 1824 as a maker of harmoniums. Still in business in 1909.

Vocalion Organ Co. Jackson and Beacon Streets, Worcester, Massachusetts, USA. Originally the Hamilton Vocalion Organ Manufacturing Co. (qv) founded in 1886 by Baillie-Hamilton (qv), a Scot who had devised the Vocalion organ in conjunction with inventors Herman Smith and John Farmer. Tied in through corporation with the Munroe Organ Reed Co and ultimately built tone ranks for the Aeolian Orchestrelle player reed organ until absorbed into the Aeolian empire. See also Mason & Risch Vocalion Co.

Waddington & Sons. New Station Street, Leeds, Yorkshire. Founded in 1840. Described as piano and organ makers at 9 Woodhouse Lane. In 1900 listed as agents for the Hamilton American organ. The principle branch of the business was in York at 44-46 Stonegate where founder's sons William Henry and Walter Waddington claimed an establishment date of 1838. Branches listed in Blythe, Cardiff, Crook, Hanley, Liverpool, Manchester, Middlesborough, Newcastle-upon-Tyne, South Shields, Spennymoor and Sunderland.

Wallis & Son Ltd, Joseph. 133/135 Euston Road, and 50 Isledon Road, London. Established in 1848. Early makers of harmoniums who also imported from France. Wallis, in advertisements, described himself as 'late foreman to Alexandre Père et fils'. Maintained the sole agency for Christophe & Étienne (qv) harmoniums from the mid 1860s to 1914. The business became a limited liability company in 1889. The son of the founder, James Wallis, became managing director. He was crippled and lived in a wheelchair. He founded The Society of Musical Instrument Manufacturers & Wholesale Importers, later to become The Musical Instrument Trades' Protection Association, of which he was president until his death in 1902. He was succeeded as head of the Wallis business by H. E. H. Standish, secretary to the company since 1889, who himself died at the age of fifty-three on 7 December 1915. He in turn was succeeded by George

Wallis. The business of Wallis manufactured harmoniums and American organs as well as the sale of imported instruments. In 1895, Wallis advertised a portable table organ which was the subject of a British Patent (No. 8827 of 3rd May, 1895) taken out in conjunction with M. Kasriel [q.v.]. In 1898 the Wallis Auto-organ was introduced which sold for £60.

Warkhold, Hans. Weinbergsweg 5, Berlin N54, Germany. Harmonium maker, fl.1909.

Warren, C. S. *see* Baillie-Hamilton.

Warren, S. R. Montreal, Quebec, Canada. Founded in 1878 by Samuel Russell Warren who had been apprenticed as a pipe-organ builder in Boston. Moved to Toronto where, with his son Charles S. Warren, he set up as S. R. Warren & Son. In 1897, the business was absorbed by D. W. Karn (qv).

Waterloo Organ Co. Waterloo, New York, USA. Makers of American organs established in 1861 by A. C. Reed and Malcolm Love. The business was listed in 1900 but gone by 1909.

Waters, Horace. 247 Broadway, New York (1850); 481 Broadway (1864), New York, USA. Described as 'Organ and Melodeon Manufacturer'. Began in business c.1850. Appears to have ceased trading sometime after 1880. An early maker of quality instruments.

Weaver Organ & Piano Co. Corner Broad and Walnut Streets, York, Pennsylvania, USA. Also with a branch in Lancaster in the same State. Established in 1870 originally as J. O. Weaver at 304 West Market Street, York. J. Oliver Weaver introduced the York-style Cottage Organ, claiming it to be 'the handsomest in the world'. The company was run by M. B. Gibson in 1909. It seems to have ceased trading c.1912. In 1902, the UK agency was given as care of 53 Darwen Road, Blackburn, Lancashire, this address being that of Edwin Smith & Co. (qv).

Wedlake, Henry Thomas. 8 Berkeley Road, Near Chalk Farm Station, Regent's Park, London. Born March 1826, Wedlake was apprenticed to organ builder John Gray, then worked with Mitchell & Groves and thence to Gray & Davison. Whilst there he learned that Boosey & Co had joined Evans in the harmonium-manufacturing business and needed a foreman. He held this job until 1862 when Boosey and Evans parted company. During this time he was granted British Patent No 1068 of 27 April 1861 for a harmonium combining two wind pressures - lower pressure for the bass reeds and higher pressure for the treble with the ability to supply from the high-pressure feeders to the low-pressure chest if needed. At the time of this patent, he gave his address as 327 Euston Road and 58 Warren Street. He then became a builder of church pipe organs and reed organs at the Berkeley Road address. He retired at the turn of the century. During a long and busy life, he spent much time in pipe-organ building but also worked extensively on reed organs. In *Musical Opinion* for February 1903, he wrote:

May I state that I was the first to bring [the Vocalion] to perfection in this country? It came about thus: Mr. Whyte took up the manufacture in conjunction with Mr. Baillie Hamilton. On seeing the first model, I advised that the profession be not invited as the model was not fit. Mr. Whyte and Mr. Baillie Hamilton then agreed to my terms for taking the matter in hand, which were that my plans were not to be interfered with. Dr. C. W. Pearce was I think the first to play on the completed instrument, and he pronounced it to be a great success. I constructed a harmonium for Mr. Pichler (a Hungarian). It had a pedal, possessed numerous tone devices and mechanical actions, and cost seven thousand pounds. Its owners highly complemented me, and I must say that the construction of the instrument required very careful attention from yours &c.

Wedlake appears to have been a tetchy person at the best of times and not to have missed an opportunity to write to the trade press about his achievements. The figure of £7,000 is astronomical for such an instrument in those days. One cannot imagine how such a figure could be claimed or justified. See also Baillie-Hamilton; Pichler.

Wemer, K. 29 Privatstr, Leipzig, Germany. A maker of harmoniums and reed organs, fl.1930.

Werdauer Harmoniumfabrik Max Horn. 1 Turnhallenstr, Werdau, Germany. Makers of harmoniums and reed organs listed in 1930.

Western Cottage Organ Co. Established in Mendota, Illinois, USA in 1865, moved to Ottawa, Illinois, in 1875. Founded by F. R. Wolfinger and H. D. Cable. Later changed name to Chicago Cottage Organ Co (qv) and ultimately became The Cable Co.

Wetzel & Sohn. 1 Haller Str, Hamburg, Germany. Makers of reed organs, fl.1930.

Wheatstone, William. 20 Conduit Street, Regent Street, London. Established in 1750. Later as C. Wheatstone & Co. Described as inventors and patentees of the concertina, Wheatstone also made harmoniums in large numbers and appears to have been the first British maker to use that name for the reed organ. At the Great Exhibition of 1851, exhibited a variety of concertinas and 'portable harmoniums, for producing expression, which can be played alone, or be placed in front of the key-board of a pianoforte, and played by the same performer; adapted for wooden or stringed instrument solo, or part music'. Was awarded the exhibition prize medal for harmoniums. See also Rock Chidley; George Jones; Francis Pichler.

Whight & Co, George. 143 Holborn Bars, London (1886). Described as 'Licensees and Importers of Automatic Musical Instruments and all kinds of Perforated Music Paper (Wholesale and for Exportation)'. Handled both the first White & Wilcox automatic organs and the first first Aeolian player reed organs in Britain. See references in text under Aeolian, and George Whight.

Whitaker & Frisbie. New Haven, Connecticut, USA. A business begun in 1847 by David Whitaker and William Frisbie as melodeon-makers. H. Q. Goodman bought into the business whereupon it was restyled Goodman & Frisbie; then a Dr. Baldwin acquired Frisbie's interest and the firm became Goodman & Baldwin. In 1856, John L. Treat and Nelson Lindsley acquired the business, renaming it Treat & Lindsley. Eight years later a Mr Davis of Worcester, Massachusetts, bought out Lindsley's interest and changed the name to Treat and Davis. When Davis died, Nelson Lindsley bought the Davis share and the business reverted to Treat & Lindsley. In 1865 it changed to B. Shoninger, operated by Simon B. Shoninger (qv). The business disappeared after 1885.

White Manufacturing Co, A. L. 215 Englewood Avenue, Chicago, Illinois, USA. Established in 1900. Makers of folding harmoniums, fl.1930.

Whitney & Currier. Quincy, Illinois, USA. Business begun by August H. Whitney c.1855 and later as the A. H. Whitney Organ Co. His sons Frank and J. W. were also in business separately manufacturing reed organs well into the 1880s. Manufactured reed organs under the name Palace. On the cessation of that business, the name Palace was taken up by Loring & Blake (qv), also Taber (qv). In 1901 London agents were J. Perino, Great Russell Street.

Whomes & Sons. 240-242 Broadway, Bexley Heath, Kent. Makers and patentees (as Whomes, Whomes & Whomes) of reed organs and in particular the invention of the Orgapian, a combined piano and reed organ. Numerous patents were taken out for improvements to reed organs, one (British Patent No 8769 of 1915) being in the names of Edmund Whomes, E. de Gruchy Whomes and Walter S. Whomes. See also references under Linard, also Robinson for similar instruments. Whomes was also well-known as a maker and distributor of electric blowers for organs and harmoniums. By 1929, the business was re-styled Whomes Ltd and is still operating today as a radio, television and hi-fi store.

Wick Organ Co. Chicago, Illinois, USA. Established in 1866 by Peter S. Wick. Makers of American organs. Extant in 1900, but gone by 1909.

Wiest, Anton. Josephstadt Langen Gasse No 59, Vienna, Austria. Name on label found on a barrel and finger harmonium dating from c.1860.

Wikstrom och Nord Orgelfabrik. Kristinehamm, Sweden. Harmonium and reed organ makers, fl.1930.

Wilcox & White (Angelus Piano & Organ Co). Meriden, Connecticut, USA. Henry Kirk White, an organ-builder from Brattleboro, Vermont, started in business making melodeons in New London in 1845. In 1853, moved to Washington, New Jersey, and in 1865 was employed by the Estey Organ Co (qv). Together with a Meriden silver-plate manufacturer Horace C. White, he set up as Wilcox & White in 1876 (some sources say 1877),

making a variety of roll-playing organettes including instruments for the Mechanical Orguinette Co, precursor of Aeolian (qv). Was reorganised in 1897. Makers of American organs, the Angelus combined reed organ and piano-player, and in 1888 introduced the Symphony player reed organ which at one time rivalled Aeolian's Orchestrelle. All early Symphony player organs were F-F compass and used a special suction action featuring a vacuum pouch system later used in the Angelus piano-player and player-piano action. Supplied an instrument Style 125 to Prince Henry of Prussia (brother of the emperor) early in 1894 as a climax to forty-seven years in organ-making by its founder. In May 1894 introduced a true piano-cased reed organ which possessed extremely novel features. Stop-knobs and swell controls were dispensed with, these operations being transferred to four small buttons in the keyboard thumper rail which operated large pneumatic motors to select the various functions. These apparently only required the lightest touch to operate, a second touch cancelling the functions selected. The large foot treadles were also dispensed with, normal-looking piano pedals being provided, the movement of which was sufficient to pump the wind. The compass was a full $7\frac{1}{3}$ octaves C to E. Claimed to be the outcome of many months of experimentation, the machine was virtually indistinguishable in appearance from a piano. In 1901, sold a Symphony player organ fitted up in a Hungarian ash case to the king of Greece and, the same year, an Angelus in bird's eye maple to the king of Portugal. The London distributors for Wilcox & White were initially George Whight (qv) but by 1914 were Sir Herbert Marshall & Sons Ltd, 233 Regent Street.

Williams Organ & Piano Co. 1427 Carroll Avenue, Chicago, Illinois, USA, also at Centreville, Iowa. Established in 1855 by J. W. Williams for the manufacture of melodeons and pianos. By 1909 was at 57, Washington, W. Chicago. Made reed organs under the brand names 'Epworth' and 'Williams'. By 1930 as the Williams Piano & Organs Co, 180 Wabash Avenue, Chicago.

Willis, J. 'Willis's Royal Musical Repository, Removed from St. James's-street, to 75, Lower Grosvenor-street, within a few Doors of Bond-street' (*The Musical World*, March, 1836). Believed only an agent specialising in pianos 'by all the approved Makers'. References to 'Willis's Seraphines' would suggest that his name appeared on some instruments.

Willis Piano & Organ Co. Halifax, Nova Scotia, Canada. Makers of reed organs, fl.1909. Factory in Stellarton, branch in Charlottetown, Prince Edward Island.

Wisker, E. R. Oriel, Byron Road, Wealdstone, Middlesex. In 1915 was granted British Patent No 18,794 on 5 May 1914, for a new action for organ and harmonium builders which claimed to solve the difficulty of the 'one-man orchestra' adding 'it will be of considerable utility for cinemas and similar entertainments'. *Musical Opinion*, September, 1915, described it in these words: 'These improvements consist of a simple application of the law of centrifugal force by means of which a striker, when actuated by the depression of the key, is made to operate in a selective manner... depending entirely on the force with which the key is struck. In this was *p*, *mf*, *f*, phrasing and expression, are obtained from the keyboard as in the pianoforte...' A very helpful description, that! In truth this was a significant innovation which was presented too late to the reed organ market for it to have too much effect, bearing in mind that there was a war on. A 'piano-forte' device, it was a simple double-touch device which varied the loudness of the sound by the degree of key pressure.

Wissmann, R. Nurtinger Str 17, Kircheim, Teck, Germany. A maker of harmoniums in business in 1940.

Witkowski, M. A. 12 Percy Street, London, W. An energetic agent during the early years of this century who handled many instruments including H. Hildebrandt's 'Weihe' organs and harmoniums. Witkowski founded his piano and organ agency in 1890 at 80/82 Fore Street, later moved to 32 Newman Street and, in February of 1913, moved to new premises at 12 Percy Street, Tottenham Court Road. He showed a piano and harmonium combination instrument in February that year which was intended for use in the silent picture house, 'picture palace' or kinema. The piano or organ could be played independently or together, and the organ had three sets of reeds representing 16ft, 8ft, and 4ft. There was also a tremolo. One was on show in Witkowski's showroom but it seems that few, if any, can have been sold in Britain. See also under Neugebauer Nachfolger.

Wolf, H. & H. 2 rue St Joseph, and 1 rue St Marc, Quimper, Finistere, France. Harmonium and reed-organ maker, fl.1909.

Woods & Co, George. Boston, Massachusetts, USA. George Woods began in business making melodeons with E. P. Carpenter (qv) and Samuel Jones at Brattleboro in 1853; then began on his own at 494 Tremont Street, Boston, and, two years later, at 608 Washington Street. He adopted a novel form of percussion and in some measure pre-empted Mustel's invention of the Celeste stop and the Scotsman Machell's Dulcitone (a purely percussion instrument playing special tuning forks) in that he added a register offering 2½ octaves in the treble which played on tuning forks. He remained in business until c.1885. In 1876, Harrison & Harrison, pianoforte, harmonium and American organ agents and importers of Great Midlands Music Warehouse, Colmore Row & Bennett's Hill, Birmingham, advertised: 'American organs manufactured at Cambridgeport, Massachusetts, U.S.A. by Messrs. Woods & Co.' Described as 'sole agents for the Midlands Counties of England.'

Woodstock Organ Co. Woodstock, Ontario, Canada. Established in 1876 as manufacturers of reed organs.

Ceased trading before 1900 and was absorbed into the business of D. W. Karn (qv).

Worcester Organ Co. Worcester, Massachusetts, USA. There were two quite separate companies formed under this name. The first was established in 1872 and subsequently was acquired by William B. Taber who renamed it, by 1877, The Tabor Organ Co. The second Worcester Organ Co. was established in 1883 for the manufacture of American organs. It was operated as a subsidiary of the Edwin P. Carpenter business (qv). Fl.1900, not listed 1909.

Worcester Reed Organ Works, Nederlandische Orgelfabriek. 185 Arnhemsche Weg, Amersfoort, Holland. Makers of American organs and harmoniums, fl.1930.

Yannane Gakki-Ten. 4 4-chome, Ginza, Kyobashi-ku, Tokyo, Japan. Makers of harmoniums, fl.1930.

Yardley, C. H. 95a Tavistock Road, Plymouth, Devon. Harmonium maker, fl.1930.

Zachariassen & Co. J. A. Nystad, Finland. Established

Programme of Promenade Concert, Curzon Hall, Birmingham, 20th July 1876

in 1870 by the brothers Zachariassen and Dr. Alex G. Zachariassen for the manufacture of church organs and harmoniums.

Zanferli, Luigi. Via S. Faustino, Brescia, Italy. Harmonium maker in business c.1909.

Zimmermann, Jules Heinrich. Querstr 26/28, Leipzig, Germany. With factory at Sedanstr 17. Established in 1886. Manufacturers of reed organs and pianos as well as mechanical musical instruments. London branch at 4 Wells Street, Oxford Street.

Zuja, Blasius. Zerotingasse 270, Ungarisch-Brod, (Mähren), Austro-Hungaria (later in Czechoslovakia).

Established in 1884 for the manufacture of barrel organs. By 1920 was listed as a maker of reed organs. Fl.1932.

Zuleger, A. Königsplatz 4, Leipzig, Germany. Alfred Zuleger set up in business in 1872 as an agent and distributor of all types of musical instrument. By 1830, the business was advertising the Harmonola reed organ but although it was made to Zuleger patents, it is uncertain that it was actually constructed by the company.

Zwahlen, Louis. New York, USA. A musical instrument maker who secured an American Patent on 5 May 1832 for a 'Seraphina or harmonicon organ'. No further details are available.

"Musical Opinion", January 1902

Carr's Special High-Class Organs.

Manufactured by the

Celebrated Fort Wayne Organ Company

INDIANA, U.S.A.

NEW STYLE.

Combination Action.
No. 314.

Fifteen Stops.

	ft.			ft.
Bourdon Bass	...16	Celeste	...	... 8
Diapason ...	... 8	Flute ...	...	... 4
Viola	... 4	Flutina	...	... 4
Violina ...	... 4	Cello ...	...	..16
Dulcet Bass	... 8	Celestina ...		... 8
Melodia ...	... 8	Dulcet Treble		... 8
Vox Humana,		Bass Coupler,		
	Treble Coupler.			

Seven Sets of Reeds,
VIZ:—

Two sets of two Octaves each,
Four sets of three Octaves each,
And one Octave of Sub-Bass,

**With Knee Swell and Patent Grand
Organ Swell.**

This Organ has a 16 ft. Row right
through, *i.e.*, Bourdon Bass connected
with Cello Set.

THIS magnificent Organ is the handsomest and finest instrument I have had the pleasure of offering my customers at such a low price. It is 78 inches high, 47 inches wide, 23 inches deep. Massive Walnut Case, highly finished, Engraved Panels, Fancy Carvings, large Bevelled Mirror in Top, handsome Stop Knobs, Handles, Music Desk, Sliding Fall Board, &c., &c. Wonderful combination of Tone, beautiful in design, and solid in construction. This Organ will give immense satisfaction to every purchaser.

SPECIAL PRICE £17:17:0 NETT CASH.
The Best Organ in the Market at the Price.

The above Organs are Free Liverpool, Packing Case included.

Department store catalogue, c.1900

Reed Organ Specifications

a) General list of reed organ stops.

The following is a brief description of some of the stops used in Mason & Hamlin American organs, taken from the Mason & Hamlin manual of 1901. The descriptions of tonality and the substitution recommendations are those of Mason & Hamlin and the position of the stop in the organ, ie whether it is pedals, bass or treble, is indicated together with the speaking pitch *as normally found* since it varies on certain individual organs.

Aeoline	8ft treble	Very string-like and sympathetic
Anglet	8ft treble	Similar to dulciana
Barytone	32ft treble	Full tone, but reedy
Bassett	16ft bass	Rich, pervading tone
Bassoon	16ft bass	Very powerful
Bourdon	16ft bass	Full and round
Bombardon	16ft pedals	A very deep 16ft in the pedals
Campanella	4ft treble	Small bells
Celeste	8ft treble	Produces a beautiful effect
Celestina	8ft treble	Soft celeste
'Cello	16ft treble	Powerful
Clarina	8ft treble	Soft reed
Clarion	8ft bass	Soft, bright tone
Clarionet	16ft treble	Resembles clarionet
Concerto	8ft treble	Brilliant
Cor anglais	8ft treble	Similar to cremona
Cornet Echo	2ft bass	Very soft echo effect
Cornettino	2ft bass	String tone
Cremona	8ft bass	Soft and rich
Delicante	8ft treble	Brilliant
Diapason	8ft treble	Round, full tone
Dolce	8ft bass	Softer than melodia: sometimes a soft stop on the viola (4ft)
Dulciana	8ft treble	Similar to diapason, but softer
Echo	8ft treble	A mechanical stop on the celeste
Echo horn	8ft treble	Soft, echo effect
Fagotte	8ft bass	Reedy
Flute	4ft treble	Brilliant, but not reedy
Gamba	8ft bass	Smooth and pipe-like
Gemshorn	2ft bass	Soft, rich tone
Harp Aeolienne	2ft bass	Closely resembles Aeolian harp
Hautboy	8ft treble	Reedy. Effective solo stop

Kalophon	8ft treble	Reedy
Melodia	8ft bass	Same quality as the diapason
Nachthorn	8ft treble	Soft, reedy tone
Pedal bass	16ft pedals	Deep, round and full
Piano organ	8ft treble	A set of bells
Piccolo	2ft treble	A set of reeds one octave higher than the flute
Principal	4ft treble	Very bright and clear
Royal jubilante	16ft treble	Very fine solo stop. Large round tone
Saxhorn	4ft bass	A bright set of fine quality
Sub-bass	16ft bass	Very deep and powerful
Sub-bourdon	32ft treble	Beautiful solo stop
Viola	4ft bass	Same character as flute set
Viola dolce	4ft bass	(In some styles), need not be in when full power is wanted
Viol etheria	8ft treble	Soft. reedy
Violetta	4ft bass	Very soft, smooth tone, for accompaniment
Violone	16ft pedals	A round, smooth 16ft in the pedals
Vox angelet	8ft treble	Soft, sweet tone
Vox angelica	8ft treble	A soft stop on the Flute
Vox jubilante	8ft treble	Very effective as a solo, but imparts a peculiar brilliancy to all
Wald flute	2ft treble	Very clear and penetrating, but very delicate, making a fine solo stop when used with the vox humana, dolce(+)tremulant, and other stops. An octave higher than flute.

b) General list of American organ stops, their pitches and makers

The following is a list of the more common stop names found on American organs and harmoniums. Those special to the Mustel organ and the French style of stop nomenclature are indicated in the first column with the accepted stop abbreviation. Each stop is listed with the name of one maker who used that name. This does not imply that that maker was the sole user (though with patented stops, this was indeed so), but is offered as a guide to identification of style. Stops without names were generic and common to many makers.

Ac	Accouplement [coupler] (Mustel)			Choral 8ft [treble] (Estey)
	Aeoline 8ft (Bell)			Clarabella 8ft [treble] (Mason & Hamlin)
	Aeolian harp 2ft (Mason & Hamlin)			Clarinet 8ft [treble] (Sherlock-Manning)
	Aeolsharfe 2ft (Mannborg)	2		Clarinette 16ft (Estey)
	Aoline 8ft (Bell)			Clarion 4ft (Smith American Organ Co)
	Baritone 16ft (Smith)	3		Clarion-fifre 4ft (Mustel)
7	Baryton 32ft			Clarionet 16ft (University)
9	Basse de flute 4ft (Mustel)			Clarionette 16ft [treble] (Estey)
	Bassett 16ft [treble] (Estey)			Clarone 8ft [treble] (Clough & Warren)
4	Basson 8ft			Contra basso 16ft (Clough & Warren)
4	Basson-hautbois 8ft (Mustel)			Contra fagotto 16ft [treble to bourdon] (Smith)
	Bassoon 8ft (Dominion; Smith)	C		Contrebasse, 16ft (Mustel)
	Bassoon 16ft (Story & Clark)	5		Contrebasson 16ft (Mustel)
2	Bourdon 16ft (Estey)	1		Cor anglais 8ft [treble] (Sherlock-Manning)
2	Bourdon-clarinette 16ft (Mustel)	1p		Cor anglais [percussion] 8ft
	Bourdon treble 16ft (Dominion)	1		Cor anglais-flute 8ft (Mustel)
	Campanella [top 3 octaves percussion] (Burdett)	1p		Cor anglais-flute [percussion] 8ft (Mustel)
	Celeste 8ft [treble] (Imperial			Coranglais 4ft (Burdett)
	Cello 16ft [treble] (Sherlock-Manning)			Cornet echo 2ft [bass] (Estey)

186

Cornettino 2ft [bass] (Estey)
Corno 16ft (Mason & Hamlin)
Cremona 8ft (Chicago Cottage)
Cremona 16ft (Bell)
7 Cromorne 32ft (Mustel)
Delicante 8ft (Estey)
Diapason 8ft (Mason & Hamlin)
Diapason dolce 8ft (Mason & Hamlin)
Dolce corno 4ft (Burdett)
Double diapason 16ft [bass] (D'Almaine)
Double diapason 16ft [treble] (D'Almaine)
Dulcet 4ft (Dominion)
Dulcet 8ft (Chicago Cottage)
Dulcet treble (8ft)
Dulciana 8ft [treble] (Estey)
Echo 8ft (Dominion)
Echo horn 8ft [treble] (Smith American Organ Co)
English horn 8ft (Mason & Hamlin)
English horn dolce 8ft (Mason & Hamlin)
Euphone 16ft (Bell)
Euphone echo 8ft (Burdett)
Ex Expression (Mustel)
Fagotte 8ft (Bell)
3 Fifre 4ft (Mustel)
Flugel horn 2ft (Dominion)
Flute 4ft (Mason & Hamlin)
1p Flute [percussion] 8ft
1 Flute 8ft
Flute d'amour 2ft (Chase)
Flute d'amour 4ft (Estey)
Flute d'amour 8ft [treble] (Mannborg)
9 Flute douce 4ft (Mustel)
O Forte expressif (Mustel)
FF Forte fixe (Mustel)
Gamba 8ft [bass] (Estey)
Gemshorn 2ft [bass] (Clough & Warren)
Gemshorn 4ft [swell treble] (Estey)
Gemshorn 8ft [treble] (Karn)
Grand jeu (Mustel)
Grand organ (Harnmona)
Grand solo 4ft+8ft+16ft mixture [treble] (Smith)
Harp aeolian 2ft [bass] (Estey)
Harp angelica 2ft (Packard)
8 Harpe éolienne [double reeds] 8ft (Mustel)
5 Harpe éolienne [double reeds] 2ft
4 Hautbois 8ft
Hautboy 2ft [bass] (Sherlock-Manning)
Hautboy 4ft [treble] (Bridgeport)
Hautboy 8ft [treble] (Bell)
Highland pipe 2ft [bass] (Karn)

Horn 8ft and 4ft composite (Story & Clark)
Kalophon 8ft [treble] (Smith)
Keraulophon 8ft [swell] (Mason & Hamlin)
La perfection 8ft [treble] (Story & Clark)
Melodia 8ft (Mason & Hamlin)
Melodia 8ft [treble] (Harnmona)
Melodia dolce 8ft (Mason & Hamlin)
Met Metaphone (Mustel)
5 Musette 16ft (Mason & Hamlin)
Oboe 8ft (Estey)
Open diapason 16ft (University)
Ophicleide 8ft (Estey)
Ophicleide 16ft (Palace)
Piano 8ft (Hamilton)
pp Pianissimo 8ft (Mustel)
Piccolo 2ft (Bell)
Piccolo 4ft (Mason & Hamlin)
Piccolo duetto 8ft+4ft [treble] (Smith)
Pipe cello 16ft [treble] (Story & Clark)
Pipe diapason 8ft (Packard)
Principal 4ft (Chicago Cottage; Smith)
Principal 8ft [treble] (Karn)
Pr Prolongment [1 octave 1/2] (Mustel)
Pr Prolongment [3 octaves 1/2] (Mustel)
Pr Prolongment [12 notes] (Mustel)
Regal 8ft [treble] (Estey)
Roman pipe 2ft [treble] (Story & Clark)
Royal jubilante 16ft (Estey)
Salicional 8ft (University)
Saxhorn 4ft (Bell)
Saxophone 16ft [treble] (Wallis; Smith)
Schalmei 8ft (Mannborg)
Seraphone 8ft [treble] (Mason & Hamlin)
Sub Bass 16ft [13 notes] (Mason & Hamlin)
S Sub-bass [17 notes] 16ft (Mustel)
Trombone 16ft (University)
Trumpet 8ft (Estey)
Tuba-mirabilis 8ft (Estey)
Vacuum viola 4ft [bass] (Story & Clark)
Vibrator [vox humana tremolo] (Mannborg)
Viola 4ft (Mason & Hamlin)
Viola da gamba 8ft [bass] (Karn)
Viola dolce 4ft (Mason & Hamlin)
Violetta 4ft (Estey)
Violette 2ft (Bell)
Violette 4ft (University)
Violina 2ft [bass] (Sherlock-Manning)
Violina 4ft [bass] (Fort Wayne)
Violine 8ft [bass] (Bell)
Violincello 16ft (Hamilton)

	Voix celeste 8ft (Malcolm)		Vox etheria 8ft [treble] (Clough & Warren)
6	Voix celeste [double reeds] 8ft (Mustel)		Vox jubilans 8ft (Mannborg)
6	Voix celeste [double reeds] 16ft		Vox jubilante 8ft (Estey)
	Voix humane 2ft [bass celeste: two sets] (Karn)		Wald flute 2ft (Estey)
	Vox angelet 8ft [treble] (Clough & Warren)		Wald flute 8ft [bass + treble] (Smith)
	Vox angelica 8ft (Dominion)		Wald flute violina 2ft (Estey)

In the above list, no differentiation is made between front or back rows in the organ, nor are derivative stops indicated since these tend to vary from maker to maker. The following observations, however, may help to determine derivatives. Cello is usually the cremona muted; Aoline is the treble hautboy muted, also the dulciana muted; Celeste is the treble oboe muted and flattened; Clarinet is the treble cor anglais muted; Echo is usually the treble celeste, melodia, dulciana or diapason muted. Malcolm used muted dulcet and dulciana with vox celeste to make the Dulcet. Mason & Hamlin's Musette is the second 16ft treble set, when Clarinet is added it forms a Voix Celeste. Story & Clark's Pipe Cello is the treble 16ft muted, the tone coming from the 'qualifying tubes'. Sherlock-Manning used the treble cor anglais muted to produce Seraphone. Invariably, stops such as viol d'amour, viola, echo, piano and hautboy are formed from various mutes and combinations. Incidentally, Mason & Hamlin often spelled their sub bass coupler as 'base'.

HARMONIUM STOPS WHICH MAY BE SUBSTITUTED
FOR AMERICAN ORGAN STOPS
(according to Mason & Hamlin)

Harmonium stops may be substituted for organ stops	American organ stops
For (1) or cor anglais	diapason, english horn, gamba bass, or dulciana
For (1) or flute	melodia, gamba, treble, diapason treble or clarabella
For (2) or clarinette	clarinet, or corno
For (2) or bourdon	bourdon or contra-basso
For (3) or Fifre	flute or wald flute
For (3) or clarion	viola or flute dolce
For (4) or hautbois	seraphone or gamba
For (4) or bassoon	diapason (or if drawn, add viola) or bassoon
For (5) or musette	euphone, musette (or seraphone 16ft), clarinet or corno
For (6) or voix-celeste	vox humana, viol d'amour and flute, or voix celeste
For (7) or harpe éolienne	viola (play as high as possible), or aeolian harp
For (G) or grand jeu	full organ knee swell or full organ foot pedal
For (E) or expression	knee swell or automatic swell
For (T) or tremolo	dolce tremulant, euphone, or clarionet and vox humana, or voix celeste and vox humana, or tremulant
For (S) or sourdine	viola (and play octave lower than the music is written) and add eolian harp, or viola-dolce *only*

c) Reed-organ stops and keyboard divisions.

Dulcet and Dulciana	Mechanical stops which obtain the subdued effects from 8ft pitch
Forte	Opens swells, augments the tone

Forte, Dia, Mel.	Increases the power of diapason and melodia stop when drawn. When the knee swell is pushed open, the forte stops do not act at all
Forte, Vio, Ser, Fl	Has no sound in itself, but increases the power of viola, seraphone or flute stops if either [sic] be drawn
Grand organ (knee)	Brings into use all the reeds in the organ at once
Knee swell	Same effect as forte, only more gradual if desired
Manual coupler	In organs with two manuals, so connects them that, when a key on the lower manual is depressed, it also depresses the corresponding key of the upper manual
Octave coupler	When any key is depressed, its octave above is also depressed, thereby doubling the tone
Pedal coupler	In organs having pedal keys, so connects the manual that, when the pedal is depressed, its corresponding key in the manual is depressed and responds also
Pedal to manual	Connects the pedals with the manuals
Vox humana	Imparts to the tone a thrilling wave-like effect

HARMONIUM STOPS AND STOP CONTROLS

The following is a short list of stops and mechanical stop controls found on harmoniums (see also the Mustel stops in the main list):

Flageolet	No 3 treble (Hopkinson)
$\frac{1}{2}$ Grand jeu	All the stops of the front organ (Debain)
Jeux doux	A quiet 8ft bass stop (Alphonse Rodolphe)
Lointain	Debain's name for the sourdine
Petite expression	Expression valve slightly open (Cramer)
Saxophone	A bass 8ft stop (Debain)
Soprano	Treble 8ft stops, quiet (Debain)
Sourdine	Pianissimo, softly voiced mute
Tremblant	Debain's name for the tremolo, a mechanical device to impart a wavering tone by fluctuating the supply of wind. (Debain often showed the compass of a stop in staff notation on the stop-face).

The petit expression is a novelty: it opens the expression valve a very small amount and offers a subtle shade of tone. Significantly, the expression stop is not one which appears on American organs, possibly because it requires special technique to play properly and most American manufacturers were more concerned with producing a mass market instrument.

THE DIVISION OF THE KEYBOARD

The following is an analysis of some of the dated instruments in the collection of Phil and Pam Fluke, whose private museum is at the Victoria Hall, Saltaire, Shipley, West Yorkshire, and other instruments from the author's records. From this it is possible to see the surprising variation in preferences for division of the harmonium and American organ keyboard. Generally speaking, it was the French who introduced the E/F break in the CC compass, but this was not exclusively followed; there were many attempts to ameliorate some of the claimed disadvantages of the CC compass by moving the break, while others who favoured the FF compass sought to do the same.

In considering this alphabetical list, it should be remembered that some instruments featured a 'straight

189

through', divisionless manual; but the majority divided the compass somewhere in the octave around or below middle C.

Maker	Date	Compass	Break	Country of Origin
Aeolian	1898	C X 5	G#/A	America
Alexandre	1892	C X 5	E/F	France
Bauer	1886	C X 5	E/F	Great Britain
Bell (Guelph)	1898	F X 5	G#/A	Canada
Clough & Warren	1880	F X 5	G#/A	America
Clough & Warren	1889	C X 5	G#/A	America
Couty & Richard	1880	C X 5	E/F	France
Doherty	1901	F X 5	E/F	Canada
Estey	1881	F X 5	B/C	America
Estey	1883	C X 5	E/F	America
Malcolm	1898	C X 5	G#/A	Great Britain
Mason & Hamlin	1903	C X 5	B/C	America
Mustel	1897	C X 5	E/F	France
Mustel	1882	C X 5	E/F	France
Mustel	1897	C X 5	E/F	France
Ramsden	1875	C X 5	A#/B	Great Britain
Smith American	1888	F X 5	B/C	America
Smith American	1887	F X 5½	G/G#	America
Trayser	1875	C X 5	E/F	Germany
Whomes	1924	F X 5	B/C	Great Britain
Woods	1873	F X 5	B/C	America

Here is the same table, this time expressed chronologically. Note how the old FF compass survived in some places until surprisingly late.

Maker	Date	Compass	Break	Country of Origin
Woods	1873	F X 5	B/C	America
Ramsden	1875	C X 5	A#/B	Great Britain
Trayser	1875	C X 5	E/F	Germany
Couty & Richard	1880	C X 5	E/F	France
Clough & Warren	1880	F X 5	G#/A	America
Estey	1881	F X 5	B/C	America
Mustel	1882	C X 5	E/F	France
Estey	1883	C X 5	E/F	America
Bauer	1886	C X 5	E/F	Great Britain
Smith American	1887	F X 5½	G/G#	America
Smith American	1888	F X 5	B/C	America
Clough & Warren	1889	C X 5	G#/A	America
Alexandre	1892	C X 5	E/F	France
Mustel	1897	C X 5	E/F	France
Mustel	1897	C X 5	E/F	France
Aeolian	1898	C X 5	G#/A	America
Malcolm	1898	C X 5	G#/A	Great Britain
Bell (Guelph)	1898	F X 5	G#/A	Canada
Doherty	1901	F X 5	E/F	Canada
Mason & Hamlin	1903	C X 5	B/C	America
Whomes	1924	F X 5	B/C	Great Britain

This time the list is presented showing the tonal break, extending from the unusual B/C division at one end through to G#/A at the other with the far more common E/F in the centre.

Maker	Date	Compass	Break	Country of Origin
Whomes	1924	F X 5	B/C	Great Britain
Woods	1873	F X 5	B/C	America
Estey	1881	F X 5	B/C	America
Mason & Hamlin	1903	C X 5	B/C	America
Smith American	1888	F X 5	B/C	America
Alexandre	1892	C X 5	E/F	France
Bauer	1886	C X 5	E/F	Great Britain
Couty & Richard	1880	C X 5	E/F	France
Doherty	1901	F X 5	E/F	Canada
Estey	1883	C X 5	E/F	America
Mustel	1897	C X 5	E/F	France
Mustel	1882	C X 5	E/F	France
Mustel	1897	C X 5	E/F	France
Trayser	1875	C X 5	E/F	Germany
Amith American	1887	F X $5\frac{1}{2}$	G/G#	America
Aeolian	1898	C X 5	G#/A	America
Bell (Guelph)	1898	F X 5	G#/A	Canada
Clough & Warren	1880	F X 5	G#/A	America
Clough & Warren	1889	C X 5	G#/A	America
Malcolm	1898	C X 5	G#/A	Great Britain
Ramsden	1875	C X 5	A#/B	Great Britain

"Musical Opinion", October 1898

APPENDIX 2

Tuning and Regulating
Mason & Hamlin Organs

Mason & Hamlin published a useful booklet on the servicing of their American organs. Written by J C Spanswick, this ran to many editions and offered useful advice which not only applied to their own instruments but to others as well. From Spanswick's own copy the significant parts of this are reproduced on the following pages with the original page numbers retained.

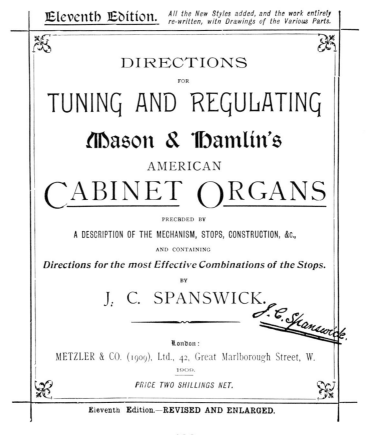

Eleventh Edition. *All the New Styles added, and the work entirely re-written, with Drawings of the Various Parts.*

DIRECTIONS

FOR

TUNING AND REGULATING

Mason & Hamlin's

AMERICAN

CABINET ORGANS

PRECEDED BY

A DESCRIPTION OF THE MECHANISM, STOPS, CONSTRUCTION, &c.,

AND CONTAINING

Directions for the most Effective Combinations of the Stops.

BY

J. C. SPANSWICK.

London:

METZLER & CO. (1909), Ltd., 42, Great Marlborough Street, W.

1909.

PRICE TWO SHILLINGS NET.

Eleventh Edition.—**REVISED AND ENLARGED.**

Construction.

THE following are the essential parts of Mason & Hamlin's Cabinet Organs, together with an explanatory description of each.

The handsomely finished Cases into which the various parts are fitted are constructed on acoustic principles, and the wood used being solid black walnut of the best quality obtainable, and various other woods carefully selected and prepared, they will stand any trying influence of temperature.

The Bellows, which are of two kinds, are used for drawing air from the Air-chamber. The principal one, named the Exhaust, is placed in a perpendicular or horizontal position, extending from end to end, in the lower part of the case. Attached to this are smaller bellows called Lifters or Exhausters, which are connected (by means of bands or straps passing over rollers) with the foot-boards, and in pedal organs with a handle at the side. In the former case a performer can himself use the Exhausters by simply pressing his feet on the foot-boards; but in the latter case, an assistant is required to work the handle. The foot-lever in some pedal organs can only be used when the handle is at the top of the guide.

The opening and closing of the Exhausters draw the air from the Exhaust, which in turn draws the supply from the Air-chamber or Air-chest.

The Air-chamber is a shallow box made of pine, occupying the entire space immediately above the Exhaust, with which its lower side is connected. The upper side of this box is called the Sounding Board, and apertures, corresponding to the size of the reeds, are cut in a row along the whole length of the upper surface.

The Reeds or Vibrators are arranged immediately over these apertures, being small in the higher or treble notes, and gradually enlarging towards the lower or bass notes. Over the reeds is glued the Tube Board, which consists of a number of tubes or cells joined together, into which each reed is inserted; the tubes also correspond to the length and size of each reed.

The air, previous to entering the Air-chamber and Exhaust, must necessarily pass through these tubes and through the reeds, which are thereby set in vibration, remaining so as long as the current of air is passing. This would cause all the reeds to sound together, but the Valves and Keys serve to obviate this difficulty. A valve is a narrow strip of wood, covered first with cloth and then with leather, which is placed over each aperture on the Sounding Board, and being pressed close by a spring excludes all air. Each valve is constructed to work upon a centre, and is opened by a pin, when its corresponding key is pressed down.

A performer working the foot-boards only would soon empty the Air-chamber and Exhaust, and so force the organ and seriously damage it, especially if no safety-valve were provided; but on pressing a key or note, a valve is opened, and the air allowed to pass in, thus causing the reed to vibrate, and so producing sound.

The Stops, until drawn forward, shut off by a mechanical contrivance all air from any particular set of reeds. In the Mason & Hamlin Organs there are from one to fourteen sets of reeds, and as many as thirty-two stops, by which all communication with the Air-chamber is regulated.

In an organ with one set of reeds no stop is required, and there are then forty-nine reeds in a four-octave, and sixty-one in a five-octave organ.

The Swells, which in some styles are moved by the knee, also by blowing, and in the pedal organs by the foot, raise a cover extending over all the reeds, and in this way the volume of sound is increased.

DRAWING No. I.

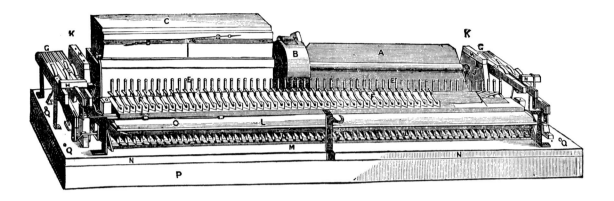

FRONT VIEW OF MASON & HAMLIN ORGAN

(*i.c.*, ACTION BOARD AND ATTACHMENTS).

(**The Case** removed, also Key Frame, Stop Board, Roller Board, &c., &c., Swell open. Octave Coupler **Levers**,
Front View of Reed Cells, showing ends of Reed Blocks.)

A Vox-Humana Fan. B Vox-Humana Motor. C Sub-Bass Box or Cover. D Spring on Sub-Bass Box. E Push Pins (on which the Keys rest). F Wire Levers (operated by buttons from Keys), connecting each note with Octave above. G Stop Levers. H Connection over Stop Levers (operated by Full Organ Knee Pedal). I Key Frame Supports, with hooks attached. J Blocks (in which are slots) into which the Pin on which Key Frame works is secured. K Blocks which secure Key Frame. L Swell Board or Swell Cover (operated by right knee). M Reeds, and Front of Tube Board. N Action Board (showing also front of Air Chest), to the lower part of which the Bellows are attached. O Spring on Swell Board. P Air Chest or Receiver. Q Action Screws (see Drawing No. 2, letter L, and Drawing No. 3).

DRAWING No. 2.

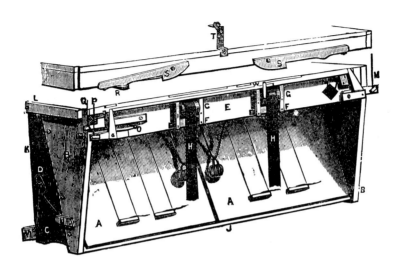

FRONT VIEW OF MASON & HAMLIN ORGAN ACTION

(*i.e.*, BELLOWS AND ATTACHMENTS).

(The Case removed, also the Stop Board, Roller Board, and Key Frame.)

A Lifters or Feeders (showing Outside Valves). **B** End Brackets. **C** End of Suction Bellows (Exhaust or Reservoir). **D** Bellows Spring (open). **E** Roller or Pulley Rail. **F** Roller Pivot Supports. **G** Roller or Pulleys. **H** Pedal Straps. **I** Lifter Springs. **J** Middle Board of Bellows. **K** Back Board of Bellows. **L** Side Blocks or Action Blocks (to remove the Action from the Case, take out the large screws which pass through these blocks—see letter Q, Drawing No. 3). **M** Wire Connection to Stop Levers connected with Full Organ Knee Pedals. **N** Full Organ Knee Pedal Spring (bass). **O** Ditto Treble Spring. **P** Wire Connection to Knee Swell. **Q** Wire Connection to Octave Coupler. **R** Button to hold up Full Organ Catch. **S** Catch to hold Knee Swell or Full Organ Knee Pedal fully open, when full power of any stop or of all the stops are desired. **T** Key-frame Support, with hook attached. **U** Bearing or Guide for Spring. **V** Support for Spring on Back Board. **W** Wood Levers worked by Knee Swell and Full Organ Knee Pedal.

DRAWING No. 3.

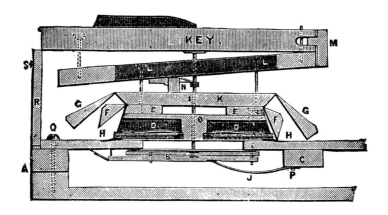

SIDE SECTION OF MASON & HAMLIN ORGAN ACTION.

(UPPER PART.)

(The Side Section of Bellows, which is screwed to Sounding Board and Air Chest, is given in Drawing No. 4.)

A Air Chest or Wind Chest, Sounding Board and Action Board (through which in some Styles the large screw passes to secure the Action to the Case). B Self-adjusting Reed Valve (showing Valve Stem hinged at the end, Guide Pins, and Cloth and Leather Seat, or Covering). C Spring Block. D Tube Board (Air Chamber) or Tube Hole or Reed Cell. E Strips of wood on top of Tube Board to which are hinged the Stop Valves. F Stop Valves. G Swell Boards. H Reeds or Vibrators. I Push Pin or Pitman. J Reed Valve Spring. K Top of Swell Box (through which pass the Push Pins). L Key Frame. M Back Catch of Key Frame. N Octave Coupler (showing end of Coupler Rail and Wire Lever touching the shoulder on the Push Pin). O Centre of Tube Board through which the Push Pin passes. P Screw for regulating weight of touch, and which secures the Valve Spring. Q Action Screw. R Lock Rail or Key Slip (end of). S Screw passing through Lock Rail.

DRAWING No. 4

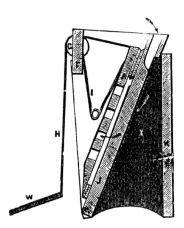

SIDE SECTION OF MASON & HAMLIN ORGAN ACTION.

(LOWER PART OF BELLOWS.)

A Side View of Lifter or Feeder (showing the arrangement of the Wind or Air Openings into Suction Bellows, Exhaust or Reservoir). **F** Roller-pivot Support on Pulley Rail. **G** Roller or Pulley. **H** Pedal Strap. **I** Lifter Spring. **J** Middle Board of Bellows. **K** Back Board of Bellows. **W** Foot Board or Blow Pedal. **X** Interior of Suction Bellows (the Exhaust, Reservoir, or Suction Bellows is covered with "rubber cloth," or "mackintosh").

When you press down the Foot Board (**W**) you tighten the Pedal Strap (**H**) stretched from the Lifter, "Feeder," "Pump" or "Exhauster" (**A**) across the Pulley (**G**). The Lifter is thus opened, and in opening sucks out the air from the Bellows, creating a "vacuum." When the Bellows are not in use, its sides are kept apart by stiff Springs, and when the air inside the Bellows is "sucked" or drawn out, the sides are brought together, and the Springs, by forcing apart the sides again, draw the air into the Bellows through the Reeds on the top of the Air Chest. When the Stops are opened and the Keys depressed, the Bellows are replenished with air passing through the Reeds, Air Chest, &c., &c

The Mason & Hamlin "Liszt" Organ.

DRAWING No. 5.

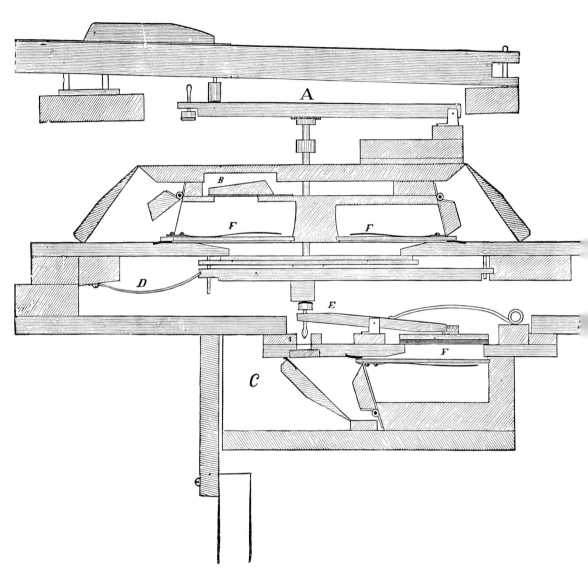

SHOWING "LISZT" ORGAN PATENTS.

(ALL INVENTED AND USED EXCLUSIVELY BY MASON & HAMLIN.)

A represents one of a set of RADIATING LEVERS, by which an enlarged set of "Liszt" reeds is brought within the compass of the ordinary key-board. All "Liszt" reeds are constructed on this enlarged scale, and but for the Radiating Levers could not be brought into use. *Patented Nov. 13th, 1877.*

B DOLCE STOP.—This stop differs materially from similar stops in other organs. It affords a Dolce that *is a Dolce,* and is produced by a peculiarity in *construction,* and not by a mere modification of some other stop. *Patented Jan. 30th, 1877.*

C VENTRILLO CHEST.—Perhaps the most valuable of the "Liszt" patents. It is an acoustically constructed air chamber, located under instead of over the wind chest, and containing an enlarged or "Liszt" scale of reeds of 16 feet pitch. *Patented March 10th, 1874.*

This, the Corno set, produces the tone most characteristic of the "Liszt" organ, and is emphatically the most artistic and musically satisfactory tone ever produced from reeds.

D IMPROVED TOUCH.—A decided point of superiority of the "Liszt" organs will be found in their improved KEY-ACTION, *patented June,* 1880, which is certainly one of the greatest practical improvements ever made in organs. It consists in a construction and arrangement of the springs (D) operating the valves admitting air to the reeds, upon a new principle, securing these advantages :—

1. The force necessary to press each key is reduced, on an average, nearly one-half, so rendering the action of the keys very light and easy to the player.

2. The gradation of force in pressing the key is reversed with very great advantages. As formerly constructed, the force necessary to depress the key was continually greater as the key descended ; more and more power must be expended by the finger as it went down, the greatest pressure being necessary at its lowest point. By the MASON & HAMLIN IMPROVED KEY-ACTION this is reversed, the greatest power being necessary when the key is started, and continually less as the key goes down.

3. The action is very elastic, giving quickest possible response and return.

4. It is strong, not likely to get out of order, and very durable.

By this patent the action is made much easier, especially when coupled. Without question this improvement affords the "Liszt" organs a *touch not equalled in any organ in the world.*

THE "PEDAL POINT" STOP IN THE "LISZT" ORGAN.

The "Pedal Point" attachment. By means of mechanism, set in operation by the knee of the performer, any one of the keys in the lowest octave, when depressed, remains down after the finger is removed, until any other key in that octave is touched, the latter key then remaining down in place of the former; thus allowing the player to manipulate as much or as little of the remaining portion of the key-board as he wishes, and at the same time affording him an excellent "organ point," which may be varied as he sees fit. A slight movement of the knee will at any moment easily disconnect the mechanism, the lower octave of keys then acting in their usual and regular manner. Several notes, instead of one, may be made to continue sounding by depressing their corresponding keys, and some remarkably charming and striking effects are thus afforded when a two feet or four feet stop is drawn.

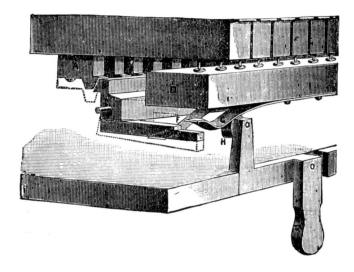

A Small Block screwed to underside of Key. B Catch or Latch. C Pivot of Catch or Latch. D Key Frame (showing key pins and front of keys). E Pedal-point Knee Stop. F Spring. G Spring. H Roller.

When the pedal-point knee stop E is moved from right to left, the roller H is carried with it. A rail—the length of one octave—is pivoted at C, and at B the rail is cut, to form a latch or catch. Each of the keys within the range of the octave is provided with a latch or catch, of which one is shown at the point where A meets B. The spring F pressing an arm upward keeps the latch in position for acting. If a key within the octave is depressed, the rail is moved, and the small block A catches under latch or catch B. The spring F causes this action to take place.

The spring G, much stronger than the spring F (when the pedal-point stop is pressed the other way), is allowed to press upon the lever. This draws back the latch-block, so that any key held down is released and rises to its place, and any new key pressed down will not stay there. When, however, the latch-block is allowed to act, one or more keys within its range can be depressed simultaneously, and will then be held down. Every new key thus depressed releases all the others.

To regulate the pedal point, adjust the buttons or small blocks A.

ONLY GOLD MEDAL AT THE LEADING EXHIBITIONS.

Mason & Hamlin American Cabinet Organs.

———◦⁙◦———

THE FOOT BOARD, FOOT PEDALS, OR BLOWERS.
(SEE DRAWING No. 4.)

These, after much use, sometimes produce a disagreeable squeaking sound.

They are attached to the front rail by hinges, through which are inserted iron pins. To remedy this very annoying defect, it is necessary to lay the organ on its back and apply some grease or machine oil.

Frequently the creaking noise in the foot pedals is caused by their working against the bottom rail. To remedy this, raise the pedal by inserting a card under each hinge.

It often occurs that the iron hinge-pin sticks firmly to the brass hinge. To rectify this, unscrew the pedal rail and the pedal board, which is done by removing the screws. In some styles the screws in the hinges can be reached by bringing the foot board close to the rail; two holes will be found in the middle of the rail, under each of the hinges in the pedal boards. The organ must be turned on its end or on its back to see the holes. The hinge-pin will now be seen, and the application of a little oil or grease will probably stop any creaking.

If this has not the desired effect, take out the pin of the hinge, by inserting a screwdriver under the points of the pin, which is turned down into the rail, and file the iron pin, so that the hinge will work easily. Apply oil before replacing the parts. (See also Bellows Action.)

THE PEDAL STRAP OR METAL CONNECTING RODS.
(Working the Exhausters or Lifters.)
(SEE DRAWINGS Nos. 2 & 4.)

The PEDAL STRAP wearing out. The old piece can be slipped out, and a new one put in, without removing the action from the case. Turn the organ on the end carefully, and reach in to the top of the lifters, where the webbing is held by a wedge of wood behind a piece of iron wire. Slip the piece out, and be careful the new piece goes into the same position.

The PEDAL STRAP passes over a roller, which revolves on an iron pin. These rollers produce a squeaking sound when the instrument has been for some time in a damp place, the pins becoming corroded with rust. To rectify this, it is necessary to take out the pin, roller, &c., and supply some grease mixed with blacklead. Oil must in no case be put to these parts. The slip below the knee-swells can often be unscrewed to get at the rollers. If necessary, the action can be taken out (see letter L, Drawing No. 2). Care must be taken to replace the washers or rings placed each side of the roller, to avoid friction with the sides of the brackets in which it works.

The METAL CONNECTING RODS take the place of the pedal strap in the smallest organs. Apply grease to the parts where friction takes place if creaking occurs. Springs are placed at the side or in small holes, to keep the lifters shut.

THE EXHAUSTERS OR LIFTERS.

(Sometimes miscalled Bellows or Feeders—worked by Straps over Rollers or Metal Rods.)

(SEE DRAWING No. 2.)

The Lifters or Exhausters open from the top, and are made to close by springs inserted in a hole at the top of the Lifter. These springs are kept in position by a guide, or fork, which is fastened to the beam which runs across the lower part of the action and into which the pedal strap rollers are inserted. Access to these springs can be had usually by taking out the thin slip below the knee pedals or by turning the organ on its end. When the action is of the horizontal style, these springs are placed at each side of the Lifter, and the metal rod pulls down the Exhauster or Lifter from its centre. The metal rod is secured by a button. Noises in these springs and parts can be altered by using oil when the bearings are metal, and tallow where the contact is between wood and metal. They seldom require any attention; the only derangement that can occur is by the valves or leather curling up from excessive damp. In this case it is necessary to apply to some mechanic or to an organ-builder, who could put new leathers. These leathers or valves are placed both outside and inside the Lifters. Care should be taken that the leather is kept perfectly flat.

The joints or hinges of the Lifters, when worn or swollen by damp, are liable to produce a squeaking or grating sound from the friction of two pieces of wood working together. This can only be rectified by cutting open the part affected, and placing leather between the joints, so that the edges work on the leather instead of the wood.

To take off the Lifters, to get to the leather valve on the middle board of the bellows, the edges of the rubber should be unglued along the edge by using a damp cloth, and melting the glue by a warm iron. This should only be attempted by experts, and only in the factory. The effect of the leather being curled up is an unpleasant springy sensation when the foot is placed on the blow pedal, and consequent loss of wind and power. Should a Lifter at any time be split or broken, it should be glued up, and a batten screwed on to strengthen it.

THE BELLOWS ACTION.

(Called also the Exhaust, the Bellows, the Suction Bellows.)

(SEE DRAWING No. 4.)

This contracts when the lifters (or pumps) are worked, and is ready to accept the wind as it passes through the reeds and air chest. The sides of the Exhaust or Suction Bellows (when the Bellows are not in use) are kept apart by stiff springs. If the air inside the Bellows is sucked out the sides are brought together, and the spring, by forcing the sides apart again, draw the air into the Bellows through the reeds on the top of the air chest. The strength of the tone is influenced by the pressure exerted by the springs, and by the quickness with which the blow pedals, and consequently the lifters, are worked. There is a screw in the centre of the middle board of the Bellows Action, and when the sides of the Bellows are brought together this screw opens an escape valve (seen on the outside of the back board), which prevents overblowing.

Sometimes a disagreeable snapping noise is heard in the Bellows. This is caused by the parts of the mechanism that move with the Bellows becoming dry and grating under the slow motion. It may be in the Bellows springs or in the work connected with the automatic swell. Everything liable to produce this defect can be seen with the back out : and a little oil applied to the coil of the Bellows springs or to the automatic swell connections will relieve the difficulty. The bearings of the Bellows springs (letter U, Drawing No. 2) at the ends may be looked after, and a little tallow applied safely.

THE WIND CHEST OR AIR CHEST.

(SEE DRAWING No. I.)

The thin board attached to the top of the bellows and the board on which the reeds rest form the Air Chest or Wind Chest. On the upper side of the Air Chest is glued the tube board or cavity board into which the various reeds are inserted. On the under side are the valves, which are opened by the push pin and the key.

ESCAPE OF WIND, so that a chord cannot be played, even when working the foot pedals very fast, is caused by the valve board becoming forced up, so that the screws round it do not hold. The screws must be replaced with larger ones.

Or the board above the exhaust or bellows action may be split, which can be seen by taking out the bellows action and taking off the valve board. If so, this must be glued, and forced into its position. Then glue wooden buttons across the joint, and cover the whole of the fracture with thin leather or canvas. This will only be found when the organ has a bad fall in transit.

VALVES ADMITTING AIR TO REEDS.

(Called Stop Valves.)

These fit closely over the reed cells or air chambers in the tube board, and are connected with the stops. When a stop is drawn one of these Valves is raised, thus allowing the air to pass through the reeds and into the air chest (of course, supposing that the blow pedals are being used, and that a key is being held down). The Stop Valves are hinged with strong canvas, and are tacked and glued to the hinge strip over the tube board, two screws passing through a small metal plate to complete the hinge. Sometimes brass hinges are used, but the canvas hinge is preferable, owing to its durability and to its presenting the least chance of jarring after use.

The Stop Valves are covered with soft leather, and are fitted with utmost care.

If a stop will not shut off the sound, but continues to admit air to the reeds after it is shut in, the defect may proceed from several causes.

1. A chip or piece of wood may prevent the Stop Valve closing firmly. Remove the obstruction.
2. The spring may have become bent so as to be powerless. It consists of a long piece of brass wire with the ends bent opposite ways ; one end is fastened into the wooden cover and the other into the action. It should by no means be taken out, unless it is impossible to make the Stop Valve air-tight in any other way, as it requires very great care to replace it. New springs can be had by sending the broken pieces. The spring may be strengthened by giving it an extra turn before replacing it, or by shortening. Replace it very carefully, together with its cloth rests.

3. The Valves, from damp, may have become swollen and fixed against the side of the division in the tube board. In this case file the Valve at the end. The obstruction being removed, the Valve will work freely.

4. The Stop Valve itself may have *cast* or warped, a new one can then be inserted at the factory.

5. The stop action may prevent them closing.

6. The Full Organ connection may catch. In either case, carefully examine the various wire and wooden connections.

7. The Stop Valve may be hinge-bound; if so, loosen very slightly the canvas under the thin metal plates, after unscrewing them.

8. Should the occasional whistling of a single note occur, it may be cured by drilling a very small hole close to the point and through the reed block.

Another way is by "bleeding" the defective reed cell; this can be done by making a small bradawl hole through the back of the reed cell into the valve opening, and thus draw off the extra wind (see the dotted lines at C, Fig. 2).

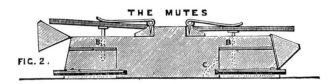

THE MUTES

FIG. 2.

SOUNDING OF NOTES at the treble end without the stop being drawn, in the Flute and Melodia stops, is caused by the *mute* (B, Fig. 2, a wooden pin passing through the tube board) becoming swollen, or not dropping when the stop slide is shut. The swells must be taken quite off, and the *mutes* eased or the spring strengthened.

ESCAPE OF WIND after a stop is pushed in is caused by the Pneumatic or Suction Valve (Fig. 1, seen at the end of the tube board, under the stop shutter) remaining open. Work it forwards and backwards several times, and the escape will cease. See also that no chip or grit is under the Suction Valve, and that the small spring connected with the Viola Dolce stop (under the action board) is in its place.

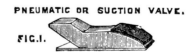

PNEUMATIC OR SUCTION VALVE.

FIG. I.

The Pneumatic or Suction Valve (Fig. 1) supersedes the Mutes (Fig. 2), which are usually found in the older styles. At the same instant that a stop is drawn, the Pneumatic Valve in connection therewith closes by the weight attached to it (see Fig. 1, Letter A). Providing the Stop Valves are air-tight, and yet a rush of air is noticeable (and also two sounds from different reeds occur from one key), it is possible that the tube board is unglued in some unseen part; in that case the only way is to send the organ to the factory, where it will be treated as on pages 32 and 33.

REED VALVES.

Under each Reed the board is mortised, leaving a hole for the air to pass through to make the Reed sound. These mortise holes vary in length (see Figs. 4 & 5), and are covered by a valve which is

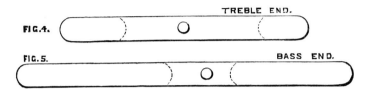

(Length of Valve Openings on under side of Mortise or Sounding Board.)

opened by the key in playing and closed by a spring when the pressure of the finger is removed from the key. If it were not for these valves all the Reeds would sound at the same time. These Reed Valves in the Mason & Hamlin Organ have centre-pressure and are self-adjusting.

In the "Liszt" Organs (Styles 501, 503, 506, 507, 514, 515, 516, 517, 518, 519, 520, 521, 522, 601, 605, 606, 800, 801, 802, 804, 900, 901, 902, 904, 1200, 1202), and several others, to get at the regulating screws for adjusting the Reed Valves and Levers in the VENTRILLO CHEST (connected with the Contra-Bass and Corno stops), turn the organ on its back or end, remove the panel behind the knee pedals, also a strip of wood marked B.

The strip B under the Action is painted black.

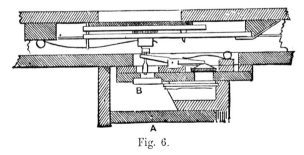

Fig. 6.

The bottom board of the Ventrillo Chest must be taken out by unhooking the hooks or removing the screws which secure it. (In some styles the action must be taken from the case before this can be done.) There will now be seen a row of holes, in each of which is the flattened end of a brass screw, and by using the little key (see page 23) sent with the organ, these screws can be turned to bring the inside levers to the right adjustment (see Fig. 7). Use the greatest care in replacing every part.

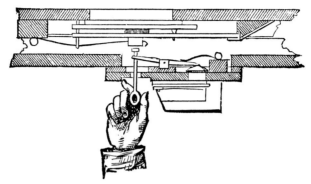

Fig. 7 repre-ents the parts **A** and **B** as removed, and the Key inserted as in the process of regulation.

Ciphering in Corno or Contra-Bass stops (in consequence of unusual swelling of the wood) will be easily altered by turning these small brass screws. Sometimes, however, the connections between the Reed Valves and the keys are swollen, and prevent the valves closing ; or they will not open enough. These must be eased.

New Reed Valve springs can be obtained by sending the broken parts.

To get at these valves, take the bellows action quite out of the case and remove the valve board, which is secured by screws round the edge of it. The valve is kept in position by a spring, which can be regulated by turning the screw which holds it, or by bending the spring. Should a particle of wood, grit, or some hard substance get under the Reed Valve and prevent it closing, it will cause the notes to continue to sound after the finger has left the key (usually termed ciphering. In such cases the Reed Valve must be taken out after gently removing the spring, or in the older styles by moving the spring on one side.

> In the largest organs there are levers, or wood connections, which are attached to these Reed Valves, and which open (at the same time) other valves in different positions. If these levers are tight between the pins which guide them to their positions, the guide pins must be slightly moved, or the dark mark (where the pin rubs) on the side of the lever filed away.

Directions for adjusting valves of Sub-Bass when the wood is affected by the atmosphere. The box over the Sub-Bass must first be removed, which can be done after loosening screws at either end in the brass slots. Move the box back out of the slots, and the action of the Sub-Bass Valves can now be seen by pressing a key which operates upon them. If the valve does not open high enough, turn it up and take out the pin and lengthen it by a turn or two of the screw in the end of the pin. If the pin is too long, so that the valve is kept too far from its seat, *turn the screw in a little*—in either case, adjust the length of pin to do its proper duty, and test it by the action of the key.

The brass flanges and centre-pointed bearings, used in the Sub-Bass actions in the "Liszt" Organ connections, Seraphone Valves, and Corno Valves may require occasionally the minutest drain of oil, bu this should be avoided if possible. A flat-headed screw should, in preference, be turned which would loosen the brass flange and so give room for the lever to work freely.

In the "Queen's" Model (Style 512), to regulate the Reed Valves of the Musette, Viola, and Piccolo sets, remove the black strip on the top of the action, and there will be seen a row of holes, in which is the flattened end of a brass screw, and by using a little key (sent with the organ), these screws can be turned to bring the inside levers to the correct adjustment. Use the greatest care in replacing every part. The panel at the back must be lowered before the black strip can be reached.

THE STOPS, OR DRAW KNOBS.

(Placed in the Stop Board, or Name Board.)

A stop when drawn raises the stop valve, which admits the air to the reed chambers. By means of a long roller, roller board, wooden levers, and wire cranks and levers, inserted in the end of the stop valves, the connection from the stop is made at either end of the action, or in any part of the larger organs ; the method varying with the different styles of instrument.

Should any of the wood levers or cranks stick from damp, unscrew them and file away that part which is swollen. (The reeds would then speak when the stops are closed.)

The stop-action levers being of wood, in the latest styles, must be reduced in thickness if swollen —the cloth bearings also. A spring judiciously added underneath these levers may be of use if they are still sluggish.

When the Full Organ Knee Stop is used it should be pressed AT ONCE to the left, as far as it will go ; if moved only part way, or slowly, a rush of air will be heard passing through the pneumatic valves, and, the stops being only partly open, the organ will sound out of tune.

COMPASS AND PITCH. The usual compass of the Mason & Hamlin Organ is five octaves. The larger instruments, and some with the Sub-Bass and Octave Coupler, are constructed with the C scale ; others with the F scale. The C scale is the old standard scale. The F scale is comparatively new ; and, giving four more notes in the bass, allows the lower octave to be used in imitation of pedal notes. The F scale is most useful in connection with the Harp Eolienne, Viola Dolce, for, by playing an octave lower, the effect of a *swell* organ is obtained ; while solo stops may be used with the right hand above the division. In an organ having the Octave Coupler coupling upwards and the F scale, any music may be played as written, and NOT an octave higher, as usually advised.

These organs are tuned to what is termed the Philharmonic pitch, so that they may be used in an orchestra, or with a pianoforte.

The CHARACTER OF THE SOUND TO BE OBTAINED FROM the Mason & Hamlin organs depends upon the different STOPS used. Thus the Diapason and Melodia give the 8-feet tone ; or, in other words, it would require an organ pipe 8 feet in length to produce the lowest C note on that stop. Other stops give other tones, such as the 4-feet and 16-feet tones.

" A Treble Stop " runs from middle F or C upwards, varying according to compass or scale.

" A Bass Stop " runs from middle E or B downwards to the lowest note.

When an instrument has no draw stops, the Melodia and Diapason are always on.

" Mechanical Stops " have no sound in themselves, and are usually labelled in red.

The following are the stops to be found in the organs. (When the mechanism of any stop is very complicated, a short description is given; and in one or two cases its special derangements are noted; otherwise, for the derangements, consult pages 17-23, 32, 33, 46, 47, &c.)

The AUTOMATIC SWELL communicates with the bellows and with the swells over the reeds, and produces a *crescendo* or *diminuendo* at pleasure. The handiness of this stop is shown in the quickness with which the full power, or a very soft tone, may be obtained. This stop is usually placed at the bass end of the organ: in the two-manual instruments, however, it will be found in the centre of the key-board, between the two rows of keys. In the latter case it appears with two knobs, marked "ON" and "OFF"; "ON" representing full power, "OFF" softness. It should be mentioned that the blowing ought to be proportioned to the volume of sound required. In the latest styles the draw stop is omitted, and the automatic swell is put on with the combination swell (see page 30).

BARYTON SOLO. A treble stop of 16-feet tone. It imitates the round notes of the baritone voice. The construction is similar to that of the Euphone.

BASSOON (found in Style 603). Similar in quality to Diapason Treble of 8-feet tone.

BOURDON. A stop of 16-feet tone. It sometimes runs throughout the key-board, and at others is divided into halves; BOURDON TREBLE and BOURDON BASS. It is similar in tone to its namesake in the pipe organ.

BOURDON PEDALS. This stop acts on the pedals only, which in compass are two and a half octaves, CCC to F, thirty notes, and the tone produced by the lowest note is equal to that of an organ pipe 16 feet in length. (The earlier Mason & Hamlin pedal organs have a compass of two octaves and one note, CCC to D.) Sometimes marked PED. BOURDON, 16 feet; also PED. OPEN DIAPASON, 16 feet.

BOURDON DOLCE, 16 feet. A soft pedal stop.

CLARINET. A treble stop of 16-feet tone. Its natural bass is Bourdon; this stop is voiced with the smoothest possible quality, and the use of large vibrators gives it a deep sonorous quality of tone.

CLARIONET. Found in Styles 547, 551, &c. A treble stop, 16 feet. Reedy tone for solos.

CORNO. This stop (found in Style 501) controls an enlarged and improved set of reeds in the treble, of 16-feet tone, mounted in what is termed a VENTRILLO CHEST, placed on the under side of the wind chest. The tones are deep, resonant, and pervading; large and dignified, yet smooth and mellow, and every note speaks when its key is pressed with almost percussive promptness. The levers (connected with the self-adjusting reed valves, which operate on the reeds) are mounted on brass flanges, having double-pointed centre bearings, so that they are almost frictionless; besides being thoroughly reliable and unaffected by variations of temperature. Motion is imparted to these levers by the ordinary valves, ample and simple means being provided for the adjustment of each to the other.

CONTRA BASSO. This stop (found in Style 501) forms the corresponding bass stop to the Corno. It is of 16-feet tone, and has the same characteristics; forms a foundation to any stop used with it; and furnishes a Sub-Bass running through the lower half of the manual.

COUPLERS. The MANUAL COUPLER connects the two rows of keys in the two-manual organs, thus doubling a note or chord. This gives great additional power.

The OCTAVE COUPLER when drawn connects the corresponding note in either the octave below or the octave above with the note played. The distribution of power is thus regulated and doubled.

The CONSTRUCTION is simple, and does not easily get out of order. The button of each key is connected by a zigzag wire lever with the piston of the key an octave below or above. The two keys thus work together. When the stop is drawn, the row of wire levers is raised, so as to be acted on by the buttons under the keys ; otherwise the levers are out of reach of the buttons.

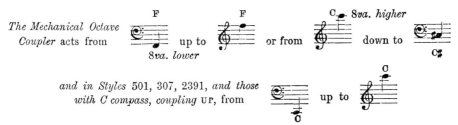

The Mechanical Octave Coupler acts from ... up to ... or from ... down to ...

and in Styles 501, 307, 2391, *and those with C compass, coupling* UP, from ... up to ...

The note thus indirectly played will not fall, as might be expected, unless the note a further octave below, or above, be also pressed down. The top octave or bottom octave differs in this respect.

For organs with the octave coupler coupling *down.* The lowest note C should not be connected with the octave coupler stop ; for its octave above, if coupled with the lowest C, would be overbalanced in power, when the Sub-Bass stop is drawn, *e.g.*, second C from bass-end if coupled to its sub-octave would give :—

1. Its own note.
2. That of the Sub-Bass.
3. The octave below.
4. The Sub-Bass note of the octave below.

When using this octave coupler stop, it is necessary to play the treble an octave higher, and if the Sub-Bass stop be used as it usually is, in conjunction with this stop, it is also necessary to play the lower bass notes in octaves to ensure a full effect.

For organs with the octave coupler stop coupling *up.* In some organs, and in those styles with the Bourdon and Clarinet stops, the octave coupler connects with the note played the corresponding note in the octave *above*—which gives great power and very full, pipe-like effects.

The 16-feet set of vibrators when used with the octave coupler is equal to one set of 16 feet, and one of 8 feet ; the 8-feet set of vibrators, with octave coupler, is the same as one 8-feet set and one 4-feet set. Both these sets of vibrators used together with the octave coupler give the equivalent of one set of 16 feet, two sets of 8 feet, and one set of 4 feet.

The advantage of coupling upwards. Brilliancy of tone, and music can be played as written. This octave coupler stop in organs not by Mason & Hamlin is miscalled sometimes "Harmonic," or "Harmonic attachment."

In Styles 2341, 2346, 2268, and some others, two octave couplers are provided, each operating from the centre of the key-board ; the treble coupler operating in an *upward*, and the bass coupler in a *downward* direction. These instruments are very popular, as they admit of the effect of the coupler being restricted to either the treble or bass portions of the instrument as desired.

The PEDAL COUPLER. By means of this one may, without using a hand, play with the foot pedals the notes in the two-and-a-quarter or two-and-a-half octaves of the bass of the lower manual. No sound, of course, will issue unless a sounding stop also be drawn.

Its CONSTRUCTION is simple. A wood button is fixed by a screw to the top of the pedal trackers ; on this is an iron lever, which runs zigzag to the key-board ; this rests on a piston, which passes through the upper manual, and presses down the keys of the lower one when the foot is placed on a pedal.

By using the Manual Coupler in conjunction with this stop, and at the same time *not* using any of the stops of the lower row, but only of the upper row, a very soft bass can be obtained. In fact, although both rows of keys are depressed, only the upper one speaks.

DIAPASON, or DIAPASON BASS. The bass stop, giving the 8-feet tone. This is the standard pitch ; its natural treble is the Melodia.

DIAPASON DOLCE. Subdued tone. 8-feet. (See English Horn Dolce.)

DIAPASON TREBLE gives the 8-feet tone. The same as the Melodia, but of purer quality.

DOLCE TREMULANT. In Style 802. 8-feet pitch *throughout*. Upper manual.

DOLCE TREMULANT. A stop in Style 502, takes the place of the Viol d'Amour, and, being of 16-feet tone, adds greatly to the variety of the organ, especially as it can be used in combination with either of the other solo stops.

DULCET. In Styles 1200 and 802. Throughout, swell, 8-feet. (See English Horn Dolce.)

DULCIANA. Similar in tone to Diapason Treble. Of 8-feet tone. Very subdued.

ENGLISH HORN. A bass stop in Style 501 of 8-feet pitch, similar to Diapason, but more horn-like in character, and resembling the Clarabella of a pipe organ.

ENGLISH HORN DOLCE and MELODIA DOLCE. 8-feet pitch. A modification of the English Horn and Melodia. Are to the organ what the *muted* strings are to the orchestra, producing a *subdued* quality of tone, and are excellent as accompaniment to solo stops. Also for full harmony for responses in Church services. These stops *must not be drawn* when the full power of the organ is desired.

EUPHONE. A treble stop of 16-feet tone (except in Styles 43 and 500, when it runs throughout the register, and is of 8-feet tone). It has a reed-like tone, and is capable of great effects, especially when modified by the Vox Humana.

The REEDS of this stop are always at the back of the instrument. The keys, by means of buttons, work wire levers, which are in connection with pistons immediately over the reed valves. To REGULATE THE VOLUME OF SOUND, turn the buttons, which work on screws, in or out. Care must, however, be taken not to bring them too high or too low, or the proper level of the keys will be disturbed.

To REMOVE THE STOP, slightly remove the wire levers, and a button will be seen fastened against the hinges at the back, usually at the left, secured by one, or sometimes by two, screws. Take this off, and, raising the front edge of the levers sufficiently to clear the pins, slide to the left till free.

EXPRESSION (found only in Styles 43 and 500). This stop breaks the communication between the notes and the exhaust-bellows. The slightest motion now, imparted by the feet of the player, gives a special accent.

FLUTE. A treble stop, 4-feet tone ; also called Principal Treble. Its natural bass is Viola.

FLUTE DOLCE. 4-feet throughout. Upper manual (Style 802). On swell in Style 1200.

FLUTE D'AMOUR (to be found in Style 71). This works on a set of pipes of 8-feet tone, from middle C upwards. The great difficulty of having pipes working together with reeds has been that their pitch is differently affected by changes of temperature. This has been surmounted by Messrs. Mason & Hamlin, by the employment of a valve, or cover, extending over all the pipes, and regulating one of the openings to each, so that by the simple turning of a screw, the pitch of all can be raised or lowered sufficiently to compensate for atmospheric changes.

FORTE I. This stop opens the swell over No. 1, Melodia and Diapason stops, and keeps open the swell till the stop is pushed in. It will be found at the bass end. In Style 501, I. Forte opens the swells over English Horn, Voix Céleste, and Melodia ; and also acts on the Seraphone and Voix Céleste in some organs.

FORTE II. This stop opens the swell over No. 2, Viola and Flute stops, and keeps open the swell till the stop is pushed in. It will be found at the treble end. In Style 501, II. Forte opens the swell over Viola, Piccolo, and Seraphone. In some styles II. Forte will act on Seraphone and Voix Céleste. This stop will not increase the power of Viola if Viola Dolce stop is drawn.

FORTE to Lower or Upper Manual in styles with two key-boards explains itself.

FORTE to Solo Stops (found in Style 701). This stop opens a cover, extending over the Gamba, Musette, and Saxaphone stops, and therefore increases the power of each. In some styles the knee swell does not act on these stops, but in others the knee and automatic swell both act, when the Forte stop is not drawn.

GAMBA. In two manual organs, throughout : 8-feet. On " great " or lower key-board.

GAMBA BASS. ⎱ Stops of 8-feet tone are found in the Concert Organ (Styles 43 and 500), and
GAMBA TREBLE. ⎰ resemble the Melodia and Diapason, but are brilliant in tone and of a purer quality. (See also Viol di Gamba.)

HAUTBOY. Sometimes divided into HAUTBOY TREBLE and HAUTBOY BASS. A stop of 8-feet tone ; of brighter tone than Gamba Bass and Treble.

KERAULOPHON. In two and three manual organs, 8-feet throughout. On the swell.

MELODIA. A treble stop giving the 8-feet tone. Its bass stop is the Diapason.

MELODIA DOLCE. (See English Horn Dolce, page 26.)

MUSETTE. A treble stop, very reed-like, of 16-feet tone.

OCTAVE COUPLER. See Couplers, pages 24, 25.

PEDAL COUPLER. See Couplers, page 25.

PIANO HARP. This stop is found in Styles 74, 302, and 328, and consists of three and a half octaves of steel tongues, firmly fixed between metal plates, and secured to a sound board. They are attached to the upper part of the manual, and made to sound by a pianoforte action connected with the keyboard when the stop is drawn. The Piano Harp is of 8-feet pitch, and can be played alone, or in combination with any stop or combination of stops, and will rarely require tuning. It is useful as a solo stop, and imparts to the organ an element of life and brilliancy, its sweet tone blending with the reed changes its entire character, and adds immensely to the power.

PICCOLO. A set of reeds in the treble of Style 501, of 4-feet pitch, corresponding to the Flute, as often used, but of improved quality.

PRINCIPAL BASS. ⎱ Other names for Viola and Flute, but found in the large organs.
PRINCIPAL TREBLE. ⎰

SALICIONAL or VIOL D'AMOUR. 8-feet throughout. Swell. Two and three-manual organs.

SERAPHONE. A marked and effective treble stop of 8-feet tone, of a delicate, soft quality, yet possessing great brilliancy. The reeds are ingeniously arranged and peculiarly tuned, and after long and careful experiment have been adjusted to give two qualities of tone. A subdued, soft tone with slight blowing, and a bright, ringing quality, when heavy pressure is given from the foot blowers.

SUB-BASS or SUB-BASE. This stop, bringing into use an independent set of large and powerful bass reeds, affects only the lowest octave, and gives the 16-feet tone. Although played with the keys, the Sub-Bass resembles the pedal notes of an organ, and is thus especially useful for ladies, and those who dislike playing the pedals. Its connection with the keyboard commences at the lowest C in the Diapason set, and extends to its octave above. In some styles the action closely resembles that of the

Octave Coupler. In others, a wire thumbscrew connected with the key and reed valve opens a pallet over the reeds, and so lets in the air. In the MASON & HAMLIN organ with F compass and Sub-Bass, the lowest octave and a half, or twenty notes, give the Sub-Bass tone, *if the Octave Coupler* be also drawn.

This important improvement is owing to the position upon the air chamber, and to the construction, lately improved. A small wooden pin (connected with the reed valves, and operated by the key) lifts up a short lever, which is centred on the Sub-Bass pallet. The Sub-Bass pallets are mounted on brass flanges, having double pointed centre-bearings, and thus are frictionless, instantaneous in action, and are unaffected by temperature. The Sub-Bass pallet when raised allows the reeds to vibrate. The shade above the Sub-Bass must be removed before the action can be seen; the shade is fastened by two angle plates, or by two screws passed through the shade. (Also see page 22.)

TREMULANT. This stop, when drawn, allows the wind to pass through the small bellows enclosed in the square box to be seen on the top of the valve-board. A trembling sound is thus given to any stop used in connection with it. In some organs, not by MASON & HAMLIN, this stop is miscalled Vox Humana, although incapable of the latter's varied effects.

VIOLA. A bass stop of 4-feet tone. Its natural treble is the Flute.

VIOLA DOLCE. A mechanical stop affecting the Viola set of reeds. This stop subdues the tones of the Viola, by the swell-board being divided and pressed firmly over the reed board by a strong spring. It acts upon the stop-valve and also upon the swell-valve, which cover the Viola reed chambers; subduing the tones and furnishing a set of 4-feet reeds in the bass of great delicacy and sweetness, especially valuable as an accompaniment for any treble stop used as a solo. It secures the softest possible effect, without sacrifice of promptness of speech, and is useful as a solo stop for soft interludes. It can also be used to produce, by means of the Full Organ stop, the effects such as are secured by combinations of the upper and lower manuals of a two-manual organ. When the full power of the organ is wanted, this stop should not be drawn.

VIOL D'AMOUR, sometimes called SALICIONAL. 8-feet soft, reed tone, upper manual, throughout. In some organs Viol d'Amour is a soft stop of the same pitch, compass, and construction as the Euphone. It has, however, a strong swell, to which only a small quantity of air is admitted. It imitates well the pathetic tone of the violin, and is useful for soft passages, or as an echo to the Euphone.

VIOL DI GAMBA, or GAMBA. A treble stop of a reed-like quality of tone, and of 8-feet pitch.

VIOLONCELLO PEDALS. This stop acts upon the pedals alone, which are in compass two octaves and a half, CC to F, thirty notes. Its lowest note is of 8-feet tone. The earlier MASON & HAMLIN pedal organs are in compass two octaves and one note, CC to D.

VOIX CELESTE. A treble stop of 8-feet tone is an improvement on other stops of this name or character. When played loud, it has the ring of a clarion; when soft, the delicacy of the Eolian harp. In some styles, by the peculiarity of the tuning, one of the sets of reeds forming the Voix Céleste sounds very slightly *above* the normal pitch and one very slightly *below*. But in most MASON & HAMLIN organs it is composed of two sets of 8-feet reeds in the treble. As now used, this stop retains and increases all the charms which have rendered it so popular, while it avoids the real objections which have existed to it in other forms. As commonly constructed, one of the two sets of reeds forming this stop is tuned a little above or below the normal pitch, so producing the peculiar tone-wave desired. This is objectionable, because one of the sets of reeds in the organ must always be out of tune, and so offensive to a sensitive musical ear. In this new Voix Céleste both sets of reeds are precisely in tune.

Only when used together as a Céleste one of them is slightly changed in pitch, and a peculiarly fine effect is produced by the mode of admitting air to its chambers, and by the reflection of its tones.

This stop is called by various misleading names, in organs not by MASON & HAMLIN, such as "Kalophon," "Vox Argentine," Vox Angelique," "Concerto," "Orchestral," "Vaolete," "Jubilante," "Concert Flute," and probably others.

VOIX CÉLESTE in Style 1400 is a treble stop of 16-feet tone, and is produced by causing two sets of reeds of 16 feet, slightly differing in pitch, and peculiarly voiced, to sound together. One set of reeds is tuned a little above the pitch of the Clarinette stop, and the other a little below, so that when played with any other stop, the blending of the tone-wave is perfected. The common mode of producing it is to have one set of reeds at the normal pitch, and one considerably above or below, which brings this stop so much out of tune as to make it offensive to a highly cultivated ear.

VOX HUMANA. This stop has no sound in itself, but acts upon the air in a peculiar manner, giving brightness with a slightly tremolo and charming wave-like effect ; varying according to pressure. Thus a wonderful approach to the sympathetic tones of the human voice is given.

The MASON & HAMLIN Vox Humana entirely changes the reed tone, for by it a fan is caused to revolve rapidly in the interior of the organ, imparting to the tones of any stop in use a peculiar wave, similar to that which the best vocalists give to their voices, in order to produce deeper expression. It affects some stops more than others : thus affording variety. The Flute, Viola, and most Solo Stops— Seraphone, Voix Céleste, Euphone, Viol d'Amour, Gamba, Saxaphone, Musette—are generally the stops most affected. The Vox Humana is usually drawn by an ordinary stop in the name-board, sometimes by pushing in a little knob marked "OFF," at the side of the ivory tablet in the name-board marked "Vox Humana." This causes a similar knob marked "ON" to come out on the other side. By pushing in the latter, this stop is thrown out of use. The Vox Humana in the MASON & HAMLIN organs varies from all others, especially by the employment of a Regulator (patented), which is essential to its high excellence, as it controls the rapidity of the succession of the waves of tone produced, thus producing an admirable emotional and flowing effect.

It is composed of a wheel inside a box, air-tight but for two apertures. This is termed the motor. A current of air passes through the box and works the wheel. This wheel turns a spindle, on which turns a fan placed just at the back of the reeds. It would be well to mention that the working of the fan on the axis is ensured by a small pin, which passes through the spindle, and, being bent, enters the fan close by where the spindle enters. In the latest styles, the fan fits on a brass cross-piece in the spindle, and can be easily unscrewed, if required.

If the fan works slowly, owing to dryness or corrosion of the bearings, apply tallow with blacklead, and in very rare cases a minute drain of oil, to the spindle. Sometimes the apertures in the box become filled with dust, or dampness causes the wooden flanges of the wheel to swell. In the former case, clean them out ; in the latter, shave away the wood. The motor can be taken out after raising the lid of the organ, or taking out the fall-board, and by taking out three screws that fasten the motor to the wind-chest ; detach or unscrew the brass strap that connects the slide with the lever on the name-board. Either side of the motor can be taken off, and examination will reveal any difficulty that may occur. Sometimes the fan will not work properly, owing to the small valve in the action-board under the motor not opening, as it ought to do, about one-eighth of an inch. See to the obstruction, and, if necessary, file away the wood. Sometimes the brass wire-spring becomes weak : this can be strengthened by taking out the screw that fastens it on, and bending it. Care must be taken to replace it in the slot.

ESCAPE OF WIND, when the stop is not being used, is often caused by the wooden rod that works the valve becoming tight ; take it out, and reduce the size with glass paper. If a journey causes the stop to stick, it is owing to the brass spring on the lever of the stop becoming bent, or getting out of place; or, more rarely, by the screws that hold the wooden guides of the lever becoming bent. If a noise is caused by the button on the outside of the motor becoming loose, give the screw a turn to the right. If the fan buzzes, probably the standard is too far from the motor; bend it in, and fasten it by tightening the screws. A minute drain of oil to the spindle will cure it, if all other remedies fail.

Wald Flute. A 4-feet bright tone, throughout, upper manual.

Automatic Bellows Swell. By this swell, most admirable for its capacity for light and shade, a player can produce with little practice perfect *crescendos* and *diminuendos*. This is effected simply by blowing. It prevents the instrument from sounding out of tune, by counteracting the effect of the varying pressure of wind, and is not liable to get out of order. This swell is found in the four-octave organs, and in the earlier Mason & Hamlin organs, but has been superseded by the combination knee swell.

Automatic Swell. This is connected with the bellows of the organ, and is operated by the ordinary process of blowing, without any unusual motion of hands or feet. To increase in loudness, it is only necessary to blow faster; to diminish, blow more slowly, or stop blowing until the desired softness is attained. In organs having both the knee and automatic swell, to use the latter it is only necessary to fold the knee swell lever closely against the front of the organ, where it will be held by a spring. When the knee swell lever is in position for use, the automatic swell is not in use.

Catch (for Full Organ Knee Stop or Knee Swell). This is applied to the Full Organ stop, and in some cases to the knee swell. When either of these is pressed to the right or left, a lever (the catch) falls and holds the stop or swell open. A slight elevation of the knee lifts the catch, and suffers the swell or stop to close. A button is provided under the key-board, at either end, by which the catch can be prevented from operating, when this is desired.

Combination Knee Swell. This swell has the advantage of combining with it the automatic bellows swell. The knee pedal or swell will be found fastened by a spring under the key-board. There are three positions of the knee pedal :—

1. Pressed close to the panel, or flat against the front of the organ, the automatic bellows swell is on, and therefore the blowing must be proportioned to the volume of sound required. Any power can thus be obtained.
2. Loose—softest possible tone.
3. Open to the right—full power.

In two-manual organs two of these knee pedals or swells are found, of which the one at the treble end acts on the lower set of keys; the one at the bass on the upper set.

If this swell does not act, proceed as described under *Knee Swell*.

With this swell is usually found a small button under the key-board, which, when turned, allows a catch or lever to fall. If the swell passes this lever, it is held there till released by the knee or hand.

To take off the Swells. Having removed the key-board, take out the screws and the brass fittings from the various stops that go across the swells. In organs with the knee swell, the wire connecting the knee pedal and the swells must be removed. To do this, turn the button just above the wire, and the button below the action-board, fastened to the supports of the bellows. To find the button, take out the back, or turn the organ on to its bass end.

Where there is the Hautboy stop, remove the small brass hook that fastens down the key-board. Raise the swells, so that they may pass from under the brass lever at either end, and they may be lifted out.

FOOT SWELLS. When the swell is at the top of the opening made for it, it is closed ; when at the bottom. it is open. It can be fastened open by sliding it into the notch to the left. In the two-manual organs, of the two-foot swells, the one at the treble end acts on the lower row ; the one at the bass on the upper.

BALANCE SWELL supersedes these (see page 57), for in old pedal organs there are two projecting iron levers, of which the one nearest the bass (except in Styles 800 and 1200) is the blower (to be used instead of the handle at the back) ; the other near the treble end is the swell, and acts on both rows of keys. In solo passages the lower manual, as giving more tone, is preferable.

FULL ORGAN. FOOT PEDAL. Composition pedal, at .bass end, throws on all stops.

FULL ORGAN is a knee stop opposite the left knee of the player. On being pressed to the left as far as it will go, all the sounding stops and the octave coupler are brought into use. It returns by a spring. It is of great use to conceal changes from stop to stop. Full Organ Knee Stop does not bring into operation the Eolian Harp, Voix Céleste, or either of the three Dolces, for each of these five stops throws the instrument *slightly out of tune.* The combination (knee) swell may well be used at the same time, and thus the full power is obtained.

A small wooden button may usually be found under the key-board to the left, which, when turned, allows a catch or lever to fall. If the stop passes this lever, it is held there till released by pressing upwards with the knee or hand.

THE KNEE STOP. This stop in Styles P, Q, and 216 brings into play an extra set of reeds of 4-feet tone. These styles have the automatic bellows swell always on, and the performer can thus, by blowing fast, obtain full power, without taking his hands off the keys. When the stop is pressed to the right, only one set of reeds is on ; when to the left, both sets are on.

THE KNEE SWELL, or Pedal, opens the swells over the reeds, whereby the player has complete control over the organ, obtaining the most perfect *crescendo* or *diminuendo* at will. To open it, keep it pressed to the right. The knee swell affects all the sounding stops when the Fortes are in, except Viola Dolce and Sub-Bass.

When I. Forte is drawn, the knee swell affects the Viola, Flute, and Seraphone stops.

When II. Forte is drawn, the knee swell affects the Melodia, Voix Céleste, and Diapason.

If the knee pedal does not work easily, it may be owing to the wood swelling. If so, unscrew it, and shave away the wood on the top part of it. Sometimes, however, the fault is in the guides on which the swells work : to get at these, take out the key-board in the manner described under the various styles, and ease them where necessary.

THE KEYS.

These, being made of soft wood, are more sensitive to atmospheric changes than other parts of the mechanism. They are liable to stick in the mortises or holes in which the pins work at either end. To remedy this, move the key up and down a number of times, pressing it firmly to the right and left, so that the aperture may be a little enlarged. If this does not cure it, remove the " back catch " or back rail of the action, which holds the keys in place and is secured by five screws ; take out the key that sticks, and, on carefully observing the aperture in which the key-pin works, a dark mark will be seen on either side of it. If this mark be filed away the key will not stick. If the aperture is covered with cloth, or what is technically termed *bushed,* insert the small end of a tuning fork, and press it firmly against the part where the dark mark appears. If in a journey the key-pin has become bent, straighten it with the pliers.

In Organs with Stops, to take out a key, the board containing the stops must be unscrewed, the rail at the back of the keys must then be removed, and the key lifted out. If the key is made too loose on the pins, the note is apt to jar or rattle when struck.

Cases occur where the front rail warps inward and catches the key when pressed down ; in this case the whole of the keys must be taken out and the rail cut away with a chisel or rough file.

The keys may stick down by the fret or lock-board under them pressing too closely against the fronts. To alter this, loosen the screws at each end of the lock-board and place a small piece of cloth or cardboard just above the screw-hole. If the sticking is more in the centre of the key-board than at the ends, and it is from the rubbing of the lock-rail on the fronts of the keys, remove the lock-rail and insert a screw into the key-frame near the centre. By turning this screw in or out the lock-rail may be kept at a proper distance from the keys.

When a key will not rise, it does not follow that the fault lies in the key, but it is as likely that the push-pin underneath is swollen. A little glass-paper will cure this (see Drawing No. 1, letter E, and Drawing No. 3).

To Regulate the Depth of the Key-board Touch.

1. *To make the touch deeper.* Lower the metal standards (letter I, Drawing No. 1) by cutting away the wood under them and on which they rest, and then re-screw.

2. *To make the touch shallow.* Raise these standards by inserting veneer under them ; or cut the slot deeper in which the metal pivot is inserted ; or cut and put in a new set of push-pins. Another method would be to take off the arms of the key-frame and cut them into the frame itself deeper, then raise the stop-board so as to allow the key to rise, regulating the stop action to it by raising the brass levers on the wood levers (seen at letter G, Drawing No. 1).

To Regulate the Touch of the Two Manual Organs. Take out the key-board, and, on setting one end of it on the floor, you will observe two wooden nuts at each end of the key-frame. To make the touch DEEPER, turn the large screw out (placed at the bottom and in front of the frame), and then turn the wooden nut *down.* About one turn will be sufficient. To make the touch *more* SHALLOW, turn the large screw out at the back of the frame, and screw the nut *up* about one turn.

REEDS. SUB-BASS. Should any of the notes in the Sub-Bass not speak freely, see first whether any dust or chip has got into the reed ; and if not, it is caused by its not being quite in place. If any one projects out more than another, then press it in as far as it will go. These notes are usually in place when flush with the board beneath them.

Again, a shaving or piece of paper may have blown over the top of the reed chamber aperture. This can be seen by removing the shade placed over the Sub-Bass (by taking the screw from each angle), and the tongues of the reeds should be seen. Remove any dust or the obstruction.

In some Sub-Bass actions, the pin which raises the lever must be lengthened by gluing a small cloth washer under the lever, at the point where the pin touches, should the Sub-Bass notes not speak quickly. A regulating screw will be found in most styles.

In the " Liszt " Model, Style 501, the buttons under the action board must be raised for each note. They will be seen when the board is unscrewed and lifted off. (See pages 41 and 42.)

REED CHAMBERS LEAKING. This will allow two notes to sound at the same time ; cause them (as it is termed) to run one into the other, and so make a confusion of sounds. This can only be caused through extreme damp, severe atmospheric changes, or want of ventilation. To remedy this, take off the valve board. It is then necessary to gently force off the tube board (containing the reed chambers), level it, scrape off the old glue from the sounding board and re-glue it. It will be necessary to take out all the reeds, the reed valves, the valve springs, and all other parts which will be in the way of the cramps or hand screws.

This must only be done in the manufactory, where every appliance for heating clamps and other necessaries are in constant use, and must not be attempted by any unskilful person.

SPRINGS. There are various kinds used, such as valve springs, pedal or feeder springs, exhaust bellows springs, and springs for closing the swell shutters. If at any time one of these springs should break, the broken one should be sent as a guide. If the metal spring works noisily on its wooden bearings, use a little grease.

A noise, when the Automatic Swell is in use, is sometimes caused by the friction of the swell springs on the shutter.

STOPS BECOMING FIXED. When this occurs, so that they will not move either in or out, it is caused by the brass slide, which works under the cover of the reed chambers, being drawn out too far. The cover must be raised and the slide pushed in.

STOPS PULLING OUT. Sometimes it is only a screw has worn loose, which can be seen at once and replaced with a larger one. The Bourdon pedal stop pulling out too far, is from the block on the slide coming off. This must be re-glued and screwed, but it will be better to take out the reed slide and shave the edges, for the damp has caused the wood to swell. The back, pedal trackers, and action cover must be removed before access to the slide can be had.

STOPS REMAINING ON. Sometimes a stop remains on ; that is, when it is pushed in the sound still continues when a key is pressed down, resulting often in a slight whistle on some notes. To remedy this, see that the wooden cover extending over the reed chambers is firmly pressed down in every part. If this is not air-tight, it will allow the stop to sound, and must be made to close.

Sometimes a chip, or piece of wood, may prevent this closing firmly ; or the spring may have become bent, so as to be powerless. It consists of a long piece of brass wire, with the ends bent opposite ways. One end is fastened into the wooden cover and the other into the action. It should by no means be taken out, unless it is impossible to make the cover air-tight in any other way, as it requires very great care to replace it.

If, however, no other means will succeed, take it out and twist each point a little to the left. Replace it very carefully, together with its cloth rests. This must not be attempted by any unskilled person. If the spring is slightly shortened, it may prevent the sounding of the stop.

The stop action levers being of wood in the latest styles, must be reduced in thickness if swollen. The cloth bearings also. A spring judiciously added underneath these levers may be of use if still sluggish.

NOTES SOUNDING at the treble end without the stop being drawn, in the Flute and Melodia stops, is caused by the *mute* (a wooden pin passing through the stop slide) becoming swollen, or not dropping when the stop slide is shut. The swells must be taken quite off, and the *mutes* eased, or the spring strengthened.

VOX HUMANA derangements (page 29).

ESCAPE OF WIND after a stop is pushed in, is caused by the suction valve (seen at the end of the tube board, under the stop shutter) remaining open. Work it forwards and backwards several times, and the escape will cease.

THE REEDS, OR VIBRATORS.

The Reeds, or Vibrators, are fixed in the tube-board air-chambers in rows, divided bass and treble, and are got at either from the front or back of the organ, according to the style of the particular instrument, and every reed is lettered F, G, A, B, C, D, E. In some models each reed is numbered; thus, C is numbered 8; C sharp, 9; D, 10; D sharp, 11; E, 12; F, 1; F sharp, 2; G, 3; G sharp, 4; A, 5; A sharp, 6; B, 7; and so on in each octave.

THE REEDS OF A MASON & HAMLIN ORGAN.

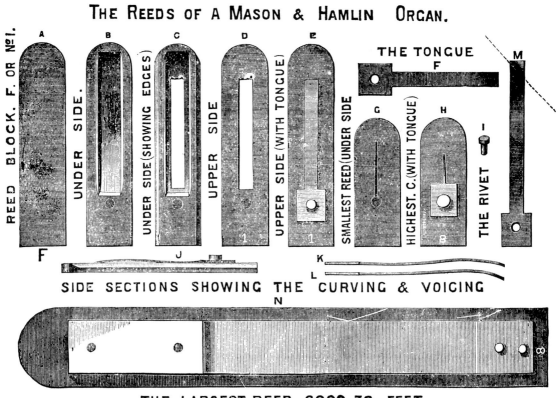

SIDE SECTIONS SHOWING THE CURVING & VOICING

THE LARGEST REED. CCCC. 32 FEET.

As the reeds are the actual tone-producers of the instrument, they constitute its most important part, and in their manufacture and subsequent preparation for use necessarily demand considerable care and attention. The materials used are those which have been found best adapted for the production of an even, round quality of tone, and the processes of manufacture are conducted upon principles deduced from untiring experiments, and confirmed by experience now extending over many years.

The block (see Fig. A) is first stamped from a sheet of brass about ⅛-inch thick, and is then milled on the under side (Figs. B and C) to facilitate the passage of air and to permit of the reed speaking promptly. The tongue (Fig. F) is next cut, from metal specially rolled, then bored for the

and finally rivetted to the block. These processes are conducted by the aid of machinery for the purpose of ensuring uniformity of tone quality. The removal of the marks of the machinery is performed by hand-filing, and the reed, if necessary, is brought to " pitch " by a further filing of the tongue, a process requiring to be accomplished with great evenness, in order not to injure the vibratory curve. Each reed 's correctly pitched by the aid of a tuning machine, or by means of a tuned instrument, the keys of which are held down by a small weight as required.

The process of manufacture here explained is common to all reeds used in the American Organ ; but the size of the reeds and the thickness of their blocks and tongues vary, according as the pitch is high or low, from Figs. G, H, to Fig. N ; this last producing a note equal to that of a pipe 32 feet in length. Reeds also vary in size and pattern, and in the relative proportions of their tongues and blocks, according to the different registers in which they are to be used, and the corresponding qualities of tone it is desired they shall produce. The reeds represented in the illustrative figures are mostly those used in the 8-feet register, which is found in both large and small organs.

VOICING.

As formerly used, reeds were quite flat and straight, and produced the thin tone which characterized the instruments in which they were employed. About forty years ago, Mr. Emmons Hamlin discovered that, by bending and twisting the tongue, the quality of tone was modified and could be greatly improved. This discovery enabled him to develop his system of voicing (by which the American Organ has been rendered so popular), and the *voicing of reeds* has now become an art, widely adopted in America. Factories exist and tuners are employed exclusively for the voicing of reeds ; and the various systems of voicing now in vogue will, in a large measure, account for the different qualities of tone found in the organs of different makers.

The Mason & Hamlin system of voicing differs from the systems of other makers. It differs also according to the different descriptions of reeds (see page 34) requiring to be voiced. In a small handbook it is not practicable to give details of the methods peculiar to each description of reed ; nor, indeed, is this necessary, as reeds for the Mason & Hamlin organs procured in this country will be found to be voiced ready for use. The following notes, however, descriptive of the method applicable to register Melodia-Diapason, are given for the guidance of tuners abroad, who not infrequently have to prepare reeds for themselves.

The necessary tools comprise a fine file (with a " safe " edge), a small pair of round-nosed pliers, and a " bender," or burnisher, which is a piece of thin half-round steel, about 2 inches long, and $\frac{3}{8}$ inch wide on the face, near the handle, graduated to a point at the farther end.

Commencing with the lowermost reed in the row, and holding it by its rivetted end in the left hand, the tongue is, by means of the bender, bent upwards from about the middle of its length and then downwards to the point. The bender is then placed between the tongue and the block, at a distance of about half an inch from the point of the tongue. The right-hand corner of the point of the tongue is then taken between the pliers (in the right hand) at the angle (see dotted line, Fig. M) of about 45 degrees, and curled downwards until it assumes the shape (Fig. K). The thumb is then moved backwards, followed by the pliers at right angles to the tongue, which is bent until it assumes the shape (Fig. L). The reed is then turned, bringing the point of the tongue towards the operator, and the tongue further bent with the pliers until it assumes the final shape (Fig. J). The reed is then held in the position in which it appears in Fig. J, and if the bending has been properly performed, the under surface of the tongue towards the point, and the upper surface of the tongue at the heel, will, upon the tongue being gently depressed, both be just level with the upper surface of the block. Care should be taken that the openings on each side, between the tongue and the block, are equal; the heel of the tongue cannot fit too closely, provided it does not touch the block.

As the reeds dealt with become smaller, the bend and twist are correspondingly reduced, until the tongues of the smallest reeds are left straight. The points and edges of the tongues are cleaned up with the file, so that the tongues will pass through the blocks without any burr. The bender, or burnisher, is very useful for clearing off filings and burnishing edges.

When placed in the tube-board the reeds should be tested singly, from the lowermost upwards, and should produce a round, even quality of tone. Any unevenness will be due to inequality in the bending of the tongue, which can only be remedied when, by practice and the exercise of a little patience, it has been ascertained what adjustment is required. It should be remembered that a straight tongue is harsh, and that softness of tone will be exactly proportionate to the degree in which a tongue has been bent.

It may be added that a close-fitting reed speaks promptly, but is unsatisfactory in tone, and that an open-fitting reed produces a good tone, but is sluggish in speech. Also, that no two tuners voice exactly alike.

TUNING.

When the several rows of reeds have been voiced and placed in the tube-board air-chambers, the reeds require a final tuning before the organ is ready for use. This is done upon the system known as "equal temperament," now generally adopted in tuning pianos and other key-board instruments. The requisite tools comprise a sharp, thin, narrow "fine-cut" file, sharpened at the end, so as to be available for either filing or scraping; and a thin slip of brass or steel for placing between the tongue and block of the reed, while the reed is being tuned.

In tuning, particular attention is required to the following points :—The pressure upon the bellows, when in use, must be kept as nearly as possible at half pressure throughout the entire process. A reed is sharpened by filing or scraping the point, or free end, of the tongue; and flattened by filing or scraping at the foot or heel. Filing is best for reeds in Styles A to 4402, and most American Organs; and scraping for reeds in the Orchestral Organ, Style 1400. In filing or scraping care must be taken not to injure the curve of the tongue, or the voicing will suffer; and for this reason the tool must be kept sharp.

A tuner need not possess a musical ear, but it is necessary he should be able to detect and measure the rate of duration of the beats, waves, or pulsations which are produced by the sounding together of two notes which are not in unison; as it is by producing, augmenting, or diminishing these beats that tuning is accomplished. The first and most important part of the process consists in laying what are termed "the bearings"; i.e., in tuning an octave (sometimes more) called "the scale," so as to form a groundwork from which the tuning of the rest of the instrument may proceed. The scale is always laid in the row of reeds which form the Diapason register; and is generally commenced at middle C (sometimes A above), as it is at this part of the instrument that the beats are best heard.

Scale commencing on Middle C. The following is the scale now generally used. The open note in each case represents a note already tuned ; the closed note is that which has to be tuned to its predecessor, flat or sharp, in the proportion indicated.

In using this scale, first tune C to the pitch of a tuning-fork, or ascertain that C accords in pitch with the rest of the organ. Then sound C with G and listen for beats. If no beats are produced, G must be flattened until about 2 beats occur in a second. If, on the other hand, beats are heard, ascertain whether G is flat or sharp by noting the rate of their occurrence, first with both keys well down, and then with the G key allowed to rise slowly. If as the key rises the beats become more frequent, G is flat ; if they become less frequent it is sharp ; and G must be sharpened or flattened until, with both keys well down, it produces about two flat beats per second. Proceed in this way to the note C sharp, leaving each note flat with its predecessor in about the following proportions per second :—G, 2 beats ; D, $1\frac{1}{2}$ beats ; A, 1 beat ; E, 2 beats ; B, $\frac{1}{2}$ beat ; F sharp, $\frac{1}{2}$ beat ; C sharp, 2 beats ; G sharp is tuned perfect to C sharp, i.e., these notes when sounded together should produce no beat.

Starting again from C, the remaining notes of the scale are *sharpened*, each with its predecessor, in about the following proportions per second :—F, 2 beats ; B flat, 1 beat ; E flat, $\frac{1}{2}$ beat. When the scale has been tuned correctly, G sharp (the last note tuned in the first division) and E flat (the last note tuned in the second) should be perfect, or smooth.

The following chords, which should all sound equally smooth, may be used to test the scale, as the tuning proceeds.

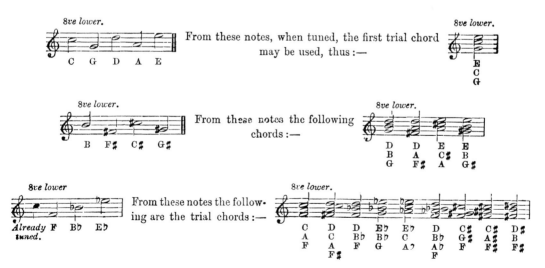

The scale being finished, the rest of the key-board is tuned by octaves, each note being left perfect, and the remaining stops are tuned perfect to the Diapason set of reeds.

Note.—For exceptionally fine tuning, and to ensure the several stops being properly *tempered* for separate use, EACH REMAINING STOP may be first tuned independently by the process above described, and such adjustments then made throughout the stop as may be necessary to ensure smoothness when it is in use with stops already tuned. When this course is adopted, it is desirable, before tuning the higher and lower reeds, to test the scale or bearings of the second (or subsequent) stop, and make each note perfect with the note in the stop (or stops) already tuned which is operated by the same key.

THE OLD OR LONG SCALE. The following is the old or long scale, here inserted because it is useful as a guide, in tuning by octaves, after the bearings have been laid by the scale already given; if preferred, it may be used in its entirety.

Trial Chords.
All must be equally smooth.

The white notes are supposed to be tuned, and the black tuned in progressions of 5th and Octaves. Each 5th must be a shade flat and each Octave perfect.

The scale can be tried in the chord F, A, C, E, B, and B flat. When these are agreeable, the remainder is nearly sure to follow smoothly.

COMBINATION SCALE. The following is another scale, the use of which ensures the brevity of the scale first given, and the accuracy in tuning by octaves afforded by the long scale :--

FIRST DIVISION.   SECOND DIVISION.
8ve lower.

Tune pitch C in unison with a tuning fork, and middle C in unison with pitch C. The closed notes as far as B are tuned flat, each with its predecessor, in about the following proportions, per second :--G, $\frac{2}{3}$ beat ; D, $\frac{2}{3}$ beat ; A, $\frac{3}{4}$ beat ; E, $\frac{3}{4}$ beat ; B, 1 beat. All the closed notes in the second division are sharpened, each with its predecessor, about one beat per second.

When the scale has been correctly tuned, B and F sharp upon being sounded together should produce about one beat per second ; and this should disappear upon the B key being allowed to rise half its depth. If the result is otherwise, it will be necessary to ascertain the extent to which, and the direction in which, the B and F sharp interval is incorrect, and then carefully go over the scale again, making such adjustments as may be required.

The scale having been carefully completed, the rest of the key-board is tuned by octaves, each note being tested by its fourth and fifth, thus :—

8ve lower.
F   Being tuned.   F♯   G

F   Try it with   A♯ C A♯ F   F♯   B C♯ B F♯ G   C D C G
Already   its fourth   Already   Already
tuned.   and fifth.   tuned.   tuned.

and so on ; and, if necessary, adjusted so that it will beat equally with either. If, in ascending, the note beats more rapidly with its fourth than its fifth, it requires flattening, and *vice versâ*. If, in descending, the note beats more rapidly with its fourth than its fifth, it requires sharpening, and *vice versâ*.

How to Take the Organ Apart.

TO GET TO THE ACTION AND MECHANISM.

How to take an Organ apart. It often happens that slight derangements occur which can be easily remedied, and to assist, the following directions are given, which will apply, as far as it is possible, to all kinds of American Organs, and to every style made by the Mason & Hamlin Organ Company, from Styles A to Z, and from Styles 1 to 4402, unless otherwise specified in the index (pages 3, 4, and 5 and 42), the slight variations in the different styles being easily understood.

Except, then, where express instructions are given under the particular style, the following is the best mode of opening an organ. The only tools necessary are a little iron hook (called a reed-hook), which will be found secured in the organ, at the back of the key-board, and a screwdriver.

To get at the Reeds. Remove the lock-rail, which is beneath and in front of the keys, after having taken out the screw at each end. Open the swell, and the reed-chambers will be seen.

Should the organ have stops, the Melodia and Diapason reeds will be seen when those stops are drawn. (The only exceptions are in the two-manual and pedal organs, and in the "Queen's" Model [Style 512], when Clarinet, Bourdon, and Sub-Bass reeds are in the front, and in Style 2,391 [the 16-feet reeds], Clarinet and Bourdon.) The reeds for the Viola, Flute, Seraphone, Musette, Clarionet, &c., &c., are at the back; this can be unscrewed, or the hinged part lowered by turning the knobs, buttons, or wires which secure it at the back or ends. With the swell raised, and by drawing the corresponding stops, the reeds can be reached.

The following list gives the names of all the stops found in small organs, and how the reeds of the stops can be reached: from the front, Clarabella and Dulciana, Melodia and Diapason; from the back, Clarionet and Viola Dolce, Oboe and Viola; Voix Céleste, from the front and back.

To reach the Viola set of reeds in those styles which have a Sub-Bass, it may be necessary to remove the Sub-Bass box altogether, which is done by taking out the screws in the slotted end of the brasses which hold down the Sub-Bass.

To reach the Viola set in those styles with Eolian Harp, it may be necessary to remove the box containing the Eolian Harp set. This may be done by loosening the screws in the slotted end of the brasses which secure the box to the action, and moving the box to one side to release it from the screws.

The Eolian Harp set is inside the long narrow box, which will at once be seen on removing back of organ, and the reeds can be drawn out, when the stop is drawn and the top of the box raised.

To reach the Sub-Bass reeds, remove the back of the organ, or lower the hinged portion; loosen the screws at ends that secure the box over the Sub-Bass reeds, slide the box forward and remove it; on pressing the key the Sub-Bass valve will rise. It then can be turned back and the reed drawn out. In returning the box to place, be careful to have the iron lever that opens the Sub-Bass stop-valve in proper position behind the button.

In Styles 547 and 551, Action 86, the box over the Clarionet must be unscrewed to get at these reeds, which are at the back of Flute reeds.

In Action 87, the Bourdon Clarinet set occupies the position of the Diapason Melodia set in the other styles, and the Diapason Melodia set the position of the Viola Flute set.

In Actions 50 and 86 the Seraphone set is over the Flute set, and the Eolian Harp is over the Viola set.

CHANCEL ORGANS (Styles 434, 350, 4402, &c). The exterior swell must be removed to get at the back sets of reeds. To do this, unscrew the top and the swell, take off the leather buttons, and then disconnect.

EXTERIOR SWELL. A device by which the case of the organ, at the back or on the top, can be opened and shut by the performer at will, thus confining and subduing the tone, or allowing it to escape as fully as though the top of the organ were opened. Similar in construction to the Venetian swell-box of a pipe organ.

To TAKE OUT A REED. The reeds should be drawn out of the chambers in which they are confined, by means of the reed-hook, as shown in the cut.

In catching hold of the reed, great care must be taken not to press the reed-hook against the reed; neither must it be inserted so far as to catch the end of the tongue. Be careful also not to let it slip from the rivet, which might injure the reed chamber. If a reed should adhere firmly to the chamber, start it in a little by a sharp tap on the end of the block. It will then be easy to draw it out.

If a note is dumb, it is only from a minute piece of wood which has caught in the reed; the obstruction can be removed by a slight blow on the reed-block.

To TAKE OUT THE BACK. Remove the screws which hold it. The upper part is usually hinged, and can be lowered or lifted out by turning or removing the fastenings which secure it.

To TAKE THE TOP OFF. After lowering the hinged part of the back, take out from each end, *inside the organ*, a round-headed screw which passes through the end blocks on the under-side of the top. Two screws must be removed in some cases. All Extended Tops, Cabinets, and Etagère Tops are usually screwed on from outside, and will require no explanation. Sometimes extra screws are also placed through the under-side of the flat surface, on which the top rests; these must be taken out before the top can be lifted off.

To TAKE OUT A KEY. Unscrew and remove the fall-board. Lower the hinged part of the back. Remove the top of the organ, after taking out a screw at each end on the under-side, which secures it to the case. Unscrew and remove the shelf above fall-board. Unscrew and remove the lamp shelves. Unscrew the roller-board and name-board, and remove them together. In styles having the stop-work at the back of the keys, it will be necessary to remove the stops before the name-board can be taken out. To do this, take out the screws which secure them to the levers. The keys are now seen, and if one is to be taken off to get at the push-pin underneath, remove the catch from the back edge of the key-frame, when any key can be taken out and all faults of sticking or rattling of the keys can now be remedied.

This will apply in some styles :—Remove the round-headed screws at each end of the name-board and the small blocks above the stop-board, take out the screw from Tremulant stop. The stop-board can now be lifted up out of the way. Next remove the five screws in the long slip at the back of the keys (if a *short* screwdriver is not at hand, it will be necessary to take the back out—described above), and any key may be lifted out.

By detaching the Vox Humana and unhooking the key-frame in octave coupler organs, the entire key-frame can be raised, and, by taking off the blocks which secure the arms at the back of the key-frame, it can be taken out altogether.

If the lock-rail should be bound by the case so as to be difficult to remove, it can be relieved by inserting wedges underneath, between the action and case, one at each end, driving them just enough to free the rail, when it can be easily removed.

To TAKE OUT THE KEY-BOARD. Remove the key blocks at each end, which are secured by a screw in the end of the back of the block ; then lift out the keys, Nos. 1, 2, and 3 (F, F sharp, and G), from the bass end ; Nos. 32 and 33 (C and C sharp), and the top key, No. 61 (F), and under each vacancy will be found two screws, which remove. Take the screws out of the brass or iron supports at the treble end at the back and front of the key-board, and it can then be removed.

To TAKE OUT THE STOP BOARD. Remove the two round-headed screws by which it is hinged, after taking out the small screw from each end of the name-board, and the blocks from over the stop-board.

To TAKE OFF THE DESK. The desk may be removed by taking out one of the two screws found under the top of the stop-board, under the desk-blocks.

To TAKE OUT THE BELLOWS ACTION. Take off the top and back completely ; and, turning the organ on the end, DISCONNECT THE PEDALS by unscrewing the wooden buttons which secure the webbing to the foot pedals. Set it upright again, and remove the stop-board ; and take out four *large* round-headed screws, to be found round the action-board, and the whole of the interior can be taken out from the back.

To TAKE OFF THE VALVE BOARD. Remove the round-headed screws and washers to be found round the top edge of the valve-board, and the six flat-headed screws in front ; REMOVE THE CONNECTING WIRE at the bass end OF THE KNEE SWELL (by turning a button at the top of the swell and one below the action-board, secured to the standard of the bellows), and the valve-board can be removed.

Care must be taken, when replacing it, that the Tremulant stop piston is put into its valve, and into the hole covered with leather, over which the stop works. If the Tremulant box is taken off (it will slide off sideways, by turning one screw), care must be taken, in replacing it, that the hole in the box comes over that in the valve-board.

The following should be particularly noted for all organs with stops :—Great care should always be taken to have the stop fully open when taking out or putting in a reed, otherwise serious injury might be caused to the stop. The position of each set of reeds may be seen on drawing the stop, or on pressing the stop-lever. In large organs, in order to get at the reeds of either set, it is necessary to remove the corresponding swell, which is fastened down by two or three screws, on removing which it can be lifted out.

If, while the name-board is up, either of the brass slides should be drawn so far out as to allow the stop to close behind it, the stop must be raised and the slide put in place *before* lowering the name-board. Also, be careful to have every part remain in place while the name-board is up ; also. that the stops do not change their places. They would better be drawn out before raising the name-board.

A careful person might be able to get at the Viola Flute set, in Styles B, C, F, H, L, P, Q, R, T, V, 21, 45, 60, 202, 203, 210, 214, 218, 232, 235, and 304, for the upper part in D, E, S, and some other styles not particularly mentioned, by raising the top, drawing the stops, then opening the back swell, and passing the reed-hook carefully over the rivet of the reed. Remove the fan or Tremulant box, and the back if in the way ; but in the larger organs, as a rule, it will be found better to first take out the key-board, remove the action of Sub-Bass or Euphone, and then replace the key-board. In all cases draw the corresponding stop, or hold down the stop-lever, to reach the reeds.

In many organs (Styles 10, 12, 46, 47, 48, 73, 75, 77, 301, 302, 400, &c.) the lid or cover can be removed very easily by going to the back of the instrument and loosening the middle screw (it need not be taken out) in the plate of iron over each hinge ; then, with a slight blow of the hand, start the lid up, and it can be taken off out of the way.

To reach the Octave or Viola and Flute set of reeds, remove the back of case. The top and back will come out together upon taking out the screws from the back. Open the swell, and on drawing the Viola and Flute stops the reeds will be accessible.

When taking off the stop-board, disconnect the stops where the brass levers and the wooden levers work together, by removing the screws and washers.

When taking out the bellows action, the stop action must be disconnected from the sides of the case, by taking out the two screws from the centre, on which the brass stop-levers work.

The REVOLVING FALL can be detached from its hinge by a short, sharp pull *upwards* at each end, and removed, after unscrewing the shelf above it.

To TAKE THE ACTION OUT OF THE CASE. Take out the back and turn the organ on one end, and detach the pedal straps. Turn organ back and take out FOUR LARGE SCREWS, two at each end (see *Drawings No. 1, letter Q, and No. 2*), unscrew and remove the thin panel (under the wind-chest) near the Knee Swell and Full Organ pieces, which need not be removed. The panel will slide down behind these. (It may be necessary, to get at these screws, to turn up the outside lever at each end. These levers are easily lifted out ; a brass pin will have to be removed from end of the lever at treble end, easily seen from the back.) After having turned out the large screws, draw the action out at the back of the case. With the action out of the case, access is had to the feeders, rollers, swell action, bellows, springs, and an examination made for the purpose of finding squeaks, rattles, leaks of wind, &c., will probably be successful.

A few cases are made with a separate rail to which the Knee Swell pieces are attached. Two screws hold this rail in place, which taken out will release the rail ; take it out, and access is had to joints that need oiling under the wind-chest. Most cases are made with a thin piece at the back of the irons, which hold Knee Swell piece and Full Organ piece ; remove this thin piece to oil the joint under wind-chest.

To go further and open the action, rest it with the front on a chair, and take out the row of screws around the edge, and disconnect, underneath the action, all wires or straps that connect through with the work above. Having the action open, the fault of the pallets can be corrected, and ciphering altered. In putting the organ together again, it will be necessary to proceed carefully in inverse order as nearly as possible. In styles that have both the knee and automatic swell, be sure, in sliding the action back into the case, to see that the pin that operates the automatic swell enters the hole in the front of the case.

DIRECTIONS FOR PUTTING TOGETHER MASON AND HAMLIN MISSION ORGANS. Style 120—211.

1st. Turn organ upside down—*i.e.*, on its top or lid.
2nd. Unhook *four* brass hooks, 2 on each side of case.
3rd. Draw up pedal board with pedals.
4th. Slip the *four* corner posts into the iron sockets.
5th. Draw down *two* brass braces or rods at the back, and fasten to posts.

6th. Turn organ up into position, and connect wires to blow pedals, and slip pedals into *their* sockets.
7th. Pull down brass knee-swell at right hand of organ under the case, and it will be ready for use.

STYLES 109 and 110. BABY ORGAN. Take out the screws and remove the *upper part* of the back; raise the *swell*, and the reeds can be withdrawn.

Directions for setting up or putting together. There are four principal parts, viz., the BODY, or ACTION; the two END SUPPORTS, or LEGS; the RAIL, with pedals attached. Secure (near the exhausters), by four small screws, the thin wooden slip (to do this it is best to turn the organ on its top). Rest one end of the action on a chair. Take one of the supports (after screwing on the handles) and place it against the end of the action, allowing the dowel or fillet to enter the hole or groove made for it. The edge of the support which has the *short* leg should be sent to the front. One round-headed screw turned in from the inside at the top, over the name-board, will secure the support. Next set up the other support in the same way. Lay the organ upon its back, and screw the pedal-rail to the front leg of each support. Fix the wire pedal rods in the holes, putting one end in the pedal first, and move the pedal, so that the other end of the rod can be put in the hole of the block on the bellows. Turn each button over the pedal-rod to keep it in place. The buttons need not be taken off. Screw on the knee pedal. Stand the organ upright, and it is ready for use. To take it apart for packing, it is only necessary to reverse the order.

Should the knee pedal stick, take off a shaving from the bottom edge of the front of organ, or with glass-paper reduce that part which catches the wire, or, if necessary, bend the wire so that it works freely.

STYLE 501. "LISZT" ORGAN (and Styles 503, 504, 505, 506, 507, 508, 509, 522, 523). To reach the front reeds (Melodia and English Horn), remove the lock-rail, held by a screw at each end, raise the swell and draw the corresponding stops.

To get at the Piccolo reeds, remove the back of the organ, raise the swell, when, on drawing the stop in name-board, the reeds can be seen.

To get at the Seraphone set, remove the top and back of the organ. The reeds of this set are in a box under the fan. This box can be removed by loosening the screws that secure it to the tube-board. On pressing the key the valve will rise, and can then be turned up and the reeds drawn out.

To get at the Sub-Bass reeds, remove the top and back of the organ, loosen the screws that hold the Sub-Bass box in place, and remove it. The valve can then be turned up and the reeds drawn.

To get at the Viola reeds, it may be necessary to remove the Sub-Bass and Eolian Harp tubes. To do this, loosen the screws that hold down the brasses, and the Sub-Bass can be lifted out. To remove the Eolian Harp tube, take out the screw in the slotted part of the brass at one end, loosen the screws a little in the brasses at the other end, and slide the box away from them. The key-frame and stop-board can easily be removed together if necessary; unhook the brass hooks at front, raise the front edge, and take it out after removing the small blocks over stop-board and over the pin on each arm of key-frame. The key-frame can be lifted up to get at octave coupler, &c., &c., if the blocks (seen when the desk-shelf is taken off) are turned.

To reach the Eolian Harp reeds, remove the strip over the levers at back of roller-board. Each valve can then be turned up, and the reed will be seen.

To reach the Corno and Contra-Basso reeds, unscrew the thin slip behind the knee pedals, and if these stops are drawn, the reeds can be seen. (See Drawing No. 5, page 14.)

STYLE 512 (Action 70, Case 136). To get at the Clarinet and Bourdon sets of reeds, remove the lock-rail after taking out the screw at each end, draw the corresponding stops, open the knee swell, and the reeds are seen.

To get at the Sub-Bass set of reeds, remove the lock-rail as above ; draw the stop and open the knee swell. To get at the Melodia and Diapason reeds, lower or take out the wire panel in the back of organ, draw these stops, open the knee swell, and the reeds can be seen. To get at the Musette, Viola, and Piccolo sets of reeds, lower or remove the wire panel, as above ; now raise the swell, draw the corresponding stops, and the reeds may be seen.

For Regulating the Valves of the Musette, Viola, and Piccolo sets, lower or remove the panel at back ; remove the black strip on top of the action, and you will see a row of holes, in which is the flattened end of a screw, and by using the little key sent with organ these screws can be turned to bring the inside levers to the right adjustment. Use the greatest care in replacing every part.

STYLES 510 and 525. To get at the front reeds (Diapason and Melodia), it is only necessary to remove the lock-rail and raise the swell.

Section 1. To get at the other reeds, raise the top of the organ and allow it to fall back as far as it will go. Remove the fall-board by taking out the screw in the hinge at each end. Remove the shelf over the fall-board by taking out a screw in each end and drawing it forward. Remove the pedal coupler by taking out the two back screws in each end.

Section 2. To get at the reeds of the Contra-Basso, Corno, Viola Flute, and Seraphone sets, proceed as in Section 1. Next remove the Vox Humana fan by taking out the pin which holds the rod in place at the left, raising it up and towards the left, when it will become detached. Remove the bar containing the push-pins at the back, near the bass end of the stop-action or roller-board, after taking out the two screws in each brass which holds the bar to the roller-board. Disconnect the wire which is attached to the Vox Humana box to connect it with the wooden angle on the roller-board, by turning the wooden button, which is on the angle, sufficiently to allow the wire to be drawn up. Remove the lock-rail under the keys. Unhook the key-frame by drawing forward a hook (at each end of the frame underneath), and pushing the front one off the screw in the frame. Remove the two blocks to which the shelf over the fall-board was screwed. Raise the key-frame as high as it will go and prop it up. If it is found inconvenient to do this, and it becomes desirable to remove the key-frame altogether, it can be done by taking off the blocks over the hinges of the arms at the back. The Contra-Basso and Corno, Flute and Seraphone reeds can now be reached, the Seraphone set being over the Flute. To reach the Viola set, it will probably be found necessary to remove the wire coupler. Take off the block at the right-hand side and raise the ends of the wires upright so as to clear the pins. By moving the coupler to the right a short distance, it will become detached.

Section 3. To get at the Bourdon Pedal reeds proceed as in Section 1. Next remove the upright wire at the bass end by turning off the wooden button at the top end, which will allow the wire to be drawn out. Turn the wooden arm towards you as far as it will go. Remove the wooden button at treble end of the coupler bar, and turn the bar from you out of the way. Turn back the three buttons on the top of the box which secure the cover, and upon raising it the valves will be seen. These being raised will allow access to the reeds. Retrace the steps in the same order when putting the organ together.

Two Manual Organs, and Styles 800, 801, 802, &c., &c. Turn back or remove the top lid, and remove the fall-board and shelves together. Take off the lock-rail. Turn up the pedal coupler, after taking out the screw at each end which holds the iron hook in place, and throwing off the hooks. Then prop the coupler up, or, if this is not convenient, remove it altogether ; then, with the reed-hook.

unfasten the key-frame secured by three hooks. The frame may then be raised sufficiently to draw forward and remove from the organ, with name-board and stop-action all on.

Any reed (except pedal reeds) in sets, having registers in the stop-boxes at the ends, can now be reached, by first finding the position of the set by drawing the register or stop and observing the stop action. Then open the swell, and the reed may be drawn. The reeds of the Diapason Melodia and Viola Flute sets may also be reached in the same manner. The first-named set is in the back, and the latter in the front, of the second tube.

To reach the reeds of the Pedal and Eolian Harp sets, the key-frame need not be taken out; but after turning up the pedal coupler, turn up in a similar manner, or remove, the level bar immediately under it. Then remove the long box covering the pedal reeds by turning off the hook at each end. By turning up the valves over the pedal reeds, or the top of the Eolian Harp box, the reeds of these sets can now be reached.

For Contra-Basso, Corno, and Musette sets, follow directions for getting at the Ventrillo set. (See pages 14, 15, 21, and 22.)

The Octave Coupler is between the two banks of keys. Remove the fret slip between the banks, unhook the brasses at ends of key-frame, and raise the upper key-board, when the coupler will be seen.

If it becomes necessary to get at the valves (pallets) in styles having the Ventrillo set, it can be done by removing the tube-board of that set, screwed on underneath. To do this the front of Case 85 will have to be removed, when the screws around the edge of the tube-board frame can be seen. In cases where the front cannot be removed the action will have to be taken from the case at the back. (See also pages 41 and 42.)

Directions for taking PEDAL ORGANS, STYLES 800, 802, *&c., in pieces, for convenience in placing in rooms, approach to which is through narrow doors or passages.* Remove the upper lid, after easing the screws in the two iron clamp plates, over hinges at the back of case. Remove the fall and lock board, after taking out the two flat-head screws in top above the fall-board, and two round-head screws in upright piece above the top; fold the fall and lock board, and take away. Remove the stop-box covers, at each end of the key-board, after taking out the oval-head screws. Remove the lock-rail, held by screws at each end. Remove the front panelled board over the pedals, with the two brackets attached, by taking out the screws and pulling it forward to relieve it from the dowel pins that hold it in position. Remove the pedal-rail, through which the swell, blow, and full organ pedals pass, after removing screws at each end: draw the pedal key-frame out as far as it will go, turn up the two wooden buttons on each back end of the pedal-frame, and it can be taken from the case. Remove blow-handle, from back of case, after unscrewing the fulcrum from the case, and taking the bolt out at the joint near the lower end. Remove back board of case, but do not take out the screws in the top and bottom rail, until the action is out of the case. Remove indicator, by unscrewing it from the bellows. Remove the pedal-rod frame, with rods all in, after taking out the three screws in the guide, by lifting the frame out of position. Remove action, take out the upper flat-head screws, in each iron plate attached to the two brackets at the top of the action, at the back, also the round-head screws in the legs of the action, at the bottom at back, and draw the action away from the back of the case. Remove iron lever under bellows if in the way. Place the case on its back and remove the front rail and lever bar from the bottom. Replace case in former position, and remove the top and bottom rail on the back. Remove the iron and wooden rails remaining in front, which completes the taking apart.

The screws in the case to be removed are all round-head with washers, unless otherwise specified.

STYLE 901 (Action 33A, Case 116). To take out key-board :--

1. Raise the top and let it rest against the wall.

2. Turn the button (inside) at each end of the panel above the fall-board, and remove the two oval-head screws in fall-board, and it can be taken out.

3. Unscrew the lock-rail and remove it (the Melodia and English Horn reeds can be reached if those stops are drawn).

4. The large checks, forming a part of the case at each end of the keys, will come off after removing screws, marked 1, on inside of cheeks at top, and also the large screw with a red washer under the head, which is underneath the lock-rail moulding at each oval in front.

5. The Diapason, Keraulophon, and Clarinet sets of reeds are in the upper wind-chest, and with the lid and fall-board off can be got at.

6. The *Eolienne Harp and Flute* sets of reeds are in the upper wind-chest, but under the *upper* stop-action board, which takes out as follows:—Remove four screws in the upper stop-action board having red washers under the heads. The large cheeks should be off, as per clause 4, and then lift up and out the *upper* part of name-board, with stops and upper stop-action board all intact.

7. The *Eolienne Harp* set is covered by a box; to remove this, loosen screws at each end and slip it off, and the reeds are in view.

To get at the Sub-Bass and other reeds of lower manual:—Loosen screws marked 2 in stop-lever board, and push back the iron latches from under the head of the screw. Take out a round-head screw at each end of the lip of the name-board outside, and lift out the name-board and stop-lever board all together. Unhook key-frame at each end, raise it slightly in front, draw it forward and out.

Proceed now as in Style 501 (page 43).

The Contra-Basso and Corno sets of reeds can be reached after removing the rail, or strip with wire gauze panels, just at the back of the Knee Swell and Full Organ boards, by taking out four screws and drawing this piece straight down, then on moving the swell-board and drawing the stops the reeds of Corno and Contra-Basso can be seen. If it becomes necessary to regulate the connection between the valves of these sets and the keys, in consequence of unusual swelling or shrinking of the parts so that the valves are held open or do not open enough, remove the bottom of the Ventrillo chest A, after unhooking it at each end, next remove a thin strip B, in front of row of reeds, held by small round-head screws, which is inserted in a groove; the strip out, there is seen a row of holes, in each of which is the flattened end of a screw, and by using the little key sent with the organ, these screws or jacks can be turned to bring the inside levers to the right adjustment.

STYLE 904 (on Pipe Organ principle, stops drawing throughout). TWO MANUALS. Proceed as in Styles 800, 901, and 501. Being a new style, a complete list of stops is given, and a brief description of the new stops, on pages 54 and 55.

STYLE 1200 (Action 63, Case 126). To get at the Hautboy and Bassoon sets of reeds, remove the lock-rail after taking out the screw at each end. Next remove the swell by taking out the screws, and by drawing the stops the reeds can be pulled out.

To get at the reeds of the Clarion, Piccolo, Saxophone, and Seraphone reeds, which are in the upper chest, directly under the lid, raise the lid, remove the panel over the fall-board after taking out the screws at each end, and lifting it out. Now draw the corresponding stops, and the reeds can be pulled out.

To reach the Basset Horn, Trumpet, and Musette sets, take out the screw at each end of the fall-board, fold it up and remove it with the desk attached. Now by opening the swells the reeds can be pulled out.

To reach the Contra-Basso and Corno sets, open the swell under the wind-chest on the front of the organ. By drawing these stops the reeds can be pulled out.

To reach the Sub-Bourdon and Violoncello pedal reeds, unscrew and remove both parts of the back, draw the corresponding stop, and the reeds will be found over lowest wind-chest, in front of the pedal rods.

To reach the Bourdon pedal reeds, it will be necessary to remove the upper wind-chest. To do this remove the fall-board and front panel as previously explained. Also take off the upper section of the back ; then take out screw No. 5, which holds the iron latch at each end of the wind-chest at the back, push the latches aside, take out the screws in the stop-box shelves, and remove them. You now raise the upper chest at the back a little, push it forward about half an inch, and lift it out. Next remove the pedal coupler by unscrewing at each end, turn up the lever-bar immediately under it, and turn up the cover of the box held in place by buttons. This being done, the valves can be turned up and the reeds drawn.

To get at all of the remaining sets, Diapason, Melodia, Viola, Flute, English Horn, Clarabella, and the Dolce stops, take off the key-slip from under the upper set of keys, unhook the key-frame by drawing forward the brass hooks at each end, slightly raise the upper key-board, draw it forward and out, the name-board and stop-rail coming with it. Remove the lock-rail, then unfasten the lower key-frame, which is secured by three hooks at the front ; it can then be raised sufficiently to draw forward and be taken from the organ. The reeds in these sets can now be reached by drawing the register and observing the stop action. The swells will have to be removed or turned up to draw the reeds. In replacing key-frame of styles which have been used well, see that the upper levers do not catch the lower ones.

To remove stop-boxes for getting at any of the parts beneath, proceed as follows :—Take off small shelves over second row of stops ; the large shelves over boxes being off, you can then loosen the set screws holding wires in stop-knobs, and draw them out. Take out screws that fasten the boxes to ends of case, and take the boxes out. Care should be taken that the stops when put back are in their proper places.

Provision is made for attaching and oiling the blow-handle in the following manner :—Take out the back, or the screws in panel at the back of organ. This will enable you to fix the handle in place and secure the same by means of bolts, as provided with the handle.

To Regulate Pedal Coupler or Manual Coupler. Should pedal coupler or manual coupler stick, having removed upper key-board as explained above, and the stop-boxes, press down the foot pedal (marked pedal coupler) and follow its action from the upper part to its connection below, seen when front panel below key-board is taken out. Any part which is swollen, or wood crank that does not return easily, should be unscrewed and woodwork filed away or eased.

This organ can be taken apart and passed through a space 2 feet 8 inches wide.

Directions for taking Style 1200 *in pieces for convenience in passing it through narrow doors and passages.* First take out the screws and remove the pedal-rail and panel over pedal key-board ; then unbutton the pedal-frame and draw it out. Next remove small pieces screwed to case at each end of Contra-Basso and Corno swell. Next fold up the fall, and remove the lock-rail held by screws at each end ; also take out screws that connect the iron braces on the front edge of the wind-chest to ends of the case. Next take out screws and remove stop-box shelves ; then loosen tapped set screws, holding iron wires in stop-knobs and draw them out. Take out screws that fasten the boxes to the ends of the case, and take the boxes out. Care should be taken that the stops, when put back, are in their proper places. Next remove front panel over upper key-board, held by screws at each end ; then take off back. Unscrew the fall-board and remove it, or the lid and fall will come off together by taking out two screws in each end of the rail to which the lid is hinged, and slipping a bolt at each end of lid in front. Next remove the blow-handle and connecting bars to exhausters ; disconnect the indicator, and take out screws in iron braces that are fastened to the bottom rail of case, and also to each end of the case and back edge of wind-chest ; then take out screws, and remove wooden props that hold the action down at each end of case ; then remove the pieces of guide-rails that hold the pedal-rods in position, and take out rods. The action is now ready to draw back and out ; but in doing so the Full Organ coupler and swell pedals should be depressed to allow them to draw under front rail of case. The action when removed can be passed through an opening thirty-two inches wide. Place the case on its back, and remove the front rail and lever-bar from the bottom. Replace case in former position, and remove bottom rail on the back, and also wooden rail in front, which completes the taking apart. To put together again, reverse the order of the directions.

STYLE 1400. The mechanism of this organ is very complicated, and it would be best to employ a skilful workman.

To get at the reeds, unscrew the fall-board, or take the pins from the hinges at the back, and remove the top. Loose the brass and wood buttons at the top of the fret-work, and turn the two wood buttons at the inside of the back of the case. Lift out the shade and fret-work. Two large iron hooks may be seen at the side of the action near the back of the case. Unhook these, and the action can be lifted over, in a horizontal position, on a stool.

The rows of reeds can now be seen, and are placed thus, Bass commencing near the front of organ :— 1, Percussion and Cor Anglais ; 2, Bourdon ; 3, Clarion ; Harpe Eolienne, two rows in an upright position—(a) sharp set, (b) flat set ; 4, Bassoon.

At the treble end the rows of reeds are :—1, Percussion or Flute ; Voix Céleste, two rows in an upright position—(a) sharp set, (b) flat set ; 2, Clarinette ; 3, Piccolo ; 5, Musette ; 6, Baryton, both placed vertically ; 4, Hautbois.

The keys may be reached by unfastening the hook at each side of the stop-board, and raising it, the pallets by unhooking those hooks under the key-board.

The bellows may be reached by removing the panelled back secured by two screws, and the rockers and bellows-action may be seen on turning the organ on the end.

To reach the expression and double expression reservoirs, the floating valve-board can be lifted out, and access can then be also obtained to the stop-valves.

STYLE 1400. COMBINATION OF STOPS.

1. Vision Scene, in Gounod's *Faust.* French Horn Solo, with the dreamy accompaniment of violins and harp. By the use of stops, Clarinette in the right hand, and the Harpe Eolienne in the left, the effect is excellent.

2. " Serenade " from *Don Giovanni.* Use Percussion stop ; imitate guitar, by playing very staccato ; play the melody in either the right or left hand.

3. " The heart bowed down," *Bohemian Girl* (Balfe). The stops, Musette and Percussion, in the right hand, and Clarion or Cor Anglais as an accompaniment in the left, will represent accurately the oboe solo introduced in the above-named opera. Produce tremolo effect by an almost insensible tremulous movement of the right foot and knee.

4. Introduction to Mendelssohn's *Midsummer Night's Dream*. Play this with Harpe Eolienne stop, using the Forte Expressif and Expression stops.

5. Beethoven's *Pastorale*. A lovely effect may be had by the use of the Musette, Percussion, Clarinette, or Hautbois stops in that part of the symphony where the wind instruments imitate the bird-voices.

6. Rossini's "Prayer" from *Mosè in Egitto*. Use the Baryton stop in the right hand, Percussion in the left, and vary the melody with Flute and Clarinette stops, &c.

7. "Clarinette obbligato," in the overture to *Zampa*. Play Clarinette and Musette in the right hand, Forte Expressif and Expression stop accompanying with Percussion or Clarion in the left hand.

8 "Kermesse" from Gounod's *Faust*. Play accompaniment on Harpe Eolienne, the melody on the Musette, Clarinette, and Percussion stops.

9. Introduction to *William Tell* (Rossini). Begin with the Percussion and Bassoon stops for violoncello effect; produce echoes by use of Expression stop, &c.

10. Waltz music. Use the Baryton and Piccolo stops; vary the effect by the addition of Percussion, &c., &c.

11. March from the *Prophète* (Meyerbeer). With the Baryton, Musette, Hautbois, Clarinette, and Percussion in the right hand, with Percussion and Clarion in the left, and Harpe Eolienne. In this the Grand Jeu is also effective.

12. A perfect imitation of the bagpipes may be had by the use of stops Bassoon, Clarion, Harpe Eolienne, and Forte in left hand, and Fifre, Hautbois, and Musette in right hand.

THE DOUBLE TOUCH, or DOUBLE ENFORCEMENT, is an arrangement on the key-board, and allows the two sets of reeds Nos. 3 and 4 to speak before the Nos. 1 and 2. When the keys are pressed *about a third of the distance down*, the back valves open sufficiently to allow the Nos. 3 and 4 reeds to speak first, then by still further depressing the key, the Nos. 1 and 2 follow. By this arrangement many orchestral effects can be produced. For instance, by drawing Nos. 1, 2, and 3 in the bass, and No. 2 in the treble, the melody can be played with great expression, and an accompaniment of 16 ft. pedal note, with a 4 ft. tone *pianissimo* movement on the No. 3 stop. The addition of the 8 ft. Percussion gives immediate articulation to the 16 ft. or Bourdon. The "double touch" is also useful for *glissando* passages, and for *accenting* any note in any position, or for making prominent the treble, alto, tenor, or bass part in four-part music. The double touch allows of still further expression, and virtually converts a single manual into a double manual instrument.

"THE PERCUSSION" stops draw on a set of pianoforte hammers acting on the Flute and Cor Anglais. The great charm of this invention consists in the instantaneous articulation, combined with the soft velvety quality of tone produced by the broad and thick reeds.

THE HARPE EOLIENNE is after the same model as the Voix Céleste, but more delicately voiced. The pitch is of 2 ft. tone, and the compass extends from lowest C in bass to middle E. The *timbre* resembles that of the harp, the zither, or two violins played in unison. Great charm is found in the subdued and mysterious effects when used with the swells loose; other effects equally delightful can be produced, quite orchestral and operatic, such as the violins in the Prison Scene from *Faust*, the Prayer from *Semiramide*, &c., &c.

THE MUSETTE is an imitation of the French instrument of that name, and suitable for pastorale melodies, or to strengthen and brighten the tone of the Clarinette.

THE BARYTON appertains to the 32 ft. register, *i.e.*, two octaves below the Flute or Hautbois, and the lowest note, if carried down to CC in bass, would be equal to a pipe of 32 ft. in length.

TO CLEANSE AND POLISH THE CASE.

1. Thoroughly clean the organ from dust and dirt. A small brush with moderately stiff bristles will be found useful in removing dust and dirt from carved work, corners, &c. If the case is very dirty, it may be necessary to use soap and water and a scrubbing-brush to dissolve and remove the dirt. In this case, clear water must be afterwards used to remove the soap, and the case be quite dry before the polish is applied.

2. Obtain some good polish; the following receipt makes an excellent one:—One half-pint of turpentine, one half-pint of raw linseed oil, one tablespoonful of alcohol, or methylated spirits of wine. Put together in a bottle and compound by thorough shaking.

3. Saturate a piece of cotton, flannel, or any other soft cloth, with the polish, and carefully rub the whole surface of the organ with the soft side. The rule is to see that every part of the surface is wet with the polish, but to use as little as possible in doing this.

4. With a piece of the dry, clean flannel, rub *hard and dry;* especially attending to all the crevices and corners. A small stick will be found useful to press the flannel into and rub these. The principal secret in successfully polishing an organ is in thus rubbing carefully and hard every portion of its surface, immediately after the polish has been applied. The object is to get off as much of the polish as possible, and leave the organ as dry and smooth as may be in every part. A Mason & Hamlin Organ occasionally so treated will grow handsomer by age.

Directions for Use.

THE SEAT. It will be found much easier to blow if a sufficiently high seat be used; and this is all the better if the top inclines somewhat towards the organ.

BLOWING. Set the feet firmly upon the blow-pedals, the heels being even with the lower edge. Cause each pedal to move steadily down or up, as far as it will go at each movement, one foot ascending while the other is descending.

To OBTAIN THE FULL POWER of the organ, the bellows must be fully supplied with wind, and the swell opened by moving the swell lever (which is just below the key-board, near the centre) to the right, by pressure of the knee.

Attention is asked to this point, because where complaint is made of lack of power, it commonly arises from imperfect blowing. It is much easier to supply the instrument fully with wind, by moving the pedals all the way up, or down, than when they are moved but a little way. Do not attempt to keep time with the feet, as in playing softly the pedals require to be moved slower than when you play with full power. The construction is so substantial, that there is no danger in forcing the bellows moderately; and this is, indeed, necessary for the most brilliant effects. Whenever there is disappointment in power or volume of tone of a Cabinet Organ, it almost always comes from a failure to use the bellows properly and efficiently; yet by attending to the above directions a little practice will enable any one to master it fully, and to produce the most perfect *crescendos* and *diminuendos* conceivable; to go from the faintest whisper to the full power of the organ, or the reverse, at will; or to maintain any degree of loudness; in short, to command every variety of expression.

SWELLS. In instruments having the Automatic Swell, the rule to be kept in mind is *the more rapid the blowing, and the greater the pressure upon the bellows, the louder the tone;* the slower the blowing, and the less the pressure upon the bellows, the softer the tone. A little practice will thus give every one perfect control of the degree of loudness of an organ having this swell, without removing the feet from the blow-pedals. The blowing should be steady, one foot descending while the other is ascending, except where a *forzando* effect is required. For this press the pedal *suddenly*, at the instant the keys are struck, or, for still more sudden force, press both pedals at once energetically.

Sometimes on Styles 1, 3, 21, 45, 27, 28, 48, 103, and 216, the Automatic Swell is always in use, as it is not necessary for any effect to turn it off.

In styles having the Knee Swell, by pushing with the knee the lever in the centre of the organ, beneath the keys to the *right*, the swell is opened ; by suffering it to return to its place, it is closed.

The following suggestions as to manner of use, though adapted especially to particular styles of organs, which are named, are yet applicable to most American organs.

To OBTAIN SOFTEST TONES from any stop or stops, leave the SWELL shut, and blow very gently ; only sufficiently to produce the tones.

For CRESCENDO, or increase of tones, gradually increase the blowing, and at the same time slowly press the KNEE SWELL to the right.

For DIMINUENDO, reverse this, blowing more slowly or even stopping the blowing for the moment, at the same time suffering the swell gradually to close.

It is an easier matter to supply the instrument fully with wind, if the player will but move the pedals *all the way up, or down.* A partial or half-way stroke of the blow-pedal will not suffice in *forte* playing. Do not fall into the common error of using a *short and fast* stroke. Far better results will be obtained if a *long* and relatively *slow* stroke be employed. Too much stress cannot be given to this point, for it is the SECRET OF GOOD BLOWING.

THE FULL ORGAN KNEE STOP is below the key-board, at the left of the player, and by being pressed to the left as far as it will go, brings into use all the stops necessary to secure the full power of the organ. It may be held open by a CATCH similar to that used for the KNEE SWELL, and operating in the same way. The FULL ORGAN KNEE STOP is very useful in enabling the player to bring out the full power of the chorus stops in the organ without having any stops drawn in the name-board ; or to change from any stop or stops which may be in use to the full power of the organ without removing his hands from the keys, by simply pressing this stop to the left with the knee. By suffering it to return, all stops are thrown out of use except such as remain drawn in the name-board. Changes in the stops drawn in the name-board may be conveniently made while the FULL ORGAN is in use. *When used, the* FULL ORGAN KNEE STOP *should always be pushed to the left as far as it will go, thus fully opening the stops. If pushed but half way, some of the stops are but half opened, and sound out of tune.*

LEGATO. In playing the organ it is very important that each key should be held down during the full length of time of the tone to be produced. When the notes to be played follow each other without the intervention of a *rest,* and the passage is not *staccato,* the finger holding down one note should not be raised until the exact point of time at which the finger producing the following note descends. This is especially important in playing sacred and slow music generally, producing that *legato* effect which is so beautiful upon this instrument.

IMITATIONS OF OTHER INSTRUMENTS. In solo effects, imitations of orchestral instruments, &c., play always within the compass, and in the style of music peculiar to the instrument or instruments represented. Thus the Violin should usually be strictly *solo*, and with the varying expression (produced by the blowing) which we are accustomed to hear in a violin well played. In imitating horn, flute, bassoon, &c., play such melodies as are adapted to, and commonly heard from, these instruments.

DESCRIPTION AND USE OF THE DIFFERENT STOPS. Melodia draws the treble, and Diapason the bass of one full set of eight feet reeds (8 ft. pitch). These stops may be called the basis or foundation of the organ tones ; they are of a fine round and smooth quality, and form a good accompaniment in song for female voices. They are the first to be drawn when full harmony is desired. Flute draws the treble, and Viola the bass, of one full set of four feet reeds (4 ft. pitch), and may be added to give brilliancy and power.

Use Diapason and Melodia stops in soft playing ; add Flute, and you have two sets of reeds in the right hand and one in the left ; good for *solo* with soft accompaniment. Add Viola to above, and you have *full organ*. Good effects are produced by (1) Flute in right hand, and Diapason in left ; (2) Viola and Diapason in left hand, and Melodia in right ; (3) Viola and Flute in right hand (playing melody), with accompaniment an octave lower than written, with left hand. Close Harmony low down the key-board.

Add Bass Coupler for pedal effect. Add Treble Coupler for full power.

TO OBTAIN THE EFFECT OF TWO ROWS OF KEYS. Draw Viola Dolce and Flute Stops. Play on LOWEST OCTAVES *below* middle C. Remove the hands from key-board, press suddenly FULL ORGAN knee stop, and play in the centre of key-board, or as written. The swell can be used to produce more marked effects. Again take off the hands from key-board, let the FULL ORGAN knee stop return quickly, and finish, as at first, on two lowest octaves.

Add Eolian Harp and a new effect is obtained. Add Clarionet in Styles 547 and 551.

ORGAN EFFECTS.

1. SOFT DIAPASON OR DULCIANA. Vox Humana off. Draw stops Diapason and Melodia ; play in smooth, connected, *legato* style.

2. FULL ORGAN. Vox Humana off. Draw all stops ; blow quickly, but steadily ; use full chords, and the effect will be similar to that of a pipe organ. By bringing the Vox Humana on, the power and brilliancy is much increased.

SOLO AND ORCHESTRAL EFFECTS.

3. FLUTE. Vox Humana off. Draw stops Melodia and Viola. Play *solo* simple melody, with right hand on two highest octaves, F to F, using left hand for accompaniment.

Play in same manner with Flute stop drawn in place of Melodia, and you have a good imitation of Piccolo Flute. Then add Clarionet (Styles 547, 551, &c.), and it imitates flute, clarinette, and piccolo.

4. VIOLIN. Vox Humana on, Draw Flute and Viola ; play solo with right hand on two highest octaves F to F ; accompaniment with left hand ; and a remarkable imitation of the violin is produced. The varying expression obtained by the Automatic Swell, and the power to force the bellows, is especially valuable here. Add Seraphone for second violin effect.

5. VIOLIN AND CLARIONET. Vox Humana on. Draw stops Melodia, Flute, and Viola ; play solo with right hand and accompaniment with left.

6. FRENCH HORN. Vox Humana on. Draw stops Diapason and Flute, and play solo with right hand on octave below middle C. Play accompaniment with left hand *above* (hands crossed) on highest octave. The effect is a horn solo, with violins in *tremolo*.

7. HUMAN VOICE. Vox Humana on. Draw stops Flute and Viola ; play melody on the middle octaves, with accompaniment below or above ; the blowing should be even, and sufficiently rapid to keep the fan briskly in motion. A familiar psalm-tune played in this manner, with staccato accompaniment, or of violins in *tremolo* (as in horn solo), has a good effect.

COMBINATIONS OF STOPS (STYLES 469, 447, 431, 547, 551, &c., &c.).

1. For softest possible effect, draw stops Melodia Dolce and Diapason Dolce. Blow lightly, and do not open knee swell. Play in harmony with both hands.

2. For more volume, draw stops Melodia and Diapason, shutting off Melodia Dolce and Diapason Dolce stops, and playing in harmony, both hands, using right-hand knee swell at discretion.

3. For still more volume, add stops Viola and Flute to stops named in No. 2.

4. For more colour to above combination in treble, add stop Voix Céleste to Nos. 2 and **3.**

5. For increased power, add stops Sub-Bass and Octave Coupler, and blow faster.

6. A good combination is Viola and Diapason Dolce, and Flute and Melodia Dolce.

7. For soft effects, draw stop Eolian Harp and play accompaniment with left hand, in harmony, on lowest two and half octaves of key-board. Play solos with right hand, single notes, using right knee swell to vary expression.

Solos can be played on the following **stops** :—

(1) Melodia Dolce.
(2) Melodia.
(3) Flute.
(4) Seraphone.
(5) Voix Céleste.

(6) Melodia and Flute.
(7) Seraphone and Flute.
(8) Vary the left-hand accompanying stops, using sometimes Eolian Harp or Viola Dolce, or both together.

8. The right-hand solos must not extend lower than middle C, which will give **two and a half** octaves of keys for such playing, and leave two and a half octaves for left hand accompanying up to middle B, not beyond it.

9. For full power of organ, press left-hand knee lever to the left as far as it will go, and draw Voix Céleste stop ; open right-hand knee swell by pressing to right as far as it will go ; blow rapidly, but firmly.

Add Clarionet in Styles 547 and 551.

The Stops should be kept closed when the organ is not is use.

THE MASON & HAMLIN "LISZT" ORCHESTRAL CABINET ORGAN.

STYLES 501, 503, 520, 522, 523, 901, 904, &c.

The directions, although specially given under this organ, will suit all organs in which those of the respective names occur.

THE EXPRESSION depends entirely upon the proper use of the bellows and knee swell. With all the stops drawn, and the swell closed, a *pianissimo* effect may be produced by very gentle blowing ; and then a grand *crescendo* by more rapid blowing, and the gradual opening of the swell.

In using the Viola Dolce and Seraphone, much depends upon the government of the blow pedals. It requires special study with reed organs to use these well.

COMBINATIONS OF STOPS.

1. For softest possible effect, draw stops Melodia Dolce and English Horn Dolce. Blow lightly, and do not open knee swell. Play in harmony, both hands.

2. For more volume, draw stops Melodia and English Horn, shutting off Melodia Dolce and English Horn Dolce stops, and playing in harmony, both hands, using right-hand knee swell at discretion.

3. For still more volume, add stops Viola and Piccolo to stops named in No. 2.

4. For more colour to above combination in treble, add stop Voix Céleste to Nos. 2 and 3.

5. For increased power, add stops Corno and Contra-Basso, and blow faster.

6. A rich combination is Contra-Basso and English Horn Dolce, and Corno and Melodia Dolce.

7. For solo effects, draw stop Eolian Harp, and play accompaniment, with left hand, in harmony on two lowest octaves of key-board. Play solos with right hand, single notes, using right knee swe to vary expression.

Solos can be played on the following stops :—

(1) Melodia Dolce.

(2) Melodia.

(3) Corno.

(4) Piccolo.

(5) Seraphone.

(6) Voix Céleste.

(7) Melodia and Piccolo.

(8) Corno and Piccolo.

(9) Seraphone and Piccolo.

(10) Corno and Voix Céleste.

(11) Corno and Piccolo.

(12) Corno, Voix Céleste, and Piccolo. Add Vox Humana at pleasure.

(13) Vary the left-hand accompanying stops, using sometimes Eolian Harp or Viola Dolce, or both together.

8. The right-hand solos must not extend lower than middle C, which will give three octaves of keys for such playing, and leave two octaves for left hand accompanying up to middle C, not beyond it.

9. Pedal Point stop affects lowest octave of keys only, and is effective when playing harmony on stops Corno and Contra-Basso, English Horn and Melodia, or Full Organ. The note must be touched with a slight staccato movement. One note is raised automatically immediately another is put down. In order to render the stop operative, press the knee-block to the left. To disconnect, press it to the right. A Stop-knob (Pedal Point) in name-board will sometimes be found.

10. In using the 16 ft. set (Corno and Contra-Basso), best effects are produced by playing the music for the right hand an octave higher than written, and by playing single notes in octaves with the left hand.

11. For full power of organ, press left-hand knee lever to the left as far as it will go, and draw Voix Céleste stop ; open right-hand knee swell by pressing to right as far as it will go ; blow rapidly, but firmly.

12. In playing Full Organ the Contra-Basso stop must be drawn to secure its effect. It is not always operated on by Full Organ knee stop.

DESCRIPTION AND COMBINATIONS OF STOPS, TWO MANUAL ORGANS (Style 904).

Swell (Upper) Manual.

Flute Harmonique	4 ft.	61 Notes.	Brilliant, but not reedy.
Flute Dolce	4 ft.	61 Notes.	Soft, for accompaniment.
Keraulophon	8 ft.	61 Notes.	Full tone, but slightly reedy.
Dulciana	8 ft.	61 Notes.	Similar to Diapason, but softer.
Sub-Bass	16 ft.	13 Notes.	In this model on upper manual only.
Viol d'Amour or Salicional	8 ft.	41 Notes.	Soft, reedy, stringy tone.
Eolian Harp	8 ft.	41 Notes.	Closely resembles Eolian Harp.

(Two sets of 5 Octaves each, two sets of 41 Notes each, and one set of 13 Notes.)

Great (Lower) Manual.

FLUTE	...	...	...	...	4 ft.	61 Notes.
DIAPASON	...	...	...	..	8 ft.	61 Notes.
VOIX CÉLESTE	...	...	...	8 ft.	61 Notes.
GAMBA	...	...	...	...	8 ft.	61 Notes.	OCTAVE COUPLER *(up) to Swell.*
CORNO	...	...	...	...	16 ft.	61 Notes.
MUSETTE	...	...	...	...	16 ft.	37 Notes.	Full tone, slightly reedy.

GAMBA ... 8 ft. 61 Notes. OCTAVE COUPLER *(up) to Swell.*

CORNO ... 16 ft. 61 Notes. (See page 57.)

MUSETTE ... 16 ft. 37 Notes. Full tone, slightly reedy.

(Four sets of 5 Octaves each, and one set of 37 Notes.)

Throughout.

SWELL TO GREAT OR COUPLER.

VOX HUMANA.

KNEE SWELL.

KNEE STOP. Full Organ, brings into use all the Stops at once, except Eolian Harp, Vox Humana, and Couplers.

Total Number of Sets of Reeds.

Six sets of 5 Octaves each,

Two sets of 41 Notes each,

One set of 37 Notes, and

One set of 13 Notes.

1. *For the softest effect.* Play on Upper Manual or Swell, draw stop Viol d'Amour, play in chords, both hands. For a soft pedal effect, draw stop Sub-Bass, and use lowest octave. For variety and Organ effect, add Eolian Harp, also Flute Dolce ; and for brilliancy, Flute Harmonique. For Choir Organ, or to accompany voices, use Dulciana, and add Keraulophon for power.

2. *For more power* vary expression by means of knee swell.

The knee swell is operated by a lever at the right of the performer. When pressed to the right (by the knee) the swell is opened, and the volume of sound *increased* producing *the crescendo* (◁). By allowing the lever to return, the contrary effect, *diminuendo* (▷), is produced. (A catch falls and holds the swell open when fully pressed to the right, keeping the swell open as long as desired. By this arrangement the player is not obliged to hold the knee swell open with the knee, and the legs are thus entirely free for blowing. To release and close the swell, *raise the knee slightly*, which will lift the catch. A button is provided underneath the key-board by which the catch can be fastened up, as some players do not care to use it.)

3. On Great Organ or Lower Manual draw Diapason, play in full harmony, varying expression by means of the knee swell. For more variety add Flute to this combination and Voix Céleste ; also for still greater power add Corno and Gamba, add Octave Coupler and Swell to Great, and for increase of tone press *Full Organ* (knee stop) to the left.

Full Organ is a mechanical combination of the full power brought on by pressing the left knee lever. It allows the stops to be prepared or arranged so that the full power can be obtained by the pressure of the knee lever. For example, draw Voix Céleste. This gives a soft Choir Organ. Press knee lever, and you have full power ; allow knee lever to return, and the stops will be found as first prepared.

4. For solo effects, all the stops in the Great Organ can be used separately or in combinations, namely, Corno singly or Corno and Flute ; Diapason singly or Diapason and Flute ; Gamba singly or Gamba and Flute ; Musette singly, Voix Céleste singly, or these two in combination. The best combinations for left-hand accompaniment to solos are stops Viol d'Amour or Salicional singly ; Viol d'Amour or Salicional and Flute Dolce combined ; Eolian Harp or Flute Dolce singly or combined.

5. Add Swell to Great and Vox Humana.

6. Add Octave Coupler at pleasure.

7. When using the Corno set in Great Organ in harmony, the best effects are produced by playing the music for the right hand an octave higher than written, and by playing single notes or octaves with the left hand.

FULL POWER OF PEDAL ORGANS.

To develop the full power of Pedal Organs the bellows must be worked by a second person, using the hand lever at the back of the instrument. *Particular care should be taken to keep the indicator up to the* TOP *of its channel—that is, to keep the bellows fully supplied with wind.* If it be suffered to fall below this, less power will be obtained. When the bellows is worked by the foot pedals, the lever at the back should remain *up* as high as it will go.

DESCRIPTION AND USE OF THE DIFFERENT STOPS (Styles 800 and 804).

SWELL ORGAN. (*Upper Manual.*)

KERAULOPHON (8 ft. pitch—61 notes). A set of reeds corresponding to Stopped Diapason. A full, smooth quality of tone.

VIOL D'AMOUR or SALICIONAL (8 ft. pitch). A set of reeds with a smooth, round quality of tone, subdued in character, forming a nice accompaniment to solo stops, also for full harmony for responses in church services, &c.

DOLCE TREMULANT (8 ft. pitch). A beautiful, soft, wavy tone. Used with care, may be made very effective in giving deep expression.

WALD FLUTE (4 ft. pitch). A set of reeds of a smooth, woody quality of tone.

FLUTE DOLCE (4 ft. pitch—two lower octaves in the bass). This is the softest stop in the organ, and from its mechanical action, its delicate and beautiful nature, it is used exclusively to accompany (in harmony) the solo stops.

EOLIAN HARP (2 ft. pitch—two lowest octaves in the bass). Two sets of reeds tuned to produce a beautiful effect either as a solo or accompaniment.

GREAT ORGAN. (*Lower Manual.*)

DIAPASON (8 ft. pitch). This set of reeds may be called the basis or foundation of the organ tones. It is of a fine, round, and smooth quality, and is the first to be used when full harmony is desired.

FLUTE (4 ft. pitch). This stop draws a set of reeds which are tuned an octave higher than Diapason. Used in connection with it, great brilliancy and power is added.

GAMBA (8 ft. pitch). A stringy yet brilliant tone of peculiar beauty, sometimes called by the Italian name "Oboe," a high-toned instrument similar to the Clarionet, only thinner. A delightful solo set.

CORNO (16 ft. pitch). A set of reeds of an enlarged scale—a noble tone, full, deep, and resonate ; fundamental in character, voice not unlike the lower tones of French Horn or Trombone ; resembling the 16 ft. Diapason of Pipe Organs.

VOIX CÉLESTE (8 ft. pitch). A bright, musical tone, approaching the Vox Humana in character.

CLARINET (16 ft. pitch—3 octaves in the treble). A delicately voiced solo set, closely resembling the instrument for which it is named. Flute Dolce is a good accompaniment for the left hand.

PEDAL ORGAN.

VIOLONCELLO PEDALS (8 ft. pitch). A set of reeds of a rich stringy quality, effective as a basis or groundwork for high organ accompaniment with one or both feet.

BOURDON PEDALS (16 ft. pitch). A heavy Sub-Bass of a deep dignified character, used principally when the full power of the organ is desired.

BOURDON PEDALS DOLCE (16 ft. pitch). This stop is of the same character as the Bourdon Pedals, except in power, being much softer, and is effective as a basis or groundwork for light organ accompaniment with one or both feet.

COUPLERS, &c.

.The Octave Coupler couples each key of the LOWER manual with the reed an octave above in the UPPER manual (without using the manual coupler), thereby giving a variety of combinations. When using it, play upon the lower manual of keys.

The Full Organ Pedal enables the performer to change instantly from any stop or combination to the full power of the organ, and return as instantly. It is held by a *catch* when pressed down to its full extent and to the right, and can be released at will.

Swell to Great couples the Upper Manual to the Lower.

Swell to Pedals couples the Upper Manual to the Pedals.

Great to Pedals couples the Lower Manual to the Pedals.

The Foot Swell enables the performer to obtain any degree of loudness. It is a BALANCE PEDAL, and will, therefore, remain stationary at any point. To obtain full power, press with the toe as far as possible. To render it inactive, press in same manner with the heel.

COMBINATIONS OF STOPS.

The upper manual is designated "Swell Organ," as in Pipe Organs.

The lower manual is designated "Great Organ," as in Pipe Organs.

Containing 545 reeds (equivalent to 545 pipes in a Pipe Organ). Built on a general plan of a Pipe Organ.

The organ must be fully supplied with wind by the blower, the indicator being kept within half an inch from the top when playing full organ. In soft playing, however, the indicator should be kept within an inch *from the bottom*.

1. For the softest possible effect, draw stop Viol d'Amour or Salicional, play in harmony, both hands. For a soft pedal effect, draw stop Swell to Pedals; add pedal Bourdon Dolce for deeper bass effect.

2. For more volume, shut off Viol d'Amour or Salicional, and draw Keraulophon; vary expression by aid of the Balanced Swell pedal, used by the right foot. For more volume add Wald Flute.

3. In Great Organ, draw Diapason with pedal stop Bourdon Dolce, and play in full harmony, varying expression by use of the Balanced Swell pedal. For more volume, add Flute to this combination, and for more colour in the treble, add Voix Céleste; for still greater power, add Corno and Gamba; and for an increase of tone, draw mechanical stops Great to Pedals, Swell to Great, and Octave Coupler; then for full organ, press left-foot pedal down, bring it to the right and catch it in the slot; open the Balanced Swell pedal as far as it will go, and with a full supply of wind by the blower the full power of the organ will be obtained.

4. For solo effects, all the stops in the Great Organ can be used separately or in combinations; namely, Corno singly or Corno and Flute; Diapason singly or Diapason and Flute; Gamba singly or Gamba and Flute; Clarinet singly, Voix Céleste singly, or these two in combination. Best combinations for left-hand accompaniment to solos are stops Viol d'Amour or Salicional singly, Viol d'Amour or Salicional and Flute Dolce combined, Eolian Harp or Flute Dolce singly or combined. Dolce Tremulant singly.

5. When using the Corno set in Great Organ, in harmony, best effects are produced by playing the music for the right hand an octave higher than written, and by playing single notes or octaves with the left hand.

Forerunners of the
Keyboard Reed Organ

Of the many names given to early reed organs, some were fanciful, others classical. Some makers, mostly of French origin, were really venturesome in the names they created for their instruments. The following is a selection of those which were to earn a place in the history and development of the harmonium and American organ, but how significant a part they played varies greatly. The popularity of a concept which endured for more than a century (at least in the minds of the inventors), and concerned the combination of reed organs with pianos, is matched by the number of such inventions. That they were not a commercial proposition is an unfortunate consequence; however fanciful the name, they all tended to go the same way - into oblivion. One wonders what happened to all these instruments. Some are known to be preserved in museums, but these are only a tiny proportion of the many whose names are listed below, where each is provided, where possible, with a brief description. Some of the descriptions, taken from Marcuse, are extremely vague, suggesting that the author translated literally from Sachs without making sense of the words. Where feasible, Sachs' descriptions have been re-translated.

Aelodicon	Voight of Schweinfurt perfected the Organo-violine of Eschenbach and the Aeoline of Schlimbach and came up with this instrument in 1820.
Aeolodicon	Name given to several imitations and improvements of the Aeoline (qv), first by van Raay, Amsterdam, 1825, then Friedrich Sturm (1797-1883) from Suhl in Saxony in 1835. This last-mentioned had two rows of reeds of 8ft and 4ft pitch and a 6-octave F compass. It was also known as Windharmonica. It is to Sturm that credit must go for the encasement of a free-reed instrument with bellows and keyboard into a piano-like case.
Aeol-harmonica	Free-reed instrument invented by Reinlein in France and played in public at Stuttgart in 1828.
Aeolian pianoforte	Generic name for combined piano and reed organ.
Aeolidion	Reed organ by von Ickley of Bremen, Germany, c.1826.
Aeoline	Reed organ built by Bernard Eschenbach in 1816.
Aeoline	Free-reed keyboard instrument built by the piano and organ builder Johann Caspar Schlimbach of Ohrdruf, in 1816. Bellows and a swell effect were controlled by the knees. The compass was 6 octaves and the tone extended from that of a flute in the treble to that of a contrabassoon in the bass. Eschenbach gave details of the instrument to Voit who began producing a series of imitations under the name Aeolodicon. In 1841, Bollermann of Dresden combined the Aeoline with a piano. Schlimbach was the cousin of Bernard Eschenbach.
Aeolo-melodicon	Reed organ designed by a Professor Hoffmann of Warsaw, patented there in

	1824. Was built by Fidelis Brunner of Warsaw and used metal tubes over reed cavities as tonal enhancers. A form of créscendo was obtainable by overblowing. The following year, Brunner patented an improved version called the Choraleon which was more powerful and suited to church use.
Aeolopantalon	Combined reed organ and piano - apparently owing something in its invention to the Aeolo-melodicon - invented in Warsaw by Joze Dlugosz who obtained a five-year patent for it in 1824. Either instrument could be played independently or together. Marcuse says that Chopin performed on it in public in 1825.
Aeolsklavier	Variation on reed organ, almost an Aeolian harp - invented by Schortmann of Buttelstedt, Germany c.1822. Keyboard instrument comprising upright wooden reeds which are excited by having wind blown against them. Said to have produced an extremely soft tone.
Aerophone	Small free-reed organ built by Johann Christian Dietz, Paris, c.1829.
Angelophone	Free-reed organ patented by Leferme in France on 28 February 1859. Name also given to a folding harmonium built to their patent of 29 July 1891 by Christophe & Étienne, Paris.
Annexe-piano	Small reed organ by Alexandre of Paris made to attach under the keyboard of a piano. Introduced in second half of the nineteenth century. Comprised 3-octave keyboard with three registers: flute, oboe and voix celeste.
Antiphonel	Automatic manually operated player attachment for pianos, reed organs and pipe organs introduced by Alexandre Debain of Paris in 1846. Described and illustrated in Ord-Hume *Pianola*.
Apollolyra	Free-reed wind instrument invented by Ernst Leopold Schmidt of Heiligenstadt in Eichfeld in 1832. Marcuse refers to a contemporary source which identified it as an improved Psallmelodikon (qv) in which tones are produced using 16 keys and 4 tone-holes and having a 4-octave compass. 44 free reeds controlled by keys.
Aspirophone	Reed organ patented by Alexandre Debain, Paris, on 29 July 1870.
Cartonium	Free-reed automatic organ shaped like a small harmonium and built by Joseph-Antoine Teste of Nantes, France. Patented 16 July 1861 and 1864. Operated on suction after the style of the American organ.
Choraleon	*see* Aeolo-melodicon
Choriphone	Church harmonium patented 7 February 1887 by Dumont and exhibited by Dumont & Lelièvre of Paris. Marcuse says that the instrument 'contained a special pedal to give the illusion of a bowed double bass'.
Clavaeoline	Free-reed organ of Aeoline type perfected by Carl Schmidt of Pressburg (Bratislava) in 1826.
Clavi-accord	Compact portable harmonium invented by Ludovico Gavioli, Paris. Patented in England on 16 July 1855 (British Patent No 1592). Keyboard instrument pumped by wrist-operated bellows.
Claviphone	Free-reed harmonium-type instrument patented by Le Toulat of France in 1847. Also name of small harmonium invented by Dumont & Lelièvre and shown at the Paris Exposition of 1889. Marcuse says 'the bellows were actuated by depressing the keys'.
Concordia	A variety of the Physharmonica invented in England in 1834.
Elodikon	Free-reed keyboard instrument made by Heinrich Baltzer, a watchmaker in Frankfurt, c.1840. Had 6-octave F compass.
Enharmonium	Name used by Hans von Bülow to describe various enharmonic instruments including experimental harmonium devised by Shohe Tanaka in 1889 and

built by Johann Kewitsch of Berlin. This instrument could be tuned to pure intervals and had 20 keys to the octave. Name also applied to Bosanquet's harmonium which had 53 microtones to the octave. Helmholtz had one of these built for him by Schiedmayer. This had two manuals and was used for demonstration and not performance.

Harmonichorde	Combined piano and reed organ.
Harmonicor	Free-reed instrument patented in Paris by Jaulin on 31 December 1861. Arranged in the form of a horn with 27 piston valves arranged in the form of a keyboard.
Harmonieorgel	Harmonium patented in 1892 by Johann Kewitsch having key fronts slightly lower than the key backs, the forward portion sounding a note tuned one systonic comma higher than the rear portion so that pure thirds could be played.
Harmoniflute	Instrument made by Mayer-Marix in Paris and exhibited in 1856. A portable instrument with 3 octaves of *anches vibrantes* (vibrating reeds) and a compass from F to F. Played with a keyboard.
Harmonino	Small harmonium intended to be placed upon a piano and played along with it. First shown in London at the Great Exhibition of 1851.
Harmoniphon	Small Physharmonica designed to replace the cor anglais and patented on 19 August 1836 by Paris, Lecrosnier & Tremblai of Dijon. Marcuse described it as having two octaves and being actuated by bellows or by a flexible mouth tube, compass c1 to d3. This is, however, incorrect: the 18-note compass included a short bass octave and a chromatic one to c2.
Harmoniphrase	Harmonium for playing chords invented by Dumont & Lelièvre of Paris and exhibited at Paris in 1889.
Harmonium	Name given to developed free-reed pressure organ by Alexandre Debain.
Harmoniumklavier	Combined piano and reed organ invented by C. S. Warmholz of Eisleben, Germany, c.1830.
Harmonium-pianino	Combined piano and reed organ made by G. A. Buschmann in Hamburg.
Harmoniumzither	Combined reed organ and zither made by M. L. Buschnigg in Leipzig in 1902.
Kallistorganon	Free reed keyboard instrument patented 23 April 1830 by Silvestre, Mirecourt, France.
Linardion	Combined piano and reed organ invented by Dr Linard of Vienna. Patented by Buschek in France on 6 March 1889 and shown in London in July 1890.
Mediophone	Harmonium made in France by Dumont & Lelièvre in 1889.
Melodeon	American name for the harmonium; is found spelled 'melodeon' or 'melodion'. Also late nineteenth and early twentieth century English name for the accordeon.
Melodieorgue	Small harmonium patented in France on 10 April 1860 and in England (No.628, 14 April 1861) by William Edward Gedge (for improved bellows) on 14 March 1861.
Melodina	Harmonium invented by J. L. N. Fourneax and Lazard, music teacher, of Paris, and patented on 26 March 1855.
Melodium	Small portable harmonium made from 1844 onwards in America. Also an early name for the genus American organ.
Melophilon	Small reed organ having 'special bellows' patented by Piron of Paris on 31 August 1846.
Melophone	Reed organ made by Jaquet in 1834.

Odestrophedon	Free-reed keyboard instrument patented in France on 7 February 1842 by Reverchon and Merlavaud of St Étienne, Loire.
Oeriphone	Free-reed instrument of the Aeoline family invented in 1828 by Johann Christian Dietz.
Orchestrina di camera	Series of free-reed instruments patented by W. E. Evans of London on 29 October 1862 and intended to represent the various instruments of the orchestra
Organino	Instrument invented by Alexandre Debain, Paris, and patented on 9 August 1840. Two reeds one octave apart per note (experimental).
Organochordon	Combined piano and reed organ built in the early 1890s by Gustav Adolf Buschmann, Hamburg. Three manuals and pedals. Instrument said to be imitative of all orchestral instruments.
Organo-harmonica	Improved form of seraphine with thin steel reeds, invented in London by W. E. Evans.
Organo-lyricon	Combined piano and harmonium with two manuals invented by de St Pern, an amateur musician, in 1810. Featured registers which imitated wind instruments.
Organophone	Hipkins, writing in the 5th edition of *Grove's Dictionary* (1959), refers to an instrument having this name designed by Alexandre François Debain. May be the same as the Organino (qv).
Organo-piano	Combined piano and reed organ by Achilles Müller and shown at the Paris Exposition in 1834. Had two manuals. Also the name of an instrument by Rönisch shown at the London Exhibition of 1900.
Organo-violine	Free-reed keyboard instrument invented by Bernard Eschenbach of Königshoven, c.1814. Had compass of 6 octaves.
Orgapian	Combined piano and reed organ made by Whomes of Bexleyheath.
Orgue à cent francs	Popular name for the Alexandre organ built in Paris by Jacob Alexandre and his son in 1874 and having wider, stronger reeds than the normal American organ. Its name, the 'hundred-franc organ', reflects its market price.
Orgue à percussion	Improved orgue expressif made by Martin of Paris, which claimed a clearer attack, ie more prompt speech.
Orgue excelsior	Improved form of harmonium invented by Gilbert de Sailly and R. de la Bastille of Paris in 1892.
Orgue expressif	Free-reed organ invented by Gabriel Joseph Grenié (1756-1837) and fitted with a control which allowed variable air pressure to be directed to the reeds by bypassing the air reservoir bellows. First used in 1810. Had a 5-octave F compass and four bellows worked by two pedals. After Debain took the name 'harmonium' for his own instruments, 'orgue expressif' became the generic name for other makers' harmoniums. Around 1845, the term was also used by Theodore Achille Müller of Paris for folding reed organs for travellers.
Orgue-melodium	Free reed organ made by Alexandre and his son in Paris, c.1843.
Orgue-orphonium	Described by Marcuse as 'a powerful *orgue expressif* with 7 stops, patented by Gavioli *jeune* of Paris on 4 February 1869'.
Orgue phonochromatique	Another form of improved orgue expressif patented in Paris on 7 June 1855 by Lorenzi.
Orpheal	Combined piano and reed organ invented in 1910 by Georges Cloetens of Brussels.
Orphei	Harmonium patented by Ligier in France on 3 June 1864 having bellows which were operated by a hand crank.

Orthotonophonium	Enharmonic pressure reed organ designed by Arthur von Oettingen (1836-1920) from Dorpat, who later was a Professor of Physics at Leipzig. The instrument was built to his design in 1914 by Schiedmayer of Stuttgart and has 57 notes, but 53 notes to each octave (ie the compass was a chromatic 57 notes, yet each of the octaves within this compass was divided into 53 separate notes).
Panorgue	Combined piano and reed organ invented by Jaulin of Paris and having the organ component under the keyboard of the piano.
Pansymphonikon	Combined piano and reed organ made by Peter Singer of Salzburg in 1839. Also known as the Polyharmonion.
Physharmonica	Small free reed instrument devised in 1818 by Anton Haeckel, Vienna. A diminutive Aeoline intended to be used with a pianoforte. Had a 4-octave compass and bellows worked by two pedals.
Piano a prolongment	Combined piano and reed organ by Alexandre of Paris in the latter half of the nineteenth century.
Piano diphone	Two-manual piano combined with free reed organ patented by Rousseau in France on 24 May 1881.
Piano melodieux	Combined piano and reed organ with a seven-octave compass, invented by Leopold Guerin of Paris, c.1883.
Piano-melodium	Combined piano and reed organ by Jacob Alexandre of Paris and shown at the Paris Exposition of 1855. Had two keyboards, the upper one for the piano and the lower one for the harmonium.
Pianon	Harmonium in the form of a small table with keyboard invented by Carl Kühn of Vienna, c.1873. Marcuse says 'the bellows were worked by depressing the keys, so that no pedal was required'.
Poikilorgue	A version of the orgue expressif invented by Aristide Cavaillé-Coll and first shown at the Paris Exposition of 1834. In the form of a small square piano with one rank of reeds, C compass, two pedals; large bellows operated by the left foot while the right foot could vary the wind pressure, thereby creating expression.
Polyharmonium	*see* Pansymphonikon.
Psallmelodikon	Described by Marcuse as 'an improved New Tschang invented in 1828 by Weinrich of Heiligenstadt near Erfurt, in the form of a flattened cylinder with free reeds, 26 keys, 6 front and 2 rear fingerholes.' See also Apollolyra.
Royal Seraphine	*see* Seraphine.
Seraphine	Free-reed keyboard instrument, precursor of the harmonium, improved upon by John Green of London as the Royal Seraphine and patented between 1839 and 1851. Who first used the name 'seraphine' is uncertain but it may well have been Green himself in 1834. Had five octaves, F compass, and was capable of crescendo and decrescendo.
Seraphone	Free-reed keyboard instrument patented by C. F. Pietschmann in France on 26 September 1876.
Symphonium	Free-reed keyboard instrument which could be combined with a piano, patented by Alexandre-François Debain of Paris on 28 October 1845. Also name given by Wheatstone to first mouth-organ.
Terpodion	Keyboard free-reed friction instrument made by Johan David Buschmann of Friederichrode near Gotha in 1817.
Triolodeon	Improved melodeon-type free reed instrument invented by Cornelius van Oeckelen of Holland c.1858.
Triphonium	Combination zither and harmonium invented by Robert Lechleitner of

	Lechtal, Tyrol, c.1878. Produced flute and harmonium tones by means of flue pipes and reeds in addition to the string tones of the zither (Marcuse).
Trylodeon	Improved harmonium invented by Joseph Poole Pirsson and patented in 1860 by Richard A. Brooman (British Patent No 2066. The depth of touch controlled a variable number of reeds so that registration was accomplished by the pressure exerted by the player on the keys.
Uranion	Free-reed instrument built in 1810 by J. D. Buschmann having $5\frac{1}{2}$ octaves.
Violo-clave	Harmonium patented by Morin de la Guerrière in 1847.
Vocalion	Invented either in part or collectively by John Farmer, Herman Smith and John Baillie-Hamilton c.1874-82 (various patents). Is generally attributed to the last-mentioned and, while he may not have been the inventor of the actual Vocalion concept, he took the credit for its later development and manufacture.
Windharmonica	*see* Aeolidicon.

CABINET ORGAN.
Length, 4 feet 8 in.   Height, 8 feet 4 in.   Depth, 2 feet 5 in.   Weight, 362 pounds.

CABINET ORGAN.
Length, 4 feet.   Height, 8 feet.   Depth, 2 feet.   Weight, 278 pounds.

"Great Industries of the United States", 1872

Bibiliography

ALLIHN, M. *Die Hausinstrument Klavier und Harmonium* Quedlinburg. 1891
    Wegweiser church die Harmonium-Musik, Berlin. 1894
BEKKER, L. J. de. *Stokes' Cyclopaedia of Music and Musicians.* Chambers, Edinburgh, 1911
BIE, OSKAR. *Intime Musik.* Berlin, 1904
    Klavier, Orgel und Harmonium. Leipzig, 1910, 1921
BOEHM, E. *Das Harmonium im akademischen Unterricht.* Berlin, 1895
BOWERS, Q. DAVID. *Encyclopaedia of Automatic Musical Instruments.* Vestal Press, New York, 1972
British Patent Office, *Musical Instruments,* 1870-1920, Abridgement Class 88, HMSO, London
BUSCHMANN, H. *Chr. F. L. Buschmann, der Erfinder der Mund-und der Handharmonika.* Trossingen, 1938
CERFBERR DE MEDELSHEIM, A. *Les orgues expressif.* Paris, 1867 and 1873
CONSTANT, PIERRE. *Les facteurs d'instruments de musique.* Paris, 1893
DIETZ, C. 'Sur l'aerophone, nouvel instrument inventé par M. Dietz', *Review Musicale,* VI, 1830, p536
DOLGE, ALFRED. *Pianos and Their Makers.* Covina Publishing Co, Covina, California, 1911 (facsimile
    edition Dover Publications, New York, 1972)
    Men Who Have Made Piano History (Pianos & Their Makers, Vol 2). Covina Publishing Co, Covina,
    California, 1913 (facsimile ed. Vestal Press, Vestal, New York, 1980)
E(ARL), S.G. *How To Repair the Player Piano.* Musical Opinion (publishers), London, 1920
ENGEL, G. *Das mathematische Harmonium.* Berlin, 1881
FAUST, OLIVER C. *Technical Treatise on the Construction, Repairing and Tuning of the Organ.* Boston, 1949
FETIS, F.-J. *Fabrication des instruments de musique.* Paris, 1856
FLUKE, PHIL and PAM. *Victorian Reed Organs & Harmoniums,* (catalogue), Bradford, 1st ed 1982; 2nd
    ed 1985
FOURNEAUX, J.-L. N. *Petit traité sur l'orgue-expressif.* Paris, 1854
    Traité théorètique et practique de l'accord des instruments a sons fixes. Paris, 1867.
FOX, JOSEPH. *Mechanical Music in the American Home, Music & Automata,* Vol 1, No 3, 1984
    'The Aeolian Orchestrelle', *Music & Automata,* Vol 1, No 4, 1984
GELLERMAN, ROBERT F. *The American Reed Organ.* Vestal Press, Vestal, New York, 1973
GIVENS, L. *Rebuilding the Player Piano.* Vestal Press, Vestal, New York, 1963
Great Industries of the United States, (various authors), Burr & Hyde, Hartford, Connecticut, 1872
GROVES, SIR GEORGE (ed). *Dictionary of Music.* London, 1st ed, 1879-82
HALL, KING. *The Harmonium.* Novello's Music Primer and Educational Series, Novello, London, (c.1890)
HARDING, ROSAMOND. *The Piano-Forte.* Cambridge, England, 1933
Harmoniumfreund, der, 13, Berlin, 1927-30
HARTMAN, L. *Das Harmonium.* Leipzig, 1913
HAASTERT, J. VAN. *Cornelis Jacobus van Oeckelen, Kunstwerker,* Utrecht, 1980
Historique du procès en contrefaçon des harmoniums-Debain. Paris, 1845
KARG-ELERT, S. *Die Kunst des Registrierens.* Berlin, 1911-14
Kurzgefasste Anleitung zu Kunstgemasser Behandlung das Harmoniums der Herren J. & P. Schiedmayer in
    Stuttgart. Stuttgart, 1854
LANGWILL, LYNDESAY G. *An Index of Musical Wind Instrument Makers.* Edinburgh, 6th ed, 1980
LEDERLE, J. *Das Harmonium, seine Geschichte, Construktion ....* Freiburg, 1884
LUCKHOFF, W. (ed). *Das Harmonium.* Leipzig, 1900
    Die Aufgabeen einer modernen Hausmusik-Padagok und das Harmonium. Berlin, 1908

McTAMMANY, JOHN. *The Technical History of the Player*. New York, 1915, facsimile ed Vestal Press, New York, (c.1968)

MARCUSE, SIBYL. *A Comprehensive Dictionary*. Country Life, London, 1966
A Survey of Musical Instruments. David & Charles, Devon, 1975

MERSENNE, M. *Harmonie universelle*. Paris 1636-7

MICHEL, N. E. *Michel's Organ Atlas*. California, 1970
Historical Pianos. California, 1970

MILE, R. A. *Das deutsch-amerikanische Harmonium*. Hamburg, 1905

MILNE, H. F. *The Reed Organ*. Musical Opinion, London, 1930

MONICHON, PIERRE. *Petite Histoire de l'Accordeon*. Enterprise Générale de Fabrication et de Publicité, Paris, 1958

Musical Box Society of Great Britain. *The Music Box* (journal), London 1962-79

Musical Opinion & Music Trade Review. London, 1880-1930

Musical Times, The. London, 1844-90

Musical World, The. London, March-December, 1836

MUSTEL, A. *L'orgue expressif ou harmonium*, Paris, 1903

NUGUES, E., POUGET, H. C.; MARTIN, CH. *Practical Manual for the Piano and Harmonium Tuner* ('Pinet's Harmonium Tuner'), Leon Pinet, Paris, 1913

ORD-HUME, ARTHUR W. J. G. *Player Piano - The History of the Mechanical Piano and How to Repair It*. Allen & Unwin, London, 1970
Clockwork Music - An Illustrated History of Mechanical Musical Instruments. Allen & Unwin, London, 1970
Barrel Organ - A History of the Mechanical Organ and how to Restore It. Allen & Unwin, London, 1975
Restoring Pianolas and Other Self-playing Pianos. Allen & Unwin, London, 1983
Pianola: The History of the Self-Playing Piano. Allen & Unwin, London, 1984

Ord-Hume Library Collection, Files 3.A100-109; 3.B100-108

Orgel-und Pianobau-Zeitung. Berlin, 1872-85

PINET, LEON. *see* Nugues, Pouget and Martin

PINOEL, F. *L'orgue expressif de salon*. Rouen, 1893

PRATT, WALDO SELDEN (ed). *The New Encyclopedia of Music and Musicians*. Macmillan, New York, 1945

PRESLEY, HORTON. *Restoring & Collecting Antique Reed Organs*. Tab Books, Summit, Pennsylvania, 1977

PROMBERGER, J. *Theoretische-praktische Anleitung zur Kenntnis und Behandlung der Physharmonika*. 1830

REINHARD, A. *Etwas vom Harmonium*. Berlin, 1895
Das Harmonium von heute. Berlin, 1903

RIEHM, W. *Das Harmonium; sein Bau und seine Behandlung*. Carl Simon, Berlin, 1897

RIMBAULT, E. F. *The Harmonium*. London, 1857

ROEHL, HARVEY. *Player Piano Treasury*. Vestal Press, Vestal, New York. 1st ed, 1961; 2nd, revised ed, 1973

SACHS, CURT. *Real-Lexikon der Musikinstrumente*. Berlin, 1913, revised 2nd ed, Dover Publications, New York, 1964.
'Zur Frühgeschichte der durchschlagended Zunge', *Zeitschrift für Instrumentenbau*, Leipzig, 1912-13

SCHOLES, PERCY A. *The Mirror of Music, 1844-1944*. London, 1947

SPILLANE, DANIEL. *History of the American Pianoforte*. Spillane, New York, 1890

TEUCHERT, E., and HAUPT, E. W. *Musik-instrumentenkunde in wort und bild*. 3, Leipzig, 1911

TOPFER, J. G. *Die Theorie und Praxis des Orgel-Baues* (ed M. Allihn). Weimar, 1855-88, p732 *et.seq*

TURGAN. *Les grandes usines: l'orgue expressif de MM Alexandre, pere et fils*. Paris, 1846.

WENNEIS, F. 'Monatszeitschrift für Neurungen und Fortschritte auf dem Gebeite des Kunstharmonium sowie des gesamten Instrumenten-Bauwesens', *Der Aufschwung*, i-ii, 1925-7

WHITING, ROBERT B. *Estey Reed Organs on Parade*. Vestal Press, New York, 1981

WOODCROFT, BENNET. *Alphabetical Index of Patentees of Inventions*. 1854, new ed Evelyn, Adams & Mackay, London, 1969

Acknowledgements

I would like to express thanks to the large number of people who have, over the years, provided me with information, pictures and assistance in the preparation of this work. I have drawn heavily on contemporary literature since this is the finest way to bring home the immediacy of developments in the reed organ business. My prime research material has been the pages of *The Musical Times* and that most valuable work of all, *Musical Opinion* which methodically charted the progress of the musical instrument trade and industry for so many years. Indeed, the first announcement of this book appeared in the form of a letter seeking readers' help published in *Musical Opinion* as long ago as 1972. To those periodicals I extend my eternal gratitude for their meticulous and assiduous work in times past.

From that early published letter, I received offers of help from a great number of musicians, historians, enthusiasts, organ owners and collectors of ephemera. To all these I extend my grateful thanks, acknowledging in particular the assistance received from Phil and Pam Fluke of Shipley, West Yorkshire, two rare enthusiasts who have amassed a fine collection of instruments which are now on permanent display in the Victoria Hall, Saltaire, forming what is probably the world's first dedicated reed-organ museum. Thanks to their generosity, this book contains many illustrations for which they have been responsible including numerous photographs of their organs taken specially for me by their special photographer, Konrad Ronkowski.

Thanks also go to very many friends and correspondents who have contributed. Among these are Desmond J. Keen of Great Missenden; Herbert F. Watts of Messrs George Osmond, organ-builders of Taunton; Claes Friberg of Rungsted-Kyst, Denmark; Professor Macarius Kastner of Lisbon; Dr Robert Talbot of Lyon, France; Douglas Berryman formerly of the West Cornwall Museum of Mechanical Music and now of Frome, Somerset; the late Sir Malcolm Sargent; Dr Jan-Jaap Haspels of the Nationaal Museum van Speelklok tot Pierement, Utrecht; Dr Rene de Mayer, director of the musical instrument collection, Brussels.

A. Foster of R. F. Stevens Ltd, reed organ builders, London; Norman Shorrock of Birkenhead; Frank H. Miller of Dorking; the late Archibald Brummer of the Aeolian Company, London; the late T. S. Paulford, the London musical-instrument industry historian; Paul Bradbury of Chicago, and Anne Dolman, also of that city; K. T. Dawes of Bristol and J. S. Dawes of Cleveland, Ohio; Paul Jenkinson of Birmingham; C. Lindars of East Grinstead; A. D. Ellis of Cliftonville, Margate; collectors Keith C. Jarrett of Solihull and Ian Thompson of Oxford; reed-organ builder J. E. Burggy of Ipswich; the late Howard and Helen Fitch of Summit, New Jersey; Everson Whittle of Preston; George Berry of Beaconsfield; Manfred Haug of Matthias Hohner, AG, Trossingen, Germany, and Ralph E. Haller of the London office; Messrs Louis Renner of Stuttgart, Germany.

Louis Jacot of Jacot Reed Organs, Evesham; the late Roy Mickleburgh of Bristol; the late Frank Moltzer of Bennekom, Holland; the late William Latey QC of London; David Wright, Boston, Lincolnshire; the late Dr C de Vere Green; the late Lew Brodski of Los Angeles; Mrs P. Haward, secretary, Franklin House Committee, National Trust of Australia (Tasmania); Cynthia Crombie, Launceston, Tasmania; C. M. Maxfield of Waltham Cross; J. C. Day of Thibouvilly-Lamy Ltd, London; L. Gillett of Enfield, Middlesex; R. H. S. Carpenter of Cambridge; R. E. Lloyd of Hollywood, Florida; David K. H. Davies of London; R. L. Mitchell of J. George Morley, Lewisham; Mr Mullineux of Rushworth & Dreaper, Liverpool; the British Library (Patents Division); the New York Public Library; the Logan Library, Philadelphia; U.S. Patents Office, New York; the Public Records Office, London; R. Kalonaitis, University of Vilnius, Lithuania; the Lenin Library, Moscow; David Schneider, historian, Connecticut; Edwin B. Holt, reed organ builder, Manchester; Tony Morgan, London instrument restorer; Professor James M. Bratton, Denver, Colorado.

In the way of things, I am sure I have omitted somebody: should that prove so, my apologies.

Index

This index includes references in Chapter 10 *Index of Makers* which may not directly be identifiable with a maker's name. To find information about a maker or brand of instrument, consult both the Index and the alphabetical listing in Chapter 10. Only in exceptional circumstances are brand names of organs listed in that Chapter: they should be sought primarily in this Index. Plate references are indicated by page and plate, eg 46[16,17].